Praise for *Head First OOA&D*

"*Head First Object-Oriented Analysis and Design* is a refreshing look at the subject of OOA&D. What sets this book apart is its focus on learning. There are too many books on the market that spend a lot of time telling you why, but do not actually enable the practitioner to start work on a project. Those books are very interesting... that the future of software development

...finished reading... ...ges to get across the essentials of object-oriented analysis and ... ...ven several lectures on good software design, all in a fast-paced, easy to understand way. The thing I liked most about this book was its focus on why we do OOA&D—to write great software! By defining what great software is and showing how each step in the OOA&D process leads you towards that goal, it can teach even the most jaded Java programmer why OOA&D matters. This is a great 'first book' on design for anyone who is new to Java, or even for those who have been Java programmers for a while but have been scared off by the massive tomes on OO Analysis and Design."

> **— Kyle Brown, Distinguished Engineer, IBM**

"Finally a book on OOA&D that recognizes that the UML is just a notation and that what matters when developing software is taking the time to think the issues through."

> **— Pete McBreen, Author,** *Software Craftsmanship*

"The book does a good job of capturing that entertaining, visually oriented, 'Head First' writing style. But hidden behind the funny pictures and crazy fonts is a serious, intelligent, extremely well-crafted presentation of OO Analysis and Design. This book has a strong opinion of how to design programs, and communicates it effectively. I love the way it uses running examples to lead the reader through the various stages of the design process. As I read the book, I felt like I was looking over the shoulder of an expert designer who was explaining to me what issues were important at each step, and why."

> **— Edward Sciore, Associate Professor, Computer Science Department**
> **Boston College**

"This is a well-designed book that delivers what it promises to its readers: how to analyze, design, and write serious object-oriented software. Its contents flow effortlessly from using use cases for capturing requirements to analysis, design, implementation, testing, and iteration. Every step in the development of object-oriented software is presented in light of sound software engineering principles. The examples are clear and illustrative. This is a solid and refreshing book on object-oriented software development."

> **— Dung Zung Nguyen, Lecturer**
> **Rice University**

Praise for other *Head First* books by the authors

"When arriving home after a 10-hour day at the office programming, who has the energy to plow through yet another new facet of emerging technology? If a developer is going to invest free time in self-driven career development, should it not be at least remotely enjoyable? Judging from the content of O'Reilly's new release *Head Rush Ajax*, the answer is yes…*Head Rush Ajax* is a most enjoyable launchpad into the world of Ajax web applications, well worth the investment in time and money."

> **— Barry Hawkins, Slashdot.org**

"By starting with simple concepts and examples, the book gently takes the reader from humble beginnings to (by the end of the book) where the reader should be comfortable creating Ajax-based websites... Probably the best web designer centric book on Ajax."

> **— Stefan Mischook, Killersites.com**

"Using the irreverent style common of the *Head First/Head Rush* series of books, this book starts at the beginning and introduces you to all you need to know to be able to write the JavaScript that will both send requests to the server and update the page with the results when they are returned...One of the best things about this book (apart form the excellent explanations of how the code works) is that it also looks at security issues...If you learn Ajax from this book you are unlikely to forget much of what you learn."

> **— Stephen Chapman, JavaScript.About.com**

"*Head Rush Ajax* is the book if you want to cut through all the hype and learn how to make your web apps sparkled…your users will love you for it!"

> **— Kristin Stromberg, Aguirre International**

"If you know some HTML, a dollop of CSS, a little JavaScript, and a bit of PHP, but you're mystified about what all the Ajax hype is about, this book is for you…You'll have a blast learning Ajax with *Head Rush Ajax*. By the time you've reached the end of the book, all those web technologies that didn't quite fit together in your head will all snap into place and you'll have The Ajax Power! You'll know the secrets behind some of the most popular web applications on the Internet. You'll impress your friends and co-workers with you knowledge of how those interactive maps and web forms really work."

> **— Elisabeth Freeman, The Walt Disney Internet Group**
> **Co-Author, *Head First Design Patterns* and *Head First HTML with CSS & XHTML***

"If you thought Ajax was rocket science, this book is for you. *Head Rush Ajax* puts dynamic, compelling experiences within reach for every web developer."

> **—Jesse James Garrett, Adaptive Path**

"This stuff is brain candy; I can't get enough of it."

> **— Pauline McNamara, Center for New Technologies and Education**
> **Fribourg University, Switzerland**

Praise for other *Head First* Books

"I *heart* *Head First HTML with CSS & XHTML* – it teaches you everything you need to learn in a 'fun coated' format!"

— **Sally Applin, UI Designer and Fine Artist, http://sally.com.**

"My wife stole the book. She's never done any web design, so she needed a book like *Head First HTML with CSS & XHTML* to take her from beginning to end. She now has a list of web sites she wants to build – for our son's class, our family, ... If I'm lucky, I'll get the book back when she's done."

— **David Kaminsky, Master Inventor, IBM**

"Freeman's *Head First HTML with CSS & XHTML* is a most entertaining book for learning how to build a great web page. It not only covers everything you need to know about HTML, CSS, and XHTML, it also excels in explaining everything in layman's terms with a lot of great examples. I found the book truly enjoyable to read, and I learned something new!"

— **Newton Lee, Editor-in-Chief, ACM Computers in Entertainment http://www.acmcie.org**

From the awesome *Head First Java* folks, this book uses every conceivable trick to help you understand and remember. Not just loads of pictures: pictures of humans, which tend to interest other humans. Surprises everywhere. Stories, because humans love narrative. (Stories about things like pizza and chocolate. Need we say more?) Plus, it's darned funny.

— **Bill Camarda, READ ONLY**

"This book's admirable clarity, humor and substantial doses of clever make it the sort of book that helps even non-programmers think well about problem-solving."

— **Cory Doctorow, co-editor of Boing Boing Author, "Down and Out in the Magic Kingdom" and "Someone Comes to Town, Someone Leaves Town"**

"I feel like a thousand pounds of books have just been lifted off of my head."

— **Ward Cunningham, inventor of the Wiki and founder of the Hillside Group**

"I literally love this book. In fact, I kissed this book in front of my wife."

— **Satish Kumar**

Other related books from O'Reilly

Practical Development Environments

Process Improvement Essentials

Prefactoring

Ajax Design Patterns

Learning UML

Applied Software Project Management

The Art of Project Management

UML 2.0 in a Nutshell

Unit Test Frameworks

Other books in O'Reilly's *Head First* Series

Head First Design Patterns

Head First Java

Head First Servlets and JSP

Head First EJB

Head First HTML with CSS & XHTML

Head Rush Ajax

Head First OOA&D

Head First PMP (2007)

Head First Algebra (2007)

Head First Software Development (2007)

Head First Object-Oriented Analysis and Design

Wouldn't it be dreamy
if there was an analysis and
design book that was more fun
than going to an HR benefits
meeting? It's probably nothing
but a fantasy...

Brett D. McLaughlin
Gary Pollice
David West

O'REILLY®

Beijing • Cambridge • Köln • Paris • Sebastopol • Taipei • Tokyo

Head First Object-Oriented Analysis and Design

by Brett D. McLaughlin, Gary Pollice, and David West

Published by O'Reilly Media, Inc., 1005 Gravenstein Highway North, Sebastopol, CA 95472.

O'Reilly Media books may be purchased for educational, business, or sales promotional use. Online editions are also available for most titles (*safari.oreilly.com*). For more information, contact our corporate/institutional sales department: (800) 998-9938 or *corporate@oreilly.com*.

Series Creators:	Kathy Sierra, Bert Bates
Series Editor:	Brett D. McLaughlin
Editor:	Mary O'Brien
Cover Designer:	Mike Kohnke, Edie Freedman
OO:	Brett D. McLaughlin
A:	David West
D:	Gary Pollice
Page Viewer:	Dean and Robbie McLaughlin

Printing History:

November 2006: First Edition.

 This book uses RepKover™, a durable and flexible lay-flat binding.

ISBN-10: 0-596-00867-8

ISBN-13: 978-0-596-00867-3

To all the brilliant people who came up with various ways to gather requirements, analyze software, and design code...

...thanks for coming up with something good enough to produce great software, but hard enough that we needed this book to explain it all.

Brett McLaughlin is a guitar player who is still struggling with the realization that you can't pay the bills if you're into acoustic fingerstyle blues and jazz. He's just recently discovered, to his delight, that writing books that help people become better programmers does pay the bills. He's very happy about this, as are his wife Leigh, and his kids, Dean and Robbie.

Before Brett wandered into Head First land, he developed enterprise Java applications for Nextel Communications and Allegiance Telecom. When that became fairly mundane, Brett took on application servers, working on the internals of the Lutris Enhydra servlet engine and EJB container. Along the way, Brett got hooked on open source software, and helped found several cool programming tools, like Jakarta Turbine and JDOM. Write to him at brett@oreilly.com.

Brett ↗

Gary →

Gary Pollice is a self-labeled curmudgeon (that's a crusty, ill-tempered, usually old man) who spent over 35 years in industry trying to figure out what he wanted to be when he grew up. Even though he hasn't grown up yet, he did make the move in 2003 to the hallowed halls of academia where he has been corrupting the minds of the next generation of software developers with radical ideas like, "develop software for your customer, learn how to work as part of a team, design and code quality and elegance and correctness counts, and it's okay to be a nerd as long as you are a great one."

Gary is a Professor of Practice (meaning he had a real job before becoming a professor) at Worcester Polytechnic Institute. He lives in central Massachusetts with his wife, Vikki, and their two dogs, Aloysius and Ignatius. You can visit his WPI home page at **http://web.cs.wpi.edu/~gpollice/**. Feel free to drop him a note and complain or cheer about the book.

Dave West would like to describe himself as sheik geek. Unfortunately no one else would describe him in that way. They would say he is a professional Englishman who likes to talk about software development best practices with the passion and energy of an evangelical preacher. Recently Dave has moved to Ivar Jacobson Consulting, where he runs the Americas and can combine his desire to talk about software development and spread the word on rugby and football, and argue that cricket is more exciting than baseball.

Before running the Americas for Ivar Jacobson Consulting, Dave worked for a number of years at Rational Software (now a part of IBM). Dave held many positions at Rational and then IBM, including Product Manager for RUP where he introduced the idea of process plug-ins and agility to RUP. Dave can be contacted at dwest@ivarjacobson.com.

Dave →

Table of Contents (summary)

Table of Contents (the real thing)

Intro

Your brain on OOA&D.

Here *you* are trying to *learn* something, while here your *brain* is doing you a favor by making sure the learning doesn't *stick*. Your brain's thinking, "Better leave room for more important things, like which wild animals to avoid and whether naked snowboarding is a bad idea." So how *do* you trick your brain into thinking that your life depends on knowing object-oriented analysis and design?

well-designed apps rock

1 Great Software Begins Here

So how do you *really* write great software? It's never easy trying to figure out **where to start**. Does the application actually **do what it's supposed to**? And what about things like duplicate code—that can't be good, can it? It's usually pretty hard to know **what you should work on first**, and still make sure you don't screw everything else up in the process. No worries here, though. By the time you're done with this chapter, you'll **know how to write great software**, and be well on your way to improving the way you develop applications forever. Finally, you'll understand why **OOAD** is a four-letter word that your mother actually *wants* you to know about.

> How am I supposed to know where to start? I feel like every time I get a new project to work on, everyone's got a different opinion about what to do first. Sometimes I get it right, and sometimes I end up reworking the whole app because I started in the wrong place. **I just want to write great software!** So what should I do first in Rick's app?

2

gathering requirements

Give Them What They Want

Everybody loves a satisfied customer. You already know that the first step in writing great software is making sure it does what the customer wants it to. But how do you figure out **what a customer really wants**? And how do you make sure that the customer even *knows* what they really want? That's where **good requirements** come in, and in this chapter, you're going to learn how to **satisfy your customer** by making sure what you deliver is actually what they asked for. By the time you're done, all of your projects will be "satisfaction guaranteed," and you'll be well on your way to writing great software, every time.

Todd and Gina's Dog Door, version 2.0
Requirements List

1. The
   tall
2. A b
   do
   th
3. On
   cl
   al

Todd and Gina's Dog Door, version 2.0
What the Door Does

1. Fido barks to be let out.
2. Todd or Gina hears Fido barking.
3. Todd or Gina presses the button on the remote control.
4. The dog door opens.
5. Fido goes outside.
6. Fido does his business.
7. Fido goes back inside.
8. The door shuts automatically.

The System

The dog door and remote are part of the system, or <u>inside</u> the system.

requirements change

3

I Love You, You're Perfect... Now Change

Think you've got just what the customer wanted?

Not so fast... So you've talked to your customer, gathered requirements, written out your use cases, and delivered a killer application. It's time for a nice relaxing cocktail, right? Right... until your customer decides that they really wanted something **different than what they told you**. They love what you've done, really, but it's **not quite good enough anymore**. In the real world, **requirements are always changing**, and it's up to you to roll with these changes and keep your customer satisfied.

```
public void pressButton() {
  System.out.println("Pressing the remote control button...");
  if (door.isOpen()) {
    door.close();
  } else {
    door.open();

    final Timer timer = new Timer();
    timer.schedule(new TimerTask() {
      public void run() {
        door.close();
        timer.cancel();
      }
    }, 5000);
  }
}
```

Remote.java

analysis

4 Taking Your Software into the Real World

It's time to graduate to real-world applications.

Your application has to do more than work on your own personal development machine, finely tuned and perfectly setup; your apps have to work when **real people use them**. This chapter is all about making sure that your software works in a **real-world context**. You'll learn how **textual analysis** can take that use case you've been working on and turn it into classes and methods that you know are what your customers want. And when you're done, you too can say: "I did it! My software is **ready for the real world**!"

Once I knew the classes and operations that I needed, I went back and updated my class diagram.

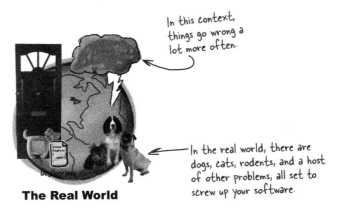

In this context, things go wrong a lot more often.

The Real World

In the real world, there are dogs, cats, rodents, and a host of other problems, all set to screw up your software.

5 (part 1)

good design = flexible software

Nothing Ever Stays the Same

Change is inevitable. No matter how much you like your software right now, it's probably going to **change** tomorrow. And the harder you make it for your software to change, the more difficult it's going to be to respond to your **customer's changing needs**. In this chapter, we're going to revisit an old friend, try and improve an existing software project, and see how **small changes can turn into big problems**. In fact, we're going to uncover a problem so big that it will take a TWO-PART chapter to solve it!

5 (interlude)

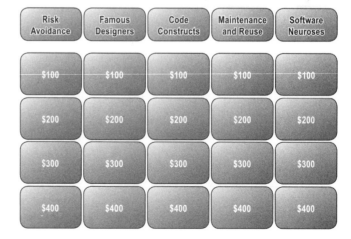

OO CATASTROPHE!
Objectville's Favorite Quiz Show

5 (part 2)

good design = flexible software

Give Your Software a 30-minute Workout

Ever wished you were just a bit more flexible?

When you run into problems making changes to your application, it probably means that your software needs to be **more flexible and resilient**. To help stretch your application out, you're going to do some analysis, a whole lot of design, and learn how OO principles can really **loosen up your application**. And for the grand finale, you'll see how **higher cohesion can really help your coupling**. Sound interesting? Turn the page, and let's get back to fixing that inflexible application.

solving really big problems

6 "My Name is Art Vandelay... I am an Architect"

It's time to build something REALLY BIG. Are you ready?

You've got a ton of tools in your OOA&D toolbox, but how do you use those tools when you have to build something **really big**? Well, you may not realize it, but **you've got everything you need** to handle big problems. We'll learn about some new tools, like **domain analysis** and **use case diagrams**, but even these new tools are based on things you already know about—like listening to the customer and understanding what you're going to build before you start writing code. Get ready... it's time to start playing the architect.

This BIG PROBLEM is really just a collection of functionalities, where each piece of functionality is really a smaller problem on its own.

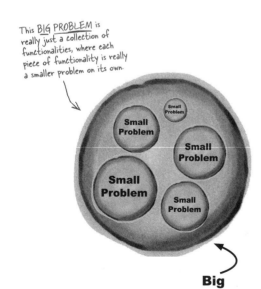

Big Problem

architecture

7

Bringing Order to Chaos

You have to start somewhere, but you better pick the *right* somewhere! You know how to break your application up into lots of small problems, but all that means is that you have **LOTS** of small problems. In this chapter, we're going to help you figure out **where to start**, and make sure that you don't waste any time working on the wrong things. It's time to take all those **little pieces** laying around your workspace, and figure out how to turn them into a **well-ordered, well-designed application**. Along the way, you'll learn about the all-important **3 Qs of architecture**, and how **Risk** is a lot more than just a cool war game from the '80s.

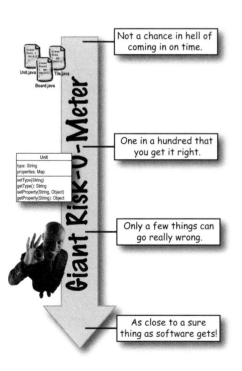

design principles

8

Originality is Overrated

Imitation is the sincerest form of not being stupid. There's

nothing as satisfying as coming up with a completely new and original solution to a problem that's been troubling you for days—until you find out someone else **solved the same problem**, long before you did, and did an even better job than you did! In this chapter, we're going to look at some **design principles** that people have come up with over the years, and how they can make you a better programmer. Lay aside your thoughts of "doing it your way"; this chapter is about **doing it the smarter, faster way.**

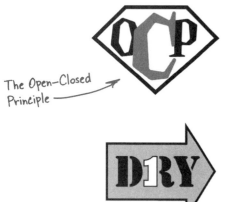

The Open-Closed Principle

The Don't Repeat Yourself Principle

The Single Responsibility Principle

The Liskov Substitution Principle

iterating and testing

9

The Software is Still for the Customer

It's time to show the customer how much you really care.

Nagging bosses? Worried clients? Stakeholders that keep asking, "Will it be done on time?" No amount of well-designed code will please your customers; you've got to **show them something working**. And now that you've got a solid OO programming toolkit, it's time to learn how you can **prove to the customer** that your software works. In this chapter, we learn about two ways to **dive deeper** into your software's functionality, and give the customer that warm feeling in their chest that makes them say, *Yes, you're definitely the right developer for this job!*

Unit

type: String
properties: Map
id: int
name: String
weapons: Weapon *

setType(String)
getType(): String
setProperty(String, Object)
getProperty(String): Object
getId(): int
setName(String)
getName(): String
addWeapon(Weapon)
getWeapons(): Weapon *

All the properties that were common across units are represented as variables outside of the properties Map.

Sam figured that id would get set in the Unit constructor, so no need for a setId() method.

Each of the new properties gets its own set of methods.

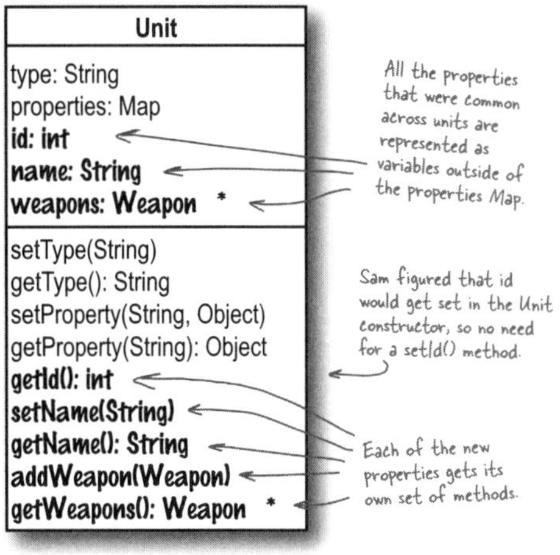

the ooa&d lifecycle

Putting It All Together

Are we there yet? We've been working on lots of individual ways to improve your software, but now it's time to **put it all together**. This is it, what you've been waiting for: we're going to take **everything** you've been learning, and show you how it's all really part of **a single process** that you can use over and over again to **write great software**.

appendix i: leftovers

The Top Ten Topics (we didn't cover)

Believe it or not, there's still more. Yes, with over 550 pages under your belt, there are still things we couldn't cram in. Even though these last ten topics don't deserve more than a mention, we didn't want to let you out of Objectville without a little more information on each one of them. But hey, now you've got just a little bit more to talk about during commercials of CATASTROPHE... and who doesn't love some stimulating OOA&D talk every now and then?

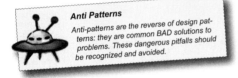

Anti Patterns

Anti-patterns are the reverse of design patterns: they are common BAD solutions to problems. These dangerous pitfalls should be recognized and avoided.

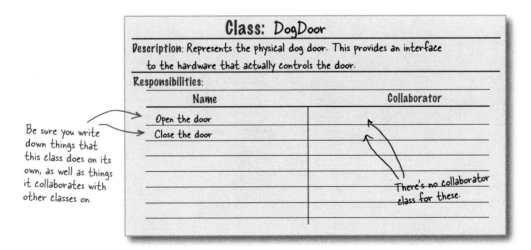

Class: DogDoor

Description: Represents the physical dog door. This provides an interface to the hardware that actually controls the door.

Responsibilities:

Name	Collaborator
Open the door	
Close the door	

Be sure you write down things that this class does on its own, as well as things it collaborates with other classes on.

There's no collaborator class for these.

appendix ii: welcome to objectville

Speaking the Language of OO

Get ready to take a trip to a foreign country. It's time to visit Objectville, a land where **objects do just what they're supposed to**, applications are all **well-encapsulated** (you'll find out exactly what that means shortly), and designs are easy to **reuse and extend**. But before we can get going, there are a few things you need to know first, and a little bit of **language skills** you're going to have to learn. Don't worry, though, it won't take long, and before you know it, you'll be speaking the language of OO like you've been living in the well-designed areas of Objectville for years.

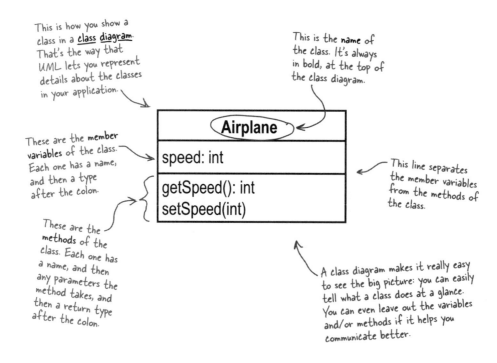

This is how you show a class in a *class diagram*. That's the way that UML lets you represent details about the classes in your application.

This is the name of the class. It's always in bold, at the top of the class diagram.

These are the member variables of the class. Each one has a name, and then a type after the colon.

This line separates the member variables from the methods of the class.

These are the methods of the class. Each one has a name, and then any parameters the method takes, and then a return type after the colon.

A class diagram makes it really easy to see the big picture: you can easily tell what a class does at a glance. You can even leave out the variables and/or methods if it helps you communicate better.

Airplane

speed: int

getSpeed(): int
setSpeed(int)

Intro

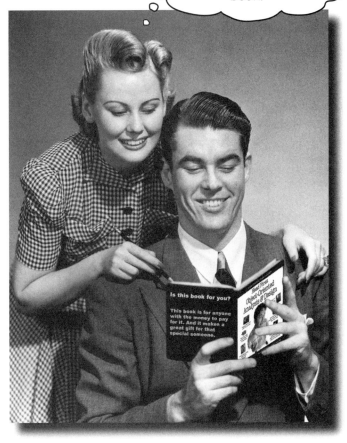

In this section, we answer the burning question:
"So why DID they put that in an OOA&D book?"

Who is this book for?

If you can answer "yes" to all of these:

(1) Do you know **Java**? (You don't need to be a guru.) ← *You'll probably be okay if you know C# instead.*

(2) Do you want to **learn, understand, remember, and apply** object-oriented analysis and design to **real world projects**, and write better software in the process?

(3) Do you prefer **stimulating dinner party conversation** to dry, dull, academic lectures?

this book is for you.

Who should probably back away from this book?

If you can answer "yes" to any *one* of these:

(1) Are you **completely new** to Java? (You don't need to be advanced, and even if you don't know Java, but you know C#, you'll probably understand almost all of the code examples. You also might be okay with just a C++ background.)

(2) Are you a kick-butt OO designer/developer looking for **a *reference* book?**

(3) Are you **afraid to try something different**? Would you rather have a root canal than mix stripes with plaid? Do you believe that a technical book can't be serious if programming concepts are anthropomorphized?

this book is not for you.

[note from marketing: this book is for anyone with a credit card.]

We know what you're thinking.

"How can *this* be a serious programming book?"

"What's with all the graphics?"

"Can I actually *learn* it this way?"

And we know what your *brain* is thinking.

Your brain craves novelty. It's always searching, scanning, *waiting* for something unusual. It was built that way, and it helps you stay alive.

So what does your brain do with all the routine, ordinary, normal things you encounter? Everything it *can* to stop them from interfering with the brain's *real* job—recording things that *matter*. It doesn't bother saving the boring things; they never make it past the "this is obviously not important" filter.

How does your brain *know* what's important? Suppose you're out for a day hike and a tiger jumps in front of you, what happens inside your head and body?

Neurons fire. Emotions crank up. *Chemicals surge.*

And that's how your brain knows...

This must be important! Don't forget it!

But imagine you're at home, or in a library. It's a safe, warm, tiger-free zone. You're studying. Getting ready for an exam. Or trying to learn some tough technical topic your boss thinks will take a week, ten days at the most.

Just one problem. Your brain's trying to do you a big favor. It's trying to make sure that this *obviously* non-important content doesn't clutter up scarce resources. Resources that are better spent storing the really *big* things. Like tigers. Like the danger of fire. Like how you should never again snowboard in shorts.

And there's no simple way to tell your brain, "Hey brain, thank you very much, but no matter how dull this book is, and how little I'm registering on the emotional Richter scale right now, I really *do* want you to keep this stuff around."

Your brain thinks THIS is important.

Your brain thinks THIS isn't worth saving.

Great. Only 637 more dull, dry, boring pages.

We think of a "Head First" reader as a <u>learner</u>.

So what does it take to *learn* something? First, you have to *get* it, then make sure you don't *forget* it. It's not about pushing facts into your head. Based on the latest research in cognitive science, neurobiology, and educational psychology, *learning* takes a lot more than text on a page. We know what turns your brain on.

Some of the Head First learning principles:

Make it visual. Images are far more memorable than words alone, and make learning much more effective (up to 89% improvement in recall and transfer studies). It also makes things more understandable. **Put the words within or near the graphics** they relate to, rather than on the bottom or on another page, and learners will be up to *twice* as likely to solve problems related to the content.

All of this is represented in a single Connection object.

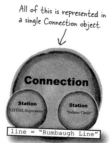

Use a conversational and personalized style. In recent studies, students performed up to 40% better on post-learning tests if the content spoke directly to the reader, using a first-person, conversational style rather than taking a formal tone. Tell stories instead of lecturing. Use casual language. Don't take yourself too seriously. Which would *you* pay more attention to: a stimulating dinner party companion, or a lecture?

> It really sucks to be an abstract method. You don't have a body.

Get the learner to think more deeply. In other words, unless you actively flex your neurons, nothing much happens in your head. A reader has to be motivated, engaged, curious, and inspired to solve problems, draw conclusions, and generate new knowledge. And for that, you need challenges, exercises, and thought-provoking questions, and activities that involve both sides of the brain, and multiple senses.

> Great software *every time*? I can hardly **imagine** what that would be like!

```
abstract void roam();
```

No method body! End it with a semicolon.

Get—and keep—the reader's attention. We've all had the "I really want to learn this but I can't stay awake past page one" experience. Your brain pays attention to things that are out of the ordinary, interesting, strange, eye-catching, unexpected. Learning a new, tough, technical topic doesn't have to be boring. Your brain will learn much more quickly if it's not.

Touch their emotions. We now know that your ability to remember something is largely dependent on its emotional content. You remember what you *care* about. You remember when you *feel* something. No, we're not talking heart-wrenching stories about a boy and his dog. We're talking emotions like surprise, curiosity, fun, "what the...?", and the feeling of "I Rule!" that comes when you solve a puzzle, learn something everybody else thinks is hard, or realize you know something that "I'm more technical than thou" Bob from engineering *doesn't*.

Metacognition: thinking about thinking

If you really want to learn, and you want to learn more quickly and more deeply, pay attention to how you pay attention. Think about how you think. Learn how you learn.

Most of us did not take courses on metacognition or learning theory when we were growing up. We were *expected* to learn, but rarely *taught* to learn.

But we assume that if you're holding this book, you really want to learn object-oriented analysis and design. And you probably don't want to spend a lot of time. And since you're going to develop software, you need to *remember* what you read. And for that, you've got to *understand* it. To get the most from this book, or *any* book or learning experience, take responsibility for your brain. Your brain on *this* content.

The trick is to get your brain to see the new material you're learning as Really Important. Crucial to your well-being. As important as a tiger. Otherwise, you're in for a constant battle, with your brain doing its best to keep the new content from sticking.

So just how *DO* you get your brain to think object-oriented analysis and design is a hungry tiger?

There's the slow, tedious way, or the faster, more effective way. The slow way is about sheer repetition. You obviously know that you *are* able to learn and remember even the dullest of topics if you keep pounding the same thing into your brain. With enough repetition, your brain says, "This doesn't *feel* important to him, but he keeps looking at the same thing *over* and *over* and *over*, so I suppose it must be."

The faster way is to do **anything that increases brain activity,** especially different *types* of brain activity. The things on the previous page are a big part of the solution, and they're all things that have been proven to help your brain work in your favor. For example, studies show that putting words *within* the pictures they describe (as opposed to somewhere else in the page, like a caption or in the body text) causes your brain to try to makes sense of how the words and picture relate, and this causes more neurons to fire. More neurons firing = more chances for your brain to *get* that this is something worth paying attention to, and possibly recording.

A conversational style helps because people tend to pay more attention when they perceive that they're in a conversation, since they're expected to follow along and hold up their end. The amazing thing is, your brain doesn't necessarily *care* that the "conversation" is between you and a book! On the other hand, if the writing style is formal and dry, your brain perceives it the same way you experience being lectured to while sitting in a roomful of passive attendees. No need to stay awake.

But pictures and conversational style are just the beginning.

Here's what WE did:

We used *pictures*, because your brain is tuned for visuals, not text. As far as your brain's concerned, a picture really *is* worth 1,024 words. And when text and pictures work together, we embedded the text *in* the pictures because your brain works more effectively when the text is *within* the thing the text refers to, as opposed to in a caption or buried in the text somewhere.

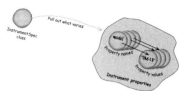

We used *redundancy*, saying the same thing in *different* ways and with different media types, and *multiple senses*, to increase the chance that the content gets coded into more than one area of your brain.

We used concepts and pictures in *unexpected* ways because your brain is tuned for novelty, and we used pictures and ideas with at least *some* **emotional** *content*, because your brain is tuned to pay attention to the biochemistry of emotions. That which causes you to *feel* something is more likely to be remembered, even if that feeling is nothing more than a little **humor**, **surprise**, or **interest.**

We used a personalized, **conversational style**, because your brain is tuned to pay more attention when it believes you're in a conversation than if it thinks you're passively listening to a presentation. Your brain does this even when you're *reading*.

We included more than 80 **activities**, because your brain is tuned to learn and remember more when you **do** things than when you *read* about things. And we made the exercises challenging-yet-do-able, because that's what most people prefer.

We used **multiple learning styles**, because *you* might prefer step-by-step procedures, while someone else wants to understand the big picture first, and someone else just wants to see a code example. But regardless of your own learning preference, *everyone* benefits from seeing the same content represented in multiple ways.

We include content for **both sides of your brain**, because the more of your brain you engage, the more likely you are to learn and remember, and the longer you can stay focused. Since working one side of the brain often means giving the other side a chance to rest, you can be more productive at learning for a longer period of time.

And we included **stories** and exercises that present **more than one point of view,** because your brain is tuned to learn more deeply when it's forced to make evaluations and judgements.

We included **challenges**, with exercises, and by asking **questions** that don't always have a straight answer, because your brain is tuned to learn and remember when it has to *work* at something. Think about it—you can't get your *body* in shape just by *watching* people at the gym. But we did our best to make sure that when you're working hard, it's on the *right* things. That **you're not spending one extra dendrite** processing a hard-to-understand example, or parsing difficult, jargon-laden, or overly terse text.

We used **people**. In stories, examples, pictures, etc., because, well, because *you're* a person. And your brain pays more attention to *people* than it does to *things*.

We used an **80/20** approach. We assume that if you're going for a PhD in software design, this won't be your only book. So we don't talk about *everything*. Just the stuff you'll actually *need*.

Here's what YOU can do to bend your brain into submission

So, we did our part. The rest is up to you. These tips are a starting point; listen to your brain and figure out what works for you and what doesn't. Try new things.

Cut this out and stick it on your refrigerator.

---

① Slow down. The more you understand, the less you have to memorize.

Don't just *read*. Stop and think. When the book asks you a question, don't just skip to the answer. Imagine that someone really *is* asking the question. The more deeply you force your brain to think, the better chance you have of learning and remembering.

② Do the exercises. Write your own notes.

We put them in, but if we did them for you, that would be like having someone else do your workouts for you. And don't just *look* at the exercises. **Use a pencil.** There's plenty of evidence that physical activity *while* learning can increase the learning.

③ Read the "There are No Dumb Questions"

That means all of them. They're not optional side-bars—***they're part of the core content!*** Don't skip them.

④ Make this the last thing you read before bed. Or at least the last *challenging* thing.

Part of the learning (especially the transfer to long-term memory) happens *after* you put the book down. Your brain needs time on its own, to do more processing. If you put in something new during that processing time, some of what you just learned will be lost.

⑤ Drink water. Lots of it.

Your brain works best in a nice bath of fluid. Dehydration (which can happen before you ever feel thirsty) decreases cognitive function.

⑥ Talk about it. Out loud.

Speaking activates a different part of the brain. If you're trying to understand something, or increase your chance of remembering it later, say it out loud. Better still, try to explain it out loud to someone else. You'll learn more quickly, and you might uncover ideas you hadn't known were there when you were reading about it.

⑦ Listen to your brain.

Pay attention to whether your brain is getting overloaded. If you find yourself starting to skim the surface or forget what you just read, it's time for a break. Once you go past a certain point, you won't learn faster by trying to shove more in, and you might even hurt the process.

⑧ *Feel* something!

Your brain needs to know that this *matters*. Get involved with the stories. Make up your own captions for the photos. Groaning over a bad joke is *still* better than feeling nothing at all.

⑨ *Design* something!

Apply what you read to something new you're designing, or rework an older project. Just do *something* to get some experience beyond the exercises and activities in this book. All you need is a problem to solve... a problem that might benefit from one or more techniques that we talk about.

Read Me

This is a learning experience, not a reference book. We deliberately stripped out everything that might get in the way of learning whatever it is we're working on at that point in the book. And the first time through, you need to begin at the beginning, because the book makes assumptions about what you've already seen and learned.

We assume you are familiar with Java.

It would take an entire book to teach you Java (in fact, that's exactly what it took: *Head First Java*). We chose to focus this book on analysis and design, so the chapters are written with the assumption that you know the basics of Java. When intermediate or advanced concepts come up, they're taught as if they might be totally new to you, though.

If you're completely new to Java, or coming to this book from a C# or C++ background, we strongly recommend you turn to the back of the book and read Appendix II before going on. That appendix has some intro material that will help you start this book off on the right foot.

We only use Java 5 when we have to.

Java 5.0 introduces a lot of new features to the Java language, ranging from generics to parameterized types to enumerated types to the **foreach** looping construct. Since many professional programmers are just moving to Java 5, we didn't want you getting hung up on new syntax while you're trying to learn about OOA&D. In most cases, we stuck with pre-Java 5 syntax. The only exception is in Chapter 1, when we needed an enumerated type—and we explained enums in that section in some detail.

If you're new to Java 5, you should have no trouble with any of the code examples. If you're already comfortable with Java 5, then you will get a few compiler warnings about unchecked and unsafe operations, due to our lack of typed collections, but you should be able to update the code for Java 5 on your own quite easily.

The activities are NOT optional.

The exercises and activities are not add-ons; they're part of the core content of the book. Some of them are to help with memory, some are for understanding, and some will help you apply what you've learned. ***Don't skip the exercises.*** The crossword puzzles are the only things you don't *have* to do, but they're good for giving your brain a chance to think about the words and terms you've been learning in a different context.

The redundancy is intentional and important.

One distinct difference in a Head First book is that we want you to *really* get it. And we want you to finish the book remembering what you've learned. Most reference books don't have retention and recall as a goal, but this book is about *learning*, so you'll see some of the same concepts come up more than once.

The examples are as lean as possible.

Our readers tell us that it's frustrating to wade through 200 lines of an example looking for the two lines they need to understand. Most examples in this book are shown within the smallest possible context, so that the part you're trying to learn is clear and simple. Don't expect all of the examples to be robust, or even complete—they are written specifically for learning, and aren't always fully-functional.

In some cases, we haven't included all of the import statements needed, but we assume that if you're a Java programmer, you know that **ArrayList** is in `java.util`, for example. If the imports are not part of the normal core J2SE API, we mention it. We've also placed all the source code on the web so you can download it. You'll find it at `http://www.headfirstlabs.com/books/hfoo/`.

Also, for the sake of focusing on the learning side of the code, we did not put our classes into packages (in other words, they're all in the Java default package). We don't recommend this in the real world, and when you download the code examples from this book, you'll find that all classes *are* in packages.

The 'Brain Power' exercises don't have answers.

For some of them, there is no right answer, and for others, part of the learning experience of the Brain Power activities is for you to decide if and when your answers are right. In some of the Brain Power exercises you will find hints to point you in the right direction.

The Technical Team

Ara Yapejian

Hannibal Scipio

Chris Austin

Technical Reviewers:

Huge thanks to our amazing trio of technical reviewers. These guys caught mistakes that we missed, let us know when we were moving too fast (or too slow), and even let us know when our jokes sucked. Several times, they turned chapters around in a matter of hours... we're not sure if that means they're really helpful, or need to get away from software development a little more. **Hannibal** in particular made our week when he let us know that the big OOA&D arrow in Chapter 10 was "Hot!" Thanks guys, this book wouldn't be nearly as solid without your hard work.

Kathy Sierra and Bert Bates:

We continue to be amazed at the insight and expertise that **Bert Bates** has about cliffs, and that **Kathy Sierra** has about dog doors. If that doesn't make much sense, don't be surprised—everything you know about almost everything gets turned on its head when you meet this pair, and yet we all came out much for the better because of their help.

Bert and Kathy did a ton of review at the eleventh hour, and we're thankful they did. Their help and guidance continues to be the heart of Head First.

Kathy Sierra

Bert Bates

Acknowledgements

My co-authors:

Because I'm doing the typing, I get to step out of "we" mode for a moment and say thanks to my co-authors, **Dave West** and **Gary Pollice**. Neither of these guys knew what they were signing up for when they came on board, but I've never been so impressed by a couple of guys willing to explain, defend, and even change their opinions and knowledge about software design, requirements and analysis, and lift shafts. They were simply incredible, writing up until the very last day, and even got me to relax and laugh until I cried on several occasions.

Our editor:

← Mary O'Brien

This book wouldn't be in your hands if not for **Mary O'Brien**. I think it's fair to say she fought more battles and paved the way for us to work without interruption more times than any of us really are aware of. Most importantly, she made this the single most enjoyable project we've worked on in our careers. Frankly, she kicked our asses a number of times, and it made all the difference. She really doesn't realize how much of an effect she has on the people she works with, because we don't tell her enough how much we respect her and value her opinions. So there, now you know, Mary. If we could put your name on the cover, we would (oh, wait... we did!).

The O'Reilly team:

These books are a team effort, never more so than on this one. **Mike Hendrickson** and **Laurie Petrycki** oversaw this project at various times, and took heated phone calls more than once. **Sanders Kleinfeld** cut his Head First teeth on this project, and managed to come out alive; better yet, he did a great job, improving the book, and we all are excited that this is just the first of many Head First books he'll be working on. **Mike Loukides** found Bert and Kathy way back when, and **Tim O'Reilly** had the foresight to turn their crazy idea into a series. As always, **Kyle Hart** is instrumental in getting these books "out there", and **Edie Freedman**'s beautiful cover design continues to amaze us all.

A particularly special thanks goes out to **Louise Barr**, the Head First Design Editor. Lou pulled several 12- and 14-hour days to help us with graphics in this book, and put together the amazing Objectville Subway Map in Chapter 10. Lou, your work has improved the learning quality of this book, and we can't thank you enough for your contributions.

Lou Barr

Special thanks

Near the completion of this book, **Laura Baldwin**, the CFO of O'Reilly, encountered some personal tragedy. It's hard to know what to say in these situations, especially because Laura has really become the backbone of O'Reilly in many ways. Laura, we are thinking and praying for you and your family, and we wish you all the very, very best in the days to come. We know you'd want nothing more than to see everyone at O'Reilly working harder than ever while you're away.

This book is certainly a testament to the people at O'Reilly continuing to deliver, and in many of our conversations, your name came up as someone we wanted to support, and not let down in any way. Your effect on this company is extraordinary, and O'Reilly and the Head First series will all be much better for the day you can return to us in full swing.

1 well-designed apps rock

Great Software Begins Here

I can hardly get over it, Sue, but since I started using OOA&D, I'm just a new man... a new man, I'll tell you!

So how do you *really* write great software? It's never easy trying to figure out **where to start**. Does the application actually **do what it's supposed to**? And what about things like duplicate code—that can't be good, can it? It's usually pretty hard to know **what you should work on first**, and still make sure you don't screw everything else up in the process. No worries here, though. By the time you're done with this chapter, you'll **know how to write great software**, and be well on your way to improving the way you develop applications forever. Finally, you'll understand why **OOA&D** is a four-letter word that your mother actually *wants* you to know about.

Rock and roll is forever!

There's nothing better than the sound of a killer guitar in the hands of a great player, and Rick's Guitars specializes in finding the perfect instrument for his discerning customers.

You wouldn't believe the selection we have here. Come on in, tell us about what kind of guitar you like, and we'll find you the perfect instrument, guaranteed!

Meet Rick, guitar aficionado, and owner of a high–end guitar shop.

Just a few months ago, Rick decided to throw out his paper-based system for keeping track of guitars, and start using a computer-based system to store his inventory. He hired a popular programming firm, Down and Dirty Coding, and they've already built him an inventory management app. He's even had the firm build him a new search tool to help him match up a customer to their dream instrument.

Rick's shiny new application...

Here's the application that the programming firm built for Rick... they've put together a system to completely replace all of Rick's handwritten notes, and help him match his customers with the perfect guitar. Here's the UML class diagram they gave Rick to show him what they did:

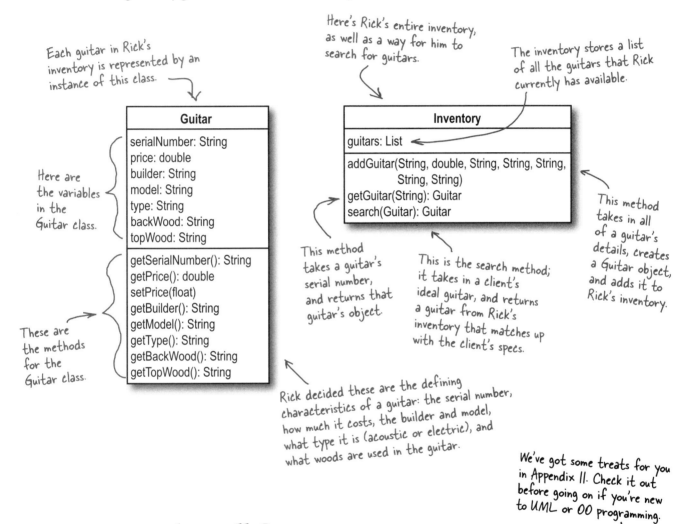

Each guitar in Rick's inventory is represented by an instance of this class.

Here's Rick's entire inventory, as well as a way for him to search for guitars.

The inventory stores a list of all the guitars that Rick currently has available.

Guitar

serialNumber: String
price: double
builder: String
model: String
type: String
backWood: String
topWood: String

getSerialNumber(): String
getPrice(): double
setPrice(float)
getBuilder(): String
getModel(): String
getType(): String
getBackWood(): String
getTopWood(): String

Here are the variables in the Guitar class.

These are the methods for the Guitar class.

Inventory

guitars: List

addGuitar(String, double, String, String, String, String, String)
getGuitar(String): Guitar
search(Guitar): Guitar

This method takes a guitar's serial number, and returns that guitar's object.

This is the search method; it takes in a client's ideal guitar, and returns a guitar from Rick's inventory that matches up with the client's specs.

This method takes in all of a guitar's details, creates a Guitar object, and adds it to Rick's inventory.

Rick decided these are the defining characteristics of a guitar: the serial number, how much it costs, the builder and model, what type it is (acoustic or electric), and what woods are used in the guitar.

We've got some treats for you in Appendix II. Check it out before going on if you're new to UML or OO programming.

New to Objectville?

If you're new to object oriented programming, haven't heard of UML before, or aren't sure about the diagram above, it's OK! We've prepared a special "Welcome to Objectville" care package for you to get you started. Flip to the back of the book, and read Appendix II—we promise you'll be glad you did. Then come back here, and this will all make a lot more sense.

Here what the code for Guitar.java looks like

You've seen the class diagram for Rick's application on the last page; now let's look at what the actual code for **Guitar.java** and **Inventory.java** look like.

These are all the properties we saw from the class diagram for the Guitar class.

```java
public class Guitar {

    private String serialNumber, builder, model, type, backWood, topWood;
    private double price;

    public Guitar(String serialNumber, double price,
                  String builder, String model, String type,
                  String backWood, String topWood) {
        this.serialNumber = serialNumber;
        this.price = price;
        this.builder = builder;
        this.model = model;
        this.type = type;
        this.backWood = backWood;
        this.topWood = topWood;
    }

    public String getSerialNumber() {
        return serialNumber;
    }

    public double getPrice() {
        return price;
    }
    public void setPrice(float newPrice) {
        this.price = newPrice;
    }
    public String getBuilder() {
        return builder;
    }
    public String getModel() {
        return model;
    }
    public String getType() {
        return type;
    }
    public String getBackWood() {
        return backWood;
    }
    public String getTopWood() {
        return topWood;
    }
}
```

UML class diagrams don't show constructors; the Guitar constructor does just what you'd expect, though: sets all the initial properties for a new Guitar.

You can see how the class diagram matches up with the methods in the Guitar class's code.

Guitar
serialNumber: String
price: double
builder: String
model: String
type: String
backWood: String
topWood: String
getSerialNumber(): String
getPrice(): double
setPrice(float)
getBuilder(): String
getModel(): String
getType(): String
getBackWood(): Stri
getTopWood(): Strin

Guitar.java

And Inventory.java...

Remember, we've stripped out the import statements to save some space.

```java
public class Inventory {
  private List guitars;

  public Inventory() {
    guitars = new LinkedList();
  }

  public void addGuitar(String serialNumber, double price,
                        String builder, String model,
                        String type, String backWood, String topWood) {
    Guitar guitar = new Guitar(serialNumber, price, builder,
                             model, type, backWood, topWood);
    guitars.add(guitar);
  }
  public Guitar getGuitar(String serialNumber) {
    for (Iterator i = guitars.iterator(); i.hasNext(); ) {
      Guitar guitar = (Guitar)i.next();
      if (guitar.getSerialNumber().equals(serialNumber)) {
        return guitar;
      }
    }
    return null;
  }
  public Guitar search(Guitar searchGuitar) {
    for (Iterator i = guitars.iterator(); i.hasNext(); ) {
      Guitar guitar = (Guitar)i.next();
      // Ignore serial number since that's unique
      // Ignore price since that's unique
      String builder = searchGuitar.getBuilder();
      if ((builder != null) && (!builder.equals("")) &&
          (!builder.equals(guitar.getBuilder())))
        continue;
      String model = searchGuitar.getModel();
      if ((model != null) && (!model.equals("")) &&
          (!model.equals(guitar.getModel())))
        continue;
      String type = searchGuitar.getType();
      if ((type != null) && (!searchGuitar.equals("")) &&
          (!type.equals(guitar.getType())))
        continue;
      String backWood = searchGuitar.getBackWood();
      if ((backWood != null) && (!backWood.equals("")) &&
          (!backWood.equals(guitar.getBackWood())))
        continue;
      String topWood = searchGuitar.getTopWood();
      if ((topWood != null) && (!topWood.equals("")) &&
          (!topWood.equals(guitar.getTopWood())))
        continue;
    }
    return null;
  }
}
```

addGuitar() takes in all the properties required to create a new Guitar instance, creates one, and adds it to the inventory.

This method is a bit of a mess... it compares each property of the Guitar object it's passed in to each Guitar object in Rick's inventory.

Inventory
guitars: List
addGuitar(String, double, String, String, String, String, String)
getGuitar(String): Guitar
search(Guitar): Guitar

```
class
Inven-
tory {

search()
```

Inventory.java

But then Rick started losing customers...

It seems like no matter who the customer is and what they like, Rick's new search program almost always comes up empty when it looks for good guitar matches. But Rick knows he has guitars that these customers would like... so what's going on?

FindGuitarTester.java simulates a typical day for Rick now... a customer comes in, tells him what they like, and he runs a search on his inventory.

```java
public class FindGuitarTester {

  public static void main(String[] args) {
    // Set up Rick's guitar inventory
    Inventory inventory = new Inventory();
    initializeInventory(inventory);

    Guitar whatErinLikes = new Guitar("", 0, "fender", "Stratocastor",
                                      "electric", "Alder", "Alder");
    Guitar guitar = inventory.search(whatErinLikes);
    if (guitar != null) {
      System.out.println("Erin, you might like this " +
        guitar.getBuilder() + " " + guitar.getModel() + " " +
        guitar.getType() + " guitar:\n   " +
        guitar.getBackWood() + " back and sides,\n   " +
        guitar.getTopWood() + " top.\nYou can have it for only $" +
        guitar.getPrice() + "!");
    } else {
      System.out.println("Sorry, Erin, we have nothing for you.");
    }
  }

  private static void initializeInventory(Inventory inventory) {
    // Add guitars to the inventory...
  }
}
```

Erin is looking for a Fender "Strat" guitar, made of Alder.

FindGuitarTester.java

```
File Edit Window Help C7#5
%java FindGuitarTester
Sorry, Erin, we have nothing for you.
```

Here's what happens when Erin comes into Rick's store, and Rick tries to find her a guitar.

I'm sorry, Rick, I guess I'll just go to that other store across town.

But I know I have a killer Fender Strat guitar. Look, it's right here:

```
inventory.addGuitar("V95693",
    1499.95, "Fender", "Stratocastor",
    "electric", "Alder", "Alder");
```

These specs seem to match up perfectly with what Erin asked for... so what's going on?

Here's part of the code that sets up Rick's inventory. Looks like he's got the perfect guitar for Erin.

Sharpen your pencil

How would you redesign Rick's app?

Look over the last three pages, showing the code for Rick's app, and the results of running a search. What problems do you see? What would you change? Write down the **FIRST** thing you'd do to improve Rick's app in the blanks below.

_____

_____

_____

What's the FIRST thing you'd change?

It's obvious that Rick's app has problems, but it's not so obvious what we
should work on first. And it looks like there's no shortage of opinion:

> Whoa... these notes from the owner says he wants his clients to have multiple choices. Shouldn't the search() method return a list of matches?

> Look at all those Strings! That's terrible... can't we use constants or objects instead?

Guitar

serialNumber: String
price: double
builder: String
model: String
type: String
backWood: String
topWood: String

getSerialNumber(): String
getPrice(): double
setPrice(float)
getBuilder(): String
getModel(): String
getType(): String
getBackWood(): String
getTopWood(): String

Inventory

guitars: List

addGuitar(String, double, String, String, String, String)
getGuitar(String): Guitar
search(Guitar): Guitar

> This design is terrible! The Inventory and Guitar classes depend on each other too much, and I can't see how this is an architecture that you'd ever be able to build upon. We need some restructuring.

Joe's fairly new to programming, but he's a big believer in writing object-oriented code.

Jill's got a rep for always delivering exactly what the customer wants.

Frank's been around for a while and really knows his OO principles and design patterns.

What would you do **first**?

How am I supposed to know where to start? I feel like every time I get a new project to work on, everyone's got a different opinion about what to do first. Sometimes I get it right, and sometimes I end up reworking the whole app because I started in the wrong place. **I just want to write great software!** So what should I do first in Rick's app?

How do you write great software, every time?

Wait a second... I hate to butt in, but what does "great software" mean? That's sort of a vague term to be throwing around, isn't it?

Good question... and there are <u>lots</u> of different answers:

The customer-friendly programmer says:

"Great software always does what the customer wants it to. So even if customers think of new ways to use the software, it doesn't break or give them unexpected results."

↱ This approach is all about making sure the customer is happy with what their app does.

The object-oriented programmer says:

"Great software is code that is object-oriented. So there's not a bunch of duplicate code, and each object pretty much controls its own behavior. It's also easy to extend because your design is really solid and flexible."

This design-focused approach optimizes code for extension and reuse, and takes advantages of design patterns and proven OO techniques.

↑ Good OO programmers are always looking for ways to make their code more flexible.

The design-guru programmer says:

"Great software is when you use tried-and-true design patterns and principles. You've kept your objects loosely coupled, and your code open for extension but closed for modification. That also helps make the code more reusable, so you don't have to rework everything to use parts of your application over and over again."

Not sure about what all that means? It's OK... you'll learn about all these things in the upcoming chapters.

 **Sharpen your pencil**

What do *you* think "great software" means?

You've seen what several different types of programmers think great software is... so who is right? Or do you have your own definition of what makes an application great? It's your turn to write down what you think makes for great software:

Write your name here...

...and write what you think great software means here.

_____ **says:**

"_____

_____

_____

_____

_____ "

Great software is...
more than just <u>one</u> thing

It's going to take more than just a simple definition to figure out exactly what "great software" means. In fact, *all* of the different programmers on page 10 talked about a *part* of what makes software great.

First, great software must satisfy the customer. The software must do what the customer wants it to do.

Win your customers over

Customers will think your software is great when it does what it's supposed to do.

Building software that works right is great, but what about when it's time to add to your code, or reuse it in another application? It's not enough to just have software that works like the customer wants it to; your software better be able to stand the test of time.

Second, great software is well-designed, well-coded, and easy to maintain, reuse, and extend.

Make your code as smart as you are.

You (and your co-workers) will think your software is great when it's easy to maintain, reuse, and extend.

Wow, if my code could do all that, then it really **would** be great software! I even think I see how you could turn this into a few simple steps that work on every project.

Great software in 3 easy steps

It may not seem easy now, but we'll show you how OOA&D and some basic principles can change your software forever.

1. Make sure your software does what the customer wants it to do.

This step focuses on the customer. Make sure the app does what it's supposed to do FIRST. This is where getting good requirements and doing some analysis comes in.

2. Apply basic OO principles to add flexibility.

Once your software works, you can look for any duplicate code that might have slipped in, and make sure you're using good OO programming techniques.

3. Strive for a maintainable, reusable design.

Got a good object—oriented app that does what it should? It's time to apply patterns and principles to make sure your software is ready to use for years to come.

Remember Rick? Remember his lost customers?

Let's put our ideas about how to write great software to the test and see if they hold up in the real world. Rick's got a search tool that isn't working, and it's your job to fix the application, and turn it into something great. Let's look back at the app and see what's going on:

Here's our test program that reveals a problem with the search tool.

```
public class FindGuitarTester {

  public static void main(String[] args) {
    // Set up Rick's guitar inventory
    Inventory inventory = new Inventory();
    initializeInventory(inventory);

    Guitar whatErinLikes = new Guitar("", 0, "fender", "Stratocastor",
                                      "electric", "Alder", "Alder");
    Guitar guitar = inventory.search(whatErinLikes);
    if (guitar != null) {
```

class
FindGui-
tar {
  main()
}

FindGuitarTester.java

Rick's app should match Erin's preferences here...

...to this guitar in Rick's inventory.

```
inventory.addGuitar("V95693",
  1499.95, "Fender", "Stratocastor",
  "electric", "Alder", "Alder");
```

So let's apply our 3 steps:

1. Make sure your software does what the customer wants it to do.

Remember, we need to start out by making sure the app actually does what Rick wants... and it's definitely not doing that right now.

2. Apply basic OO principles to add flexibility.

Don't worry too much about trying to apply patterns or other OO techniques to your app at this point... just get it to where it's working like it should.

3. Strive for a maintainable, reusable design.

If we're starting with functionality, let's figure out what's going on with that broken search() method. It looks like in Rick's inventory, he's got "Fender" with a capital "F," and the customer's specs have "fender" all lowercase. We just need to do a case-insensitive string comparison in the search() method.

Let's get a little help from some of our programmer buddies.

Frank

Jill

Joe

Frank: Sure, that would fix the problem Rick's having now, but I think there's probably a better way to make this work than just calling toLowerCase() on a bunch of strings all over the place.

Joe: Yeah, I was thinking the same thing. I mean, all that string comparison seems like a bad idea. Couldn't we use constants or maybe some enumerated types for the builders and woods?

Jill: You guys are thinking *way* too far ahead. Step 1 was supposed to be fixing the app so it does what the customer wants it to do. I thought we weren't supposed to worry about design yet.

Frank: Well, yeah, I get that we're supposed to focus on the customer. But we can at least be smart about *how* we fix things, right? I mean, why create problems we'll have to come back and fix later on if we can avoid them from the start?

Jill: Hmmm... I guess that does make sense. We don't want our solution to this problem creating new design problems for us down the road. But we're still not going to mess with the other parts of the application, right?

Frank: Right. We can just remove all those strings, and the string comparisons, to avoid this whole case-matching thing.

Joe: Exactly. If we go with enumerated types, we can ensure that only valid values for the builder, woods, and type of guitar are accepted. That'll make sure that Rick's clients actually get to look at guitars that match their preferences.

Jill: And we've actually done a little bit of design at the same time... very cool! Let's put this into action.

Don't <u>create</u> problems to <u>solve</u> problems.

Ditching String comparisons

The first improvement we can make to Rick's guitar search tool is getting rid of all those annoying **String** comparisons. And even though you could use a function like **toLowerCase()** to avoid problems with uppercase and lowercase letters, let's avoid **String** comparisons altogether:

These are all Java enums, enumerated types that function sort of like constants.

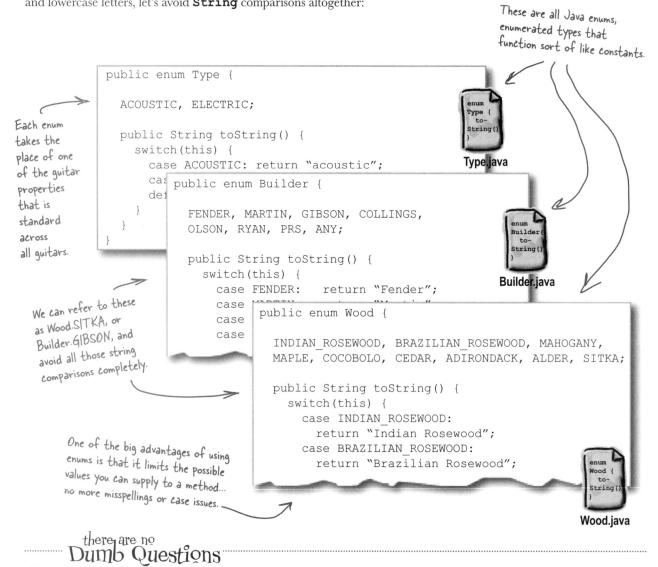

```
public enum Type {

  ACOUSTIC, ELECTRIC;

  public String toString() {
    switch(this) {
      case ACOUSTIC: return "acoustic";
      case ELECTRIC: return "electric";
      default:
    }
  }
}
```

Type.java

Each enum takes the place of one of the guitar properties that is standard across all guitars.

```
public enum Builder {

  FENDER, MARTIN, GIBSON, COLLINGS,
  OLSON, RYAN, PRS, ANY;

  public String toString() {
    switch(this) {
      case FENDER:   return "Fender";
      case MARTIN
      case
      case
```

Builder.java

We can refer to these as Wood.SITKA, or Builder.GIBSON, and avoid all those string comparisons completely.

```
public enum Wood {

  INDIAN_ROSEWOOD, BRAZILIAN_ROSEWOOD, MAHOGANY,
  MAPLE, COCOBOLO, CEDAR, ADIRONDACK, ALDER, SITKA;

  public String toString() {
    switch(this) {
      case INDIAN_ROSEWOOD:
        return "Indian Rosewood";
      case BRAZILIAN_ROSEWOOD:
        return "Brazilian Rosewood";
```

Wood.java

One of the big advantages of using enums is that it limits the possible values you can supply to a method... no more misspellings or case issues.

there are no Dumb Questions

Q: I've never seen an enum before. What is that, exactly?

A: Enums are *enumerated types*. They're available in C, C++, Java version 5.0 and up, and will even be a part of Perl 6.

Enumerated types let you define a type name, like **Wood**, and then a set of values that are allowed for that type (like **COCOBOLO**, **SITKA**, and **MAHOGANY**). Then, you refer to a specific value like this: **Wood.COCOBOLO**.

Q: And why are enumerated types so helpful here?

```
public class FindGuitarTester {

  public static void main(String[] args) {
    // Set up Rick's guitar inventory
    Inventory inventory = new Inventory();
    initializeInventory(inventory);

    Guitar whatErinLikes = new Guitar("", 0, Builder.FENDER,
      "Stratocastor", Type.ELECTRIC, Wood.ALDER, Wood.ALDER);
    Guitar guitar = inventory.search(whatErinLikes);
    if (guitar != null) {
```

We can replace all those String preferences with the new enumerated type values.

class FindGuitar { main() }

FindGuitarTester.java

The only String left is for the model, since there really isn't a limited set of these like there is with builders and wood.

```
public Guitar search(Guitar searchGuitar) {
  for (Iterator i = guitars.iterator(); i.hasNext(); ) {
    Guitar guitar = (Guitar)i.next();
    // Ignore serial number since that's unique
    // Ignore price since that's unique
    if (searchGuitar.getBuilder() != guitar.getBuilder())
      continue;
    String model = searchGuitar.getModel().toLowerCase();
    if ((model != null) && (!model.equals("")) &&
        (!model.equals(guitar.getModel().toLowerCase())))
      continue;
    if (searchGuitar.getType() != guitar.getType())
      continue;
    if (searchGuitar.getBackWood() != guitar.getBackWood())
      continue;
    if (searchGuitar.getTopWood() != guitar.getTopWood())
      continue;
    return guitar;
  }
  return null;
}
```

The only property that we need to worry about case on is the model, since that's still a String.

It looks like nothing has changed, but with enums, we don't have to worry about these comparisons getting screwed up by misspellings or case issues.

class Inventory { search() }

Inventory.java

A: The cool thing about enums is that methods or classes that use them are protected from any values not defined in the enum. So you can't misspell or mistype an enum without getting a compiler error. It's a great way to get not only type safety, but value safety; you can avoid getting bad data for anything that has a standard range or set of legal values.

Q: **I'm using an older version of Java. Am I stuck?**

A: No, not at all. Visit the Head First Labs web site at http://www.headfirstlabs.com, where we've posted a version of Rick's Guitars that doesn't use enums, and will work with older JDKs.

Let's take a look at the big picture:

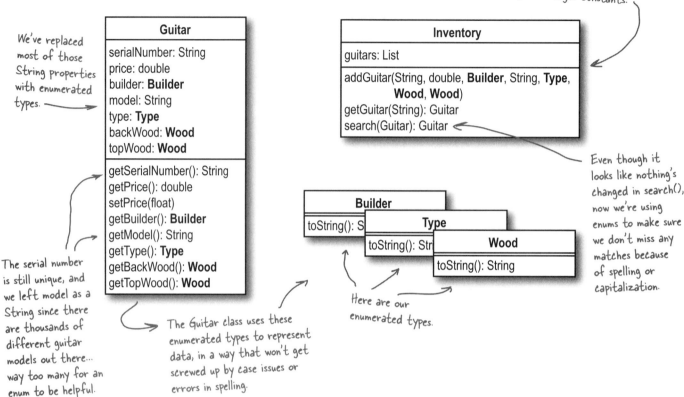

Now the addGuitar() method takes in several enums, instead of Strings or integer constants.

We've replaced most of those String properties with enumerated types.

Guitar

serialNumber: String
price: double
builder: **Builder**
model: String
type: **Type**
backWood: **Wood**
topWood: **Wood**

getSerialNumber(): String
getPrice(): double
setPrice(float)
getBuilder(): **Builder**
getModel(): String
getType(): **Type**
getBackWood(): **Wood**
getTopWood(): **Wood**

The serial number is still unique, and we left model as a String since there are thousands of different guitar models out there... way too many for an enum to be helpful.

The Guitar class uses these enumerated types to represent data, in a way that won't get screwed up by case issues or errors in spelling.

Inventory

guitars: List

addGuitar(String, double, **Builder**, String, **Type**, **Wood**, **Wood**)
getGuitar(String): Guitar
search(Guitar): Guitar

Even though it looks like nothing's changed in search(), now we're using enums to make sure we don't miss any matches because of spelling or capitalization.

Builder

toString(): S

Type

toString(): Str

Wood

toString(): String

Here are our enumerated types.

So what have we really done here?

We've gotten a lot closer to completing step 1 in building great software. Rick's problem with searches coming up empty when he's got a matching guitar in his inventory is a thing of the past.

Even better, we've made Rick's application *less fragile* along the way. It's not going to break so easily now, because we've added both type safety and value safety with these enums. That means less problems for Rick, and less maintenance for us.

Code that is not fragile is generally referred to as <u>robust code</u>.

1. Make sure your software does what the customer wants it to do.

Sharpen your pencil

Apply Step 1 to your own project.

It's time to see how you can satisfy your own customers. In the blank below, write a short description of the current project you're working on (you can also use a project you finished recently):

_____

_____

Now, write down the first thing you did when you started working on this project. Did it have anything to do with making sure your code did what the customer wanted it to?

_____

_____

_____

_____

If you started out focusing on something other than the customer, think about how you might have approached things differently if you knew about the 3 steps to building great software. What would have been different? Do you think your application would be any better or worse than it is right now?

_____

_____

_____

_____

there are no Dumb Questions

Q: So it's OK to do a *little* design when I'm working on Step 1, right?

A: Yeah, as long as your focus is still on the customer's needs. You want the basic features of your application in place *before* you start making big design changes. But while you're working on functionality, you can certainly use good OO principles and techniques to make sure your application is well designed from the start.

Q: That diagram over on page 18 is a class diagram right? Or is it class diagrams, since it's more than one class?

A: It is a class diagram, and a single diagram can have multiple classes in it. In fact, class diagrams can show a lot more detail than you've seen so far, and we'll be adding to them in the next several chapters.

Q: So we're ready to move on to Step 2, and start applying OO principles, right?

A: Not quite... there's one more thing Rick would like us to help him with before we're ready to start analyzing our code for places we might be able to improve it. Remember, our first job is to please the customer, and *then* we really focus on improving our OO design.

So I thought this was perfect, but then I realized... I have **two** guitars that Erin would love. Could you make the search tool return both of them?

Rick's happy with your improvements but he really needs the app to return <u>all</u> matching guitars, not just one.

Rick would really like Erin to be able to check out <u>both</u> of these guitars.

```
inventory.addGuitar("V95693",
    1499.95, Builder.FENDER,
    "Stratocastor", Type.ELECTRIC,
    Wood.ALDER, Wood.ALDER);
```

These guitars are almost exactly the same. Only the serial number and price are different.

```
inventory.addGuitar("V9512",
    1549.95, Builder.FENDER,
    "Stratocastor", Type.ELECTRIC,
    Wood.ALDER, Wood.ALDER);
```

Rick's customers want choices!

Rick's come up with a new requirement for his app: he wants his search tool to return *all* the guitars that match his client's specs, not just the first one in his inventory.

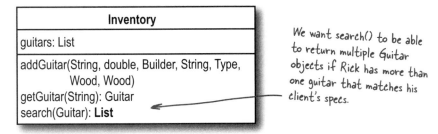

Inventory
guitars: List
addGuitar(String, double, Builder, String, Type, Wood, Wood)   getGuitar(String): Guitar   search(Guitar): **List**

We want search() to be able to return multiple Guitar objects if Rick has more than one guitar that matches his client's specs.

Code Magnets

Let's continue with Step 1, and make sure we've got the app working right. Below is the code for the search() method in Rick's inventory tool, but it's up to you to fill in the missing pieces. Use the code magnets at the bottom of the page to return all the matching guitars from Rick's inventory.

```java
public _____ search(Guitar searchGuitar) {
  _____ _____ = new _____();
  for (Iterator i = guitars.iterator(); i.hasNext(); ) {
    Guitar guitar = (Guitar)i.next();
    // Ignore serial number since that's unique
    // Ignore price since that's unique
    if (searchGuitar.getBuilder() != guitar.getBuilder())
      continue;
    String model = searchGuitar.getModel();
    if ((model != null) && (!model.equals("")) &&
        (!model.equals(guitar.getModel())))
      continue;
    if (searchGuitar.getType() != guitar.getType())
      continue;
    if (searchGuitar.getBackWood() != guitar.getBackWood())
      continue;
    if (searchGuitar.getTopWood() != guitar.getTopWood())
      continue;
    _____._____(_____);
  }
  return _____;
}
```

List LinkedList List matchingGuitars guitar ArrayList

List List matchingGuitars add matchingGuitars guitar ArrayList

LinkedList matchingGuitars

Code Magnets

Let's keep on with Step 1, and make sure we've got the app working right. Below is the code for the search() method in Rick's inventory tool, but it's up to you to fill in the missing pieces. Use the code magnets at the bottom of the page to return all the matching guitars from Rick's inventory.

You actually could have used either a LinkedList or an ArrayList here... both choices are OK.

```
public  List  search(Guitar searchGuitar) {
   List  matchingGuitars  = new  LinkedList ();
   for (Iterator i = guitars.iterator(); i.hasNext(); ) {
      Guitar guitar = (Guitar)i.next();
      // Ignore serial number since that's unique
      // Ignore price since that's unique
      if (searchGuitar.getBuilder() != guitar.getBuilder())
        continue;
      String model = searchGuitar.getModel();
      if ((model != null) && (!model.equals("")) &&
          (!model.equals(guitar.getModel())))
        continue;
      if (searchGuitar.getType() != guitar.getType())
        continue;
      if (searchGuitar.getBackWood() != guitar.getBackWood())
        continue;
      if (searchGuitar.getTopWood() != guitar.getTopWood())
        continue;
      matchingGuitars . add ( guitar );
   }
   return matchingGuitars ;
}
```

Matching guitars get added to the list of options for Rick's client.

Leftover magnets.

List ArrayList guitar ArrayList LinkedList matchingGuitars List

<hr>

there are no Dumb Questions

Q: So I'm not done with the first step until the application works like my customer wants it to?

A: Exactly. You want to make sure that the application works like it should before you dive into applying design patterns or trying to do any real restructuring of how the application is put together.

Q: And why is it so important to finish Step 1 before going on to Step 2?

A: You're going to make lots of changes to your software when you're getting it to work right. Trying to do too much design before you've at least got the basic functionality down can end up being a waste, because a lot of the design will change as you're adding new pieces of functionality to your classes and methods.

Q: You seem sort of hung up on this "Step 1" and "Step 2" business. What if I don't code my apps that way?

A: There's nothing that says you have to follow these steps exactly, but they do provide an easy path to follow to make sure your software does what it's supposed to, and is well-designed and easy to reuse. If you've got something similar that accomplishes the same goals, that's great!

Test drive

We've talked a lot about getting the right requirements from the customer, but now we need to make sure we've actually got those requirements handled by our code. Let's test things out, and see if our app is working like Rick wants it to:

Here's the test program, updated to use the new version of Rick's search tool.

```java
public class FindGuitarTester {

  public static void main(String[] args) {
    // Set up Rick's guitar inventory
    Inventory inventory = new Inventory();
    initializeInventory(inventory);

    Guitar whatErinLikes = new Guitar("", 0, Builder.FENDER,
                              "Stratocastor", Type.ELECTRIC,
                              Wood.ALDER, Wood.ALDER);

    List matchingGuitars = inventory.search(whatErinLikes);
    if (!matchingGuitars.isEmpty()) {
      System.out.println("Erin, you might like these guitars:");
      for (Iterator i = matchingGuitars.iterator(); i.hasNext(); ) {
        Guitar guitar = (Guitar)i.next();
        System.out.println("  We have a " +
          guitar.getBuilder() + " " + guitar.getModel() + " " +
          guitar.getType() + " guitar:\n    " +
          guitar.getBackWood() + " back and sides,\n    " +
          guitar.getTopWood() + " top.\n  You can have it for only $" +
          guitar.getPrice() + "!\n  ----");
      }
    } else {
      System.out.println("Sorry, Erin, we have nothing for you.");
    }
  }
}
```

We're using enumerated types in this test drive. No typing mistakes this time!

In this new version, we need to iterate over all the choices returned from the search tool.

This time we get a whole list of guitars that match the client's specs.

class FindGui-tar {
  main()
}

FindGuitarTester.java

```
File  Edit  Window  Help  SweetSmell
%java FindGuitarTester
Erin, you might like these guitars:
  We have a Fender Stratocastor electric guitar:
    Alder back and sides,
    Alder top.
  You can have it for only $1499.95!
  ----
  We have a Fender Stratocastor electric guitar:
    Alder back and sides,
    Alder top.
  You can have it for only $1549.95!
  ----
```

Yes! That's **exactly** what I want it to do.

Everything worked! Erin gets several guitar recommendations, and Rick's customers are going to start buying guitars again.

Back to our steps

Now that Rick's all set with our software, we can begin to use some OO principles and make sure the app is flexible and well-designed.

1. Make sure your software does what the customer wants it to do.

Now that the app does what Rick wants, we're finished up with this step.

So this is where we can make sure there's no duplicate code, and all our objects are well designed, right?

2. Apply basic OO principles to add flexibility.

Here's where you take software that works, and make sure the way it's put together actually makes sense.

3. Strive for a maintainable, reusable design.

Looking for problems

Let's dig a little deeper into our search tool, and see if we can find any problems that some simple OO principles might help improve. Let's start by taking a closer look at how the **search()** method in **Inventory** works:

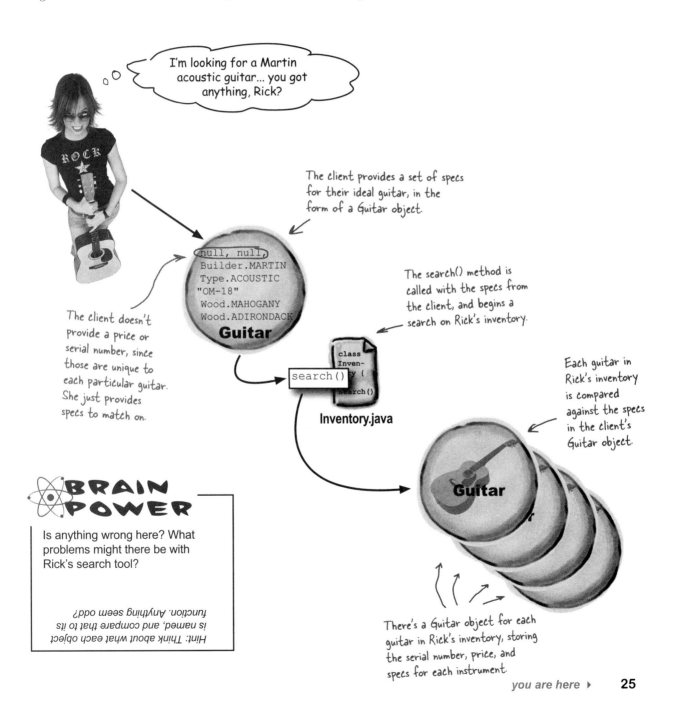

I'm looking for a Martin acoustic guitar... you got anything, Rick?

The client provides a set of specs for their ideal guitar, in the form of a Guitar object.

null, null,
Builder.MARTIN
Type.ACOUSTIC
"OM-18"
Wood.MAHOGANY
Wood.ADIRONDACK
Guitar

The client doesn't provide a price or serial number, since those are unique to each particular guitar. She just provides specs to match on.

The search() method is called with the specs from the client, and begins a search on Rick's inventory.

```
class
Inven-
tory {

  search()

  search()
```
Inventory.java

Each guitar in Rick's inventory is compared against the specs in the client's Guitar object.

Guitar

There's a Guitar object for each guitar in Rick's inventory, storing the serial number, price, and specs for each instrument.

BRAIN POWER

Is anything wrong here? What problems might there be with Rick's search tool?

Hint: Think about what each object is named, and compare that to its function. Anything seem odd?

Analyze the search() method

Let's spend a little time analyzing exactly what goes on in the **search()** method of **Inventory.java**. Before we look at the code, though, let's think about what this method *should* do.

❶ The client provides their guitar preferences. ◄──────── The client can specify only general properties of an instrument. So they never supply a serial number or a price.

Each of Rick's clients has some properties that they're interested in finding in their ideal guitar: the woods used, or the type of guitar, or a particular builder or model. They provide these preferences to Rick, who feeds them into his inventory search tool.

❷ The search tool looks through Rick's inventory.

Once the search tool knows what Rick's client wants, it starts to loop through each guitar in Rick's inventory.

❸ Each guitar is compared to the client's preferences.

For each guitar in Rick's inventory, the search tool sees if that guitar matches the client's preferences. If there's a match, the matching guitar is added to the list of choices for the client.

↖
─── All the general properties, like the top wood and guitar builder, are compared to the client's preferences.

❹ Rick's client is given a list of matching guitars.

Finally, the list of matching guitars is returned to Rick and his client. The client can make a choice, and Rick can make a sale.

Use a **textual description** of the problem you're trying to solve to make sure that your design lines up with the intended functionality of your application.

The Mystery of the Mismatched Object Type

In the better-designed areas of Objectville, objects are very particular about their jobs. Each object is interested in doing its job, and only its job, to the best of its ability. There's nothing a well-designed object hates more than being used to do something that really isn't its true purpose.

Unfortunately, it's come to our attention that this is exactly what is happening in Rick's inventory search tool: somewhere, an object is being used to do something that it really shouldn't be doing. It's your job to solve this mystery and figure out how we can get Rick's application back in line.

To help you figure out what's gone amiss, here are some helpful tips to start you on your search for the mismatched object type:

1. Objects should do what their names indicate.
If an object is named Jet, it should probably takeOff() and land(), but it shouldn't takeTicket()—that's the job of another object, and doesn't belong in Jet.

2. Each object should represent a single concept.
You don't want objects serving double or triple duty. Avoid a Duck object that represents a real quacking duck, a yellow plastic duck, and someone dropping their head down to avoid getting hit by a baseball.

3. Unused properties are a dead giveaway.
If you've got an object that is being used with no-value or null properties often, you've probably got an object doing more than one job. If you rarely have values for a certain property, why is that property part of the object? Would there be a better object to use with just a subset of those properties?

STOP! Try and solve this mystery before turning the page.

What do you think the mismatched object type is? Write your answer in the blank below:

_____

What do you think you should do to fix the problem? What changes would you make?

_____

_____

_____

You know, Rick's clients really aren't providing a Guitar object... I mean, they don't actually give him a guitar to compare against his inventory.

Encapsulation allows you to hide the inner workings of your application's parts, but yet make it clear what each part does.

New to **encapsulation**? Flip ahead to Appendix II, read that short introduction to Objectville, and then come back here and keep reading.

Frank: Hey, that's right, Joe. I hadn't thought about that before.

Jill: So what? Using a Guitar object makes it really easy to do comparisons in the search() method.

Joe: Not any more than some other object would. Look:

```
if (searchGuitar.getBuilder() !=
        guitar.getBuilder()) {
  continue;
}
```

A small fragment from the search() method in Inventory.

Joe: It really doesn't matter what type of object we're using there, as long as we can figure out what specific things Rick's clients are looking for.

Frank: Yeah, I think we should have a new object that stores just the specs that clients want to send to the search() method. Then they're not sending an entire Guitar object, which never seemed to make much sense to me.

Jill: But isn't that going to create some duplicate code? If there's an object for all the client's specs, and then the Guitar has all its properties, we've got two getBuilder() methods, two getBackWood() methods... that's not good.

Frank: So why don't we just encapsulate those properties away from Guitar into a new object?

Joe: Whoa... I was with you until you said "encapsulate." I thought that was when you made all your variables private, so nobody could use them incorrectly. What's that got to do with a guitar's properties?

Frank: Encapsulation is also about breaking your app into logical parts, and then keeping those parts separate. So just like you keep the data in your classes separate from the rest of your app's behavior, we can keep the generic properties of a guitar separate from the actual Guitar object itself.

Jill: And then Guitar just has a variable pointing to a new object type that stores all its properties?

Frank: Exactly! So we've really encapsulated the guitar properties out of Guitar, and put them in their own separate object. Look, we could do something like this...

Sharpen your pencil

Create the GuitarSpec object.

Below, you'll see the class diagram for Guitar, and the new GuitarSpec object that Frank, Jill, and Joe have been discussing. It's your job to add all the properties and methods that you think you'll need to GuitarSpec. Then, cross out anything you don't need anymore in the Guitar class. Finally, we've left you some space in the Guitar class diagram in case you think you need to add any new properties or methods. Good luck!

Guitar
serialNumber: String
price: double
builder: Builder
model: String
type: Type
backWood: Wood
topWood: Wood
_____
_____
getSerialNumber(): String
getPrice(): double
setPrice(float)
getBuilder(): Builder
getModel(): String
getType(): Type
getBackWood(): Wood
getTopWood(): Wood
_____
_____

Move anything out of the Guitar object that you think belongs in the new GuitarSpec class.

You can add extra properties and methods to Guitar if you think you need to.

GuitarSpec
_____
_____
_____
_____
_____
_____
_____
_____
_____
_____
_____
_____
_____
_____
_____
_____
_____
_____
_____

✷ If you get stuck, think about the things that are common between the Guitar object and what a client would supply to the search() method.

Sharpen your pencil
answers

Create the GuitarSpec object.

Below you'll see the class diagram for Guitar, and the new GuitarSpec object that Frank, Jill, and Joe have been discussing. It's your job to add all the properties and methods that you think you'll need to GuitarSpec. See if you made the same changes that we did.

These two properties are still unique to each Guitar, so they stay.

These are the properties that Rick's clients supply to search(), so we can move them into GuitarSpec.

We also need a reference to a GuitarSpec object for each guitar.

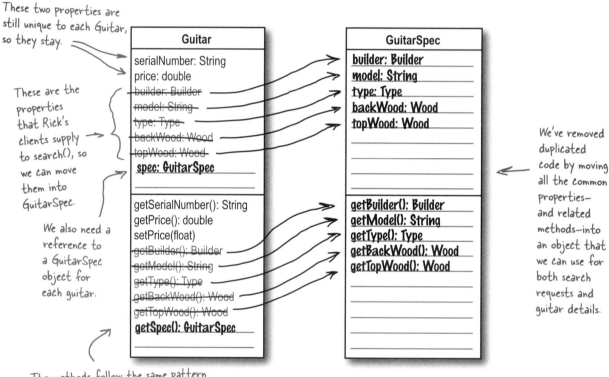

Guitar
serialNumber: String
price: double
~~builder: Builder~~
~~model: String~~
~~type: Type~~
~~backWood: Wood~~
~~topWood: Wood~~
spec: GuitarSpec
getSerialNumber(): String
getPrice(): double
setPrice(float)
~~getBuilder(): Builder~~
~~getModel(): String~~
~~getType(): Type~~
~~getBackWood(): Wood~~
~~getTopWood(): Wood~~
getSpec(): GuitarSpec

GuitarSpec
builder: Builder
model: String
type: Type
backWood: Wood
topWood: Wood
getBuilder(): Builder
getModel(): String
getType(): Type
getBackWood(): Wood
getTopWood(): Wood

We've removed duplicated code by moving all the common properties—and related methods—into an object that we can use for both search requests and guitar details.

The methods follow the same pattern as the properties: we remove any duplication between the client's specs and the Guitar object.

Now update your own code

With this class diagram, you should be able to add the **GuitarSpec** class to your application, and update the **Guitar** class as well. Go ahead and make any changes you need to **Inventory.java** so that the search tool compiles, as well.

there are no
Dumb Questions

Q: I understand why we need an object for the client to send specs to search()... but why are we using that object to hold properties for Guitar, too?

A: Suppose you just used `GuitarSpec` to hold client specs for sending to the **search()** method, and you kept the `Guitar` class just the same as it was. If Rick started carrying 12-string guitars, and wanted a **numStrings** property, you'd have to add that property—and code for a **getNumStrings()** method—to both the `GuitarSpec` and `Guitar` classes. Can you see how this would lead to duplicate code?

Instead, we can put all that (potentially) duplicate code into the `GuitarSpec` class, and then have `Guitar` objects reference an instance of it to avoid any duplication.

Anytime you see duplicate code, look for a place to encapsulate!

Q: I still am confused about how this is a form of encapsulation. Can you explain that again?

A: The idea behind encapsulation is to protect information in one part of your application from the other parts of your application. In its simplest form, you can protect the data in your class from the rest of your app by making that data private. But sometimes the information might be an entire set of properties—like the details about a guitar—or even behavior—like how a particular type of duck flies.

When you break that behavior out from a class, you can change the behavior without the class having to change as well. So if you changed how properties were stored, you wouldn't have to change your `Guitar` class at all, because the properties are encapsulated away from `Guitar`.

That's the power of encapsulation: by breaking up the different parts of your app, you can change one part without having to change all the other parts. In general, you should encapsulate the parts of your app that might vary away from the parts that will stay the same.

Let's see how we're coming along on our three steps to great software.
↓

✓ **1. Make sure your software does what the customer wants it to do.**

Here's what we're doing now: working on design.

2. Apply basic OO principles to add flexibility.

This is where you look for big problems, especially related to things like duplicate code or bad class design.

3. Strive for a maintainable, reusable design.

Remember, we've got even more design work to do in this step, so before you're done, your software is really easy to extend and reuse.

Update the Inventory class

Now that we've encapsulated away the specifications of a guitar, we'll need to make a few other changes to our code.

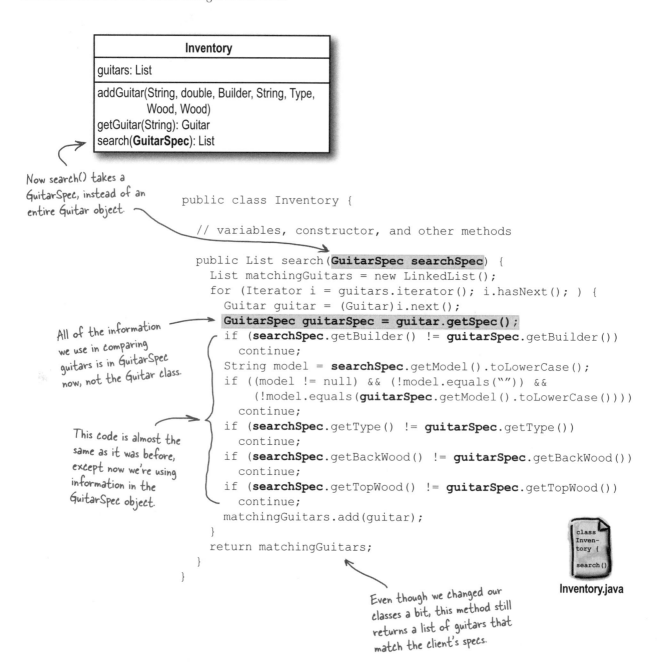

Inventory
guitars: List
addGuitar(String, double, Builder, String, Type, Wood, Wood) getGuitar(String): Guitar search(**GuitarSpec**): List

Now search() takes a GuitarSpec, instead of an entire Guitar object.

```
public class Inventory {

    // variables, constructor, and other methods

    public List search(GuitarSpec searchSpec) {
        List matchingGuitars = new LinkedList();
        for (Iterator i = guitars.iterator(); i.hasNext(); ) {
            Guitar guitar = (Guitar)i.next();
            GuitarSpec guitarSpec = guitar.getSpec();
            if (searchSpec.getBuilder() != guitarSpec.getBuilder())
                continue;
            String model = searchSpec.getModel().toLowerCase();
            if ((model != null) && (!model.equals("")) &&
                (!model.equals(guitarSpec.getModel().toLowerCase())))
                continue;
            if (searchSpec.getType() != guitarSpec.getType())
                continue;
            if (searchSpec.getBackWood() != guitarSpec.getBackWood())
                continue;
            if (searchSpec.getTopWood() != guitarSpec.getTopWood())
                continue;
            matchingGuitars.add(guitar);
        }
        return matchingGuitars;
    }
}
```

All of the information we use in comparing guitars is in GuitarSpec now, not the Guitar class.

This code is almost the same as it was before, except now we're using information in the GuitarSpec object.

Even though we changed our classes a bit, this method still returns a list of guitars that match the client's specs.

Inventory.java

Getting ready for another test drive

You'll need to update the **FindGuitarTester** class to test out all these new changes:

```java
public class FindGuitarTester {

  public static void main(String[] args) {
    // Set up Rick's guitar inventory
    Inventory inventory = new Inventory();
    initializeInventory(inventory);

    GuitarSpec whatErinLikes =
        new GuitarSpec(Builder.FENDER, "Stratocastor", Type.ELECTRIC,
                        Wood.ALDER, Wood.ALDER);
    List matchingGuitars = inventory.search(whatErinLikes);
    if (!matchingGuitars.isEmpty()) {
      System.out.println("Erin, you might like these guitars:");
      for (Iterator i = matchingGuitars.iterator(); i.hasNext(); ) {
        Guitar guitar = (Guitar)i.next();
        GuitarSpec spec = guitar.getSpec();
        System.out.println("  We have a " +
          spec.getBuilder() + " " + spec.getModel() + " " +
          spec.getType() + " guitar:\n       " +
          spec.getBackWood() + " back and sides,\n        " +
          spec.getTopWood() + " top.\n  You can have it for only $" +
          guitar.getPrice() + "!\n  ----");
      }
    } else {
      System.out.println("Sorry, Erin, we have nothing for you.");
    }
  }

  private static void initializeInventory(Inventory inventory) {
    // Add guitars to the inventory...
  }
}
```

This time, the client sends a GuitarSpec to search().

We're using the new GuitarSpec class here as well.

FindGuitarTester.java

Get Online

You can download the current version of Rick's search tool at http://www.headfirstlabs.com. Just look for Head First OOA&D, and find "Rick's Guitars (with encapsulation)".

WHY DO I MATTER?

You've learned a lot about writing great software, and there's still more to go! Take a deep breath and think about some of the terms and principles we've covered. Connect the words on the left to the purposes of those techniques and principles on the right.

Flexibility

Encapsulation

Functionality

Design Pattern

Without me, you'll never actually make the customer happy. No matter how well-designed your application is, I'm the thing that puts a smile on the customer's face.

I'm all about reuse and making sure you're not trying to solve a problem that someone else has already figured out.

You use me to keep the parts of your code that stay the same separate from the parts that change; then it's really easy to make changes to your code without breaking everything.

Use me so that your software can change and grow without constant rework. I keep your application from being fragile.

⟶ Answers on page 52.

---

there are no Dumb Questions

Q: Encapsulation isn't the only OO principle I can use at this stage, is it?

A: Nope. Other good OO principles that you might want to think about at this stage are inheritance and polymorphism. Both of these relate to duplicate code and encapsulation though, so starting out by looking for places where you could use encapsulation to better your design is always a good idea.

We'll talk about a lot more OO programming principles throughout this book (and even see a few sing in Chapter 8), so don't worry if you are still getting a handle on things at this point. You'll learn a lot more about encapsulation, class design, and more before we're done.

Q: But I don't really see how this encapsulation makes my code more flexible. Can you explain that again?

A: Once you've gotten your software to work like it's supposed to, flexibility becomes a big deal. What if the customer wants to add new properties or features to the app? If you've got tons of duplicate code or confusing inheritance structures in your app, making changes is going to be a pain.

By introducing principles like encapsulation and good class design into your code, it's easier to make these changes, and your application becomes a lot more flexible.

Getting back to Rick's app...

Let's make sure all our changes haven't messed up the way Rick's tool works. Compile your classes, and run the **FindGuitarTester** program again:

```
File Edit Window Help NotQuiteTheSame
%java FindGuitarTester
Erin, you might like these guitars:
    We have a Fender Stratocastor electric guitar:
        Alder back and sides,
        Alder top.
    You can have it for only $1499.95!
    ----
    We have a Fender Stratocastor electric guitar:
        Alder back and sides,
        Alder top.
    You can have it for only $1549.95!
    ----
```

The results aren't different this time, but the application is better designed, and much more flexible.

BRAIN POWER

Can you think of three specific ways that well-designed software is easier to change than software that has duplicate code?

Design once, design twice

Once you've taken a first pass over your software and applied some basic OO principles, you're ready to take another look, and this time make sure your software is not only flexible, but easily reused and extended.

1. Make sure your software does what the customer wants it to do.

It's time to really think about reuse, and how easy it is to make changes to your software. Here's where you can take some well-designed classes and really turn them into a reusable, extensible piece of software.

2. Apply basic OO principles to add flexibility.

Once you've applied some basic OO principles, you're ready to apply some patterns and really focus on reuse.

3. Strive for a maintainable, reusable design.

Let's make sure Inventory.java is (really) well-designed

We've already used encapsulation to improve the design of Rick's search tool, but there are still some places in our code where we could get rid of potential problems. This will make our code easier to extend when Rick comes up with that *next* new feature he wants in his inventory search tool, and easier to reuse if we want to take just a few parts of the app and use them in other contexts.

Now that you've made Rick a working search tool, you <u>know</u> he's gonna call you back when he wants changes made to the tool.

Here's the search() method from Inventory.java. Take a close look at this code.

```java
public List search(GuitarSpec searchSpec) {
    List matchingGuitars = new LinkedList();
    for (Iterator i = guitars.iterator(); i.hasNext(); ) {
        Guitar guitar = (Guitar)i.next();
        GuitarSpec guitarSpec = guitar.getSpec();
        if (searchSpec.getBuilder() != guitarSpec.getBuilder())
            continue;
        String model = searchSpec.getModel().toLowerCase();
        if ((model != null) && (!model.equals("")) &&
             (!model.equals(guitarSpec.getModel().toLowerCase())))
            continue;
        if (searchSpec.getType() != guitarSpec.getType())
            continue;
        if (searchSpec.getBackWood() != guitarSpec.getBackWood())
            continue;
        if (searchSpec.getTopWood() != guitarSpec.getTopWood())
            continue;
        matchingGuitars.add(guitar);
    }
    return matchingGuitars;
}
```

Inventory.java

Sharpen your pencil

What would you change about this code?

There's a big problem with the code shown above, and it's up to you to figure it out. In the blanks below, write down what you think the problem is, and how you would fix it.

_____

_____

_____

See what we said on page 53.

You know, I've always loved playing 12-string guitars. How hard would it be to update my app so I can sell 12-string guitars, and let my clients search for them, too?

How easy is it to make this change to Rick's application?

Take a look at the class diagram for Rick's application, and think about what you would need to do to add support for 12-string guitars. What properties and methods would you need to add, and to what classes? And what code would you need to change to allow Rick's clients to search for 12-strings?

How many classes did you have to modify to make this change? Do you think Rick's application is well designed right now?

Guitar
serialNumber: String price: double spec: GuitarSpec
getSerialNumber(): String getPrice(): double setPrice(float) getSpec(): GuitarSpec

GuitarSpec

builder: Builder
model: String
type: Type
backWood: Wood
topWood: Wood

getBuilder(): Builder
getModel(): String
getType(): Type
getBackWood(): Wood
getTopWood(): Wood

Annotate Rick's class diagram.

 Sharpen your pencil

Rick wants to be able to sell 12-string guitars. Get out your pencil, and add notes to the class diagram showing the following things:

1. Where you'd add a new property, called numStrings, to store the number of strings a guitar has.
2. Where you'd add a new method, called getNumStrings(), to return the number of strings a guitar has.
3. What other code you think you'd need to change so that Rick's clients can specify that they want to try out 12-string guitars.

Finally, in the blanks below, write down any problems with this design that you found when adding support for 12-string guitars.

_____

_____

_____

Here's a hint: you should get an answer here related to what you wrote down in the blanks back on page 37.

Inventory

guitars: List

addGuitar(String, double, Builder, String, Type,
        Wood, Wood)
getGuitar(String): Guitar
search(GuitarSpec): List

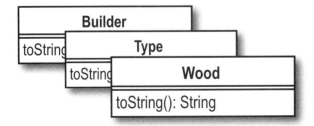

Builder

toString

Type

toString

Wood

toString(): String

⚛ **BRAIN POWER**

What's the advantage of using a numStrings property instead of just adding a boolean property to indicate if a guitar is a 12-string?

Sharpen your pencil answers

Annotate Rick's class diagram.

Rick wants to be able to sell 12-string guitars. Get out your pencil, and add notes to the class diagram showing the following things:

1. Where you'd add a new property, called numStrings, to store the number of strings a guitar has.
2. Where you'd add a new method, called getNumStrings(), to return the number of strings a guitar has.
3. What other code you think you'd need to change so that Rick's clients can specify that they want to try out 12-string guitars.

Finally, in the blanks below, write down any problems with this design that you found when adding support for 12-string guitars.

We're adding a property to GuitarSpec, but we have to change code in the Inventory class's search() method, as well as in the constructor to the Guitar class.

Here's what we came up with... did you write down something similar?

We need to change the constructor of this class, since it takes in all the properties in GuitarSpec, and creates a GuitarSpec object itself.

Guitar
serialNumber: String
price: double
spec: GuitarSpec
getSerialNumber(): String
getPrice(): double
setPrice(float)
getSpec(): GuitarSpec

This class's addGuitar() method deals with all of a guitar's properties, too. New properties means changes to this method—that's a problem.

We need to add a numStrings property to the GuitarSpec class.

GuitarSpec
builder: Builder
model: String
type: Type
backWood: Wood
topWood: Wood
getBuilder(): Builder
getModel(): String
getType(): Type
getBackWood(): Wood
getTopWood(): Wood

We need a getNumStrings() method in this class to return how many strings a guitar has.

Inventory
guitars: List
addGuitar(String, double, Builder, String, Type, Wood, Wood)
getGuitar(String): Guitar
search(GuitarSpec): List

Another problem: we have to change the search() method here to account for the new property in GuitarSpec.

Builder
toString

Type
toString

Wood
toString(): String

So that's the problem, right? We shouldn't have to change code in Guitar and Inventory to add a new property to the GuitarSpec class. Can't we just use more encapsulation to fix this?

That's right—we need to <u>encapsulate</u> the guitar specifications and <u>isolate them</u> from the rest of Rick's guitar search tool.

Even though you're adding a property only to the **GuitarSpec** class, there are two other classes that have to be modified: **Guitar** and **Inventory**. The constructor of **Guitar** has to take an additional property now, and the **search()** method of **Inventory** has to do an extra property comparison.

This constructor creates a GuitarSpec object, so every time the spec changes, this code has to change, too.

This code is <u>not</u> easy to reuse. The classes are all interdependent, and you can't use one class without using all the others, too.

```java
public Guitar(String serialNumber,
              double price,
              Builder builder,
              String model, Type type,
              Wood backWood, Wood topWood) {
    this.serialNumber = serialNumber;
    this.price = price;
    this.spec = new GuitarSpec(builder, model,
                    type, backWood, topWood);
}
```

Guitar.java

```java
public List search(GuitarSpec searchSpec) {
    List matchingGuitars = new LinkedList();
    for (Iterator i = guitars.iterator(); i.hasNext(); ) {
        Guitar guitar = (Guitar)i.next();
        GuitarSpec guitarSpec = guitar.getSpec();
        if (searchSpec.getBuilder() != guitarSpec.getBuilder())
            continue;
        String model = searchSpec.getModel().toLowerCase();
        if ((model != null) && (!model.equals("")) &&
            (!model.equals(guitarSpec.getModel().toLowerCase())))
            continue;
        if (searchSpec.getType() != guitarSpec.getType())
            continue;
        if (searchSpec.getBackWood() != guitarSpec.getBackWood())
            continue;
        if (searchSpec.getTopWood() != guitarSpec.getTopWood())
            continue;
        matchingGuitars.add(guitar);
    }
    return matchingGuitars;
}
```

Inventory.java

 Design Puzzle

It's not enough to know what's wrong with Rick's app, or even to figure out that we need some more encapsulation. Now ~~we~~ *you* need to actually figure out how to fix his app so it's easier to reuse and extend.

The problem:

Adding a new property to **GuitarSpec.java** results in changes to the code in **Guitar.java** and **Inventory.java**. The application should be restructured so that adding properties to **GuitarSpec** doesn't affect the code in the rest of the application.

Your task:

❶ Add a **numStrings** property and **getNumStrings()** method to **GuitarSpec.java**.

❷ Modify **Guitar.java** so that the properties of **GuitarSpec** are encapsulated away from the constructor of the class.

Not sure what delegation is? Check this out...

❸ Change the **search()** method in **Inventory.java** to delegate comparing the two **GuitarSpec** objects to the **GuitarSpec** class, instead of handling the comparison directly.

All you should have to do here is update your code that creates a sample inventory to use the new Guitar constructor.

❹ Update **FindGuitarTester.java** to work with your new classes, and make sure everything still works.

❺ Compare your answers with ours on page 44, and then get ready for another test drive to see if we've finally got this application finished.

there are no
Dumb Questions

Q: You said I should "delegate" comparisons to GuitarSpec. What's delegation?

A: Delegation is when an object needs to perform a certain task, and instead of doing that task directly, it asks *another* object to handle the task (or sometimes just a part of the task).

So in the design puzzle, you want the **search()** method in **Inventory** to ask **GuitarSpec** to tell it if two specs are equal, instead of comparing the two **GuitarSpec** objects directly within the **search()** method itself. **search()** *delegates* the comparison to **GuitarSpec**.

Q: What's the point of that?

A: Delegation makes your code more reusable. It also lets each object worry about its own functionality, rather than spreading the code that handles a single object's behavior all throughout your application

One of the most common examples of delegation in Java is the **equals()** method. Instead of a method trying to figure out if two objects are equal, it calls **equals()** on one of the objects and passes in the second object. Then it just gets back a true or false response from the **equals()** method.

Q: And what does delegation have to do with code being more reusable?

A: Delegation lets each object worry about equality (or some other task) on its own. This means your objects are more independent of each other, or more *loosely coupled*. Loosely coupled objects can be taken from one app and easily reused in another, because they're not tightly tied to other objects' code.

Q: And what does loosely coupled mean again?

A: Loosely coupled is when the objects in your application each have a specific job to do, and they do only that job. So the functionality of your app is spread out over lots of well-defined objects, which each do a single task really well.

Q: And why is that good?

A: Loosely coupled applications are usually more flexible, and easy to change. Since each object is pretty independent of the other objects, you can make a change to one object's behavior without having to change all the rest of your objects. So adding new features or functionality becomes a *lot* easier.

the
Scholar's Corner

delegation. The act of one object forwarding an operation to another object, to be performed on behalf of the first object.

 # Design Puzzle Solution

It's not enough to know what's wrong with Rick's app, or even to figure out that we need some more encapsulation. Now ~~we~~ *you* need to actually figure out how to fix his app so we can test it out.

The problem:

> Adding a new property to **GuitarSpec.java** results in changes to the code in **Guitar.java** and **Inventory.java**. The application should be refactored so that adding properties to **GuitarSpec** doesn't affect the code in the rest of the application.

Your task:

① Add a **numStrings** property and **getNumStrings()** method to **GuitarSpec.java**.

This is pretty easy stuff...

Don't forget to update the constructor for GuitarSpec.

```java
public class GuitarSpec {

  // other properties
  private int numStrings;

  public GuitarSpec(Builder builder, String model,
    Type type, int numStrings, Wood backWood, Wood topWood) {
    this.builder = builder;
    this.model = model;
    this.type = type;
    this.numStrings = numStrings;
    this.backWood = backWood;
    this.topWood = topWood;
  }

  // Other methods

  public int getNumStrings() {
    return numStrings;
  }
}
```

GuitarSpec.java

2 Modify **Guitar.java** so that the properties of **GuitarSpec** are encapsulated away from the constructor of the class.

```java
public Guitar(String serialNumber, double price, GuitarSpec spec) {
  this.serialNumber = serialNumber;
  this.price = price;
  this.spec = spec;
}
```

Just take in a GuitarSpec directly now, instead of creating one in this constructor.

```
class
Guitar {
  Gui-
tar()
}
```
Guitar.java

3 Change the **search()** method in **Inventory.java** to delegate comparing the two **GuitarSpec** objects to the **GuitarSpec** class, instead of handling the comparison directly.

The search() method got a *lot* simpler.

```java
public List search(GuitarSpec searchSpec) {
  List matchingGuitars = new LinkedList();
  for (Iterator i = guitars.iterator(); i.hasNext(); ) {
    Guitar guitar = (Guitar)i.next();
    if (guitar.getSpec().matches(searchSpec))
      matchingGuitars.add(guitar);
  }
  return matchingGuitars;
}
```

```
class
Inven-
tory {

search()
```
Inventory.java

Most of the code from search() has been pulled out, and put into a matches() method in GuitarSpec.java.

```java
public boolean matches(GuitarSpec otherSpec) {
  if (builder != otherSpec.builder)
    return false;
  if ((model != null) && (!model.equals("")) &&
      (!model.equals(otherSpec.model)))
    return false;
  if (type != otherSpec.type)
    return false;
  if (numStrings != otherSpec.numStrings)
    return false;
  if (backWood != otherSpec.backWood)
    return false;
  if (topWood != otherSpec.topWood)
    return false;
  return true;
}
```

Adding properties to GuitarSpec now requires only a change to that class, not Guitar.java or Inventory.java.

```
class
Guitar-
Spec {
  get-
Num-
Strings(
```
GuitarSpec.java

One last test drive
(and an app ready for reuse)

Wow, we've done a lot of work since Rick showed us that first version
of his guitar app. Let's see if the latest version still works for Rick
and his clients, and manages to satisfy our own goal of having a well-
designed, easily maintainable application that we can reuse.

*This is what
you should see
when you run
FindGuitarTester
with your new code.* →

```
File Edit Window Help ReuseRules
%java FindGuitarTester
Erin, you might like these guitars:
   We have a Fender Stratocastor 6-string electric guitar:
      Alder back and sides,
      Alder top.
   You can have it for only $1499.95!
   ----
   We have a Fender Stratocastor 6-string electric guitar:
      Alder back and sides,
      Alder top.
   You can have it for only $1549.95!
   ----
```

← *Erin gets a couple of
guitars to choose from,
and Rick is back to selling
guitars to his elite clientele.*

Congratulations!
You've turned Rick's broken
inventory search tool into a well-
designed piece of great software.

What we did

Let's take a quick look back at how we got Rick's search tool working so well:

Remember our 3 steps? We followed them to turn Rick's broken search tool into functional, well-designed software.

We started out by fixing some of the functionality problems with Rick's search tool.

1. Make sure your software does what the customer wants it to do.

We went on to add some more functionality, so that the search returns a list of guitars.

↓

While we were adding features, we made sure our design choices were really solid.

2. Apply basic OO principles to add flexibility.

We also encapsulated out the guitar properties, and made sure we could add new properties to the app easily.

↓

3. Strive for a maintainable, reusable design.

We even added delegation so that our objects are less dependent upon each other, and can be reused easily.

Remember this poor guy?

He just wanted to write great software. So what's the answer? How do you write great software <u>consistently</u>?

You just need a set of steps to follow that makes sure your software works and is well designed. It can be as simple as the three steps we used in working on Rick's app; you just need something that works, and that you can use on all of your software projects.

We call this OOA&D for short.

<u>Object-Oriented</u> <u>Analysis</u> & <u>Design</u> helps you write great software, every time

All this time that we've been talking about the three steps you can follow to write great software, we've really been talking about OOA&D.

OOA&D is really just an approach to writing software that focuses on making sure your code does what it's supposed to, and that it's well designed. That means your code is flexible, it's easy to make changes to it, and it's maintainable and reusable.

OOA&D is about writing great software, not doing a bunch of paperwork!

Customers are satisfied when their apps WORK.
We can get requirements from the customer to make sure that we build them what they ask for. Use cases and diagrams are helpful ways to do that, but it's all about figuring out what the customer wants the app to do.

We'll talk all about requirements in Chapter 2.

Customers are satisfied when their apps KEEP WORKING.
Nobody is happy when an application that worked yesterday is crashing today. If we design our apps well, then they're going to be robust, and not break every time a customer uses them in unusual ways. Class and sequence diagrams can help show us design problems, but the point is to write well-designed and robust code.

You've learned a bit about fragile apps already.

Customers are satisfied when their apps can be UPGRADED.
There's nothing worse than a customer asking for a simple new feature, and being told it's going to take two weeks and $25,000 to make it happen. Using OO techniques like encapsulation, composition, and delegation will make your applications maintainable and extensible.

Want more on delegation, composition, and aggregation? We'll talk about all of these in detail in Chapters 5, and then again in Chapter 8.

Programmers are satisfied when their apps can be REUSED.
Ever built something for one customer, and realized you could use something almost exactly the same for another customer? If you do just a little bit of analysis on your apps, you can make sure they're easily reused, by avoiding all sorts of nasty dependencies and associations that you don't really need. Concepts like the Open-Closed Principle (OCP) and the Single Responsibility Principle (SRP) are big time in helping here.

You'll get to see these principles really strut their stuff in Chapter 8.

Programmers are satisfied when their apps are FLEXIBLE.
Sometimes just a little refactoring can take a good app and turn it into a nice framework that can be used for all sorts of different things. This is where you can begin to move from being a head-down coder and start thinking like a real architect (oh yeah, those guys make a lot more money, too). Big-picture thinking is where it's at.

Chapters 6 and 7 are all about looking at the big picture, and really developing a good architecture for your applications.

This is ALL OOA&D! It's not about doing silly diagrams... it's about writing killer applications that leave your customer happy, and you feeling like you've kicked major ass.

This is **fantastic**! I'm selling guitars like crazy with this new search tool. By the way, I had a few ideas for some new features...

See? You're already getting requests for more work. Rick will have to wait until Chapter 5, though... we've got some hairier issues to tackle in the next chapter.

BULLET POINTS

- It takes very little for something to go wrong with an application that is fragile.

- You can use OO principles like encapsulation and delegation to build applications that are flexible.

- Encapsulation is breaking your application into logical parts that have a clear boundary that allows an object to hide its data and methods from other objects.

- Delegation is giving another object the responsibility of handling a particular task.

- Always begin a project by figuring out what the customer wants.

- Once you've got the basic functionality of an app in place, work on refining the design so it's flexible.

- With a functional and flexible design, you can employ design patterns to improve your design further, and make your app easier to reuse.

- Find the parts of your application that change often, and try and separate them from the parts of your application that don't change.

- Building an application that works well but is poorly designed satisfies the customer but will leave you with pain, suffering, and lots of late nights fixing problems.

- Object oriented analysis and design (OOA&D) provides a way to produce well-designed applications that satisfy both the customer and the programmer.

 OOA&D Cross

Let's put what you've learned to use, and stetch out your left brain a bit. All of the words to answer the puzzle below are somewhere in this chapter. Good luck!

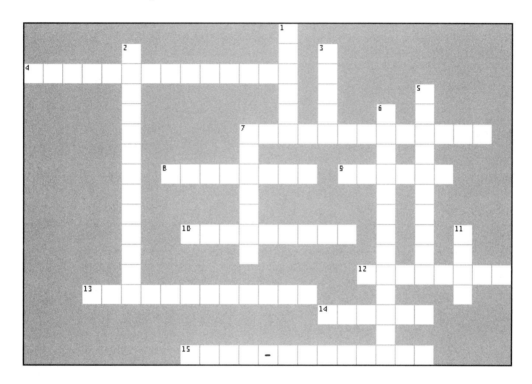

Across

4. These help you avoid solving problems someone else has already solved.

7. Customers focus on this part of your applications.

8. Objects in loosely coupled applications are more _____ than tightly coupled ones.

9. Flexible applications are usually easy to _____.

10. This is one type of code you don't want to write.

12. Your applications should be easy to _____.

13. You usually need some sort of process to write great software _____.

14. Encapsulate what _____.

15. These types of applications satisfy programmers.

Down

1. Once your application works correctly, focus on this.

2. Grouping your application into logical parts.

3. The goal of OOA&D is to help you write this type of software.

5. Use this to let objects focus on more specific tasks.

6. A good way to avoid duplicate code

7. An application that things can go wrong in easily.

11. This is a four letter word your mom will be proud you know.

WHY DO I MATTER?

You've learned a lot about writing great software, and there's still more to go! Take a deep breath and think about some of the terms and principles we've covered. Connect the words on the left to the purpose of those techniques and principles on the right.

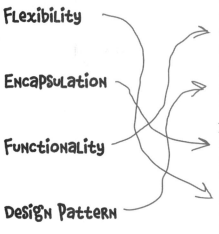

Flexibility

Encapsulation

Functionality

Design Pattern

Without me, you'll never actually make the customer happy. No matter how well-designed your application is, I'm the thing that puts a smile on the customer's face.

I'm all about reuse and making sure you're not trying to solve a problem that someone else has already figured out.

You use me to keep the parts of your code that stay the same separate from the parts that change; then it's really easy to make changes to your code without breaking everything.

Use me so that your software can change and grow without constant rework. I keep your application from being fragile.

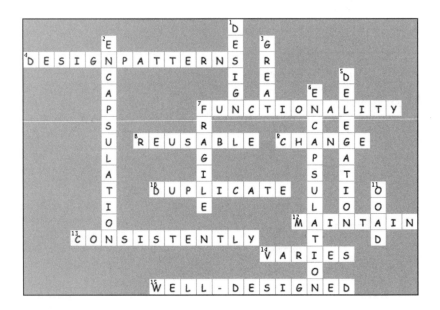

Sharpen your pencil answers

What would you change about this code?

There's a big problem with the code shown above, and it's up to you to figure it out. In the blanks below, write down what you think the problem is, and how you would fix it.

<u>Every time a new property is added to GuitarSpec.java, or the methods in GuitarSpec change,</u>
<u>the search() method in Inventory.java will have to change, too. We should let GuitarSpec handle</u>
<u>comparisons, and encapsulate these properties away from Inventory.</u>

This isn't very good design. Every time a new property is added to GuitarSpec, this code is going to have to change.

```java
public List search(GuitarSpec searchSpec) {
  List matchingGuitars = new LinkedList();
  for (Iterator i = guitars.iterator(); i.hasNext(); ) {
    Guitar guitar = (Guitar)i.next();
    GuitarSpec guitarSpec = guitar.getSpec();
    if (searchSpec.getBuilder() != guitarSpec.getBuilder())
      continue;
    String model = searchSpec.getModel().toLowerCase();
    if ((model != null) && (!model.equals("")) &&
        (!model.equals(guitarSpec.getModel().toLowerCase())))
      continue;
    if (searchSpec.getType() != guitarSpec.getType())
      continue;
    if (searchSpec.getBackWood() != guitarSpec.getBackWood())
      continue;
    if (searchSpec.getTopWood() != guitarSpec.getTopWood())
      continue;
    matchingGuitars.add(guitar);
  }
  return matchingGuitars;
}
```

`class Inven-tory {` `search()`

Inventory.java

Think about it: is Inventory really focusing on Rick's inventory? Or is it focusing on what makes two GuitarSpec objects the same? You want your classes to focus on <u>their</u> jobs, not the jobs of other classes. Comparing GuitarSpec objects is something GuitarSpec should worry about, not your Inventory class.

2 *gathering requirements*

Give Them What They Want

I hope you like it... I've been paying attention to every word you've said lately, and I think this is just perfect for you!

Everybody loves a satisfied customer. You already know that the first step in writing great software is making sure it does what the customer wants it to. But how do you figure out **what a customer really wants**? And how do you make sure that the customer even *knows* what they really want? That's where **good requirements** come in, and in this chapter, you're going to learn how to **satisfy your customer** by making sure what you deliver is actually what they asked for. By the time you're done, all of your projects will be "satisfaction guaranteed," and you'll be well on your way to writing great software, every time.

You've got a new programming gig

You've just been hired as the lead programmer at a new start-up, Doug's Dog Doors. Doug's got a pretty high-tech door under development, and he's decided you're the programmer that can write all the software to make his killer hardware work.

Here's the new sales insert that's running in all the Sunday papers this week.

Tired of cleaning up your dog's mistakes?

Ready for someone else to let your dog outside?

Sick of dog doors that stick when you open them?

It's time to call...

Doug's Dog Doors

★ Professionally installed by our door experts.

★ Patented all-steel construction.

★ Choose your own custom colors and imprints.

★ Custom-cut door for your dog.

Call Doug today at **1-800-998-9938**

Every night, Fido barks and barks at the stupid door until we let him go outside. I hate getting out of bed, and Todd never even wakes up. Can you help us out, Doug?

Todd

Gina

Todd and Gina: your first customer

Todd and Gina want more than a "normal" doggie door. Todd has everything from his plasma TV to his surround sound stereo to his garage door operating off of a remote control, and he wants a dog door that responds to the press of a button. Not satisfied with a little plastic flap letting their dog in and out, they've given Doug's Dog Doors a call... and now Doug wants you to build them the dog door of their dreams.

Let's start with the dog door

The first thing we need is a class to represent the dog door. Let's call this class **DogDoor**, and add just a few simple methods:

> Assume the DogDoor class will interface with Doug's custom door hardware.

```
public class DogDoor {

    private boolean open;

    public DogDoor() {
        this.open = false;
    }

    public void open() {
        System.out.println("The dog door opens.");
        open = true;
    }

    public void close() {
        System.out.println("The dog door closes.");
        open = false;
    }

    public boolean isOpen() {
        return open;
    }
}
```

This is pretty simple: open() opens the door...

...and close() closes the door.

This returns the state of the door: whether it's open or closed.

All this code...

...goes into DogDoor.java...

```
class
DogDoor
{
    open()
}
```

DogDoor.java

...which will control the hardware in Todd and Gina's dog door.

Fido's depending on you... not to mention Todd, Gina, and your boss, Doug.

Fido's Exit

Code Magnets

Let's write another class, Remote, to allow a remote control to operate the dog door. Todd and Gina can use the remote to open the dog door without having to get out of bed.

Be careful... you may not need all the magnets.

Yes, we know this is a really easy one. We're just getting you warmed up, don't worry.

```
public class Remote {

  private _____ door;

  public Remote(_____ _____) {
    this.door = door;
  }

  public void pressButton() {
    System.out.println("Pressing the remote control button...");
    if (_____._____()) {
      door._____();
    } else {
      door._____();
    }
  }
}
```

→ Once you're done, compare your answer with ours on page 108.

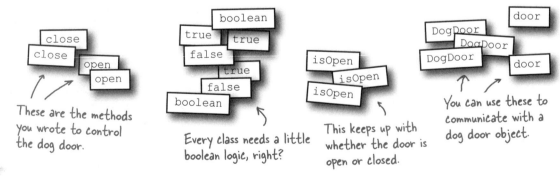

close
close
open
open

These are the methods you wrote to control the dog door.

boolean
true
true
false
true
false
boolean

Every class needs a little boolean logic, right?

isOpen
isOpen
isOpen

This keeps up with whether the door is open or closed.

DogDoor
door
DogDoor
DogDoor
door

You can use these to communicate with a dog door object.

Test drive

Let's see if everything works. Go ahead and take your
new dog door for a test drive.

❶ Create a class to test the door (DogDoorSimulator.java).

```java
public class DogDoorSimulator {
  public static void main(String[] args) {
    DogDoor door = new DogDoor();
    Remote remote = new Remote(door);
    System.out.println("Fido barks to go outside...");
    remote.pressButton();
    System.out.println("\nFido has gone outside...");
    remote.pressButton();
    System.out.println("\nFido's all done...");
    remote.pressButton();
    System.out.println("\nFido's back inside...");
    remote.pressButton();
  }
}
```

DogDoorSimulator.java

❷ Compile all your Java source code into classes.

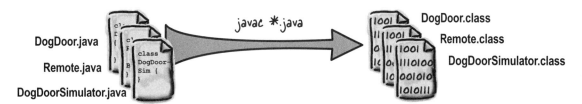

DogDoor.java
Remote.java
DogDoorSimulator.java

javac *.java

DogDoor.class
Remote.class
DogDoorSimulator.class

❸ Run the code!

```
File Edit Window Help Woof
%java DogDoorSimulator
Fido barks to go outside...
Pressing the remote control button...
The dog door opens.

Fido has gone outside...
Pressing the remote control button...
The dog door closes.

Fido's all done...
Pressing the remote control button...
The dog door opens.

Fido's back inside...
Pressing the remote control button...
The dog door closes.
```

It works! Let's go
show Todd and Gina...

But when Gina tried it...

Not so fast, there... what the heck is a rabbit doing in my kitchen?

How did a rabbit get into Gina's kitchen?

Uh oh... when Gina used the door, Fido came back in, but so did a few friends.

Sharpen your pencil

How do you think the rodents are getting into Gina's kitchen? In the blanks below, write down what you think is wrong with the current version of the dog door.

_____

_____

_____

_____

Don't go to the next page until you've written down an answer for this exercise.

There's nothing wrong with our code! Gina must have forgotten to press the button on the remote again after Fido came back in. It's not my fault she's using the door incorrectly!

But the door doesn't work the way <u>Todd and Gina</u> want it to!

Todd and Gina didn't expect to have to close the dog door, so they pressed the button on the remote only once: to let Fido out.

Even worse, in this case, the way they used the door created *new* problems. Rats and rabbits started coming into their house through the open door, and you're taking the blame.

Let's tackle Todd and Gina's dog door again, but this time, we'll do things a little bit differently. Here's our plan:

1 **Gather requirements for the dog door.**

Looks like we're going to spend a lot more time talking with Todd and Gina this time around.

2 **Figure out what the door should <u>really</u> do.**

3 **Get any additional information we need from Todd and Gina.**

4 **Build the door RIGHT!**

We're paying a lot more attention to Step 1 in writing great software this time, aren't we?

→ 1. Make sure your software does what the customer wants it to do.

So what exactly <u>is</u> a requirement, anyway?

A requirement is usually a <u>single</u> thing, and you can <u>test</u> that thing to make sure you've actually fulfilled the requirement. ➤

It's a
specific thing
your
system
has to
do
to
work correctly.

"system" is the complete app or project you're working on. In this case, your system is Todd and Gina's complete dog door setup (which includes the remote control, by the way). ➤

The dog door system has to "do" lots of things: open, close, let Fido out, keep rodents from getting inside... anything that Todd and Gina come up with is part of what the system "does."

↑

Remember, the <u>customer</u> decides when a system works correctly. So if you leave out a requirement, or even if they forget to mention something to you, the system isn't working correctly!

^{the} Scholar's Corner

requirement. A requirement is a <u>singular</u> <u>need</u> detailing what a particular product or service should <u>be</u> or <u>do</u>. It is most commonly used in a formal sense in systems engineering or software engineering.

Listen to the customer

When it comes to requirements, the best thing you can do is **let the customer talk**. And pay attention to *what* the system needs to do; you can figure out *how* the system will do those things later.

Here's what Todd and Gina say; it's your job to translate this into requirements for their door.

> Fido's about a foot tall, and we don't want him having to hurt his back leaning over to get out the door.

Gina: And we want the door to automatically close after a few seconds. I don't want to have to wake back up in the middle of the night to close the door.

You: Do you want a single button on the remote, or both an "Open" and "Close" button?

Todd: Well, if the door always closes automatically, we really don't need separate "Open" and "Close" buttons, do we? Let's just stick with a single button on the remote control.

You: Sure. So the button opens the door if it's closed, and it can also close the door if it's open, just in case the door gets stuck.

Todd: Perfect. Gina, anything else you can think of?

Gina: No, I think that's it. That's the dog door of our dreams.

Don't worry about your code at this stage—just make sure you know what the system should do.

Here's your new set of remote control and dog door plans, based on Todd and Gina's requirements.

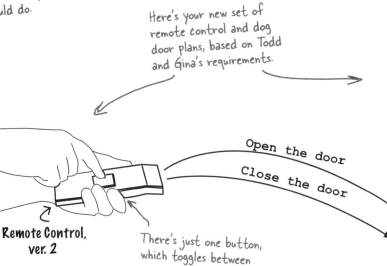

Remote Control, ver. 2

There's just one button, which toggles between opening and closing the door.

Open the door

Close the door

Dog Door, ver. 2

This opening needs to be at least 12" tall... so Fido doesn't have to "lean."

12"

Creating a requirements list

Now that we know what Todd and Gina want, let's write down our new set of requirements. We don't need anything too fancy...

Todd and Gina's Dog Door, version 2.0
Requirements List

This is just a list of the things that your customer wants the system you're building them to do.

1. The dog door opening must be at least 12" tall.

2. A button on the remote control opens the dog door if the door is closed, and closes the dog door if the door is open.

3. Once the dog door has opened, it should close automatically if the door isn't already closed.

Compare these with Todd and Gina's comments on page 63... see how we turned their words into a basic set of requirements?

We'll just close the door after a few seconds of being open.

Be sure to leave extra space... additional requirements almost always come up as you work on a project.

A special bonus prize

In addition to having a list of things you need to do to complete Todd and Gina's dog door, now you can show your boss exactly what you're working on, and what work you think is left to finish the project.

> Is this list really going to help? Todd and Gina completely forgot to tell us they wanted the door to automatically close before... won't they just forget something again?

You need to understand how the dog door will be used.

You've figured out one of the hardest parts about getting a customer's requirements—sometimes even the *customer* doesn't know what they really want! So you've got to ask the customer questions to figure out what they want before you can determine exactly what the system should do. Then, you can begin to think *beyond* what your customers asked for and anticipate their needs, even before they realize they have a problem.

In Todd and Gina's case, the system is the dog door and the remote control.

Sharpen your pencil

What sorts of things do you think Todd and Gina might not have thought about when it comes to their new dog door? Make a list of any concerns you might have in making sure Todd and Gina are happy with the new door you're building them.

_____

_____

_____

_____

_____

What does the dog door <u>really</u> need to do?

You know what Todd and Gina want the dog door to do, but it's your job to make sure that the door actually *works*. In the process, you may even come across some things that Todd and Gina want, but didn't think about on their own.

Let's write down exactly what happens when Fido needs to go outside:

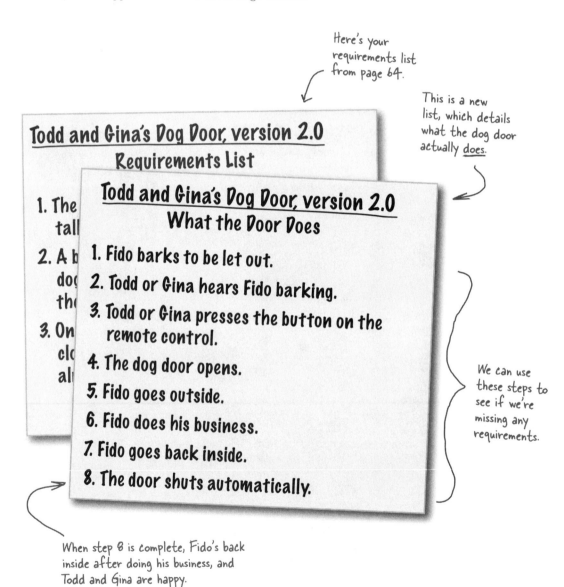

Here's your requirements list from page 64.

This is a new list, which details what the dog door actually <u>does</u>.

Todd and Gina's Dog Door, version 2.0
Requirements List

1. The
   tall
2. A b
   do
   th
3. On
   cl
   al

Todd and Gina's Dog Door, version 2.0
What the Door Does

1. Fido barks to be let out.
2. Todd or Gina hears Fido barking.
3. Todd or Gina presses the button on the remote control.
4. The dog door opens.
5. Fido goes outside.
6. Fido does his business.
7. Fido goes back inside.
8. The door shuts automatically.

We can use these steps to see if we're missing any requirements.

When step 8 is complete, Fido's back inside after doing his business, and Todd and Gina are happy.

Q: So a requirement is just one of the things that a customer wants the application you build for them to do?

A: Actually, a requirement is a lot more than just what the customer wants—although that's a good place to start. Begin by finding out what your customer wants and expects, and what they think the system you're building for them should do. But there's still a lot more to think about...

Remember, most people expect things to work even if problems occur. So you've got to anticipate what might go wrong, and add requirements to take care of those problems as well. A good set of requirements goes beyond just what your customers tell you, and makes sure that the system works, even in unusual or unexpected circumstances.

Q: And the system for Todd and Gina is just the dog door, right?

A: The system is *everything* needed to meet a customer's goals. In the case of the dog door, the system includes the door, but it also includes the remote control. Without the remote, the dog door wouldn't be complete.

And even though they aren't part of the system, Todd and Gina and Fido are all things you have to at least think about when designing the system. So there's a lot more to worry about than just the actual dog door.

Q: I don't see why I have to figure out how Todd and Gina are going to use the dog door, and what can go wrong. Isn't that their problem, not mine?

A: Do you remember the first step we talked about in writing great software? You've got to make sure your app works like the customer wants it to—even if that's not how *you* would use the application. That means you've got to really understand what the system has to do, and how your customers are going to use it.

In fact, the only way to ensure you get Todd and Gina a working, successful dog door is to know the system even *better* than they do, and to understand exactly what it needs to do. You can then anticipate problems, and hopefully solve them before Todd and Gina ever know something could have gone wrong.

Q: So I should just come up with all sorts of bad things that might happen when Todd and Gina use their door?

A: Exactly! In fact, let's do that now...

> # The best way to get good requirements is to understand what a system is supposed to do.

Plan for things going wrong

Below is a diagram of how Todd and Gina's dog door should work; all the numbers match up with the steps in our list on page 66. But things aren't always going to go according to plan, so we've written down some things that might go wrong along the way.

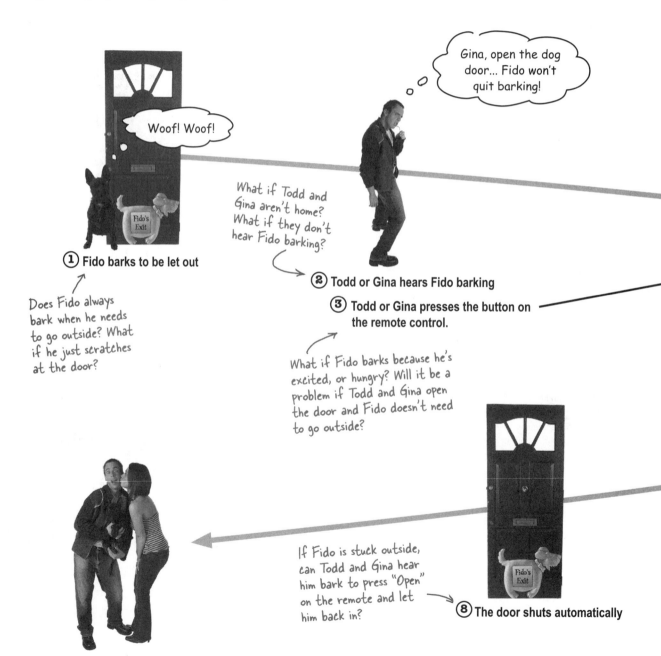

Woof! Woof!

Gina, open the dog door... Fido won't quit barking!

What if Todd and Gina aren't home? What if they don't hear Fido barking?

① Fido barks to be let out

Does Fido always bark when he needs to go outside? What if he just scratches at the door?

② Todd or Gina hears Fido barking

③ Todd or Gina presses the button on the remote control.

What if Fido barks because he's excited, or hungry? Will it be a problem if Todd and Gina open the door and Fido doesn't need to go outside?

If Fido is stuck outside, can Todd and Gina hear him bark to press "Open" on the remote and let him back in?

⑧ The door shuts automatically

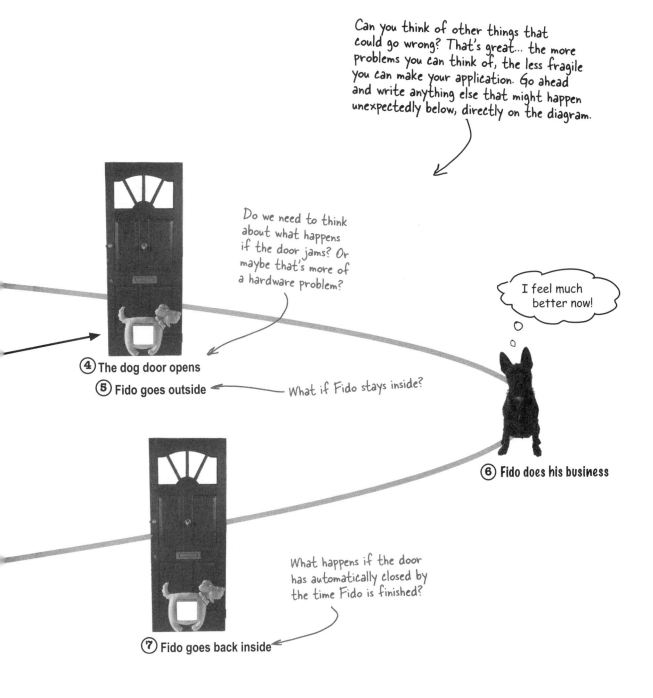

Can you think of other things that could go wrong? That's great... the more problems you can think of, the less fragile you can make your application. Go ahead and write anything else that might happen unexpectedly below, directly on the diagram.

Do we need to think about what happens if the door jams? Or maybe that's more of a hardware problem?

I feel much better now!

④ The dog door opens

⑤ Fido goes outside ← What if Fido stays inside?

⑥ Fido does his business

What happens if the door has automatically closed by the time Fido is finished?

⑦ Fido goes back inside

Alternate paths handle system problems

Now that you've figured out some of the things that can go wrong, you need to update your list of things that needs to happen to make the dog door work. Let's write down what should happen if the door closes before Fido gets back inside.

This is that same requirements list from page 64. We may need to update these later, but for now, they're still OK.

Todd and Gina's Dog Door, version 2.0
Requirements List

1. Th
    ta
2. A
    d
    t
3. O
    c

We can use these "sub-numbers" to show some sub-steps that might happen as part of Step 6.

If Fido stays outside, there are a few additional steps required to get him back inside. These extra steps are called an **alternate path**.

Todd and Gina's Dog Door, version 2.0
What the Door Does

1. Fido barks to be let out.
2. Todd or Gina hears Fido barking.
3. Todd or Gina presses the button on the remote control.
4. The dog door opens.
5. Fido goes outside.
6. Fido does his business.
   - 6.1 The door shuts automatically.
   - 6.2 Fido barks to be let back inside.
   - 6.3 Todd or Gina hears Fido barking (again).
   - 6.4 Todd or Gina presses the button on the remote control.
   - 6.5 The dog door opens (again).
7. Fido goes back inside.
8. The door shuts automatically.

All of these new steps handle the problem of the door closing before Fido can get back inside the house.

With some extra steps added, Fido can still get back inside, even though a problem Todd and Gina hadn't thought about occurred.

Hey, I took a course in college on this stuff... aren't we just writing a **use case**?

Yes! You've been writing use cases all along

When you wrote down the steps in getting Fido outside to use the bathroom, you were actually writing a **use case**.

A use case *is* what people call the steps that a system takes to make something happen. In Todd and Gina's case, the "something" that needs to happen is getting Fido outside to do his business, and then back inside.

Look! It's a use case.

↙

Todd and Gina's Dog Door, version 2.0
What the Door Does

1. Fido barks to be let out.
2. Todd or Gina hears Fido barking.
3. Todd or Gina presses the button on the remote control.
4. The dog door opens.
5. Fido goes outside.
6. Fido does his business.
   6.1 The door shuts automatically.
   6.2 Fido barks to be let back inside.
   6.3 Todd or Gina hears Fido barking (again).
   6.4 Todd or Gina presses the button on the remote control.
   6.5 The dog door opens (again).
7. Fido goes back inside.
8. The door shuts automatically.

You've actually already written the use case for Todd and Gina's dog door. ↗

(Re) introducing use cases

You've been writing a use case for almost 10 pages now, but let's take a closer look at exactly what that list of steps—the use case for Todd and Gina's dog door—is really all about:

A use case describes **what your system does to accomplish a particular customer goal.**

Use cases are all about the "what." __What__ does the dog door need to do? Remember, don't worry about the "how" right now... we'll get to that a little bit later.

We're still definitely focusing on what the system needs to "do." __What__ should happen in order to get Fido outside (and then back into the house)?

A __single__ use case focuses on a __single__ goal. The single goal for Todd and Gina is getting Fido outside without either of them getting out of bed.

If Todd and Gina decide they want to track how many times Fido uses the dog door, that would be a __different__ goal, so you'd need another, __different__ use case.

The user (or users) are __outside__ of the system, not a part of it. Fido uses the system, and he's outside of it; Gina has a goal for the system, and she's also outside of the system.

The customer goal is the __point__ of the use case: what do all these steps need to make happen? We're focusing on the customer, remember? The system has to help that customer accomplish their goal.

So we're the outsiders, huh?

The System

The dog door and remote are part of the system, or __inside__ the system.

The entire use case describes exactly what the dog door does when Fido needs to go outside.

Todd and Gina's Dog Door, version 2.0
What the Door Does

1. Fido barks to be let out.
2. Todd or Gina hears Fido barking.
3. Todd or Gina presses the button on the remote control.
4. The dog door opens.
5. Fido goes outside.
6. Fido does his business.
    6.1 The door shuts automatically.
    6.2 Fido barks to be let back inside.
    6.3 Todd or Gina hears Fido barking (again).
    6.4 Todd or Gina presses the button on the remote control.
    6.5 The dog door opens (again).
7. Fido goes back inside.
8. The door shuts automatically.

The use case ends when the customer goal is complete—that's Fido back inside, after doing his business, with Todd and Gina still comfortable in bed.

This is an alternate path, but it's still about achieving the same goal as the main path, so it's part of the same use case.

the
Scholar's Corner

use case. A use case is a technique for capturing the potential requirements of a new system or software change. Each use case provides one or more <u>scenarios</u> that convey how the system should <u>interact</u> with the end user or another system to achieve a <u>specific goal</u>.

One use case, three parts

There are three basic parts to a good use case, and you need all three if your use case is going to get the job done.

① ## Clear Value

Super Buy

Every use case must have a **clear value** to the system. If the use case doesn't help the customer achieve their goal, then the use case isn't of much use.

The use case __must__ help Todd and Gina deal with Fido.

The use case starts up when Fido barks... it stops when he's back inside, done with his business.

Start and Stop

STOP

② Every use case must have a definite **starting** and **stopping point**. Something must begin the process, and then there must be a condition that indicates that the process is complete.

In the dog door, Fido is the external initiator. He's what starts the entire process.

External Initiator

Every use case is started off by an **external initiator**, outside of the system. Sometimes that initiator is a person, but it could be anything outside of the system.

③

Use Case Magnets

Below is Todd and Gina's use case, and a magnet for each of the three parts of a good use case (one part, Start and Stop, actually has two magnets). Your job is to identify where each magnet goes and attach it to the right part of the use case.

Clear Value — **Super Buy**

Start and Stop — **STOP**

 External Initiator

↖ Hint: One of these should be <u>really</u> easy... if you look at the icons.

Todd and Gina's Dog Door, version 2.0
What the Door Does

1. Fido barks to be let out.
2. Todd or Gina hears Fido barking.
3. Todd or Gina presses the button on the remote control.
4. The dog door opens.
5. Fido goes outside.
6. Fido does his business.
    6.1 The door shuts automatically.
    6.2 Fido barks to be let back inside.
    6.3 Todd or Gina hears Fido barking (again).
    6.4 Todd or Gina presses the button on the remote control.
    6.5 The dog door opens (again).
7. Fido goes back inside.
8. The door shuts automatically.

What kicks off the use case? This is usually some action outside of the system.

Super Buy

Put the Super Buy magnet on the part of the use case that is the **clear value** to Todd and Gina.

STOP ←

Put this magnet on the condition in the use case that indicates the process should **stop**.

Who starts the use case?

Use Case Magnet Solutions

Below is Todd and Gina's use case, along with several use case magnets. Your job was to identify where each magnet goes, and attach it to the right part of the use case.

This is the **start** of the use case. Nothing begins until Fido barks.

Todd and Gina's Dog Door, version 2.0
What the Door Does

1. Fido barks to be let out.
2. Todd or Gina hears Fido barking.
3. Todd or Gina presses the button on the remote control.
4. The dog door opens.
5. Fido goes outside.
6. Fido does his business.
   6.1 The door shuts automatically.
   6.2 Fido barks to be let back inside.
   6.3 Todd or Gina hears Fido barking (again).
   6.4 Todd or Gina presses the button on the remote control.
   6.5 The dog door opens (again).
7. Fido goes back inside.
8. The door shuts automatically.

Fido is the **external initiator** in this use case.

Here's the **stop** condition... Fido is back in, and the door is closed.

STOP

Super Buy

The entire use case is of **value**, because Todd and Gina can stay in bed and still get Fido outside.

Q: **So a use case is just a list of the steps that a system has to do to work correctly?**

A: In most cases, yes. But, remember, one of the key points about a use case is that it is focused on accomplishing **one particular** goal. If your system does more than one thing—like let Fido outside *and* track how many times he's been out in an entire day—then you'll need more than one use case.

Q: **Then my system will have a use case for every goal it accomplishes, right?**

A: Exactly! If your system just does one single thing, you'll probably only need one use case. If it does ten or fifteen things, then you're going to have a *lot* of use cases.

Q: **And a use case is what the system does to accomplish a goal?**

A: Now you've got it. If you write down what the system needs to do to perform a task, you've probably got a use case.

Q: **But the use case isn't very specific. Why didn't we talk about the Remote class or the DogDoor class?**

A: Use cases are meant to help you understand what a system should do—and often to explain the system to others (like the customer or your boss). If your use case focuses on specific code-level details, it's not going to be useful to anyone but a programmer. As a general rule, your use cases should use simple, everyday language. If you're using lots of programming terms, or technical jargon, your use case is probably getting too detailed to be that useful.

Q: **Is a use case the same as a use case diagram?**

A: No, use cases are usually a list of steps (although you can write them differently, something we talk about in the Appendix). Use case diagrams are a way to show use cases visually, but we've already been working on our own diagram of how the system works (check out page 69 for a refresher). Don't worry, though, we'll still look at use case diagrams in Chapter 6.

Q: **Then how do I turn my use case into actual code?**

A: That's another step in the process of writing your application. In fact, we're going to look at how to take our use case for Todd and Gina and update our code in just a few more pages.

But the purpose of the use case isn't to detail *how* you'll write your code. You'll probably still have to do some thinking about how you want to actually put the steps of your use case into action.

Q: **If the use case doesn't help me write my code, then what's the point? Why spend all this time on use cases?**

A: Use cases *do* help you write your code—they just aren't specific about programming details. For instance, if you didn't write a use case for Todd and Gina, you never would have figured out that Fido might get stuck outside, or realize that the dog door needed to close automatically. Those all came from writing a use case.

Remember, you'll never write great software if you can't deliver an app that does what the customer wants it to do. Use cases are a tool to help you figure that out—and *then* you're ready to write code to actually implement the system your use case describes.

Checking your requirements against your use cases

So far, you've got an initial set of requirements and a good solid use case. But now you need to go *back* to your requirements and make sure that they'll cover everything your system has to do. And that's where the use case comes in:

Todd and Gina's Dog Door, version 2.0
Requirements List

1. The dog door opening must be at least 12" tall.

2. A button on the remote control opens the dog door if the door is closed, and closes the dog door if the door is open.

3. Once the dog door has opened, it should close automatically if the door isn't already closed.

Here's our list of requirements that we got from Todd and Gina...

...and here's what we know the dog door needs to do.

Todd and Gina's Dog Door, version 2.0
What the Door Does

1. Fido barks to be let out.
2. Todd or Gina hears Fido barking.
3. Todd or Gina presses the button on the remote control.
4. The dog door opens.
5. Fido goes outside.
6. Fido does his business.
   6.1 The door shuts automatically.
   6.2 Fido barks to be let back inside.
   6.3 Todd or Gina hears Fido barking (again).
   6.4 Todd or Gina presses the button on the remote control.
   6.5 The dog door opens (again).
7. Fido goes back inside.
8. The door shuts automatically.

Is anything missing?

Now you need to look over the use case and see if everything the system needs to do is covered by the requirements.

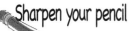

Sharpen your pencil

Do your requirements handle everything?

Below on the left is the list of things that the dog door does, pulled straight from our use case on page 78. Your job is to identify the requirement that handles each step of the use case and write that requirement's number down in the blank next to that step of the use case. If a step in the use case doesn't require you to do anything, just write **N/A** down, for "not applicable".

Here are the three requirements we have... you can use any of these for each step in the use case.

Todd and Gina's Dog Door, version 2.0
What the Door Does

1. Fido barks to be let out. _____

2. Todd or Gina hears Fido barking. _____

3. Todd or Gina presses the button on the remote control. _____

4. The dog door opens. _____

5. Fido goes outside. _____

6. Fido does his business. _____

    6.1 The door shuts automatically. _____

    6.2 Fido barks to be let back inside. _____

    6.3 Todd or Gina hears Fido barking (again). _____

    6.4 Todd or Gina presses the button on the remote control. _____

    6.5 The dog door opens (again). _____

7. Fido goes back inside. _____

8. The door shuts automatically. _____

Todd and Gina's Dog Door, version 2.0
Requirements List

1. The dog door opening must be at least 12" tall.
2. A button on the remote control opens the dog door if the door is closed, and closes the dog door if the door is open.
3. Once the dog door has opened, it should close automatically if the door isn't already closed.

Write 1, 2, 3, or N/A in each of these blanks.

Did you find any steps in the use case that you don't think you have a requirement to handle? If you think you need any additional requirements, write what you think you need to add to the requirements list in the blanks below:

_____

_____

_____

Sharpen your pencil
answers   Do your requirements handle everything?

Below on the left is the list of things that the dog door does, pulled straight from our use case on page 78. Your job was to identify the requirement that handles each step of the use case, and write that requirement's number down in the blank next to that step of the use case. You should have written down **N/A** for a step that didn't require our system to do anything.

Todd and Gina's Dog Door, version 2.0
What the Door Does

1. Fido barks to be let out.   N/A

2. Todd or Gina hears Fido barking.   N/A

3. Todd or Gina presses the button on the remote control.   2

4. The dog door opens.   2

5. Fido goes outside.   1

6. Fido does his business.   N/A

   6.1 The door shuts automatically.   3

   6.2 Fido barks to be let back inside.   N/A

   6.3 Todd or Gina hears Fido barking (again).   N/A

   6.4 Todd or Gina presses the button on the remote control. 2

   6.5 The dog door opens (again).   2

7. Fido goes back inside.   1

8. The door shuts automatically.   3

A lot of the things that happen to a system don't require you to do anything.

You might have put N/A here, since them pushing the button isn't something that's you have to handle... then again, 2 is OK, too, since they wouldn't push a button without a remote.

Did you get this one? Fido can't get outside if the opening isn't the right size.

The alternate path should have been easy once you figured out the requirements for the main path.

Did you find any steps in the use case that you don't think you have a requirement to handle? If you think you need any additional requirements, write what you think you need to add to the requirements list down in the blanks below:

No, our requirements cover everything the system needs to do. We're ready to actually write code to handle these requirements now, right?

So <u>now</u> can we write some code?

With use case and requirements in hand, you're ready to write code that you **know** will make Todd and Gina satisfied customers. Let's check out our requirements and see exactly what we're going to have to write code for:

This is something for Doug and the hardware guys to deal with... we don't need any code for this requirement.

Todd and Gina's Dog Door, version 2.0
Requirements List

1. The dog door opening must be at least 12" tall.

2. A button on the remote control opens the dog door if the door is closed, and closes the dog door if the door is open.

3. Once the dog door has opened, it should close automatically if the door isn't already closed.

We've already got code to take care this requirement.

This is what Todd and Gina added when we talked to them... we need to write code to take care of closing the door automatically.

We're getting pretty psyched about our new door. We love that you thought about Fido getting stuck outside, and took care of that, too.

Automatically closing the door

The only requirement left to code is taking care of
automatically closing the door after it's been opened. Let's go
back to our **Remote** class and handle that now:

Remote.java

```java
import java.util.Timer;
import java.util.TimerTask;

public class Remote {

    private DogDoor door;

    public Remote(DogDoor door) {
        this.door = door;
    }

    public void pressButton() {
        System.out.println("Pressing the remote control button...");
        if (door.isOpen()) {
            door.close();
        } else {
            door.open();

            final Timer timer = new Timer();
            timer.schedule(new TimerTask() {
                public void run() {
                    door.close();
                    timer.cancel();
                }
            }, 5000);
        }
    }
}
```

You'll need these two import statements to use Java's timing classes.

This checks the state of the door before opening or closing it.

The remote already has code to handle closing the door if it's open.

Create a new Timer so we can schedule the dog door closing.

All the task does is close the door, and then turn off the timer.

This tells the timer how long to wait before executing the task... in this case, we're waiting 5 seconds, which is 5000 milliseconds.

---

there are no Dumb Questions

Q: What's all this Timer stuff? Can't I just use a Java thread to close the door?

A: Sure, there's nothing wrong with using a **Thread** to close the dog door. In fact, that's all the **Timer** class does: kick off a background **Thread**. But the **Timer** class makes running a task in the future easy, so it seemed like a good choice for the **Remote** class.

Q: Why did you make the timer variable final?

A: Because we need to call its **cancel()** method in the **TimerTask** anonymous class. If you need to access variables in your anonymous class from the enclosing class (that's **Remote** in this case), those variables must be final. And, really, just because it makes things work.

Q: Why are you calling cancel()? Won't the timer quit automatically after running the TimerTask?

A: It will, but it turns out that most JVMs take forever before they garbage collect the **Timer**. That ends up hanging the program, and your code will run for hours before it actually quits gracefully. That's no good, but calling **cancel()** manually takes care of the problem.

We need a new simulator!

Our old simulator isn't that useful anymore... it assumes Todd and Gina are closing the door manually, and not letting the timer do its work. Let's update our simulator to make it work with the updated **Remote** class:t

DogDoorSimulator.java

```
public class DogDoorSimulator {

    public static void main(String[] args) {
        DogDoor door = new DogDoor();
        Remote remote = new Remote(door);

        System.out.println("Fido barks to go outside...");
        remote.pressButton();

        System.out.println("\nFido has gone outside...");
        remote.pressButton();

        System.out.println("\nFido's all done...");
        remote.pressButton();

        System.out.println("\nFido's back inside...");
        remote.pressButton();
    }
}
```

This is the same as in our earlier version, but pressing the button will open the door <u>and</u> start a timer to close the door.

Since the door's on a timer, Fido has plenty of time to get back inside before the door closes. Gina doesn't need to open the door to let Fido back in.

In the new improved dog door, Gina doesn't need to press a button to close the door. That will happen automatically now.

Here's another spot where we can get rid of some code... the door closes automatically.

Q: You lost me on that timer code. What's going on there again?

A: That's OK... you don't need to get too hung up on Java here. The point is that our use case helped us write good requirements, and our requirements made it easy to figure out how to write a working dog door. That's a lot more important than how—or even in what language—you write the dog door code.

Q: So the new simulator tests out the main path we figured out, right?

A: That's right. Flip back to page 78 and review what the dog door does... that's what the new **DogDoorSimulator** tests out. We want to make sure that Todd and Gina's new door works just like they want it to.

Q: Why aren't we testing out that alternate path we found?

A: That's a **very** good question. Let's test this version of the door, and then we'll talk more about that...

Test drive, version 2.0

It's time to see if all our hard work is going to pay off. Let's test out the new and improved dog door.

1 **Compile all your Java source code into classes.**

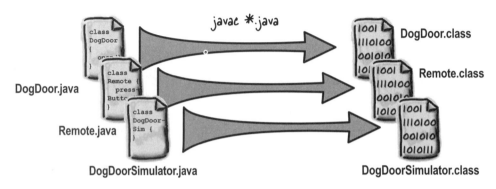

2 **Run the code!**

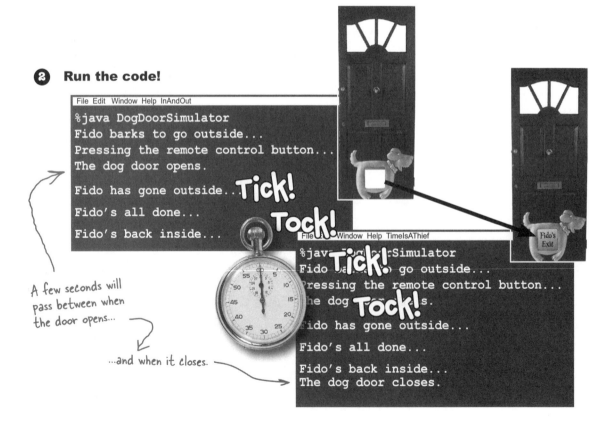

```
File Edit Window Help InAndOut
%java DogDoorSimulator
Fido barks to go outside...
Pressing the remote control button...
The dog door opens.

Fido has gone outside...

Fido's all done...

Fido's back inside...
```

A few seconds will pass between when the door opens...

...and when it closes.

```
File Edit Window Help TimeIsAThief
%java DogDoorSimulator
Fido barks to go outside...
Pressing the remote control button...
The dog door opens.

Fido has gone outside...

Fido's all done...

Fido's back inside...
The dog door closes.
```

It works! Let's go show Todd and Gina...

But I don't think we're ready to show Todd and Gina yet... what about that alternate path, when Fido stays outside and the door closes behind him?

Your system must work in the <u>real</u> world...

Good catch... we need to test alternate paths as well as the main path.

Wouldn't it be great if things worked just like you expected them to every time? Of course, in the real world, that almost never happens. Before we can show the new door off to Todd and Gina, let's take a little extra time to make sure the door works when Fido *doesn't* come right back inside after doing his business.

...so <u>plan</u> and <u>test</u> for when <u>things go</u> wrong.

BRAIN POWER

How would you change the `DogDoorSimulator` class to test for Fido staying outside longer?

SUPER BRAIN POWER

Can you come up with at least one more alternate path for Todd and Gina's dog door? Write out the use case and update the requirements list for your new alternate path, too.

Reviewing the alternate path

Let's make sure we understand exactly what happens on the alternate path, and then we can update **DogDoorSimulator** to test the new path out. Here's the original main path diagram from page 68, along with the alternate path we figured out and added to our use case:

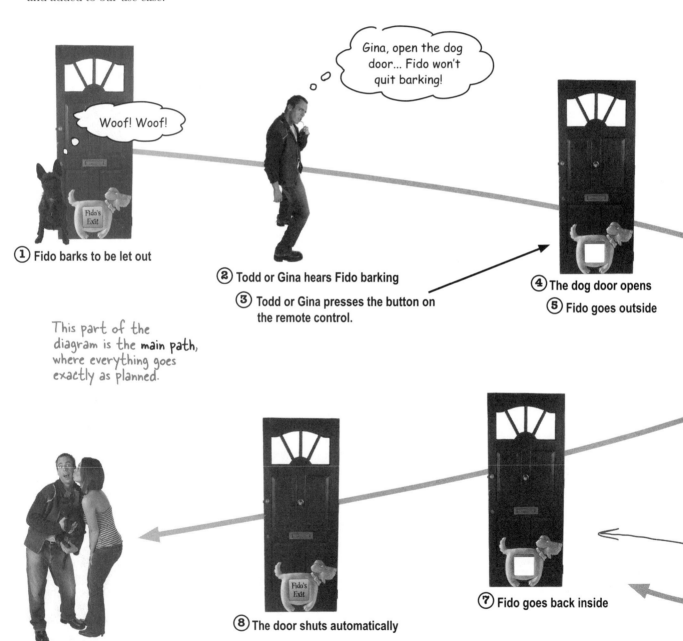

Gina, open the dog door... Fido won't quit barking!

Woof! Woof!

(1) Fido barks to be let out

(2) Todd or Gina hears Fido barking

(3) Todd or Gina presses the button on the remote control.

(4) The dog door opens

(5) Fido goes outside

This part of the diagram is the **main path**, where everything goes exactly as planned.

(7) Fido goes back inside

(8) The door shuts automatically

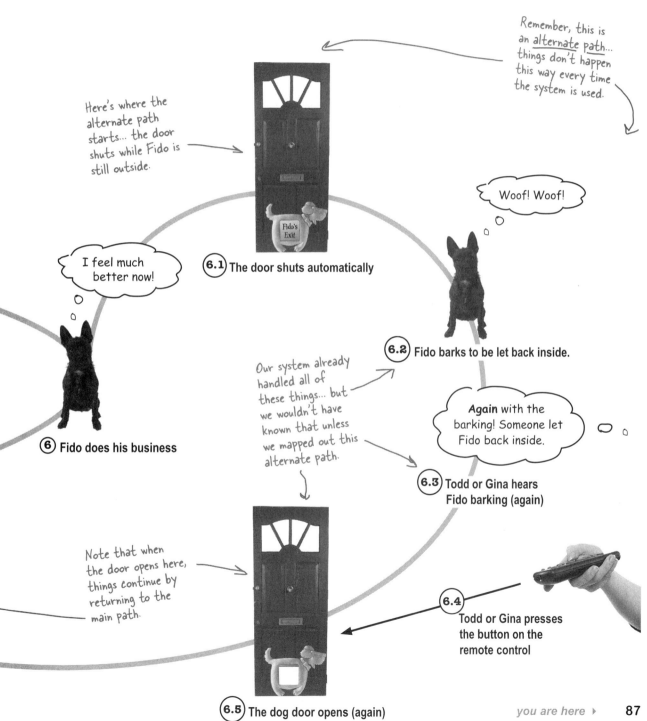

Remember, this is an <u>alternate path</u>... things don't happen this way every time the system is used.

Here's where the alternate path starts... the door shuts while Fido is still outside.

(6.1) The door shuts automatically

Woof! Woof!

I feel much better now!

(6.2) Fido barks to be let back inside.

Our system already handled all of these things... but we wouldn't have known that unless we mapped out this alternate path.

Again with the barking! Someone let Fido back inside.

(6) Fido does his business

(6.3) Todd or Gina hears Fido barking (again)

Note that when the door opens here, things continue by returning to the main path.

(6.4) Todd or Gina presses the button on the remote control

(6.5) The dog door opens (again)

Code Magnets

It's time to update the simulator, but this time it's your job to actually write some code. Below is what we have so far for DogDoorSimulator.

DogDoorSimulator.java

Your job is to match the code magnets at the bottom of the page to where they belong in the simulator. If you get stuck, check the diagram on the last page to see what's going on at each step of the way. Oh, and there's a twist... all the magents for periods, semicolons, and parentheses fell off the fridge, so you'll have to add those wherever they're needed, too.

```
public class DogDoorSimulator {

    public static void main(String[] args) {
        DogDoor door = new DogDoor();
        Remote remote = new Remote(door);
        _____
        _____
        System.out.println("\nFido has gone outside...");
        System.out.println("\nFido's all done...");

        try {
            Thread.currentThread()._____(10000);
        } catch (InterruptedException e) { }
        _____
        _____
        _____
        System.out.println("\nFido's back inside...");
    }
}
```

Here's where the alternate path begins.

We want the program to pause and let the door close automatically.

The alternate path returns to the main path right here.

System.out.println | System.out.println | System.out.println | System.out.println | System.out.println | System.out.println

← Here are the methods to use the remote control.

pressButton | pressButton | pressButton | pressButton

Here are several messages you can print out.

remote | remote | remote | remote

waitFor | wait | sleep

These are methods you can call on a Java thread.

"Fido scratches at the door." | "\nFido starts barking..."

"...but he's stuck outside!" | "...so Todd grabs the remote control."

"...but he's stuck inside!" | "...so Gina grabs the remote control."

Test drive, version 2.1

Make the changes to your copy of **DogDoorSimulator.java**, and then recompile your test class. Now you're ready to test out the alternate path of your use case:

```
File Edit Window Help InLikeFlynn
%java DogDoorSimulator
Fido barks to go outside...
Pressing the remote control button...
The dog door opens.

Fido has gone outside...

Fido's all done...
```

Tick!
Tock!

The door opens, and Fido goes outside to do his business.

But Fido starts chasing bugs, and the dog door closes while he's still outside.

Fido barks to get back inside, and Gina uses her remote control...

```
   Edit  Window Help TheOutsiders
va DogDoorSimulator
o barks to go outside...
ssing the remote control button...
he dog door opens.

Fido has gone outside...

Fido's all done...
The dog door closes.
...but he's stuck outside!

Fido starts barking...
...so Gina grabs the remote control.
Pressing the remote control button...
The dog door opens.

Fido's back inside...
```

...and Fido gets to return to air conditioning.

```
File Edit Window Help ThereAndBackAgain
%java DogDoorSimulator
Fido barks to go outside...
Pressing the remote control butt
The dog door opens.

Fido has gone outside...

Fido's all done...
The dog door closes.
...but he's stuck outside!

Fido starts barking...
...so Gina grabs the remote control.
Pressing the remote control button...
The dog door opens.

Fido's back inside...
The dog door closes.
```

Tick!
Tock!

Before long, the door closes again, keeping rabbits, rodents, and bugs safely outside.

Code Magnets Solution

Here's what we did to complete the simulator. Make sure you got the same answers that we did.

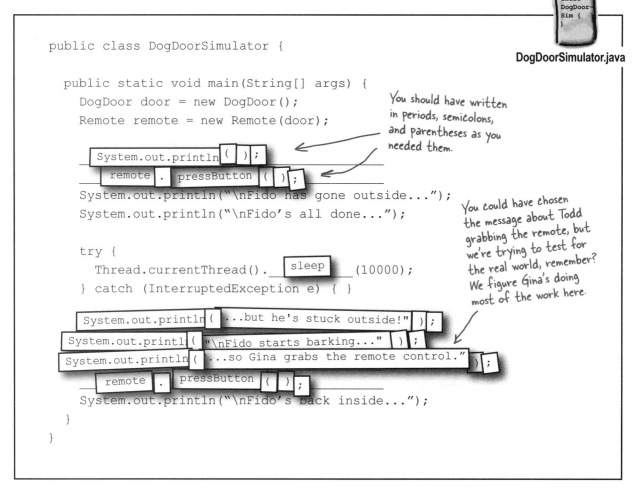

DogDoorSimulator.java

```java
public class DogDoorSimulator {

  public static void main(String[] args) {
    DogDoor door = new DogDoor();
    Remote remote = new Remote(door);
    System.out.println( ( ) );
      remote . pressButton ( ) ;
    System.out.println("\nFido has gone outside...");
    System.out.println("\nFido's all done...");

    try {
      Thread.currentThread(). sleep (10000);
    } catch (InterruptedException e) { }

    System.out.println( "...but he's stuck outside!" );
    System.out.println( "\nFido starts barking..." );
    System.out.println( "...so Gina grabs the remote control." );
      remote . pressButton ( ) ;
    System.out.println("\nFido's back inside...");

  }
}
```

You should have written in periods, semicolons, and parentheses as you needed them.

You could have chosen the message about Todd grabbing the remote, but we're trying to test for the real world, remember? We figure Gina's doing most of the work here.

Delivering the new dog door

Good use cases, requirements, main paths, alternate paths, and a working simulator; we're definitely on the road to great software. Let's take the new dog door to Todd and Gina.

> This dog door rocks! We don't have to get out of bed to let Fido out anymore, and the door closes on its own. Life is good!

Todd and Gina's nights are uninterrupted now, which makes them satisfied customers.

Fido's inside, and the rabbits, woodchucks, and mice are outside.

This was <u>exactly</u> the outcome we were hoping for way back on page 60. What a difference good requirements make, huh?

Fido's Exit

Working app, happy customers

Not only did we turn Todd and Gina into satisfied customers, we made sure their door worked when Fido did something they didn't expect—like stay outside playing.

Use Cases Exposed

This week's interview:
Getting to Know the Happy Path

HeadFirst: Hello there, Main Path.

Happy Path: Actually, I prefer to be called "Happy Path." I know a lot of books refer to me as "Main Path," but I find lots more people remember who I am when I go by "Happy Path."

HeadFirst: Oh, I apologize. Well, in any case, it's great to have you with us today, Happy Path, and you're right on time, too.

Happy Path: Thanks... I'm always on time, that's really important to me.

HeadFirst: Is that right? You're *never* late?

Happy Path: Nope, not a single time. I never miss an appointment, either. I never make a mistake, nothing ever goes unexpectedly... you can really count on me to come through just like you want, every time.

HeadFirst: That's quite a statement to make.

Happy Path: Well, it's just part of who I am.

HeadFirst: And that's how you got your name? You make people happy by always being on time and never making a mistake?

Happy Path: No, but that's close. They call me "Happy Path" because when you're hanging out with me, everything goes just as you'd hope. Nothing ever goes wrong when the "Happy Path" is at the wheel.

HeadFirst: I have to admit, I'm still a bit amazed that nothing ever goes wrong around you. Are you sure you're living in the real world?

Happy Path: Well, don't get me wrong... things definitely go wrong in the real world. But when that happens, I just hand things off to my buddy, Alternate Path.

HeadFirst: Oh, I think I see now... so things can go wrong, but that's Alternate Path's job to handle.

Happy Path: Yeah, pretty much. But I don't worry too much about that. My job is to take care of things when the sun is shining and things are going just like people expect.

HeadFirst: Wow, that must be really satisfying.

Happy Path: Well, most of the time it is. But things do tend to go wrong a lot. It seems like hardly anyone sticks with me from start to finish. Alternate Path usually gets involved at some point, but we get along well, so it's no big deal.

HeadFirst: Do you ever feel like Alternate Path is butting in? I could imagine some tension there...

Happy Path: No, not at all. I mean, we're all after the same thing: getting the customer to their goal, and making sure they're satisfied. And once we're defined well, actually coding an application is a lot simpler.

HeadFirst: Well, you heard it here folks. Next week, we'll try and catch up with Alternate Path, and get her side of the story. Until then, try and stay on the Happy Path, but remember to plan for problems!

WHAT'S MY PURPOSE

Below on the left are some of the new terms you've learned in this chapter. On the right are descriptions of what those terms mean and how they're used. Your job is to match the term on the left with that term's purpose on the right.

External _____

_____ Case

Start _____

Requirement

_____ Value

_____ Condition

_____ Path

Kicks off the list of steps described in a use case. Without this, a use case never gets going.

Something a system needs to do to be a success.

Lets you know when a use case is finished. Without this, use cases can go on forever.

Helps you gather good requirements. Tells a story about what a system does.

What a system does when everything is going right. This is usually what customers describe when they're talking about the system.

This is always the first step in the use case.

Without this, a use case isn't worth anything to anyone. Use cases without this <u>always</u> fail.

Uh oh... parts of some of the terms on the left have gone missing. You've got to use the definitions on the right to match to a term, <u>and</u> fill in the missing part of the term.

Exercise Solutions

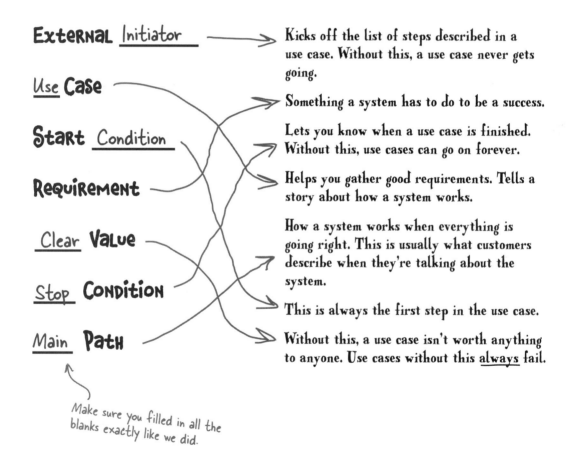

WHAT'S MY PURPOSE

Below on the left are some of the new terms you've learned in this chapter. On the right are descriptions of what those terms mean, and how they're used. Your job is to match the term on the left with what that term's purpose is on the right.

External Initiator → Kicks off the list of steps described in a use case. Without this, a use case never gets going.

Use Case → Something a system has to do to be a success.

Start Condition → Lets you know when a use case is finished. Without this, use cases can go on forever.

Requirement → Helps you gather good requirements. Tells a story about how a system works.

Clear Value → How a system works when everything is going right. This is usually what customers describe when they're talking about the system.

Stop Condition → This is always the first step in the use case.

Main Path → Without this, a use case isn't worth anything to anyone. Use cases without this __always__ fail.

Make sure you filled in all the blanks exactly like we did.

Sharpen your pencil

Time to write some more use cases.

Below are three more potential customers that are interested in Doug's Dog Doors. For each customer, your job is to write a use case to solve the customer's problem.

Doug's Dog Doors is partnering with the local security company to handle their growing customer base, and requests like this one.

Bitsie is constantly nudging open our back door, or nosing open the kitchen bay windows. I want a system that locks my dog door and windows behind me every time I enter a code, so Bitsie can't get out.

Bitsie

Kristen

Bruce is constantly barking, so I never know if he really wants out or not. Can you build a door that opens up when he scratches it with his paws?

Tex is constantly tracking mud inside the house. I want a dog door that automatically closes every time he goes outside, and stays closed until I press a button to let him back in.

John

Tex

Holly

Bruce

→ Answers on page 96.

Sharpen your pencil
       answers

Time to write some more use cases!

You've seen the customers; now let's look at the use cases. Here is how we wrote our use cases for the dog-loving folks on page 95. See if your use cases look anything like ours.

> Bitsie is constantly nudging open our back door, or nosing open the kitchen bay windows. I want a system that locks my dog door and windows behind me every time I enter a code, so Bitsie can't get out.

Bitsie

Kristen

Kristen's use case is just two steps: she enters a code, and then the dog door and the windows lock.

Kristen and Bitsie's Dog Door

1. Kristen enters a code on a keypad.

2. The dog door and all the windows in the house lock.

Even though this is a dog door, Bitsie actually has <u>no effect</u> on how the system behaves!

> Tex is constantly tracking mud inside the house. I want a dog door that automatically closes every time he goes outside, and stays closed until I press a button to let him back in.

John's request turns out to be very similar to what Todd and Gina wanted. Part of gathering good requirements is recognizing when you've already built something similar to what a customer wants.

John

Tex

Bruce is constantly barking, so I never know if he really wants out or not. Can you build a door that opens up when he scratches it with his paws?

Holly

Bruce

Holly and Bruce's Dog Door

1. Bruce scratches at the dog door.
2. The dog door opens.
3. Bruce goes outside.
4. The dog door closes automatically.
4. Bruce does his business.
5. Bruce scratches at the door again.
6. The dog door opens up again.
7. Bruce comes back inside.
8. The door closes automatically.

Some of this really wasn't laid out in what Holly said, but you should have figured it out when you thought through how her system will be used.

Even though John said Tex usually gets muddy, he doesn't *have* to get muddy... so that's really an alternate path.

We really need more information to write this use case... looks like we need to ask John some additional questions.

John and Tex's Dog Door

1. (Somehow) the dog door opens.
2. Tex goes outside.
3. The dog door closes automatically.

4. Tex does his business.
   4.1 Tex gets muddy
   4.2 John cleans Tex up
5. John presses a button.
6. The dog door opens.
7. Tex comes back inside.
8. The door closes automatically.

More Use Case Magnets

Remember the three parts of a use case? It's time to put what you've learned into action. On these pages, you'll find several use cases; your job is to match the use case magnets on the bottom of the page to the correct parts of each use case.

Clear Value **Super Buy**

Start and Stop **STOP**

 External Initiator

You can review all of these by flipping back to page 74.

Holly and Bruce's Dog Door

Bruce scratches at the dog door to be let out. The dog door automatically opens, and Bruce goes outside. The dog door closes after a preset time. Bruce goes to the bathroom, and then scratches at the door again. The dog door opens automatically, and Bruce returns inside. The dog door then closes automatically.

If Bruce scratches at the door but stays inside (or stays outside), he can scratch at the door again to re-open it, from inside or outside.

You should be able to follow these alternate use case formats without much trouble. If you get confused, check out Appendix I for the scoop on alternate use case formats.

Kristen and Bitsie's Dog Door

1. Kristen enters a code on a keypad.
2. The dog door and all the windows in the house lock.

This magnet indicates the **start** condition for a use case.

Super Buy **Super Buy** **Super Buy**

Use these magnets to indicate the **clear value** of a use case.

John and Tex's Dog Door

Primary Actor: Tex

Secondary Actor: John

Preconditions: The dog door is open for Tex to go outside.

Goal: Tex uses the bathroom and comes back inside, without getting mud inside the house.

Main Path

1. Tex goes outside.
2. The dog door closes automatically.
3. Tex does his business.
4. John presses a button.
5. The dog door opens.
6. Tex comes back inside.
7. The door closes automatically.

Extensions

3.1 Tex gets muddy.

3.2 John cleans Tex up.

Answers on page 100.

Use this magnet for the **stop condition** of a use case. How do you know when the use case is finished?

Fido here represents the **external initiator** of a use case, which kicks things off.

Use Case Magnets Solutions

Remember the three parts of a use case? It's time to put what you've learned into action. On these pages, you'll find several use cases (in different formats, no less!); your job is to match the use case magnets on the bottom of the page up to the correct parts of each use case.

Clear Value Super Buy

Start and Stop STOP

 External Initiator

Holly and Bruce's Dog Door

Bruce scratches at the dog door to be let out. The dog door automatically opens, and Bruce goes outside. The dog door closes after a preset time. Bruce goes to the bathroom, and then scratches at the door again. The dog door opens automatically, and Bruce returns inside. The dog door then closes automatically.

If Bruce scratches at the door but stays inside (or stays outside), he can scratch at the door again to re-open it, from inside or outside.

STOP

Super Buy Bruce can get outside to use the bathroom without Holly having to open and close the dog door (or even listen for Bruce to bark)

The clear value of a use case—in most formats—isn't stated in the use case, so you'll need to figure it out on your own.

Look closely for the stop condition in this style of use cases; it's usually <u>not</u> the last sentence if there are any alternate paths.

Kristen and Bitsie's Dog Door

1. Kristen enters a code on a keypad.
2. The dog door and all the windows in the house lock.

STOP

The start condition and external initiator are usually both part of the first step of a use case.

Super Buy Bitsie can't get outside without Kristen letting her out.

The stop condition is almost always the last step in the use case.

In this use case format, the external initiator is always the primary actor.

John and Tex's Dog Door

Primary Actor: Tex

Secondary Actor: John

Preconditions: The dog door is open for Tex to go outside.

Goal: Tex uses the bathroom and comes back inside, without getting mud inside the house.

Super Buy

Anytime the goal of a use case is explicitly stated, you've got your clear value.

Main Path

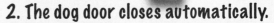

1. Tex goes outside.
2. The dog door closes automatically.
3. Tex does his business.
4. John presses a button.
5. The dog door opens.
6 Tex comes back inside.
7. The door closes automatically.

STOP

Extensions

3.1 Tex gets muddy.

3.2 John cleans Tex up.

Look for the last step in the main path, not the last step of the extensions.

Sharpen your pencil

What's the real power of use cases?

You've already seen how use cases help you build a complete requirements list. Below are several more use cases to check out. Your job is to figure out if the requirements list next to each use case covers everything, or if you need to add in additional requirements.

Kristen and Bitsie's Dog Door
Use Case

1. Kristen enters a code on a keypad.

2. The dog door and all the windows in the house lock.

Kristen and Bitsie's Dog Door
Requirements List

1. The keypad must accept a 4-digit code.

2. The keypad must be able to lock the dog door.

Here's the requirements list for Kristen's dog door. Is anything missing or incomplete based on the use case? If so, write in the extra requirements you think the door needs to handle.

Remember Kristen and Bitsie?

Holly and Bruce's Dog Door
Use Case

1. Bruce scratches at the dog door.

2. The dog door opens.

3. Bruce goes outside.

4. The dog door closes automatically.

4. Bruce does his business.

5. Bruce scratches at the door again.

6. The dog door opens up again.

7. Bruce comes back inside.

8. The door closes automatically.

Holly is psyched about life with her new dog door. It just needs to work, and she's all set!

Holly and Bruce's Dog Door
Requirements List

1. The dog door must detect scratching from a dog.

2. The door should be able to open on a command (from #1).

Is anything missing? It's up to you to make sure Holly is a satisfied customer.

Answers on page 104

Sharpen your pencil

answers

What's the real power of use cases?

In each situation below, the use case describes how the dog door should work-but the requirements aren't complete. Here are the things we saw that were missing from the requirement list, based on the ever-helpful use case.

Kristen and Bitsie's Dog Door
Use Case

1. Kristen enters a code on a keypad.

2. The dog door and all the windows in the house lock.

Kristen and Bitsie's Dog Door
Requirements List

1. The keypad must accept a 4-digit code.

2. The keypad must be able to lock the dog door **and all the windows.**

3. The keypad must be able to unlock the dog door and all the windows in the house.

This one was a little trickier... the use case doesn't mention anything about Bitsie getting back in, so really the use case and the requirements list are incomplete. Kristen wouldn't be too happy if she couldn't unlock everything, would she?

This requirement is incomplete... Kristen wants to be able to lock the doors and windows.

Be careful! Good use cases make for good requirements, but a bad-or incomplete-use case can result in BAD requirements!

Holly and Bruce's Dog Door
Use Case

1. Bruce scratches at the dog door.

2. The dog door opens.

3. Bruce goes outside.

4. The dog door closes automatically.

4. Bruce does his business.

5. Bruce scratches at the door again.

6. The dog door opens up again.

7. Bruce comes back inside.

8. The door closes automatically.

Holly and Bruce's Dog Door
Requirements List

1. The dog door must detect scratching from a dog.

2. The door should be able to open on a command (from #1).

3. The dog door should close automatically.

This is one of the same requirements as for Todd and Gina's dog door.

Tools for your OOA&D Toolbox

OOA&D is all about writing great software, and you can't do that without making sure your apps do exactly what customers want them to.

In this chapter, you learned several tools for making sure your customers are smiling when you show them the systems you've built. Here are some key tools to keep handy:

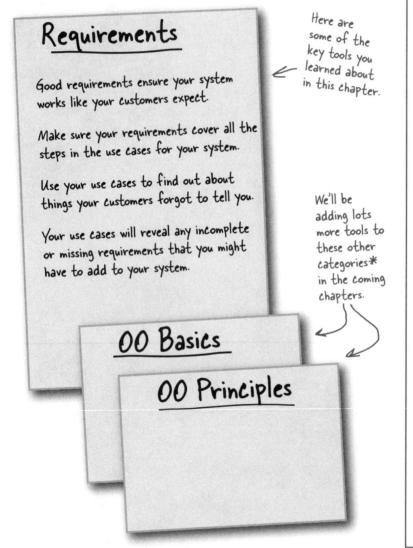

Requirements

Good requirements ensure your system works like your customers expect.

Make sure your requirements cover all the steps in the use cases for your system.

Use your use cases to find out about things your customers forgot to tell you.

Your use cases will reveal any incomplete or missing requirements that you might have to add to your system.

Here are some of the key tools you learned about in this chapter.

OO Basics

OO Principles

We'll be adding lots more tools to these other categories* in the coming chapters.

BULLET POINTS

- **Requirements** are things your system must do to work correctly.

- Your initial requirements usually come from your customer.

- To make sure you have a good set of requirements, you should develop use cases for your system.

- **Use cases** detail exactly what your system should do.

- A use case has a **single goal**, but can have multiple paths to reach that goal.

- A good use case has a **starting** and **stopping condition**, an **external initiator**, and **clear value** to the user.

- A use case is simply a story about how your system works.

- You will have at least one use case for each goal that your system must accomplish.

- After your use cases are complete, you can refine and add to your requirements.

- A requirements list that makes all your use cases possible is a good set of requirements.

- Your system must work in the real world, not just when everything gōes as you expect it to.

- When things go wrong, your system must have **alternate paths** to reach the system's goals.

---

* Readers of Head First Design Patterns will find these categories familiar... that's because OOA&D and design patterns go hand in hand.

OOA&D Cross

Across

4. The main path is sometimes called the _____ path.
5. A use case must have this (two words) to the user.
8. Requirements ensure that your system works _____.
10. In the dog door system, who was the external initiator?
13. Use cases focus on a _____ user goal.
14. When Fido is here, the dog door has hit its stop condition.
16. A use case is just a list of things that a system ____.
18. A use case tells a _____ about how a system works.
21. Use cases are easeist to understand when they're in this kind of language.
22. Good use cases make for _____ requirements.
24. A use case helps you understand how a system will be _____.
25. Use cases help you gather _____.

Down

1. A use case details how a system _____ with users or other systems.
2. When things go right, you're on this.
3. Use cases are all about the "_____" of your system.
6. Without use cases, you won't know if your requirements are _____.
7. If you have four goals in a system, you'll have at least this many use cases.
9. Good systems work in the _____ _____.
11. Fido does this to signal the start of the dog door system's use case.
12. When things go wrong, you end up on an _____ path.
15. Fido isn't part of this, but his dog door is.
17. This is what you should do to the customer to gather an initial set of requirements.

19. How many use cases are there in Todd and Gina's dog door?
20. Fido was chasing these when he got stuck outside.
23. A requirement documents this many needs.

Code Magnets Solutions

The DogDoor class is done, so all you need now is to write a class for the remote control. We've started this class below, but it's your job to finish things up. Using the code magnets at the bottom of the page, complete the code for the Remote class.

Be careful... you may not need all the magnets.

```java
public class Remote {

  private   DogDoor   door;

  public Remote(   DogDoor     door  ) {
    this.door = door;
  }

  public void pressButton() {
    System.out.println("Pressing the remote control button...");
    if ( door . isOpen ()) {
      door.  close  ();
    } else {
      door.  open  ();
    }
  }
}
```

Here's what's leftover.

isOpen   boolean
DogDoor   isOpen
true   false   true
true   open
false
close   boolean

Exercise
Solutions

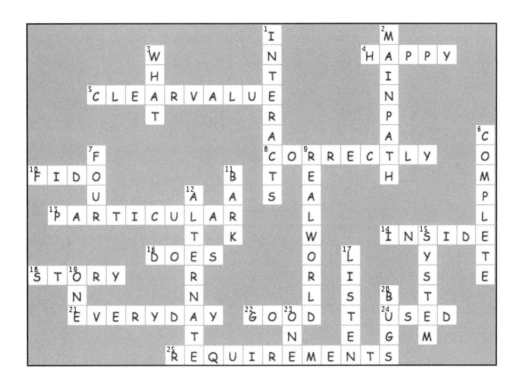

3 requirements change

I Love You, You're Perfect...
Now Change

What in the world was I thinking? I just found out he doesn't even like NASCAR.

Think you've got just what the customer wanted?
Not so fast... So you've talked to your customer, gathered requirements, written out your use cases, and delivered a killer application. It's time for a nice relaxing cocktail, right? Right... until your customer decides that they really wanted something **different than what they told you**. They love what you've done, really, but it's **not quite good enough anymore**. In the real world, **requirements are always changing**, and it's up to you to roll with these changes and keep your customer satisfied.

You're a hero!

A nice piña colada to sip on, the sun shining down on you, a roll of hundred dollar bills stuffed into your swim trunks... this is the life of a programmer who's just made Doug's Dog Doors a successful venture. The door you built for Todd and Gina was a huge success, and now Doug's selling it to customers all across the world.

Doug's making some serious bucks with your code.

But then came a phone call...

> Listen, our dog door's been working great, but we'd like you to come work on it some more...

Todd and Gina, happily interrupting your vacation.

You: Oh, has something gone wrong?

Todd and Gina: No, not at all. The door works just like you said it would.

You: But there must be a problem, right? Is the door not closing quickly enough? Is the button on the remote not functioning?

Todd and Gina: No, really... it's working just as well as the day you installed it and showed everything to us.

You: Is Fido not barking to be let out anymore? Oh, have you checked the batteries in the remote?

Todd and Gina: No, we swear, the door is great. We just have a few ideas about some changes we'd like you to make...

You: But if everything is working, then what's the problem?

We're both tired of having to listen for Fido all the time. Sometimes, we don't even hear him barking, and he pees inside.

And we're constantly losing that remote, or leaving it in another room. I'm tired of having to push a button to open the door.

Todd and Gina's Dog Door, version 2.0
What the Door (Currently) Does

1. Fido barks to be let out.

2. Todd or Gina hears Fido barking.

3. Todd or Gina presses the button on the remote control.

4. The dog door opens.

5. Fido goes outside.

6. Fido does his business.

   6.1. The door shuts automatically.

   6.2. Fido barks to be let back inside.

   6.3. Todd or Gina hears Fido barking (again).

   6.4. Todd or Gina presses the button on the remote control.

   6.5. The dog door opens (again).

7. Fido goes back inside.

What if the dog door opened **automatically** when Fido barked at it? Then, we wouldn't have to do anything to let him outside! We both talked it over, and we think this is a **GREAT** idea!

Back to the drawing board

Time to get working on fixing up Todd and Gina's dog door again. We need to figure out a way to open the door whenever Fido barks. Let's start out by...

> Wait a minute... this totally sucks! We already built them a **working** door, and they said it was **fine**. And now, just because they had some new idea, we have to make more changes to the door?

The customer is always right

Even when requirements change, you've got to be ready to update your application and make sure it works like your customers expect. When your customer has a new need, it's up to you to change your applications to meet those new needs.

Doug loves it when this happens, since he gets to charge Todd and Gina for the changes you make.

⚛ BRAIN POWER

You've just discovered the one constant in software analysis and design. What do you think that constant is?

The one constant in software analysis and design*

Okay, what's the one thing you can always count on in writing software?

No matter where you work, what you're building, or what language you are programming in, what's the one true constant that will always be with you?

(use a mirror to see the answer)

No matter how well you design an application, over time the application will always grow and change. You'll discover new solutions to problems, programming languages will evolve, or your friendly customers will come up with crazy new requirements that force you to "fix" working applications.

Sharpen your pencil

Requirements change all the time... sometimes in the middle of a project, and sometimes when you think everything is complete. Write down some reasons that the requirements might change in the applications you currently are working on.

My customer decided that they wanted the application to work differently.

My boss thinks my application would be better as a web application than a desktop app.

_____

_____

_____

> **Requirements always change. If you've got good use cases, though, you can usually change your software quickly to adjust to those new requirements.**

*If you've read Head First Design Patterns, this page might look a bit familiar. They did such a good job describing change that we decided to just rip off their ideas, and just CHANGE a few things here and there. Thanks, Beth and Eric!

Exercise

Add bark recognition to Todd and Gina's dog door.

Update the diagram, and add an alternate path where Fido barks, Doug's new bark recognizer hears Fido, and the dog door automatically opens. The remote control should still work, too, so don't remove anything from the diagram; just add another path where Fido's barking opens the door.

Woof! Woof!

Gina, open the dog door... Fido won't quit barking!

① Fido barks to be let out

② Todd or Gina hears Fido barking

③ Todd or Gina presses the button on the remote control.

④ The dog door opens

⑤ Fido goes outside

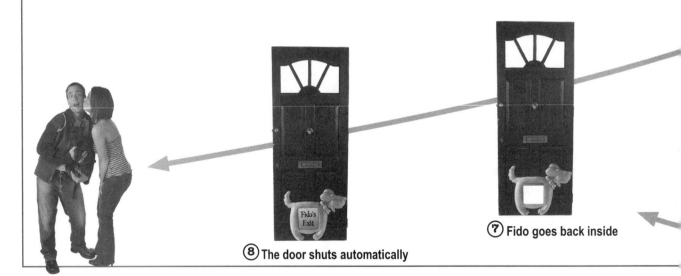

⑦ Fido goes back inside

⑧ The door shuts automatically

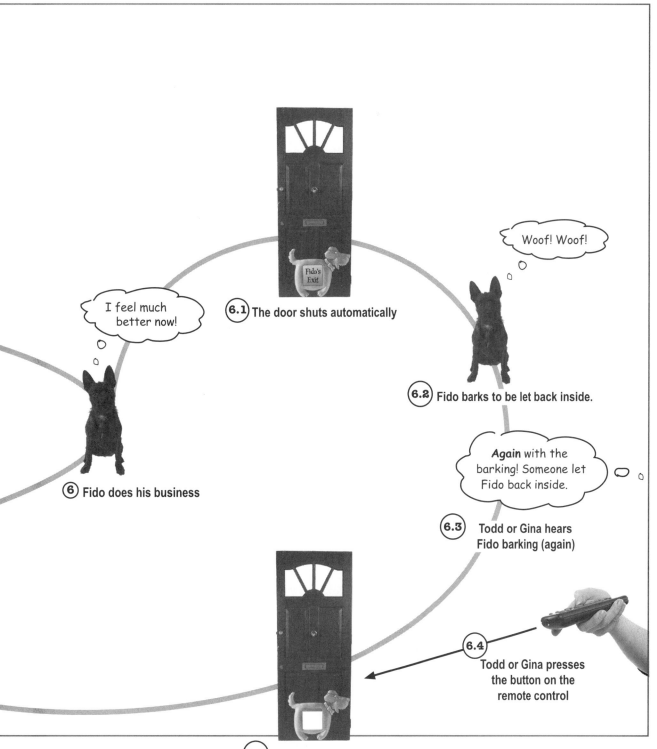

6.1 The door shuts automatically

Woof! Woof!

I feel much better now!

6.2 Fido barks to be let back inside.

Again with the barking! Someone let Fido back inside.

6 Fido does his business

6.3 Todd or Gina hears Fido barking (again)

6.4 Todd or Gina presses the button on the remote control

6.5 The dog door opens (again)

Exercise Solutions

Doug's invented hardware to recognize barks, but it's up to you to figure out how to use his new hardware in the dog door system.

Here's how we solved Todd and Gina's problem, and implemented their bark-recognizing dog door. See if you made similar additions to the diagram.

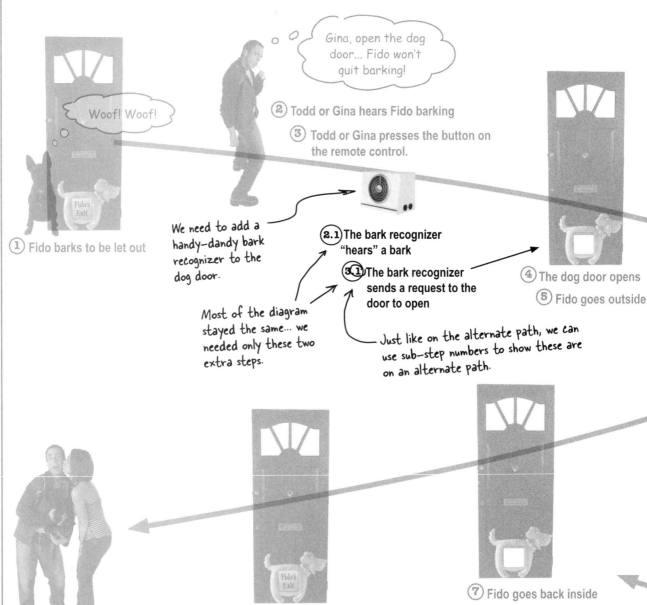

Gina, open the dog door... Fido won't quit barking!

Woof! Woof!

② Todd or Gina hears Fido barking

③ Todd or Gina presses the button on the remote control.

We need to add a handy-dandy bark recognizer to the dog door.

2.1 The bark recognizer "hears" a bark

3.1 The bark recognizer sends a request to the door to open

Most of the diagram stayed the same... we needed only these two extra steps.

① Fido barks to be let out

④ The dog door opens

⑤ Fido goes outside

Just like on the alternate path, we can use sub-step numbers to show these are on an alternate path.

⑦ Fido goes back inside

⑧ The door shuts automatically

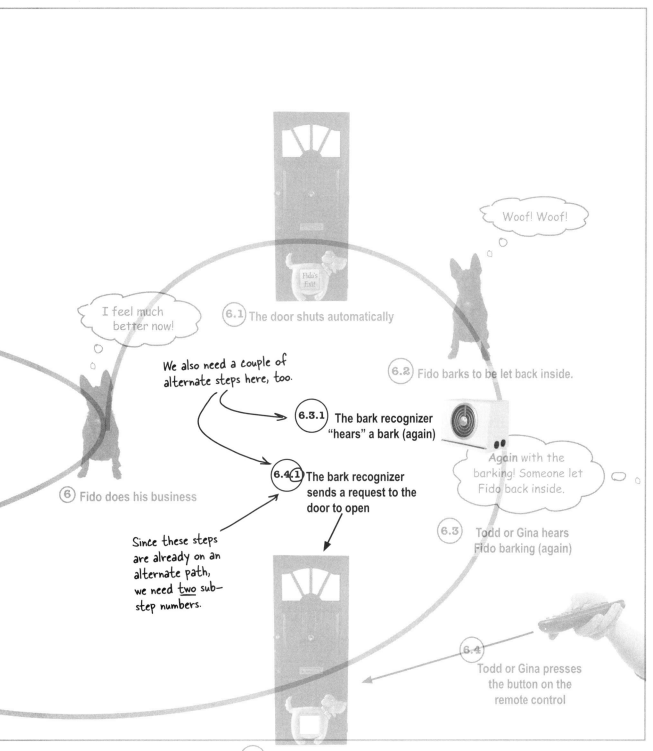

Woof! Woof!

I feel much better now!

(6.1) The door shuts automatically

(6.2) Fido barks to be let back inside.

We also need a couple of alternate steps here, too.

(6.3.1) The bark recognizer "hears" a bark (again)

Again with the barking! Someone let Fido back inside.

(6.4.1) The bark recognizer sends a request to the door to open

(6) Fido does his business

(6.3) Todd or Gina hears Fido barking (again)

Since these steps are already on an alternate path, we need <u>two</u> sub-step numbers.

(6.4) Todd or Gina presses the button on the remote control

(6.5) The dog door opens (again)

> But now my use case is totally confusing. All these alternate paths make it hard to tell what in the world is going on!

Optional Path?
Alternate Path?
Who can tell?

Todd and Gina's Dog Door, version 2.1
What the Door Does

1. Fido barks to be let out.
2. Todd or Gina hears Fido barking.
    2.1. The bark recognizer "hears" a bark.
3. Todd or Gina presses the button on the remote control.
    3.1. The bark recognizer sends a request to the door to open.
4. The dog door opens.
5. Fido goes outside.
6. Fido does his business.
    6.1. The door shuts automatically.
    6.2. Fido barks to be let back inside.
    6.3. Todd or Gina hears Fido barking (again).
        6.3.1. The bark recognizer "hears" a bark (again).
    6.4. Todd or Gina presses the button on the remote control.
        6.4.1. The bark recognizer sends a request to the door to open.
    6.5. The dog door opens (again).
7. Fido goes back inside.
8. The door shuts automatically.

There are now alternate steps for both #2 and #3.

These are listed as sub-steps, but they really are providing a completely different path through the use case.

These sub-steps provide an additional set of steps that can be followed...

...but these sub-steps are really a different way to work through the use case.

Even the alternate steps now have alternate steps.

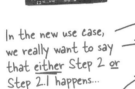

I still think this use case is confusing. It looks like Todd and Gina **always** hear Fido barking, but the bark recognizer only hears him **sometimes**. But that's not what Todd and Gina want...

Do you see what Gerald is talking about? Todd and Gina's big idea was that they wouldn't <u>have</u> to listen for Fido's barking anymore.

In the new use case, we really want to say that <u>either</u> Step 2 <u>or</u> Step 2.1 happens...

...and then <u>either</u> Step 3 <u>or</u> Step 3.1 happens.

Todd and Gina's Dog Door, version 2.1
What the Door Does

1. Fido barks to be let out.
2. Todd or Gina hears Fido barking.
   2.1. The bark recognizer "hears" a bark.
3. Todd or Gina presses the button on the remote control.
   3.1. The bark recognizer sends a request to the door to open.
4. The dog door opens.
5. Fido goes outside.
6. Fido does his business.
   6.1. The door shuts automatically.
   6.2. Fido barks to be let back inside.
   6.3. Todd or Gina hears Fido barking (again).
      6.3.1. The bark recognizer "hears" a bark (again).
   6.4. Todd or Gina presses the button on the remote control.
      6.4.1. The bark recognizer sends a request to the door to open.
   6.5. The dog door opens (again).
7. Fido goes back inside.
8. The door shuts automatically.

Here, <u>either</u> Step 6.3 <u>or</u> 6.3.1 happens...

...and then <u>either</u> 6.4 <u>or</u> 6.4.1 happens.

Use cases have to make sense to you

If a use case is confusing to you, *you can simply rewrite it*. There are tons of different ways that people write use cases, but the important thing is that it makes sense to you, your team, and the people you have to explain it to. So let's rewrite the use case from page 121 so it's not so confusing.

We've moved the steps that can occur instead of the steps on the main path over here to the right.

Todd and Gina's Dog Door, version 2.2
What the Door Does

Main Path

Now we've added a label to tell us that these steps on the left are part of the main path.

1. Fido barks to be let out.
2. Todd or Gina hears Fido barking.
3. Todd or Gina presses the button on the remote control.
4. The dog door opens.
5. Fido goes outside.
6. Fido does his business.
   - 6.1. The door shuts automatically.
   - 6.2. Fido barks to be let back inside.
   - 6.3. Todd or Gina hears Fido barking (again).
   - 6.4. Todd or Gina presses the button on the remote control.
   - 6.5. The dog door opens (again).
7. Fido goes back inside.
8. The door shuts automatically.

Alternate Paths

2.1. The bark recognizer "hears" a bark.

3.1. The bark recognizer sends a request to the door to open.

6.3.1. The bark recognizer "hears" a bark (again).

6.4.1. The bark recognizer sends a request to the door to open.

When there's only a single step, we'll always use that step when we go through the use case.

These sub-steps are optional... you may use them, but you don't have to. But they're still on the left, because they don't replace steps on the main path.

This is a little clearer: we can use Step 2, OR Step 2.1, and then Step 3, OR Step 3.1.

These steps on the right can replace Steps 6.3 and 6.4. You can only take one step to work through the use case: either the step on the left, OR the step on the right.

No matter how you work through this use case, you'll always end up at Step 8 on the main path.

If we can really write the use case however we want, can we make the bark recognizer part of the main path? That's really the path we want to follow most of the time, right?

Excellent idea!

The main path should be what you want to have happen most of the time. Since Todd and Gina probably want the bark recognizer to handle Fido more than they want to use the remote, let's put those steps on the main path:

Todd and Gina's Dog Door, version 2.3
What the Door Does

Main Path

1. Fido barks to be let out.
2. The bark recognizer "hears" a bark.
3. The bark recognizer sends a request to the door to open.
4. The dog door opens.
5. Fido goes outside.
6. Fido does his business.
  6.1. The door shuts automatically.
  6.2. Fido barks to be let back inside.
  6.3. The bark recognizer "hears" a bark (again).
  6.4. The bark recognizer sends a request to the door to open.
  6.5. The dog door opens (again).
7. Fido goes back inside.
8. The door shuts automatically.

Alternate Paths

2.1. Todd or Gina hears Fido barking.

3.1. Todd or Gina presses the button on the remote control.

Todd and Gina won't use the remote most of the time, so the steps related to the remote are better as an alternate path.

6.3.1. Todd or Gina hears Fido barking (again).

6.4.1. Todd or Gina presses the button on the remote control.

Now the steps that involve the bark recognizer are on the main path, instead of an alternate path.

Start to finish: a single scenario

With all the alternate paths in the new use case, there are lots of different ways to get Fido outside to use the bathroom, and then back in again. Here's one particular path through the use case:

Let's take this alternate path, and let Todd and Gina handle opening the door with the remote.

Todd and Gina's Dog Door, version 2.3
What the Door Does

Main Path

Each path through this use case starts with Step 1.

1. Fido barks to be let out.
2. The bark recognizer "hears" a bark.
3. The bark recognizer sends a request to the door to open.
4. The dog door opens.
5. Fido goes outside.
6. Fido does his business.
   6.1. The door shuts automatically.
   6.2. Fido barks to be let back inside.
   6.3. The bark recognizer "hears" a bark (again).
   6.4. The bark recognizer sends a request to the door to open.
   6.5. The dog door opens (again).
7. Fido goes back inside.
8. The door shuts automatically.

Alternate Paths

2.1. Todd or Gina hears Fido barking.
3.1. Todd or Gina presses the button on the remote control.

We'll take the optional sub-path here, where Fido gets stuck outside.

6.3.1. Todd or Gina hears Fido barking (again).
6.4.1. Todd or Gina presses the button on the remote control.

We're letting Todd and Gina handle opening the door again, on the alternate path.

Following the arrows gives you a particular path through the use case. A path like this is called a **scenario**. There are usually several possible scenarios in a single use case.

You'll always end up at Step 8, with Fido back inside.

there are no
Dumb Questions

Q: I understand the main path of a use case, but can you explain what an alternate path is again?

A: An alternate path is one or more steps that a use case has that are optional, or provide alternate ways to work through the use case. Alternate paths can be *additional* steps added to the main path, or provide steps that allow you to get to the goal in a *totally different way* than parts of the main path.

Q: So when Fido goes outside and gets stuck, that's part of an alternate path, right?

A: Right. In the use case, Steps 6.1, 6.2, 6.3, 6.4, and 6.5 are an alternate path. Those are *additional* steps that the system may go through, and are needed only when Fido gets stuck outside. But it's an alternate path because Fido doesn't *always* get stuck outside—the system could go from Step 6 directly on to Step 7.

Q: And we use sub-steps for that, like 6.1 and 6.2?

A: Exactly. Because an alternate path that has additional steps is just a set of steps that can occur *as part of* another step on the use case's main path. When Fido gets stuck outside, the main path steps are 6 and 7, so the alternate path steps start at 6.1 and go through 6.5; they're an optional part of Step 6.

Q: So what do you call it when you have two *different* paths through part of a use case?

A: Well, that's actually just another kind of alternate path. When Fido barks, there's one path that involves Todd and Gina hearing Fido and opening the door, and another path that involves the bark recognizer hearing a bark and opening the door. But the system is designed for one or the other—either the remote opens the door, or the bark recognizer does—not both.

Q: Can you have more than one alternate path in the same use case?

A: Absolutely. You can have alternate paths that provide additional steps, and multiple ways to get from the starting condition to the ending condition. You can even have an alternate path that ends the use case early... but we don't need anything that complicated for Todd and Gina's dog door.

> # A complete path through a use case, from the first step to the last, is called a <u>scenario</u>.

> # Most use cases have several different scenarios, but they always share the same user goal.

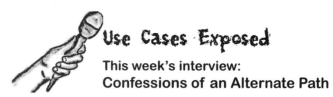

Use Cases Exposed

This week's interview:
Confessions of an Alternate Path

HeadFirst: Hello, Alternate Path. We've been hearing that you're really unhappy these days. Tell us what's going on.

Alternate Path: I just don't feel very included sometimes. I mean, you can hardly put together a decent use case without me, but I still seem to get ignored all the time.

HeadFirst: Ignored? But you just said you're part of almost every use case. It sounds like you're quite important, really.

Alternate Path: Sure, it may *sound* that way. But even when I'm part of a use case, I can get skipped over for some other set of steps. It really sucks... it's like I'm not even there!

HeadFirst: Can you give us an example?

Alternate Path: Just the other day, I was part of a use case for buying a CD at this great new online store, Musicology. I was so excited... but it turned out that I handled the situation when the customer's credit card was rejected.

HeadFirst: Well, that sounds like a really important job! So what's the problem?

Alternate Path: Well, yeah, I guess it's important, but I always get passed over. It seems like everyone was ordering CDs, but their credit cards were all getting accepted. ***Even though I was part of the use case, I wasn't part of the most common scenarios.***

HeadFirst: Oh, I see. So unless someone's credit card was rejected, you were never involved.

Alternate Path: Exactly! And the finance and security guys loved me, they just went on and on about how much I'm worth to the company, but who wants to sit there unused all the time?

HeadFirst: I'm starting to get the picture. But you're still helping the use case, right? Even if you're not used all the time, you're bound to get called on once in a while.

Alternate Path: That's true; we all do have the same goal. I just didn't realize that I could be important to the use case and still hardly ever get noticed.

HeadFirst: Well, just think... the use case wouldn't be complete without you.

Alternate Path: Yeah, that's what 3.1 and 4.1 keep telling me. Of course, they're part of the alternate path for when customers already have an account on the system, so they get used constantly. Easy for them to say!

HeadFirst: Hang in there, Alternate Path. We know you're an important part of the use case!

Sharpen your pencil

How many scenarios are in Todd and Gina's use case?

How many different ways can you work your way through Todd and Gina's use case? Remember, sometimes you have to take one of multiple alternate paths, and sometimes you can skip an alternate path altogether.

Todd and Gina's Dog Door, version 2.3
What the Door Does

Main Path

1. Fido barks to be let out.
2. The bark recognizer "hears" a bark.
3. The bark recognizer sends a request to the door to open.
4. The dog door opens.
5. Fido goes outside.
6. Fido does his business.
   6.1. The door shuts automatically.
   6.2. Fido barks to be let back inside.
   6.3. The bark recognizer "hears" a bark (again).
   6.4. The bark recognizer sends a request to the door to open.
   6.5. The dog door opens (again).
7. Fido goes back inside.
8. The door shuts automatically.

Alternate Paths

2.1. Todd or Gina hears Fido barking.
3.1. Todd or Gina presses the button on the remote control.

6.3.1. Todd or Gina hears Fido barking (again).
6.4.1. Todd or Gina presses the button on the remote control.

Check out our answers on the next page

We've written out the steps we followed for the scenario highlighted above to help get you started.

1. _1, 2.1, 3.1, 4, 5, 6, 6.1, 6.2, 6.3.1, 6.4.1, 6.5, 7, 8_

2. _____

3. _____

4. _____

5. _____

6. _____

7. _____

8. _____

You might not need all of these blanks.

Sharpen your pencil
answers
How many scenarios are in Todd and Gina's use case?

How many different ways can you work your way through Todd and Gina's use case? Remember, sometimes you have to take one of multiple alternate paths, and sometimes you can skip an alternate path altogether.

Todd and Gina's Dog Door, version 2.3
What the Door Does

Main Path

1. Fido barks to be let out.
2. The bark recognizer "hears" a bark.
3. The bark recognizer sends a request to the door to open.
4. The dog door opens.
5. Fido goes outside.
6. Fido does his business.
  6.1. The door shuts automatically.
  6.2. Fido barks to be let back inside.
  6.3. The bark recognizer "hears" a bark (again).
  6.4. The bark recognizer sends a request to the door to open.
  6.5. The dog door opens (again).
7. Fido goes back inside.
8. The door shuts automatically.

Alternate Paths

2.1. Todd or Gina hears Fido barking.

3.1. Todd or Gina presses the button on the remote control.

6.3.1. Todd or Gina hears Fido barking (again).

6.4.1. Todd or Gina presses the button on the remote control.

This is just the use case's main path.

These two don't take the optional alternate path where Fido gets stuck outside.

1. 1, 2.1, 3.1, 4, 5, 6, 6.1, 6.2, 6.3.1, 6.4.1, 6.5, 7, 8

2. 1, 2, 3, 4, 5, 6, 7, 8

3. 1, 2.1, 3.1, 4, 5, 6, 7, 8

4. 1, 2.1, 3.1, 4, 5, 6, 6.1, 6.2, 6.3, 6.4, 6.5, 7, 8

If you take Step 2.1, you'll always also take Step 3.1.

When you take 6.3.1, you'll also take Step 6.4.1.

5. 1, 2, 3, 4, 5, 6, 6.1, 6.2, 6.3.1, 6.4.1, 6.5, 7, 8

6. 1, 2, 3, 4, 5, 6, 6.1, 6.2, 6.3, 6.4, 6.5, 7, 8

7. <nothing else>

8. <nothing else>

Let's get ready to code...

Now that our use case is finished up, and we've figured out all the possible scenarios for using the dog door, we're ready to write code to handle Todd and Gina's new requirements. Let's figure out what we need to do...

> I think we should recheck our requirements list against the new use case. If Todd and Gina's requirements changed, then our requirements list might change too, right?

Any time you change your use case, you need to go back and check your requirements.

Remember, the whole point of a good use case is to get good requirements. If your use case changes, that may mean that your requirements change, too. Let's review the requirements and see if we need to add anything to them.

Go ahead and write in any additional requirements that you've discovered working through the scenarios for the new dog door on page 128.

Todd and Gina's Dog Door, version 2.2
Requirements List

1. The dog door opening must be at least 12" tall.

2. A button on the remote control opens the dog door if the door is closed, and closes the dog door if the door is open.

3. Once the dog door has opened, it should close automatically if the door isn't already closed.

Finishing up the requirements list

So we need to handle the two new alternate paths by adding a couple extra requirements to our requirements list. We've gone ahead and crossed off the steps that our requirements already handle, and it looks like we need a few additions to our requirements list:

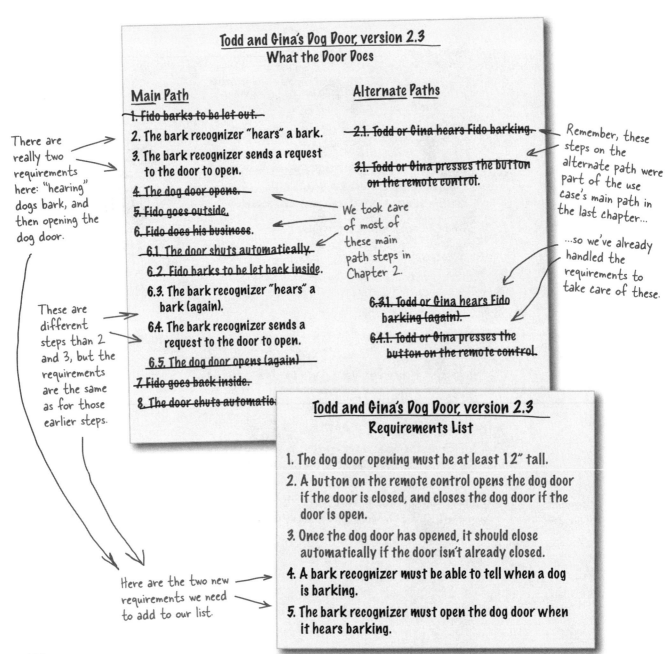

Todd and Gina's Dog Door, version 2.3
What the Door Does

Main Path

1. ~~Fido barks to be let out.~~
2. The bark recognizer "hears" a bark.
3. The bark recognizer sends a request to the door to open.
4. ~~The dog door opens.~~
5. ~~Fido goes outside.~~
6. ~~Fido does his business.~~
   6.1. ~~The door shuts automatically.~~
   6.2. ~~Fido barks to be let back inside.~~
   6.3. The bark recognizer "hears" a bark (again).
   6.4. The bark recognizer sends a request to the door to open.
   6.5. ~~The dog door opens (again)~~
7. ~~Fido goes back inside.~~
8. ~~The door shuts automatic...~~

Alternate Paths

2.1. ~~Todd or Gina hears Fido barking.~~

3.1. ~~Todd or Gina presses the button on the remote control.~~

6.3.1. ~~Todd or Gina hears Fido barking (again).~~
6.4.1. ~~Todd or Gina presses the button on the remote control.~~

There are really two requirements here: "hearing" dogs bark, and then opening the dog door.

We took care of most of these main path steps in Chapter 2.

These are different steps than 2 and 3, but the requirements are the same as for those earlier steps.

Remember, these steps on the alternate path were part of the use case's main path in the last chapter...

...so we've already handled the requirements to take care of these.

Here are the two new requirements we need to add to our list.

Todd and Gina's Dog Door, version 2.3
Requirements List

1. The dog door opening must be at least 12" tall.
2. A button on the remote control opens the dog door if the door is closed, and closes the dog door if the door is open.
3. Once the dog door has opened, it should close automatically if the door isn't already closed.
4. A bark recognizer must be able to tell when a dog is barking.
5. The bark recognizer must open the dog door when it hears barking.

<u>Now</u> we can start coding the dog door again

With new requirements comes new code. We need some barking, a bark recognizer to listen for barking, and then a dog door to open up:

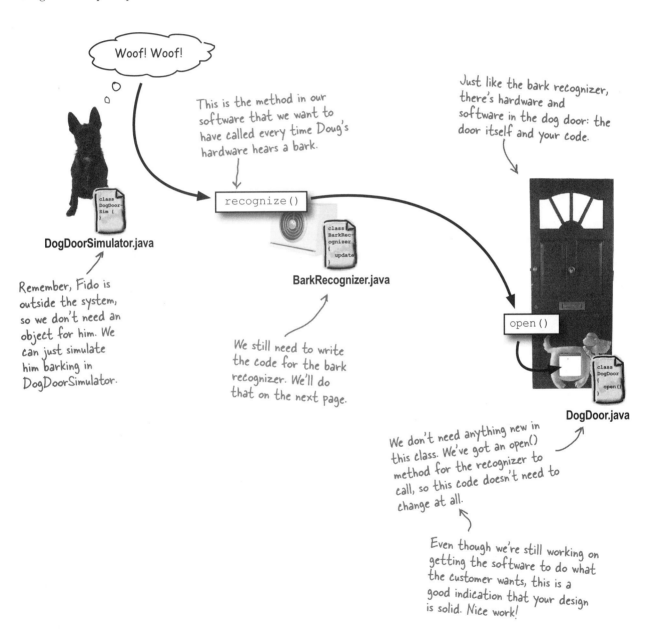

Woof! Woof!

This is the method in our software that we want to have called every time Doug's hardware hears a bark.

Just like the bark recognizer, there's hardware and software in the dog door: the door itself and your code.

recognize()

DogDoorSimulator.java

BarkRecognizer.java

Remember, Fido is outside the system, so we don't need an object for him. We can just simulate him barking in DogDoorSimulator.

We still need to write the code for the bark recognizer. We'll do that on the next page.

open()

DogDoor.java

We don't need anything new in this class. We've got an open() method for the recognizer to call, so this code doesn't need to change at all.

Even though we're still working on getting the software to do what the customer wants, this is a good indication that your design is solid. Nice work!

Was that a "woof" I heard?

We need some software to run when Doug's hardware "hears" a bark. Let's create a **BarkRecognizer** class, and write a method that we can use to respond to barks:

BarkRecognizer.java

We'll store the dog door that this bark recognizer is attached to in this member variable.

The BarkRecognizer needs to know which door it will open.

Every time the hardware hears a bark, it will call this method with the sound of the bark it heard.

```java
public class BarkRecognizer {

  private DogDoor door;

  public BarkRecognizer(DogDoor door) {
    this.door = door;
  }

  public void recognize(String bark) {
    System.out.println("    BarkRecognizer: Heard a '" +
        bark + "'");
    door.open();
  }
}
```

All we need to do is output a message letting the system know we heard a bark...

...and then open up the dog door.

there are no Dumb Questions

Q: That's it? It sure seems like the BarkRecognizer doesn't do very much.

A: Right now, it doesn't. Since the requirements are simple—when a dog barks, open the door—your code is pretty simple, too. Any time the hardware hears a bark, it calls **recognize()** in our new **BarkRecognizer** class, and we open the dog door. Remember, keep things as simple as you can; there's no need to add complexity if you don't need it.

Q: But what happens if a dog *other* than Fido is barking? Shouldn't the BarkRecognizer make sure it's Fido that is barking before opening the dog door?

A: Very interesting question! The **BarkRecognizer** hears *all* barks, but we really don't want it to open the door for just *any* dog, do we? We may have to come back and fix this later. Maybe you should think some more about this while we're testing things out.

I think with this new class, we've got everything we need. Let's test out the BarkRecognizer and see if we can make Todd and Gina happy again.

First, let's make sure we've taken care of Todd and Gina's new requirements for their door:

This is another hardware requirement for Doug. For now, we can use the simulator to get a bark to the recognizer, and test the software we wrote.

> ## Todd and Gina's Dog Door, version 2.3
> ### Requirements List
>
> 1. The dog door opening must be at least 12" tall.
>
> 2. A button on the remote control opens the dog door if the door is closed, and closes the dog door if the door is open.
>
> 3. Once the dog door has opened, it should close automatically if the door isn't already closed.
>
> 4. A bark recognizer must be able to tell when a dog is barking.
>
> 5. The bark recognizer must open the dog door when it hears barking.

This is the code we just wrote... anytime the recognizer hears a bark, it opens the dog door.

Hmmm... our bark recognizer isn't really "recognizing" a bark, is it? It's opening the door for <u>ANY</u> bark. We may have to come back to this later.

Power up the new dog door

Use cases, requirements, and code have all led up to this. Let's
see if everything works like it should.

DogDoorSimulator.java

① Update the DogDoorSimulator source code:

```
public class DogDoorSimulator {

    public static void main(String[] args) {
        DogDoor door = new DogDoor();
        BarkRecognizer recognizer = new BarkRecognizer(door);
        Remote remote = new Remote(door);

        // Simulate the hardware hearing a bark
        System.out.println("Fido starts barking.");
        recognizer.recognize("Woof");

        System.out.println("\nFido has gone outside...");

        System.out.println("\nFido's all done...");

        try {
            Thread.currentThread().sleep(10000);
        } catch (InterruptedException e) { }

        System.out.println("...but he's stuck outside!");

        // Simulate the hardware hearing a bark again
        System.out.println("Fido starts barking.");
        recognizer.recognize("Woof");

        System.out.println("\nFido's back inside...");
    }
}
```

Create the
BarkRecognizer,
connect it to
the door, and
let it listen for
some barking.

We don't have
real hardware,
so we'll just
simulate the
hardware
hearing a
bark.✱

Here's where
our new
BarkRecognizer
software gets to
go into action.

We simulate
some time
passing here.

We test the
process when
Fido's outside,
just to make sure
everything works
like it should.

Notice that Todd and
Gina never press a
button on the remote
this time around.

✱The authors of this book sincerely wanted to
 include hardware that could hear dogs barking...
 but marketing insists that nobody would buy a
 book priced at $299.95. Go figure!

2 **Recompile all your Java source code into classes.**

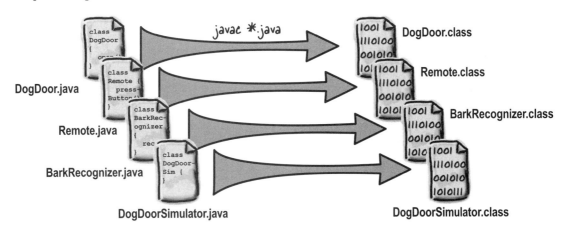

DogDoor.java

Remote.java

BarkRecognizer.java

DogDoorSimulator.java

javac *.java

DogDoor.class

Remote.class

BarkRecognizer.class

DogDoorSimulator.class

3 **Run the code and watch the humanless dog door go into action.**

```
File Edit Window Help YouBarkLikeAPoodle
%java DogDoorSimulator
Fido starts barking.
  BarkRecognizer: Heard a 'Woof'
The dog door opens.

Fido has gone outside...

Fido's all done...
...but he's stuck outside!
Fido starts barking.
  BarkRecognizer: Heard a 'Woof'
The dog door opens.

Fido's back inside...
```

A few seconds pass here while Fido plays outside.

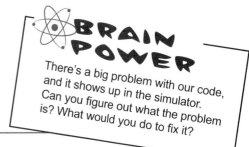

There's a big problem with our code, and it shows up in the simulator. Can you figure out what the problem is? What would you do to fix it?

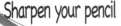

Sharpen your pencil

Which scenario are we testing?

Can you figure out which scenario from the use case we're testing? Write down the steps this simulator follows (flip back to page 123 to see the use case again):

_____

Sharpen your pencil
answers

Which scenario
are we testing?

Did you figure out which scenario from the use
case we're testing? Here are the steps from the
use case on page 123 that we followed:

1, 2, 3, 4, 5, 6, 6.1, 6.2, 6.3, 6.4, 6.5, 7, 8

BRAIN POWER

There's a big problem with our code,
and it shows up in the simulator.
Can you figure out what the problem
is? What would you do to fix it?

*Did you figure out what
was wrong with our latest
version of the dog door?*

In our new version of the dog door, the door doesn't automatically close!

In the scenarios where Todd and Gina press
the button on the remote control, here's the
code that runs:

```java
public void pressButton() {
    System.out.println("Pressing the remote control button...");
    if (door.isOpen()) {
        door.close();
    } else {
        door.open();

        final Timer timer = new Timer();
        timer.schedule(new TimerTask() {
            public void run() {
                door.close();
                timer.cancel();
            }
        }, 5000);
    }
}
```

*When Todd
and Gina press
the button on
the remote,
this code
also sets up
a timer to
close the door
automatically.*

*Remember, this timer waits
5 seconds, and the sends a
request to the dog door to
close itself.*

class
Remote {
press-
Button()
}

Remote.java

But in **BarkRecognizer**, we open the door, and never close it:

```java
public void recognize(String bark) {
    System.out.println("   BarkRecognizer: " +
        "Heard a '" + bark + "'");
    door.open();
}
```

We open the door, but never close it.

BarkRecognizer.java

Doug, owner of Doug's Dog Doors, decides that he knows exactly what you should do.

Even I can figure this one out. Just add a Timer to your BarkRecognizer like you did in the remote control, and get things working again. Todd and Gina are waiting, you know!

What do <u>YOU</u> think about Doug's idea?

> I think Doug's lame. I don't want to put the same code in the remote **and** in the bark recognizer.

Duplicate code is a bad idea. But where <u>should</u> the code that closes the door go?

> Well, closing the door is really something that the **door** should do, not the remote control or the BarkRecognizer. Why don't we have the DogDoor close itself?

Let's have the dog door close automatically <u>all</u> the time.

Since Gina never wants the dog door left open, the dog door should *always* close automatically. So we can move the code to close the door automatically into the **DogDoor** class. Then, no matter *what* opens the door, it will always close itself.

Even though this is a design decision, it's part of getting the software to work like the customer wants it to. Remember, it's OK to use good design as you're working on your system's functionality.

DogDoor.java

Updating the dog door

Let's take the code that closed the door from the **Remote** class, and put it into our **DogDoor** code:

You'll have to add imports for java.util.Timer and java.util.TimerTask, too.

```
public class DogDoor {
  public void open() {
    System.out.println("The dog door opens.");
    open = true;

    final Timer timer = new Timer();
    timer.schedule(new TimerTask() {
      public void run() {
        close();
        timer.cancel();
      }
    }, 5000);
  }

  public void close() {
    System.out.println("The dog door closes.");
    open = false;
  }
}
```

This is the same code that used to be in Remote.java.

Now the door closes itself... even if we add new devices that can open the door. Nice!

Simplifying the remote control

You'll need to take this same code out of **Remote** now, since the dog door handles automatically closing itself:

```
public void pressButton() {
  System.out.println("Pressing the remote control button...");
  if (door.isOpen()) {
    door.close();
  } else {
    door.open();

    final Timer timer = new Timer();
    timer.schedule(new TimerTask() {
      public void run() {
        door.close();
        timer.cancel();
      }
    }, 5000);
  }
}
```

Remote.java

A final test drive

You've made a lot of changes to Todd and Gina's dog door since they first called you up. Let's test things out and see if everything works. Make the changes to **Remote.java** and **DogDoor.java** so that the door closes itself, compile all your classes again, and run the simulator:

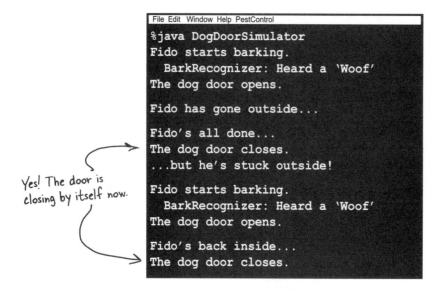

```
File Edit  Window  Help PestControl
%java DogDoorSimulator
Fido starts barking.
   BarkRecognizer: Heard a 'Woof'
The dog door opens.

Fido has gone outside...

Fido's all done...
The dog door closes.
...but he's stuck outside!

Fido starts barking.
   BarkRecognizer: Heard a 'Woof'
The dog door opens.

Fido's back inside...
The dog door closes.
```

Yes! The door is closing by itself now.

BRAIN POWER

What would happen if Todd and Gina decided they wanted the door to stay open longer? Or to close more quickly? See if you can think of a way to change the DogDoor so that the amount of time that passes before the door automatically closes can be set by the customer.

Sometimes a change in requirements reveals problems with your system that you didn't even know were there.

Change is constant, and your system should always <u>improve</u> every time you work on it.

Sharpen your pencil

Write your own design principle!

You've used an important design principle in this chapter related to duplicating code, and the dog door closing itself. Try and summarize the design principle that you think you've learned:

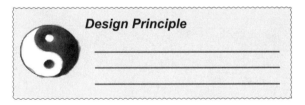

Design Principle

_____

_____

_____

You won't find an answer to this puzzle in the chapter, but we're going to come back to this a little later. Still, take your best guess!

More
Tools for your OOA&D Toolbox

You've learned a lot in this chapter, and now it's time to add what you've picked up to your OOA&D toolbox. Review what you've learned on this page, and then get ready to put it all to use in the OOA&D cross on the next page.

Requirements

Good requirements ensure your system works like your customers expect.

Make sure your requirements cover all the steps in the use cases for your system.

Use your use cases to find out about things your customers forgot to tell you.

Your use cases will reveal any incomplete or missing requirements that you might have to add to your system.

Your requirements will always change (and grow) over time.

There was just one new requirement principle you learned, but it's an important one!

OO Principles

Encapsulate what varies.

Encapsulation helped us realize that the dog door should handle closing itself. We separated the door's behavior from the rest of the code in our app.

BULLET POINTS

- Requirements will always **change** as a project progresses.

- When requirements change, your system has to evolve to handle the new requirements.

- When your system needs to work in a new or different way, begin by updating your use case.

- A **scenario** is a single path through a use case, from start to finish.

- A single use case can have multiple scenarios, as long as each scenario has the same customer goal.

- **Alternate paths** can be steps that occur only some of the time, or provide completely different paths through parts of a use case.

- If a step is optional in how a system works, or a step provides an alternate path through a system, use numbered sub-steps, like 3.1, 4.1, and 5.1, or 2.1.1, 2.2.1, and 2.3.1.

- You should almost always try to **avoid duplicate code**. It's a maintenance nightmare, and usually points to problems in how you've designed your system.

OOA&D Cross

The puzzles keep coming. Make sure you've gotten all the key concepts in this chapter by working this crossword. All the answer words are somewhere in this chapter.

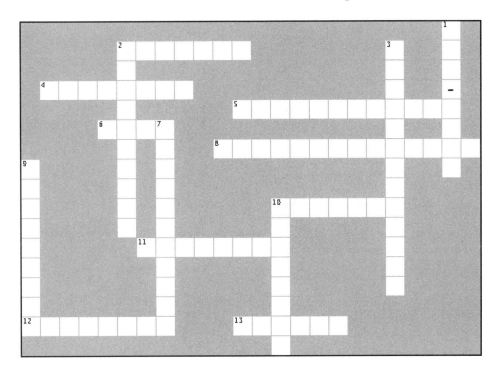

Across

2. We made this responsible for closing the dog door.
4. This is what you follow in a use case most of the time.
5. When your use case changes, these often change as well.
6. Requirements always change over ____.
8. We had to add this to our dog door to satisfy Todd and Gina.
10. When your system changes, you should always update this before writing code.
11. Use cases often have _____ scenarios.
12. Many real-world applications involve both software and this.
13. The one constant in software analysis and design.

Down

1. If a step is optional, use this in your use case.
2. Always avoid _____ code.
3. A set of steps that don't always occur in your use case.
7. Do this to things that vary.
9. The main path is also called this.
10. Every scenario in a use case shares the same ____ ____.

Exercise
Solutions

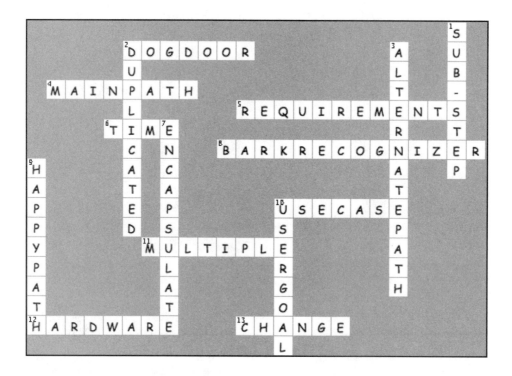

4 analysis

Taking Your Software into the Real World

I think I'm finally ready!

It's time to graduate to real-world applications.

Your application has to do more than work on your own personal development machine, finely tuned and perfectly set up; your apps have to work when **real people use them**. This chapter is all about making sure that your software works in a **real-world context**. You'll learn how **textual analysis** can take that use case you've been working on and turn it into classes and methods that you know are what your customers want. And when you're done, you too can say: "I did it! My software is **ready for the real world**!"

One dog, two dog, three dog, four...

Things are going well at Doug's Dog Doors. The version of the dog door you just developed in Chapter 3 is selling like crazy... but as more doors get installed, complaints have started coming in:

I loved your new model, with the bark recognizer. But now that you've got it installed at my house, it opens up every time the **neighbors'** dogs bark. That's **not** what I wanted when I bought this thing!

Holly

Rowlf! Rowlf!

Holly's dog door should only open when Bruce barks...

Bruce

...but it's opening up when all the other dogs in the neigborhood bark, too.

Aroooo!

Ruff! Ruff!

Yip! Yip!

Your software has a <u>context</u>

So far, we've worked on writing software in a vacuum, and haven't really thought much about the context that our software is running in. In other words, we've been thinking about our software like this:

In the perfect world, everyone uses our software just like we expect them to.

The Perfect World

Everyone is relaxed, and there are no multi-dog neighborhoods here.

But our software has to **work in the real world**, not just in a perfect world. That means we have to think about our software in a different context:

In this context, things go wrong a lot more often.

The Real World

In the real world, there are dogs, cats, rodents, and a host of other problems, all set to screw up your software.

The key to making sure things work and that the real world doesn't screw up your application is **analysis**: figuring out potential problems, and then solving those problems—*before* you release your app out into the real world.

<u>Analysis</u> helps you ensure your system works in a <u>real-world</u> <u>context.</u>

Identify the problem

The first step in good analysis is figuring out potential problems. We already know that there's a problem when there are multiple dogs in the same neighborhood:

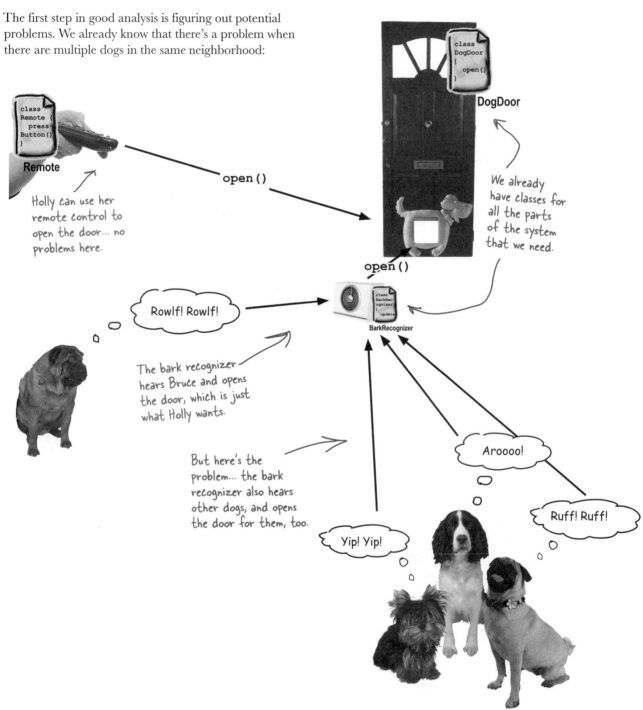

DogDoor

Remote

open()

Holly can use her remote control to open the door... no problems here.

We already have classes for all the parts of the system that we need.

Rowlf! Rowlf!

open()

BarkRecognizer

The bark recognizer hears Bruce and opens the door, which is just what Holly wants.

But here's the problem... the bark recognizer also hears other dogs, and opens the door for them, too.

Aroooo!

Yip! Yip!

Ruff! Ruff!

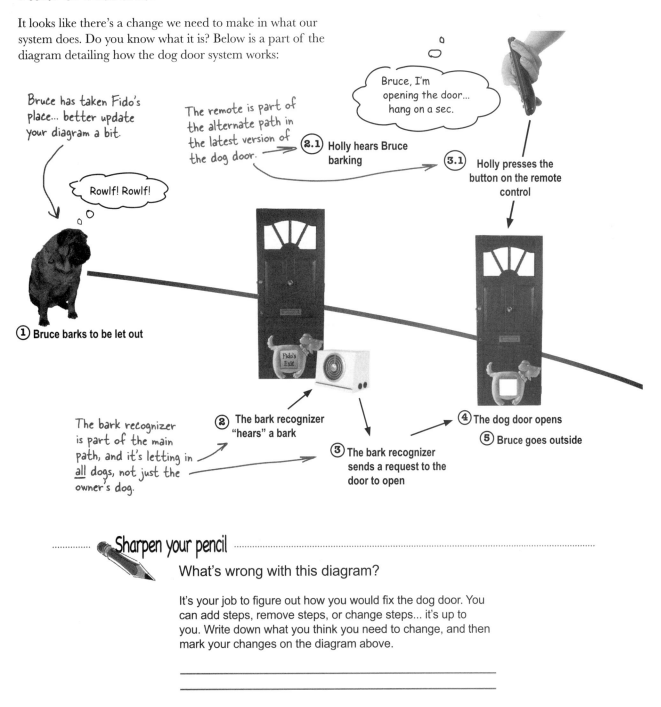

Plan a solution

It looks like there's a change we need to make in what our system does. Do you know what it is? Below is a part of the diagram detailing how the dog door system works:

Bruce has taken Fido's place... better update your diagram a bit.

Rowlf! Rowlf!

The remote is part of the alternate path in the latest version of the dog door.

2.1 Holly hears Bruce barking

Bruce, I'm opening the door... hang on a sec.

3.1 Holly presses the button on the remote control

① Bruce barks to be let out

The bark recognizer is part of the main path, and it's letting in <u>all</u> dogs, not just the owner's dog.

② The bark recognizer "hears" a bark

③ The bark recognizer sends a request to the door to open

④ The dog door opens

⑤ Bruce goes outside

..........**Sharpen your pencil**..

What's wrong with this diagram?

It's your job to figure out how you would fix the dog door. You can add steps, remove steps, or change steps... it's up to you. Write down what you think you need to change, and then mark your changes on the diagram above.

_____

_____

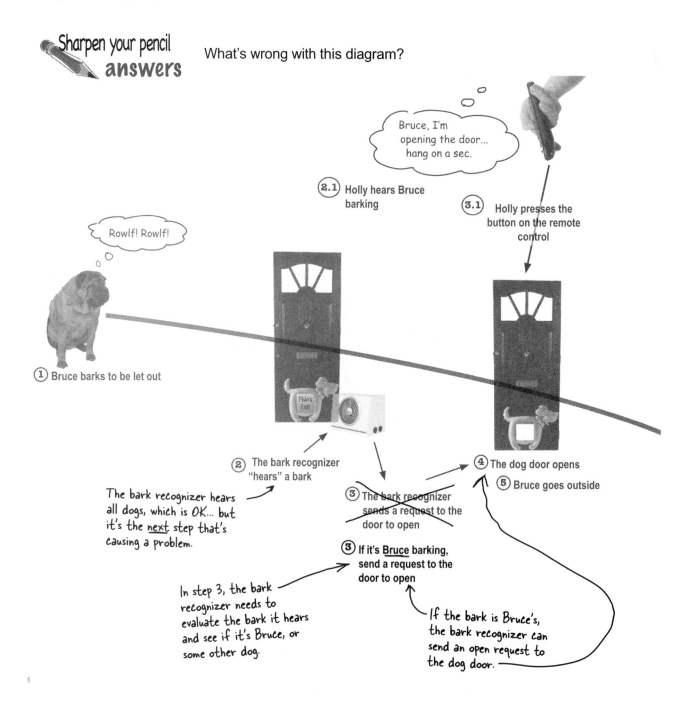

Sharpen your pencil answers

What's wrong with this diagram?

Bruce, I'm opening the door... hang on a sec.

(2.1) Holly hears Bruce barking

(3.1) Holly presses the button on the remote control

Rowlf! Rowlf!

(1) Bruce barks to be let out

(2) The bark recognizer "hears" a bark

The bark recognizer hears all dogs, which is OK... but it's the <u>next</u> step that's causing a problem.

(3) The bark recognizer sends a request to the door to open

(4) The dog door opens

(5) Bruce goes outside

(3) If it's <u>Bruce</u> barking, send a request to the door to open

In step 3, the bark recognizer needs to evaluate the bark it hears and see if it's Bruce, or some other dog.

If the bark is Bruce's, the bark recognizer can send an open request to the dog door.

there are no
Dumb Questions

Q: I came up with a different solution. Does that mean my solution is wrong?

A: No, as long as your solution kept all the dogs except for Bruce from going in and out of the dog door. That's what makes talking about software so tricky: there's usually more than one way to solve a problem, and there's not always just one "right" solution.

Q: In my solution, I turned step 3 of the original use case into *two* steps, instead of just replacing the existing step. Where did I go wrong?

A: You didn't go wrong. Just as there is usually more than one solution to a problem, there is usually more than one way to write that solution in a use case. If you use more than one step, but have the scenario with other dogs barking handled, then you've got a working use case.

Q: So these use cases really aren't that precise, are they?

A: Actually, use cases are *very* precise. If your use case doesn't detail exactly what your system is supposed to do, then you could miss an important requirement or two and end up with unhappy customers.

But, use cases don't have to be very *formal*; in other words, your use case may not look like ours, and ours might not look like anyone else's. The important thing is that your use case makes sense to you, and that you can explain it to your co-workers, boss, and customers.

Write your use cases in a way that makes sense to y<u>ou</u>, your <u>boss</u>, and your <u>customers</u>.

Analysis and your use cases let you show customers, managers, and other developers how your system works in a <u>real</u> <u>world</u> <u>context</u>.

BRAIN POWER

There's an important addition that needs to be made to the dog door system, in addition to what's shown on page 150. What is it?

Update your use case

Since we've changed our dog door diagram, we need to go back to the dog door use case, and update it with the new steps we've figured out. Then, over the next few pages, we'll figure out what changes we need to make to our code.

*We've removed all the references to specific owners and dogs, so now this use case will work for **all** of Doug's customers.*

The Ultimate Dog Door, version 3.0
What the Door Does

Main Path

Bye bye, Fido. Let's use "the owner's dog" from now on.

1. The owner's dog barks to be let out.
2. The bark recognizer "hears" a bark.

Here is the updated step that deals with only allowing the owner's dog in and out the door.

3. If it's the owner's dog barking, the bark recognizer sends a request to the door to open.
4. The dog door opens.
5. The owner's dog goes outside.
6. The owner's dog does his business.
   6.1. The door shuts automatically.
   6.2. The owner's dog barks to be let back inside.
   6.3. The bark recognizer "hears" a bark (again).

Don't forget to change this substep, too.

   6.4. If it's the owner's dog barking, the bark recognizer sends a request to the door to open.
   6.5. The dog door opens (again).
7. The owner's dog goes back inside.
8. The door shuts automatically.

Alternate Paths

Instead of Todd and Gina, or Holly, let's just use "The owner."

2.1. The owner hears her dog barking.

3.1. The owner presses the button on the remote control.

6.3.1. The owner hears her dog barking (again).

6.4.1. The owner presses the button on the remote control.

> Don't we need to store the owner's dog's bark in our dog door? Otherwise, we won't have anything to compare to the bark that our bark recognizer gives us.

We need a new use case to store the owner's dog's bark.

Our analysis has made us realize we need to make some changes to our use case— and those changes mean that we need to make some additions to our system, too.

If we're comparing a bark from our bark recognizer to the owner's dog's bark, then we actually need to store the owner's dog's bark somewhere. And that means we need another use case.

Sharpen your pencil

Add a new use case to store a bark.

You need a use case to store the owner's dog's bark; let's store the sound of the dog in the dog door itself (Doug's hardware guys tell us that's no problem for their door technology). Use the use case template below to write a new use case for this task.

The Ultimate Dog Door, version 3.0
Storing a dog bark ←

1. _____
   _____
2. _____
   _____

Since this is our second use case, let's label it according to what it describes.

You should need only two steps for this use case, and there aren't any alternate paths to worry about.

answers

Add a new use case to store a bark.

You need a use case to store the owner's dog's bark; let's store the sound of the dog in the dog door itself (Doug's hardware guys tell us that's no problem for their door technology). Use the use case template below to write a new use case for this task.

We don't need to know the exact details of this, since it's a hardware issue. ———→

The Ultimate Dog Door, version 3.0
Storing a dog bark

1. **The owner's dog barks "into" the dog door.**

2. **The dog door stores the owner's dog's bark.**

This is what we need to do... add a method to DogDoor to store the owner's dog's bark.

---

there are no Dumb Questions

Q: Do we really need a whole new use case for storing the owner's dog's bark?

A: Yes. Each use case should detail one particular user goal. The user goal for our original use case was to get a dog outside and back in without using the bathroom in the house, and the user goal of this new use case is to store a dog's bark. Since those aren't the same user goal, you need two different use cases.

Q: Is this really the result of good analysis, or just something we should have thought about in the last two chapters?

A: Probably a bit of both. Sure, we probably should have figured out that we needed to store the owner's dog's bark much earlier, but that's what analysis is really about: making sure that you didn't forget anything that will help your software work in a real world context.

Q: How are we representing the dog's bark?

A: That's a good question, and it's one you're going to have to answer next...

 **Design Puzzle**

You know what classes you already have, and you've got two use cases that tell you what your code has to be able to do. Now it's up to you to figure out how your code needs to change:

Your task:

1 Add any new objects you think you might need for the new dog door.

2 Add a new method to the **DogDoor** class that will store a dog's bark, and another new method to allow other classes to access the bark.

3 If you need to make changes to any other classes or methods, write in those changes in the class diagram below.

4 Add notes to the class diagram to remind you what any tricky attributes or operations are used for, and how they should work.

Update DogDoor to support the new use case we detailed on page 154.

We used class diagrams back in Chapter 1; they show the basic code-level constructs in your app.

DogDoor

open: boolean

open()
close()
isOpen(): boolean

Remember, these are the attributes of your class, which usually match up with the class's member variables...

Remote

door: DogDoor

pressButton()

...and these are the class's operations, which are usually the class's public methods.

BarkRecognizer

door: DogDoor

recognize(String)

Remember, Doug's hardware sends the sound of the current dog's bark to this method.

A tale of two coders

There are lots of ways you could solve the design puzzle on page 155. In fact, Randy and Sam, two developers who Doug's Dog Doors just hired, both have some pretty good ideas. But there's more at stake here than just programmer pride—Doug's offered the programmer with the best design a sparkling new Apple MacBook Pro!

17 inches of raw Apple and Intel power.

Randy: simple is best, right?

Randy doesn't waste any time with unnecessary code. He starts thinking about how he can compare barks:

> Bark sounds are just Strings, so I'll store a String for the owner's dog's bark in DogDoor, and add a couple of simple methods. Piece of cake!

Randy

Randy adds an allowedBark variable to his DogDoor class.

```
public class DogDoor {

  private boolean open;
  private String allowedBark;

  public DogDoor() {
    open = false;
  }

  public void setAllowedBark(String bark) {
    this.allowedBark = bark;
  }

  public String getAllowedBark() {
    return allowedBark;
  }

  // etc
}
```

This handles setting the bark, which was what our new use case focused on.

Other classes can get the owner's dog's bark with this method.

Here's Randy's class diagram for DogDoor.

DogDoor
open: boolean **allowedBark: String**
open() close() isOpen(): boolean **setAllowedBark(String)** **getAllowedBark(): String**

Sam: object lover extraordinaire

Sam may not be as fast as Randy, but he loves his objects, so he figures that a new class devoted to dog barks is just the ticket:

> I've got the power of objects!

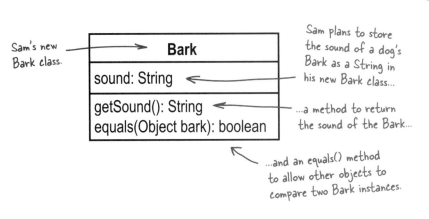

Sam's new Bark class.

Bark
sound: String
getSound(): String equals(Object bark): boolean

Sam plans to store the sound of a dog's Bark as a String in his new Bark class...

...a method to return the sound of the Bark...

...and an equals() method to allow other objects to compare two Bark instances.

Sam

Sharpen your pencil — Writing code based on a class diagram is a piece of cake.

You've already seen that class diagrams give you a lot of information about the attributes and operations of a class. Your job is to write the code for Sam's Bark class based on his class diagram. We've written just a bit of the code to help get you started.

```
public class _____ {
  private _____ _____;

  public _____(_____ _____) {
    this._____ = _____;
  }

  public _____ _____() {
    _____ _____;
  }

  _____ _____ _____(_____ _____) {
    if (_____ instanceof _____) {
      Bark otherBark = (_____)_____;
      if (this._____.equalsIgnoreCase(_____._____)) {
        return _____;
      }
    }
    return _____;
  }
}
```

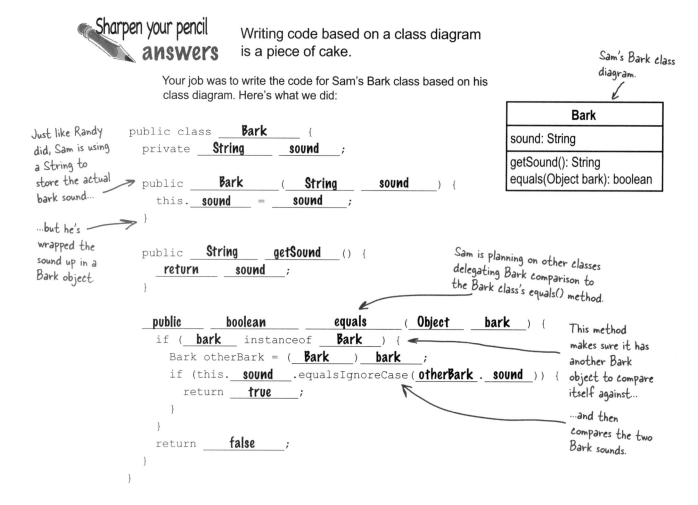

Sharpen your pencil
answers

Writing code based on a class diagram is a piece of cake.

Sam's Bark class diagram.

Your job was to write the code for Sam's Bark class based on his class diagram. Here's what we did:

Bark
sound: String
getSound(): String equals(Object bark): boolean

Just like Randy did, Sam is using a String to store the actual bark sound...

```
public class ___Bark___ {
    private ___String___ ___sound___ ;

    public ___Bark___ ( ___String___ ___sound___ ) {
        this. ___sound___ = ___sound___ ;
    }
```

...but he's wrapped the sound up in a Bark object.

```
    public ___String___ ___getSound___ () {
        ___return___ ___sound___ ;
    }
```

Sam is planning on other classes delegating Bark comparison to the Bark class's equals() method.

```
    ___public___ ___boolean___ ___equals___ ( ___Object___ ___bark___ ) {
        if ( ___bark___ instanceof ___Bark___ ) {
            Bark otherBark = ( ___Bark___ ) ___bark___ ;
            if (this. ___sound___ .equalsIgnoreCase( ___otherBark___ . ___sound___ )) {
                return ___true___ ;
            }
        }
        return ___false___ ;
    }
}
```

This method makes sure it has another Bark object to compare itself against...

...and then compares the two Bark sounds.

Sam: updating the DogDoor class

Since Sam created a new **Bark** object, he takes a slightly different path than Randy did in updating his version of the **DogDoor** class:

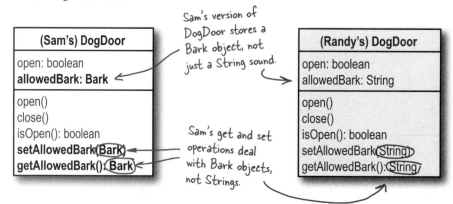

(Sam's) DogDoor
open: boolean **allowedBark: Bark**
open() close() isOpen(): boolean **setAllowedBark(Bark)** **getAllowedBark(): Bark**

Sam's version of DogDoor stores a Bark object, not just a String sound.

(Randy's) DogDoor
open: boolean allowedBark: String
open() close() isOpen(): boolean setAllowedBark(String) getAllowedBark(): String

Sam's get and set operations deal with Bark objects, not Strings.

Comparing barks

All that's left to do is add a comparison of barks into **BarkRecognizer**'s
recognize() method.

Randy: I'll just compare two strings

When the **BarkRecognizer** class gets a signal from the
hardware that a dog is barking, it also gets the bark, and
compares it to what's stored in the door:

The argument sent to recognize() is a String with the dog's bark.

```
public class BarkRecognizer {

  public void recognize(String bark) {
    System.out.println("    BarkRecognizer: "
      "Heard a '" + bark + "'");
    if (door.getAllowedBark().equals(bark)) {
      door.open();
    } else {
      System.out.println("This dog is " +
        "not allowed.");
    }
  }

  // etc
}
```

Compare the bark we get from the recognizer hardware to the bark stored in the door.

Sam: I'll <u>delegate</u> bark comparison

Sam is using a **Bark** object, and he lets that object
take care of all the sound comparisons:

Sam has the hardware guys make sure he gets sent a Bark object now, not just the String bark sound, like Randy.

```
public class BarkRecognizer {

  public void recognize(Bark bark) {
    System.out.println("    BarkRecognizer: "
      "Heard a '" + bark.getSound() + "'");
    if (door.getAllowedBark().equals(bark)) {
      door.open();
    } else {
      System.out.println("This dog is not allowed.");
    }
  }

  // etc
}
```

Sam's code lets the bark stored in the DogDoor handle comparisons. His BarkRecognizer <u>delegates</u> bark comparison to the Bark object.

Delegation Detour

Delegation in Sam's dog door: an in-depth look

Sam is doing something very similar in his **Bark** and **DogDoor** classes. Let's see exactly what's going on:

❶ The BarkRecognizer gets a Bark to evaluate.

Doug's hardware hears a dog barking, wraps the sound of the dog's bark in a new **Bark** object, and delivers that **Bark** instance to the **recognize()** method.

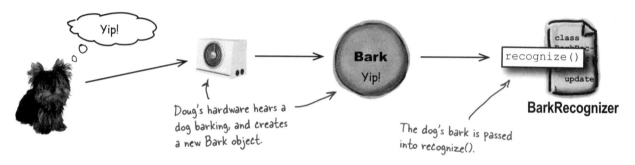

Doug's hardware hears a dog barking, and creates a new Bark object.

The dog's bark is passed into recognize().

❷ BarkRecognizer gets the owner's dog's bark from DogDoor

The **recognize()** method calls **getAllowedBark()** on the dog door it's attached to, and retrieves a **Bark** object representing the owner's dog's bark.

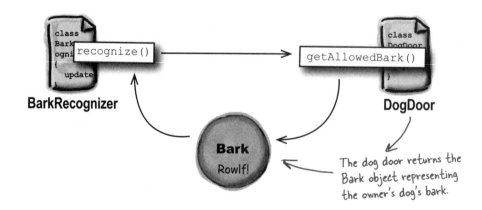

The dog door returns the Bark object representing the owner's dog's bark.

Delegation Detour

We'll come back to Sam and Randy's attemps to win the MacBook Pro once we've got a handle on delegation.

③ BarkRecognizer delegates bark comparison to Bark

The **recognize()** method asks the owner's dog's **Bark** object to see if it is equal to the **Bark** instance supplied by Doug's hardware, using **Bark.equals()**.

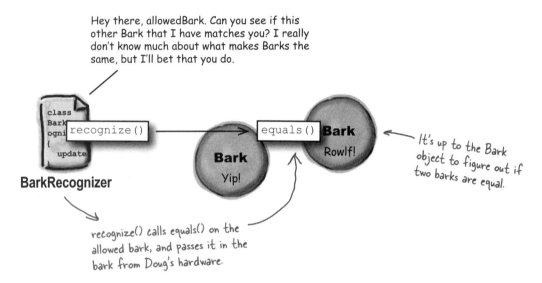

Hey there, allowedBark. Can you see if this other Bark that I have matches you? I really don't know much about what makes Barks the same, but I'll bet that you do.

It's up to the Bark object to figure out if two barks are equal.

recognize() calls equals() on the allowed bark, and passes it in the bark from Doug's hardware.

④ Bark decides if it's equal to the bark from Doug's hardware

The **Bark** object representing the owner's dog's bark figures out if it is equal to the **Bark** object from Doug's hardware... *however that needs to happen*.

The details of _how_ this comparison happens are hidden from all the other objects in the dog door application.

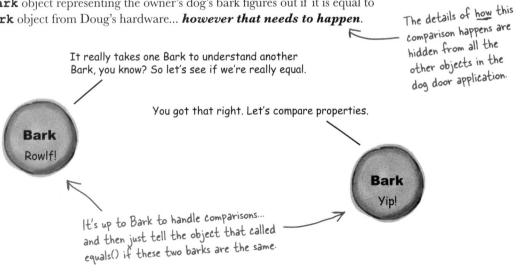

It really takes one Bark to understand another Bark, you know? So let's see if we're really equal.

You got that right. Let's compare properties.

It's up to Bark to handle comparisons... and then just tell the object that called equals() if these two barks are the same.

Delegation Detour

The power of loosely coupled applications

In Chapter 1, we said that delegation helps our applications stay loosely coupled. That means that your objects are independent of each other; in other words, changes to one object don't require you to make a bunch of changes to other objects.

By delegating comparison of barks to the **Bark** object, we abstract the details about what makes two barks the same away from the **BarkRecognizer** class. Look again at the code that calls **equals()** on **Bark**:

```java
public void recognize(Bark bark) {
  System.out.println("    BarkRecognizer: "
    "Heard a '" + bark.getSound() + "'");
  if (door.getAllowedBark().equals(bark)) {
    door.open();
  } else {
    System.out.println("This dog is not allowed.");
  }
}
```

equals() **Bark**
Rowlf!

Bark
Yip!

The details of how equals() works are shielded away from the recognize() method.

Now suppose that we started storing the sound of a dog barking as a WAV file in **Bark**. We'd need to change the **equals()** method in the **Bark** class to do a more advanced comparison of sounds and account for the WAV files. But, since the **recognize()** method delegates bark comparison, no code in **BarkRecognizer** would have to change.

So with delegation and a loosely coupled application, you can change the implementation of one object, like **Bark**, and you won't have to change all the other objects in your application. Your objects are *shielded* from implementation changes in other objects.

Delegation shields your objects from implementation changes to other objects in your software.

Back to Sam, Randy, and the contest...

With Randy's quick solution, and Sam's more object-oriented one, let's see how their applications are working out:

Rowlf! Rowlf!

Remember, Randy's bark is a String, and Sam's is an object.

Randy's code just does some simple String comparison.

```
if (door.getAllowedBark()
        .equals(bark)) {
  door.open();
}
```

```
if (door.getAllowedBark()
        .equals(bark)) {
  door.open();
}
```

Sam's code uses objects and delegation to get the job done.

Aroooo!

Yip! Yip!

Ruff! Ruff!

Randy <u>AND</u> Sam: It works!

Both Randy and Sam ended up with a working dog door that let in only the owner's dog.

We **both** got it right? So who won the laptop?

Maria won the MacBook Pro!

To both Randy and Sam's surprise, Doug announces
that Maria, a junior programmer he got to work for the
company as a summer intern, has won the laptop.

This is Maria. Try not to hate
her guts too much... maybe you
can borrow her MacBook Pro
when she's on vacation...→

Randy: Oh, this is ridiculous. My solution worked! That
laptop is mine, not some intern's!

Sam: Whatever, man. My solution worked, too, and I used
objects. Didn't you read Head First Java? An object-oriented
solution is the way to go... the laptop's mine!

Maria: Umm, guys, I don't mean to interrupt, but I'm not
sure either one of your dog doors *really* worked.

Sam: What do you mean? We tested it. Bruce barked,
"Rowlf!" and the door opened up... but it stayed shut for the
other dogs. Sounds like a working solution to me.

Maria: But did you do any analysis on your solution? Does
your door truly work in the real world?

Randy: What are you talking about? Are you some sort of
philosophy major? Is this like a "there is no spoon" sort of
thing?

Maria: No, not at all. I'm just wondering... what if Bruce
were to make a different sound? Like "Woof" or "Ruff"?

Sam: A different sound? Like if he's hungry...

Randy: ...or excited...

Maria: ...or maybe... he really needs to get outside to *use the
bathroom*. That's, ummm, sort of how things work in the real
world, isn't it?

Randy and Sam: I guess we hadn't thought about that...

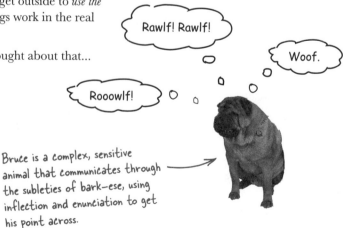

Rawlf! Rawlf!

Woof.

Rooowlf!

Bruce is a complex, sensitive
animal that communicates through
the subtleties of bark-ese, using
inflection and enunciation to get
his point across.

So what did Maria do differently?

Maria started out a lot like Sam did. She created a **Bark** object to represent the bark of a dog.

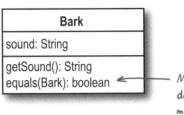

Bark
sound: String
getSound(): String equals(Bark): boolean

Maria knew she'd need delegation via the equals() method, just as Sam did.

I **knew** objects and delegation were important!

But Maria went even further: she decided that since a dog might have different barks, the dog door should store *multiple* **Bark** objects. That way, no matter how the owner's dog barks, it still gets outside:

DogDoor
open: boolean **allowedBarks: Bark [*]**
open() close() isOpen(): boolean **addAllowedBark(Bark)** **getAllowedBarks(): Bark [*]**

Here's where Maria really went down a different path. She decided that the dog door should store more than just one bark, since the owner's dog can bark in different ways.

Wondering about this asterisks? Check this out...

UML Up Close

We've added something new to our class diagrams:

Anytime you see brackets, it indicates the **multiplicity** of an attribute: how <u>many</u> of a certain type that the attribute can hold.

allowedBarks: Bark [*]

The type of the allowedBarks attribute is Bark.

And this asterisk means that allowedBarks can hold an unlimited number of Bark objects.

How in the world did you know to store multiple barks? I never would have thought about a dog having multiple barks.

It's right here in the use case...

Randy's not thrilled he lost either, but figures Maria might be his ticket to winning the <u>next</u> programming contest.

We're focusing on our main use case here, not the new one we developed earlier in this chapter.

The Ultimate Dog Door, version 3.0
Opening/closing the door

It's the <u>dog</u> that is the focus here, not just a specific bark.

<u>Main Path</u>

1. The owner's dog barks to be let out.
2. The bark recognizer "hears" a bark.
3. If it's the owner's dog barking, the bark recognizer sends a request to the door to open.
4. The dog door opens.
5. The owner's dog goes outside.
6. The owner's dog does his business.
   6.1. The door shuts automatically.
   6.2. The owner's dog barks to be let back inside.
   6.3. The bark recognizer "hears" a bark (again).
   6.4. If it's the owner's dog barking,

<u>Alternate Paths</u>

2.1. The owner hears her dog barking.
3.1. The owner presses the button on the remote control.

6.3.1. The owner hears her dog barking (again).
6.4.1. The owner presses the button on the remote control.

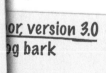

...or, version 3.0
...og bark

...rks "into"

...the

Pay attention to the <u>nouns</u> in your use case

Maria's figured out something really important: the nouns in a use case are usually the classes you need to write and focus on in your system.

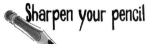

Your job is to circle each noun (that's a person, place, or thing) in the use case below. Then, in the blanks at the bottom of the page, list all the nouns that you found (just write each one a single time; don't duplicate any nouns). Be sure to do this exercise before turning the page!

The Ultimate Dog Door, version 3.0
Opening/closing the door

Main Path

1. The owner's dog barks to be let out.
2. The bark recognizer "hears" a bark.

"dog" is a noun (or you could circle "owner's dog").

3. If it's the owner's (dog) barking, the bark recognizer sends a request to the door to open.
4. The dog door opens.
5. The owner's dog goes outside.
6. The owner's dog does his business.
   6.1. The door shuts automatically.
   6.2. The owner's dog barks to be let back inside.
   6.3. The bark recognizer "hears" a bark (again).
   6.4. If it's the owner's (dog) barking, the bark recognizer sends a request to the door to open.
   6.5. The dog door opens (again).
7. The owner's dog goes back inside.
8. The door shuts automatically.

Alternate Paths

2.1. The owner hears her dog barking.

3.1. The owner presses the button on the remote control.

6.3.1. The owner hears her dog barking (again).

6.4.1. The owner presses the button on the remote control.

Write the nouns that you circled in the use case in these blanks.

_____   _____   _____

_____   _____   _____

_____   _____   _____

Sharpen your pencil answers

Your job was to circle each noun (that's a person, place, or thing) in the use case below. Here's the use case with all the nouns circled.

The Ultimate Dog Door, version 3.0
Opening/closing the door

Main Path

1. The owner's dog barks to be let out.
2. The bark recognizer "hears" a bark.

3. If it's the owner's dog barking, the bark recognizer sends a request to the door to open.
4. The dog door opens.
5. The owner's dog goes outside.
6. The owner's dog does his business.
   6.1. The door shuts automatically.
   6.2. The owner's dog barks to be let back inside.
   6.3. The bark recognizer "hears" a bark (again).
   6.4. If it's the owner's dog barking, the bark recognizer sends a request to the door to open
   6.5. The dog door opens (again)
7. The owner's dog goes back inside.
8. The door shuts automatically.

Alternate Paths

2.1. The owner hears her dog barking.

3.1. The owner presses the button on the remote control.

6.3.1. The owner hears her dog barking (again).
6.4.1. The owner presses the button on the remote control.

---

the (owner's) dog	bark recognizer	dog door
the owner	request	remote control
the button	inside/outside	bark

Here are all the nouns we circled in the use case.

OK, I get it... almost all of these nouns are the classes in my system.

Sam

Maria: That's right. That's how I figured out I needed a **Bark** class... it showed up in the use case as a noun in Steps 2 and 6.3. So I created a **Bark** class.

Randy: So that's where I went wrong... if I had looked at the use case and circled the nouns, I would have known to create a **Bark** class, too.

Maria: Probably. A lot of times, even if I think I know what classes I need, I double-check my ideas with the nouns in my use case to make sure I didn't forget anything.

Sam: But you don't need a class for some of those nouns, like "the owner" or "request," or even "inside."

Maria: That's true... you still have to have some common sense, and understand the system that you're building. Remember, you need classes only for the parts of the system you have to represent. We don't need a class for "outside" or "inside" or "the owner" because our software doesn't have to represent those things.

Randy: And you don't need a class for "the button" because it's part of the remote control—and we already *do* have a class for that.

Sam: This is all great, but I was just thinking... I came up with a **Bark** class, too, and I didn't need the use case to figure that out.

Maria: Yeah... but then you didn't end up with a dog door that really worked, did you?

Sam: Well, no... but that's just because you stored more than one **Bark** object in the dog door. What does that have to do with the use case?

Looking at the nouns (and verbs) in your use case to figure out classes and methods is called <u>textual analysis.</u>

It's all about the use case

Take a close look at Step 3 in the use case, and see <u>exact</u>ly which classes are being used:

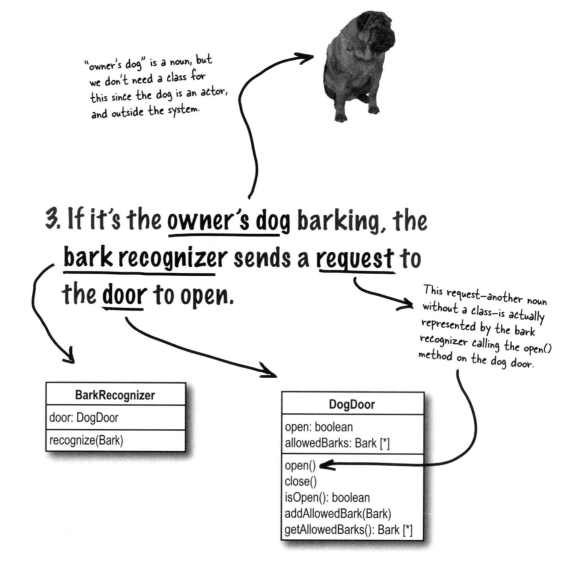

"owner's dog" is a noun, but we don't need a class for this since the dog is an actor, and outside the system.

3. If it's the <u>owner's dog</u> barking, the bark recognizer sends a <u>request</u> to the <u>door</u> to open.

This request—another noun without a class—is actually represented by the bark recognizer calling the open() method on the dog door.

BarkRecognizer
door: DogDoor
recognize(Bark)

DogDoor
open: boolean allowedBarks: Bark [*]
open() close() isOpen(): boolean addAllowedBark(Bark) getAllowedBarks(): Bark [*]

There is <u>no</u> <u>Bark</u> class here!

The classes in use here in Step 3 are BarkRecognizer and DogDoor... <u>not</u> Bark!

Wait a second... I don't buy that. What if I happened to use just a slightly different wording?

3. If the owner's dog's bark matches the bark heard by the bark recognizer, the dog door should open.

Here's Step 3 from the use case that Randy wrote for his dog door. In his Step 3, "bark" <u>is</u> a noun.

Step 3 in Randy's use case looks a lot like Step 3 in our use case... but in his step, the focus is on the noun "bark", and not "the owner's dog." So is Randy right? Does this whole textual analysis thing fall apart if you use a few different words in your use case?

What do y<u>ou</u> think?

HINT: Look closely at Randy's Step 3. Does it describe a system that works exactly the same as the system on page 170?

One of these things is not like the other...

It looks like Randy's Step 3 is actually just a little bit different than our original Step 3... so where did Randy go wrong?

Here's our Step 3, from the original use case we wrote back in Chapter 3.

And here's Step 3 from the use case that Randy came up with for the same dog door.

3. If it's the owner's dog barking, the bark recognizer sends a request to the door to open.

3. If the owner's dog's bark matches the bark heard by the bark recognizer, the dog door should open.

Focus: owner's <u>dog</u>

Our original Step 3 focuses on the owner's dog... *no matter how the dog sounds when it barks.* So if the owner's dog barks with a loud "Rowlf!" one day, but a quiet "ruff" the next, the system will let the dog in, either way. That's because we're focusing on the *dog*, not a particular bark.

Focus: owner's dog's <u>bark</u>

Randy's use case focuses on the owner's dog's bark... but what if the dog has more than one sound it makes? And what if two dogs bark in a really similar way? This step looks similar to the original Step 3, but *it's really not the same at all!*

With the right Step 3, the dog door will open for all of Bruce's barks.

With a poorly written Step 3, only one of Bruce's barks will get him in and out of the dog door.

there are no
Dumb Questions

Q: So you're telling me as long as I write use cases, all my software will work like it should?

A: Well, use cases are certainly a good start towards writing good software. But there's a lot more to it than that. Remember, analysis helps you figure out the classes from your use case, and in the next chapter, we'll spend some time talking about good design principles in writing those classes.

Q: I've never used use cases before, and I've never had any problems. Are you saying that I *have* to write use cases to create good software?

A: No, not at all. There are plenty of programmers who are good at their jobs, and don't even know what a use case is. But if you want your software to satisfy the customer more often, and you want your code to work correctly with less rework, then use cases can really help you nail your requirements down... *before* you make embarrassing mistakes in front of your boss or a customer.

Q: It seems like this stuff about nouns and analysis is pretty tricky, and I'm not any good at English grammar. What can I do?

A: You really don't need to focus too much on grammar. Just write your use cases in conversational English (or whatever language you speak and write in). Then figure out what the "things" are in your use case—those are generally the nouns. For each noun, think about if you need a class to represent it, and you've got a good start on a real-world analysis of your system.

Q: But what if I make a mistake like Randy did, and use a noun in my use case when I shouldn't?

A: Randy's mistake—using "bark" as a noun in step 3 of his use case—had nothing to do with Randy's grammar. He didn't think through the use case, and how his system would work in the real world. Instead of focusing on getting the owner's dog outside, he was worrying about one specific bark. *He focused on the wrong thing!*

When you write your use case, reread it, and make sure that it makes sense to you. You might even want to let a couple of friends or co-workers read through it, too, and make sure it will work in the real world, not just in a controlled environment.

A good use case <u>clearly</u> and <u>accurately</u> explains what a system does, in language that's easily understood.

With a good use case complete, <u>textual</u> <u>analysis</u> is a quick and easy way to figure out the classes in your system.

OK, I see what Randy's mistake was: he got hung up on a bark, not the owner's dog. But even in the correct use case, we don't **have** a Dog object. So what's the point of all this, if our analysis doesn't tell us what classes to create and use?

Textual analysis tells you what to focus on, not just what classes you should create.

Even though we don't have a **Dog** class, textual analysis gave us an important clue about what our system really needs to do: get the owner's dog in and out of the door, *regardless of how he barks*. In other words, our analysis helped us understand what to focus on... and it's *not* a specific bark.

Once you've figured that out, it makes sense to think about what a dog really does. Does a dog always bark the same way? That's when Maria figured out her real-world solution: she realized that if the owner's dog could bark in more than one way, and the point was getting the owner's dog outside, then the dog door needed to store *all* the ways that the dog could bark, not just one of them. But Maria would have never figured this out if she hadn't really analyzed her use case.

Sharpen your pencil   Why is there no Dog class?

When you picked the nouns out of the use case, one that kept showing up was "the owner's dog." But Maria decided not to create a Dog object. Why not? Below, write down three reasons you think Maria *didn't* create a Dog class in her system.

1. _____

2. _____

3. _____

Answers on page 179.

Remember: pay attention to those nouns!

Even if the nouns in your use case don't get turned into classes in your system, they're always important to making your system work like it should.

In this use case, "owner's dog" is a noun, but it's not a class...

...and even though "barking" isn't a noun in this step, we have a Bark class.

3. If it's the **owner's dog barking**, the bark recognizer sends a request to the door to open.

The point is that the <u>nouns</u> are what you should focus on. If you focus on the dog in this step, you'll figure out that you need to make sure the dog gets in and out of the dog door—whether he has <u>one</u> bark, or <u>multiple</u> barks.

Pay attention to the <u>nouns</u> in your use case, even when they aren't classes in your system.

Think about how the classes you <u>do</u> have can support the behavior your use case describes.

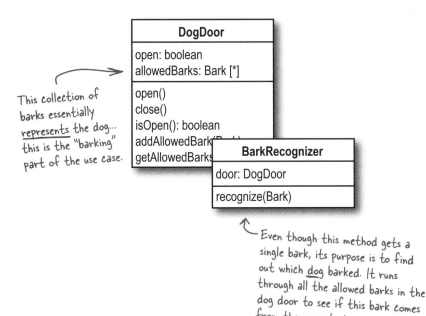

This collection of barks essentially <u>represents</u> the dog... this is the "barking" part of the use case.

DogDoor

open: boolean
allowedBarks: Bark [*]

open()
close()
isOpen(): boolean
addAllowedBark(Bark)
getAllowedBarks

BarkRecognizer

door: DogDoor

recognize(Bark)

Even though this method gets a single bark, its purpose is to find out which <u>dog</u> barked. It runs through all the allowed barks in the dog door to see if this bark comes from the owner's dog.

> It seems like if the nouns in the use case are usually the classes in my system, then the **verbs** in my use case are my methods. Doesn't that make sense?

The verbs in your use case are (usually) the methods of the objects in your system.

You've already seen how the nouns in your use case usually are a good starting point for figuring out what **classes** you might need in your system. If you look at the verbs in your use case, you can usually figure out what **methods** you'll need for the objects that those classes represent:

The DogDoor class needs to have an open() and close() method to support these verb actions.

The Ultimate Dog Door, version 3.0
Opening/closing the door

Main Path

1. The owner's dog barks to be let out.
2. The bark recognizer "hears" a bark.
3. If it's the owner's dog barking, the bark recognizer sends a request to the door to open.
4. The dog door opens.
5. The owner's dog goes outside.
6. The owner's dog does his business.
   6.1. The door shuts automatically.
   6.2. The owner's dog barks to be let back inside.
   6.3. The bark recognizer "hears" a bark (again).
   6.4. If it's the owner's dog barking, the bark recognizer sends a request to the door to open.
   6.5. The dog door opens (again).
7. The owner's dog goes back inside.
8. The door shuts automatically.

Alternate Paths

2.1. The owner hears her dog barking.
3.1. The owner presses the button on the remote control.

6.3.1. The owner hears her dog barking (again).
6.4.1. The owner presses the button on the remote control.

Here's another verb fragment: "presses the button." Our Remote class has a pressButton() method that matches up perfectly.

Code Magnets

It's time to do some more textual analysis. Below is the use case for the dog door you've been developing. At the bottom of the page are magnets for most of the classes and methods we've got in our system so far. Your job is to match the class magnets up with the nouns in the use case, and the method magnets up with the verbs in the use case. See how closely the methods line up with the verbs.

The Ultimate Dog Door, version 3.0
Opening/closing the door

Main Path

1. The owner's dog barks to be let out.
2. The bark recognizer "hears" a bark.
3. If it's the owner's dog barking, the bark recognizer sends a request to the door to open.
4. The dog door opens.
5. The owner's dog goes outside.
6. The owner's dog does his business.
   6.1. The door shuts automatically.
   6.2. The owner's dog barks to be let back inside.
   6.3. The bark recognizer "hears" a bark (again).
   6.4. If it's the owner's dog barking, the bark recognizer sends a request to the door to open.
   6.5. The dog door opens (again).
7. The owner's dog goes back inside.
8. The door shuts automatically.

Alternate Paths

2.1. The owner hears her dog barking.
3.1. The owner presses the button on the remote control.

6.3.1. The owner hears her dog barking (again).
6.4.1. The owner presses the button on the remote control.

There are lots of classes and methods at this point, so take your time.

Remote
Remote
Remote
BarkRecognizer
getSound()
ark
Bark   Bark
BarkRecognizer
Bark
BarkRecognizer
getSound()
BarkRecognizer
Remote
open()
open()
open()
open()
DogDoor
DogDoor
DogDoor
DogDoor
close()
close()
close(
close(
getAllowedBarks()
recognize()
recognize()
recognize()
recognize()
recognize()
getAllowedBarks()
getAllowedBarks()
pressButton()
sButton()
ressButton()
essButton()

Code Magnets Solutions

It's time to do some more textual analysis. Below is the use case for the dog door you've been developing. At the bottom of the page are magnets for most of the classes and methods we've got in our system so far. Your job is to match the class magnets up with the nouns in the use case, and the method magnets up with the verbs in the use case. See how closely the methods line up with the verbs.

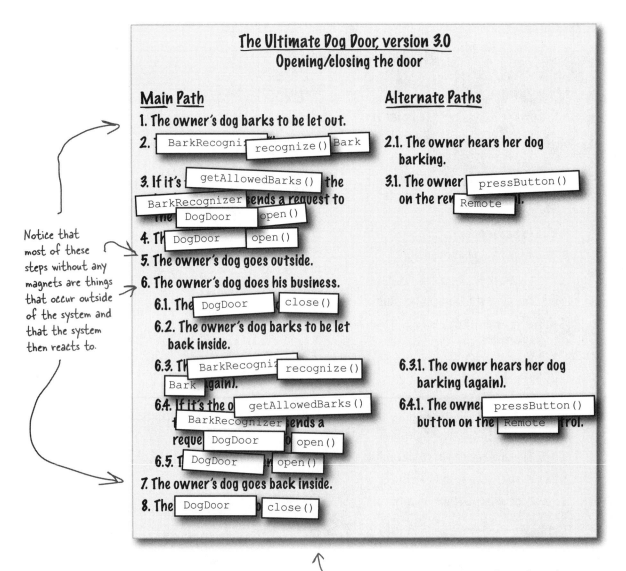

The Ultimate Dog Door, version 3.0
Opening/closing the door

Main Path

1. The owner's dog barks to be let out.
2. The `BarkRecognizer` `recognize()` the `Bark`
3. If it's `getAllowedBarks()` the `BarkRecognizer` sends a request to the `DogDoor` `open()`
4. The `DogDoor` `open()`
5. The owner's dog goes outside.
6. The owner's dog does his business.
   6.1. The `DogDoor` `close()`
   6.2. The owner's dog barks to be let back inside.
   6.3. The `BarkRecognizer` `recognize()` the `Bark` again.
   6.4. If it's the o `getAllowedBarks()` the `BarkRecognizer` sends a reque `DogDoor` `open()`
   6.5. The `DogDoor` `open()`
7. The owner's dog goes back inside.
8. The `DogDoor` `close()`

Alternate Paths

2.1. The owner hears her dog barking.
3.1. The owner `pressButton()` on the rer `Remote`

6.3.1. The owner hears her dog barking (again).
6.4.1. The owne `pressButton()` button on the `Remote` trol.

Notice that most of these steps without any magnets are things that occur outside of the system and that the system then reacts to.

The use case still makes a lot of sense with the magnets in place! That's a good sign that our classes and methods are doing exactly what they're supposed to so that the system will be a success.

Sharpen your pencil
answers

Why didn't Maria create a Dog class?

When you picked the nouns out of the use case, one that kept showing up was "the owner's dog." But Maria decided not to create a Dog object. Why not? Here are three reasons we think Maria made the right choice.

There are times when you might do this, but usually only when you need to interact with those external things. We don't need to interact with the dog.

1. The dog is external to the system, and you usually don't need to represent things external to the system.

2. Dog isn't a software object (and shouldn't be)... you usually don't represent living things with a class unless the system is going to store long-term information about that thing.

3. Even if you had a Dog class, it wouldn't help the rest of the system. For example, you can't really "store" a Dog in the dog door; that doesn't make any sense.

You could have a reference to the Dog class in your DogDoor object, but how do you store a dog within a door in the real world? Remember, what works in software doesn't always work in real life. Make sure your applications are real-world compatible!

You'll often see classes like User or Manager, but these represent roles in a system, or store credit cards or addresses. A dog doesn't fit any of those patterns.

---

there are no Dumb Questions

Q: So the nouns in the use case turn into classes, and the verbs turn into methods?

A: That's almost it. Actually, the nouns are *candidates* for classes... not every noun will be a class. For instance, "the owner" is a noun in the use case (check out Steps 2.1 and 3.1, for example), but we don't need a class for that noun. So even though "the owner" is a candidate for a class, it doesn't become a class in the actual system.

In the same way, the verbs are candidates for operations. For example, one verb phrase is "does his business," but we just couldn't bear to write a `pee()` or `poop()` method. We hope you'll agree that we made the right choice! Still, textual analysis is a really good start to figuring out the classes and methods you'll need in your system.

Q: It looks like the nouns that are outside the system don't get turned into classes. Is that always true?

A: Most of the time it is. The only common exception is when you have to interact with something outside the system—like when there's some state or behavior that the system needs to work with on a recurring basis.

In the dog door system, for example, we didn't need a class for the owner because the `Remote` class took care of all the owner-related activity. If we ever needed to track owner state, though—like if the owner was asleep or awake—then we might have to create an `Owner` class.

From good analysis to good classes...

Once I knew the classes and operations that I needed, I went back and updated my class diagram.

Maria's Dog Door Class Diagram

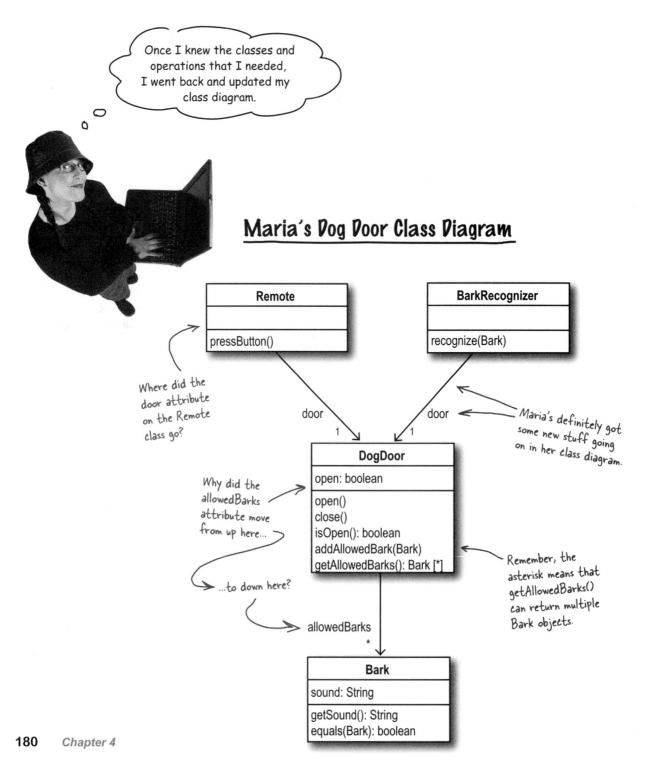

Remote

pressButton()

BarkRecognizer

recognize(Bark)

Where did the door attribute on the Remote class go?

Maria's definitely got some new stuff going on in her class diagram.

door 1   door 1

DogDoor

open: boolean

open()
close()
isOpen(): boolean
addAllowedBark(Bark)
getAllowedBarks(): Bark [*]

Why did the allowedBarks attribute move from up here...

...to down here?

Remember, the asterisk means that getAllowedBarks() can return multiple Bark objects.

allowedBarks

*

Bark

sound: String

getSound(): String
equals(Bark): boolean

UML Investigation

Maria's gone pretty crazy with her UML diagrams... do you think you can figure out what all she's done? On the diagram below, add notes to all the new things she's added, and try and figure out what the lines, numbers, and additional words all mean. We've written a few notes of our own to get you started.

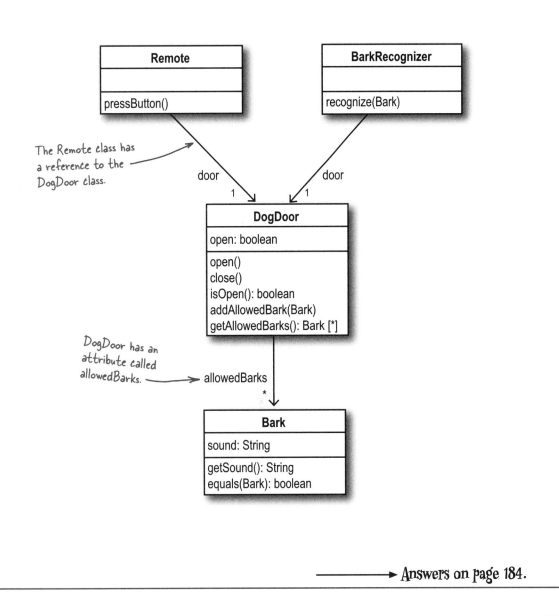

The Remote class has a reference to the DogDoor class.

Remote

pressButton()

BarkRecognizer

recognize(Bark)

door
1

door
1

DogDoor

open: boolean

open()
close()
isOpen(): boolean
addAllowedBark(Bark)
getAllowedBarks(): Bark [*]

DogDoor has an attribute called allowedBarks.

allowedBarks

*

Bark

sound: String

getSound(): String
equals(Bark): boolean

Answers on page 184.

Class diagrams dissected

**There's a lot more to a class diagram than boxes
and text. Let's see how some lines and arrows can
add a lot more information to your class diagrams.**

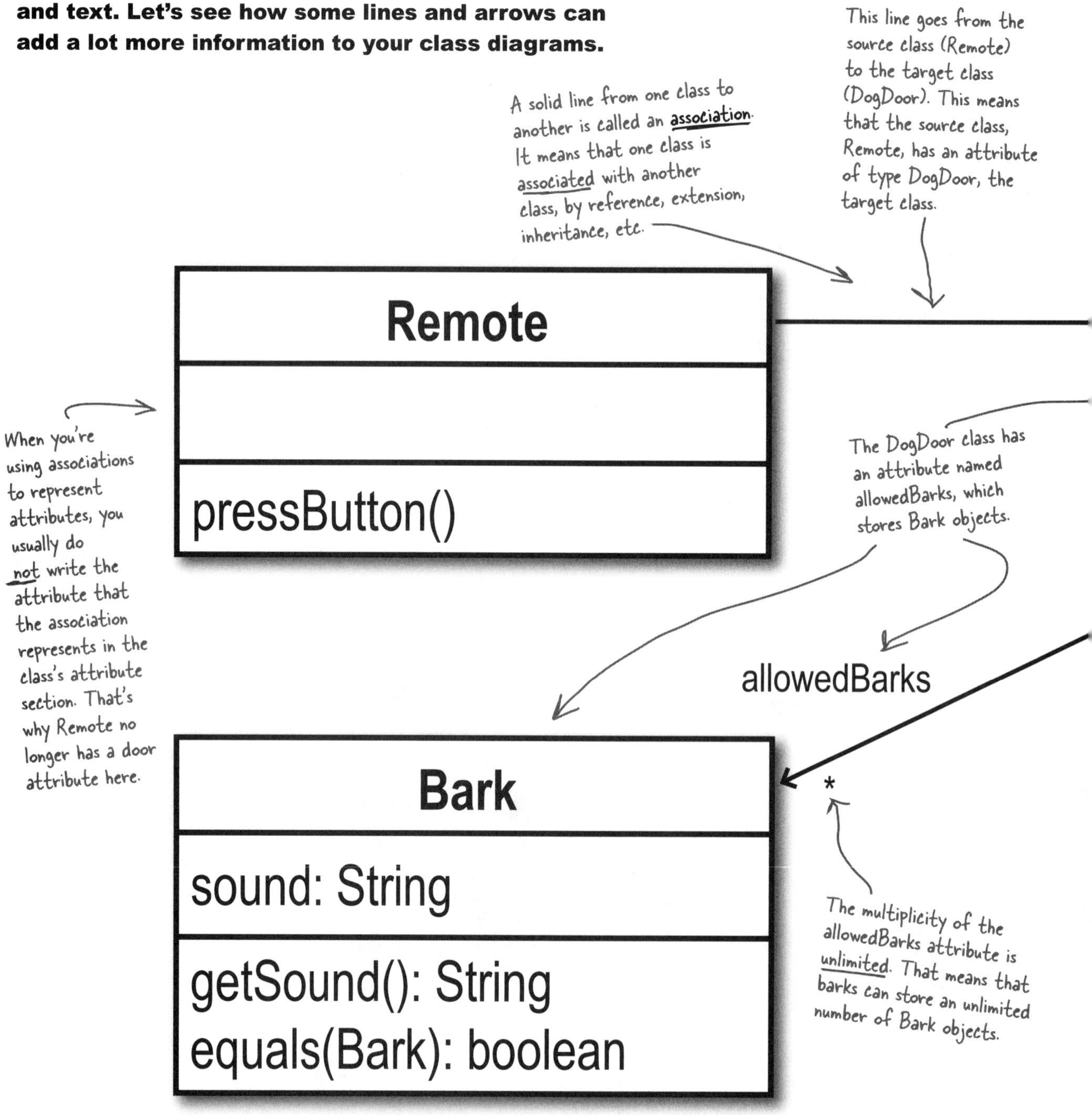

This line goes from the
source class (Remote)
to the target class
(DogDoor). This means
that the source class,
Remote, has an attribute
of type DogDoor, the
target class.

A solid line from one class to
another is called an <u>association</u>.
It means that one class is
<u>associated</u> with another
class, by reference, extension,
inheritance, etc.

Remote
pressButton()

When you're
using associations
to represent
attributes, you
usually do
<u>not</u> write the
attribute that
the association
represents in the
class's attribute
section. That's
why Remote no
longer has a door
attribute here.

The DogDoor class has
an attribute named
allowedBarks, which
stores Bark objects.

allowedBarks

Bark
sound: String
getSound(): String equals(Bark): boolean

*

The multiplicity of the
allowedBarks attribute is
<u>unlimited</u>. That means that
barks can store an unlimited
number of Bark objects.

The name of the attribute in the source class is written here, at the target end of the line. So the Remote class has an attribute called door, of type DogDoor.

This number is the **multiplicity** of this association. It's how many of the target type is stored in the attribute of the source class. In this case, the door attribute stores a single DogDoor.

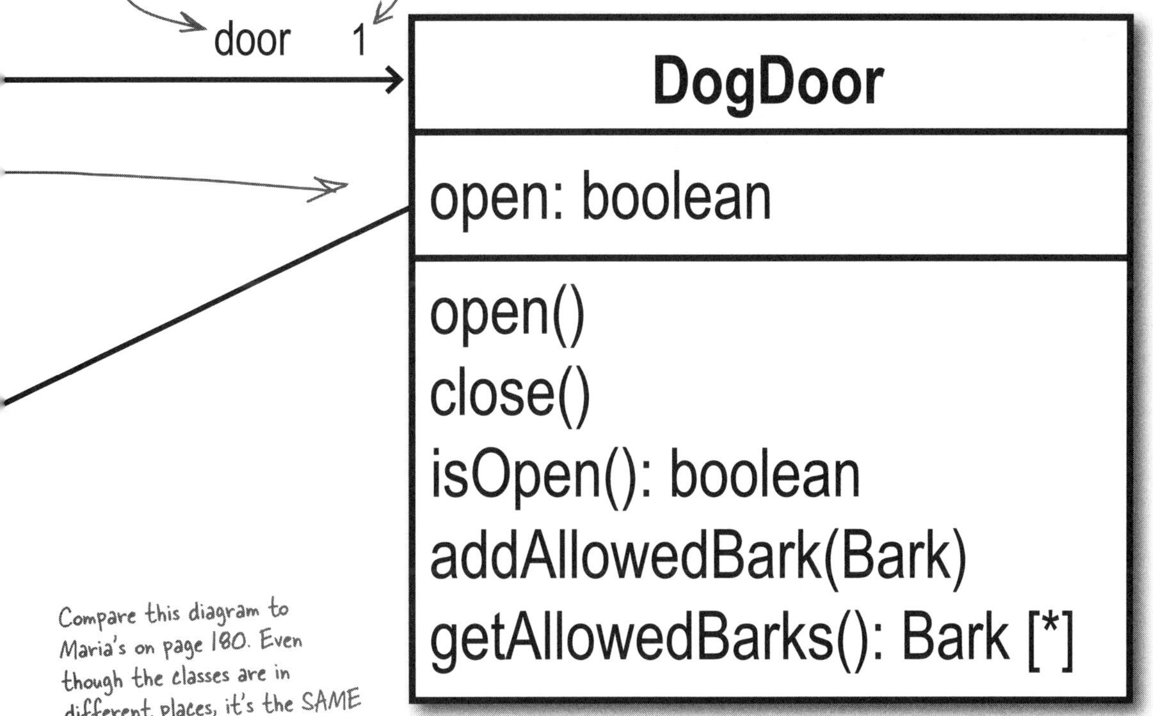

door   1

DogDoor

open: boolean

open()
close()
isOpen(): boolean
addAllowedBark(Bark)
getAllowedBarks(): Bark [*]

Compare this diagram to Maria's on page 180. Even though the classes are in different places, it's the SAME class diagram. So the position of the classes on the diagram doesn't matter.

Answers to this exercise are on page 185.

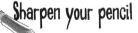

Sharpen your pencil

Based on the class diagram above, what types could you use for the allowedBarks attribute in the DogDoor class? Write your ideas below:

_____

UML Investigation Complete

Maria's gone pretty crazy with her UML diagrams... see if you can figure out everything that she's done.

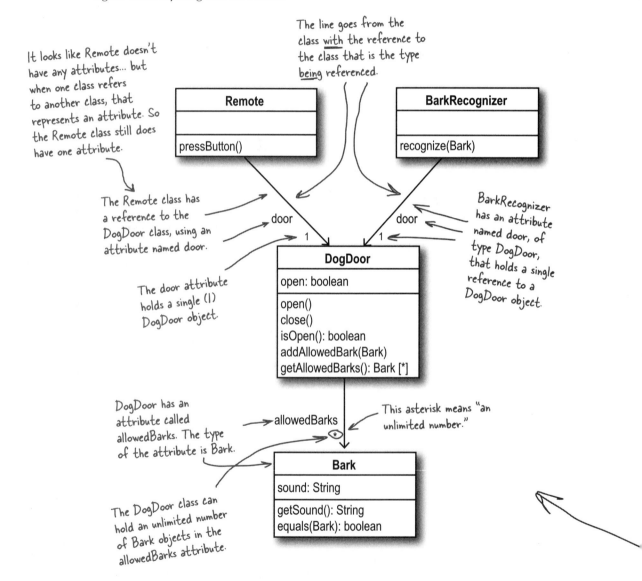

It looks like Remote doesn't have any attributes... but when one class refers to another class, that represents an attribute. So the Remote class still does have one attribute.

The line goes from the class <u>with</u> the reference to the class that is the type <u>being</u> referenced.

Remote

pressButton()

BarkRecognizer

recognize(Bark)

The Remote class has a reference to the DogDoor class, using an attribute named door.

door 1

door 1

BarkRecognizer has an attribute named door, of type DogDoor, that holds a single reference to a DogDoor object.

The door attribute holds a single (1) DogDoor object.

DogDoor

open: boolean

open()
close()
isOpen(): boolean
addAllowedBark(Bark)
getAllowedBarks(): Bark [*]

DogDoor has an attribute called allowedBarks. The type of the attribute is Bark.

allowedBarks

This asterisk means "an unlimited number."

⬥*

Bark

sound: String

getSound(): String
equals(Bark): boolean

The DogDoor class can hold an unlimited number of Bark objects in the allowedBarks attribute.

Sharpen your pencil
~~~~~~~~~ answers

Based on the class diagram below, what types could you use for the barks member variable in your DogDoor class? Write your ideas in the blank below:

List, Array, Vector, etc.

You could write any type that supports multiple values... most of the Java Collection classes would work.

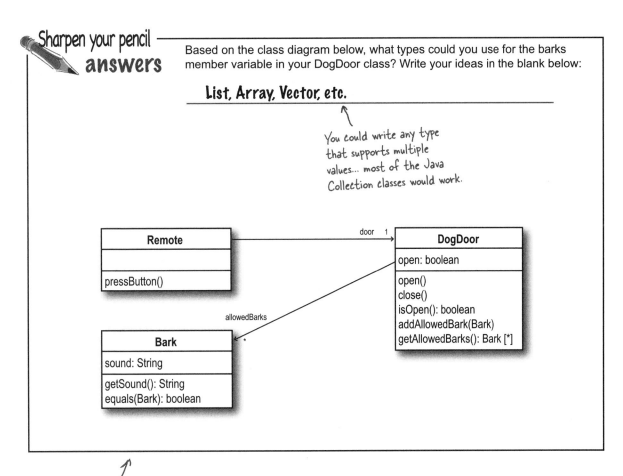

Remote
pressButton()

door 1

DogDoor
open: boolean
open() close() isOpen(): boolean addAllowedBark(Bark) getAllowedBarks(): Bark [*]

allowedBarks

Bark
sound: String
getSound(): String equals(Bark): boolean

*

Notice that this diagram, although positioned very differently, has the same classes and associations as this diagram.

I guess I'm still just not sure why you need all these diagrams...

Randy: I may have missed creating a **Bark** class, but my solution wasn't that bad, and I didn't waste a bunch of my time drawing squares and arrows.

Maria: Haven't you ever heard that a picture is worth a thousand words? Once I had my class diagram, I had a pretty good idea about how my whole system was going to work.

Randy: Well, yeah, I guess I can see that... but I had a good idea of how my system would work, too. It was just in my head, not drawn out on paper.

Sam: I think I'm starting to come around on this UML thing, Randy. I mean, once you've got the use case, it's pretty natural to do some analysis, and turn the nouns into classes. It seems like you wouldn't have to spend as much time worrying about what should be a class, and what shouldn't.

Maria: Exactly! I hate writing a bunch of classes and then finding out I did something wrong. With use cases and class diagrams, if I make a mistake, I can just scribble things out and redraw my diagram.

Remember how we said OOA&D helps you write great software, <u>every time</u>? This is one way OOA&D can help you avoid making mistakes in your code.

Randy: Well, I guess that's true. Rewriting code takes a lot more time than rewriting a use case or redrawing a class diagram...

Maria: And you know, if you ever have to work with anyone else, you're going to have to explain that system in your head to them somehow, right?

Sam: I think she's right, Randy. I've seen your whiteboard when you're trying to explain your ideas... it's a mess!

Randy: OK, even I can't argue with that. But I still think class diagrams don't tell the whole story. Like, how is our code actually going to compare barks and figure out if the dog door should open up?

Bark
sound: String
getSound(): String equals(Bark): boolean

DogDoor
open: boolean allowedBarks: Bark
open() close() isOpen(): boolean addAllowedBark(Bark) getAllowedBarks(): Bark [*]

Remote
door: DogDoor
pressButton()

BarkRecognizer
door: DogDoor
Bark)

Class diagrams aren't everything

Class diagrams are a great way to get an overview of your system, and show the parts of your system to co-workers and other programmers. But there's still plenty of things that they *don't* show.

Class diagrams provide limited type information

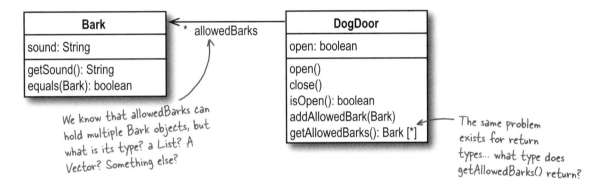

We know that allowedBarks can hold multiple Bark objects, but what is its type? a List? A Vector? Something else?

The same problem exists for return types... what type does getAllowedBarks() return?

Class diagrams don't tell you how to code your methods

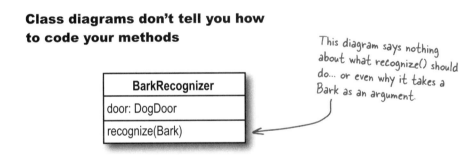

This diagram says nothing about what recognize() should do... or even why it takes a Bark as an argument.

Class diagrams only give you a 10,000 foot view of your system

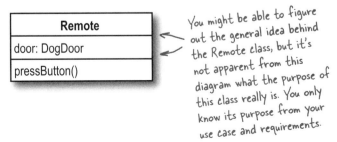

You might be able to figure out the general idea behind the Remote class, but it's not apparent from this diagram what the purpose of this class really is. You only know its purpose from your use case and requirements.

WHAT'S MISSING

Class diagrams are great for modeling the classes you need to create, but they don't provide all the answers you'll need in programming your system. You've already seen that the dog door class diagram doesn't tell us much about matching up return types; what other things do you think are unclear from this diagram that you might need to know to program the dog door?

Add notes to the diagram below about what you might need to figure out in order to program the door. We've added a note about comparing barks to get you started.

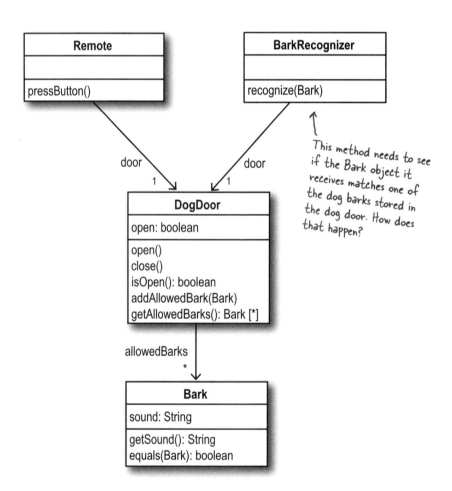

Answer on page 190

So how does recognize() work now?

Maria's figured out that her **BarkRecognizer** class should be able to compare any bark it receives against multiple allowed barks, but her class diagram doesn't tell us much about how to actually write the **recognize()** method.

Instead, we have to look at Maria's code. Here's the **recognize()** method of her **BarkRecognizer**, and how she solved the barking problem:

Iterator is a Java object that lets us walk through each item in a list.

Just like in Sam's code, Maria delegates Bark comparisons to the Bark object.

Maria's getting a whole list of Bark objects from the dog door.

We cast each item we get from the Iterator to a Bark object.

This makes sure we don't keep looping once we've found a match.

```java
public void recognize(Bark bark) {
    System.out.println("   BarkRecognizer: Heard a '" +
        bark.getSound() + "'");
    List allowedBarks = door.getAllowedBarks();
    for (Iterator i = allowedBarks.iterator(); i.hasNext(); ) {
        Bark allowedBark = (Bark)i.next();
        if (allowedBark.equals(bark)) {
            door.open();
            return;
        }
    }
    System.out.println("This dog is not allowed.");
}
```

This method represents an entire dog: all the barking sounds that the dog can make.

Maria's textual analysis helped her figure out that her BarkRecognizer needed to focus on the <u>dog</u> involved, rather than the <u>barking</u> of that dog.

```
door.getAllowedBarks()
```

```
door.getAllowedBark()
```

This method is focused on a <u>single</u> bark... on <u>one</u> <u>sound</u> the dog makes, rather than the dog itself.

Add notes to the diagram about what you might need to figure out to program the door.

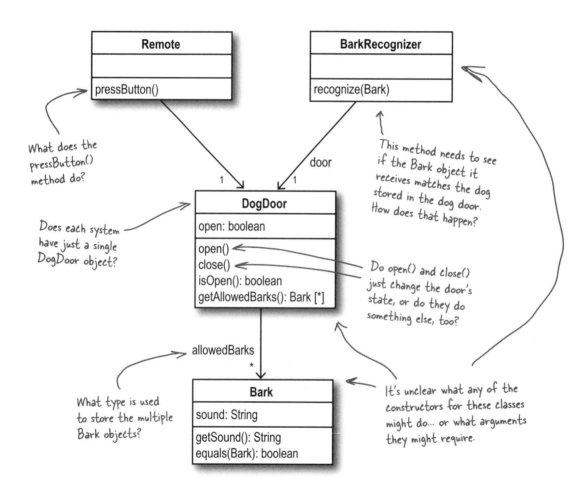

Remote

pressButton()

What does the pressButton() method do?

Does each system have just a single DogDoor object?

BarkRecognizer

recognize(Bark)

This method needs to see if the Bark object it receives matches the dog stored in the dog door. How does that happen?

door

1   1

DogDoor

open: boolean

open()
close()
isOpen(): boolean
getAllowedBarks(): Bark [*]

Do open() and close() just change the door's state, or do they do something else, too?

allowedBarks

*

What type is used to store the multiple Bark objects?

Bark

sound: String

getSound(): String
equals(Bark): boolean

It's unclear what any of the constructors for these classes might do... or what arguments they might require.

* These are just a few of the things we thought of. Your answers may be totally different, if you thought of other things that the class diagram doesn't really show.

Sam and Randy are anxious to see the code that beat them out of the MacBook Pro.

So when do we get to see the final version of Maria's dog door?

BULLET POINTS

- Analysis helps you ensure that your software works in the real world context, and not just in a perfect environment.

- Use cases are meant to be understood by you, your managers, your customers, and other programmers.

- You should write your use cases in whatever format makes them most usable to you and the other people who are looking at them.

- A good use case precisely lays out what a system does, but does not indicate how the system accomplishes that task.

- Each use case should focus on only one customer goal. If you have multiple goals, you will need to write mutiple use cases.

- Class diagrams give you an easy way to show your system and its code constructs at a 10,000-foot view.

- The attributes in a class diagram usually map to the member variables of your classes.

- The operations in a class diagram usually represent the methods of your classes.

- Class diagrams leave lots of detail out, such as class constructors, some type information, and the purpose of operations on your classes.

- Textual analysis helps you translate a use case into code-level classes, attributes, and operations.

- The nouns of a use case are candidates for classes in your system, and the verbs are candidates for methods on your system's classes.

Design Puzzle

I'll bet you expected to find all the code I wrote here, didn't you? I wish... when I was transferring files to my new MacBook Pro, almost all of the code for my dog door got corrupted. Can you help?

Maria's old computer screwed up all the code she wrote for her dog door except for **DogDoorSimulator.java**, shown on the next page. All we've got to go on are the code fragments from her solution in this chapter, her class diagrams, and what you've learned about good analysis, requirements and OO programming. It's your turn to be a hero...

The problem:

> You need to code the dog door application so that it satisfies all of Doug's new customers (that's a lot of potential sales), especially the ones with more than one dog in the neighborhood. The door should operate just as the use cases in this chapter describe the system.

Your task:

1 Start out by re-creating the dog door application as it was described in Chapter 3. You can download this code from the Head First Labs web site if you want a jump start.

2 Copy or download **DogDoorSimulator.java**, shown on the next page. This is the only file that survived Maria's laptop meltdown.

3 Make your code match up with Maria's class diagram, shown on page 180.

4 Start coding! First concentrate on getting all of your classes to compile, so you can begin testing.

5 Use the **DogDoorSimulator** class to see if things are working like they should.

6 Keep up the analysis and coding until your test class's output matches the output shown on the next page. Don't give up!

7 Once you think you've got a working dog door, check your code against ours at the Head First Labs web site. We'll be waiting.

```
public class DogDoorSimulator {

  public static void main(String[] args) {
    DogDoor door = new DogDoor();
    door.addAllowedBark(new Bark("rowlf"));
    door.addAllowedBark(new Bark("rooowlf"));
    door.addAllowedBark(new Bark("rawlf"));
    door.addAllowedBark(new Bark("woof"));
    BarkRecognizer recognizer = new BarkRecognizer(door);
    Remote remote = new Remote(door);

    // Simulate the hardware hearing a bark
    System.out.println("Bruce starts barking.");
    recognizer.recognize(new Bark("rowlf"));

    System.out.println("\nBruce has gone outside...");

    try {
      Thread.currentThread().sleep(10000);
    } catch (InterruptedException e) { }

    System.out.println("\nBruce's all done...");
    System.out.println("...but he's stuck outside!");

    // Simulate the hardware hearing a bark (not Bruce!)
    Bark smallDogBark = new Bark("yip");
    System.out.println("A small dog starts barking.");
    recognizer.recognize(smallDogBark);

    try {
      Thread.currentThread().sleep(5000);
    } catch (InterruptedException e) { }

    // Simulate the hardware hearing a bark again
    System.out.println("Bruce starts barking.");
    recognizer.recognize(new Bark("rooowlf"));

    System.out.println("\nBruce's back inside...");
  }
}
```

DogDoorSimulator.java

This is the test class from Maria's old laptop. Use this for your own dog door testing.

```
File Edit Window Help HollyLovesBruce
%java DogDoorSimulator
Bruce starts barking.
    BarkRecognizer: Heard a 'rowlf'
The dog door opens.

Bruce has gone outside...
The dog door closes.

Bruce's all done...
...but he's stuck outside!
Bitsie starts barking.
    BarkRecognizer: Heard a 'yip'
This dog is not allowed.
Bruce starts barking.
    BarkRecognizer: Heard a 'rooowlf'
The dog door opens.

Bruce's back inside...
The dog door closes.
```

Here's the output you want, which proves that the door works for Bruce, but not for other dogs.

WHAT'S MY DEFINITION

UML and use cases have a lot of terms that are similar to, but not quite the same as, the programming terms you're already familiar with. Below are several OOA&D-related terms, and their definitions... but everything is all mixed up. Connect the term to the definition, and unscramble the mess.

Noun Analysis

Multiplicity

Attribute

Class Diagram

Operation

Association

Verb Analysis

Lists all the code-level constructs, along with their attributes and operations.

This is the UML term that usually represents a method in one of your classes.

Helps you figure out the candidates for methods on the objects in your system.

Visually shows that one class has a relation to another class, often through an attribute.

Equivalent to a member variable in a class.

Describes how many of a specific type can be stored in an attribute of a class.

You do this to your use case to figure out what classes you need in your system.

OOA&D Cross

You know you love it... try another puzzling crossword
to get those new concepts lodged firmly in your brain.

Across

1. Use cases should use this kind of language.
5. Every class diagram has one of these for each member variable.
10. This focuses on putting your application into the correct context.
12. Software always works better in the testing lab than here.
13. Maria won the laptop because she paid attention to the
14. This relates one class to another
16. You write your use case so you can _____ your customers
17. Use cases should be _____ as well as easily understood.
18. UML is this type of modeling language.

Down

2. Analysis makes sure your application works in this place.
3. An operation is UML-ese for this.
4. You do this to your use cases to figure out the classes and operations in your system.
6. He replaced Fido as this chapter's star.
7. Class diagrams are a great way to get this of your system.
8. How many of a type an attribute can hold is its _____.
9. These types of diagrams are worth a thousand words to a programmer.
11. Use cases aren't formal, but they are _____.
15. Verb is to operation as this is to attribute.

Exercise Solutions

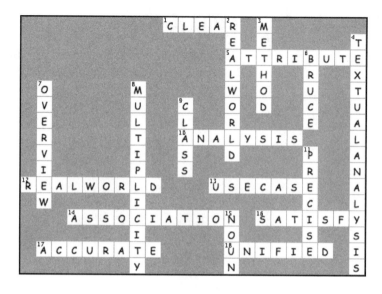

Crossword solution grid:

1 Across: CLEAR
5 Across: ATTRIBUTE
10 Across: ANALYSIS
12 Across: REALWORLD
13 Across: USECASE
14 Across: ASSOCIATION
15 Across: SATISFY
17 Across: ACCURATE
18 Across: UNIFIED

Down answers include: REALWORLD, METHOD, CLASS, OVERVIEW, MULTIPLICITY, CLASS, PRACTICES, COMMON, TEXTUALANALYSIS

WHAT'S MY DEFINITION?

UML and use cases have a lot of terms that are similar to, but not quite the same as, the programming terms you're already familiar with. Below are several OOA&D-related terms, and their definitions... but everything is all mixed up. Connect the term to the definition, and unscramble the mess.

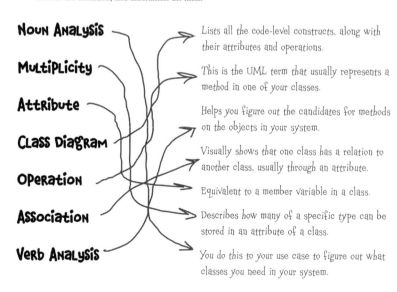

Noun Analysis

Multiplicity

Attribute

Class Diagram

Operation

Association

Verb Analysis

Lists all the code-level constructs, along with their attributes and operations.

This is the UML term that usually represents a method in one of your classes.

Helps you figure out the candidates for methods on the objects in your system.

Visually shows that one class has a relation to another class, usually through an attribute.

Equivalent to a member variable in a class.

Describes how many of a specific type can be stored in an attribute of a class.

You do this to your use case to figure out what classes you need in your system.

5 (part 1)   good design = flexible software

Nothing Ever Stays the Same

Molly, I hope we never have to grow up. Let's just stay like this forever!

Change is inevitable. No matter how much you like your software right now, it's probably going to **change** tomorrow. And the harder you make it for your software to change, the more difficult it's going to be to respond to your **customer's changing needs**. In this chapter, we're going to revisit an old friend, try and improve an existing software project, and see how **small changes can turn into big problems**. In fact, we're going to uncover a problem so big that it will take a TWO-PART chapter to solve it!

Stringed Instruments

Rick's ~~Guitars~~ is expanding

Fresh off the heels of selling three guitars to the rock group Augustana, Rick's guitar business is doing better than ever—and the search tool you built Rick back in Chapter 1 is the cornerstone of his business.

> Your software is the best—I'm selling guitars left and right. I've been getting a lot of business from Nashville, though, and want to start carrying mandolins, too. I figure I can make a killing!

Mandolins are a lot like guitars... they shouldn't be too hard to support, right?

Let's put our design to the test

We've talked a lot about good analysis and design being the key to software that you can reuse and extend... and now it looks like we're going to have to prove that to Rick. Let's figure out how easy it is to restructure his application so that it supports mandolins.

Sharpen your pencil

Add support for mandolins to Rick's search tool.

Below is the completed class diagram for Rick's guitar search app, just like it was when we finished up with Chapter 1. It's up to you to add to this diagram so that Rick can start selling mandolins, and your search tool can help him find mandolins that match his clients' preferences, just like he already can with guitars.

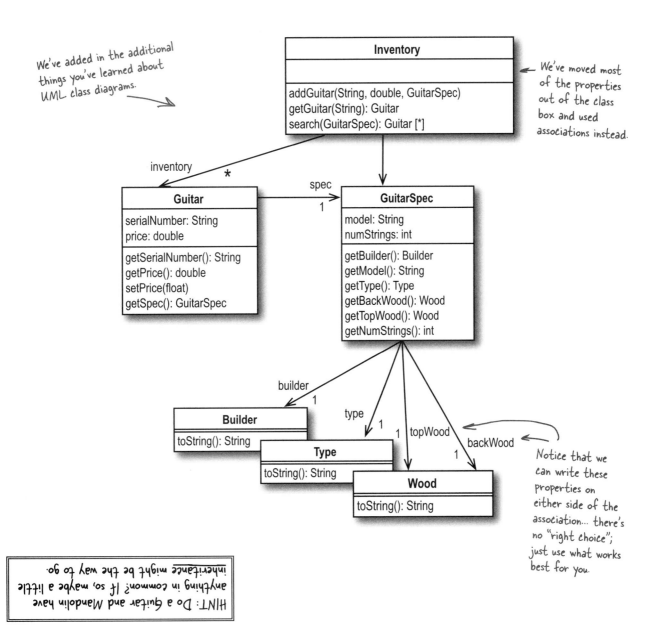

We've added in the additional things you've learned about UML class diagrams.

We've moved most of the properties out of the class box and used associations instead.

Notice that we can write these properties on either side of the association... there's no "right choice"; just use what works best for you.

HINT: Do a Guitar and Mandolin have anything in common? If so, maybe a little inheritance might be the way to go.

Add support for mandolins to Rick's search tool.

Below is the completed class diagram for Rick's guitar search app, just like it was when we finished up with Chapter 1. Here's what we did first to add support for mandolins (we'll make some more changes over the next few pages).

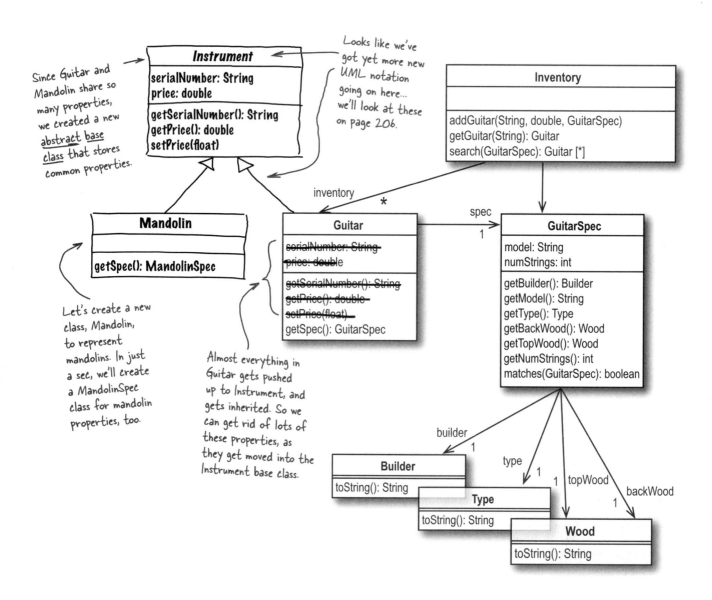

Since Guitar and Mandolin share so many properties, we created a new <u>abstract base class</u> that stores common properties.

Looks like we've got yet more new UML notation going on here... we'll look at these on page 206.

Let's create a new class, Mandolin, to represent mandolins. In just a sec, we'll create a MandolinSpec class for mandolin properties, too.

Almost everything in Guitar gets pushed up to Instrument, and gets inherited. So we can get rid of lots of these properties, as they get moved into the Instrument base class.

Did you notice that abstract base class?

Take a close look at the new **Instrument** class that we created:

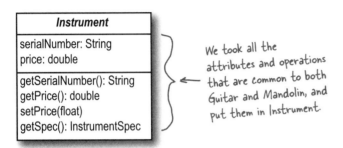

We took all the attributes and operations that are common to both Guitar and Mandolin, and put them in Instrument.

Instrument is an abstract class: that means that you can't create an instance of **Instrument**. You have to define subclasses of **Instrument**, like we did with **Mandolin** and **Guitar**:

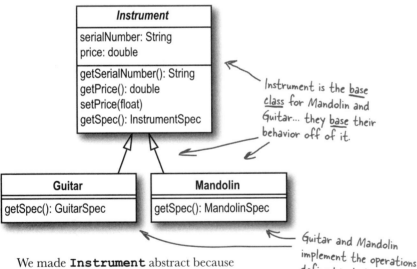

Instrument is the base class for Mandolin and Guitar... they base their behavior off of it.

Guitar and Mandolin implement the operations defined in Instrument in ways specific to a guitar and mandolin.

We made **Instrument** abstract because **Instrument** is just a *placeholder* for actual instruments like **Guitar** and **Mandolin**. An abstract class defines some basic behavior, but it's really the *subclasses* of the abstract class that add the implementation of those behaviors. **Instrument** is just a generic class that stands in for your actual implementation classes.

Abstract classes are <u>placeholders</u> for actual implementation classes.

The abstract class <u>defines</u> <u>behavior</u>, and the subclasses <u>implement</u> <u>that</u> <u>behavior</u>.

We'll need a MandolinSpec class, too

Mandolins and guitars are similar, but there are just a few things different about mandolins... we can capture those differences in a **MandolinSpec** class:

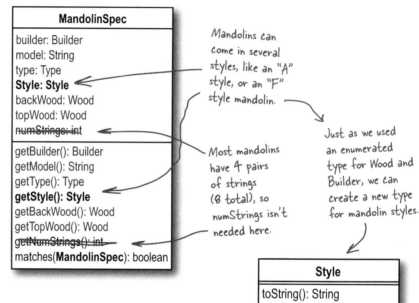

GuitarSpec
builder: Builder model: String type: Type backWood: Wood topWood: Wood numStrings: int
getBuilder(): Builder getModel(): String getType(): Type getBackWood(): Wood getTopWood(): Wood getNumStrings(): int matches(GuitarSpec): boolean

MandolinSpec
builder: Builder model: String type: Type **Style: Style** backWood: Wood topWood: Wood ~~numStrings: int~~
getBuilder(): Builder getModel(): String getType(): Type **getStyle(): Style** getBackWood(): Wood getTopWood(): Wood ~~getNumStrings(): int~~ matches(**MandolinSpec**): boolean

Mandolins can come in several styles, like an "A" style, or an "F" style mandolin.

Most mandolins have 4 pairs of strings (8 total), so numStrings isn't needed here.

Just as we used an enumerated type for Wood and Builder, we can create a new type for mandolin styles.

Style
toString(): String

It's OK if you don't know anything about mandolins, or didn't figure out the different properties in the MandolinSpec class. The main thing is that you realized we probably need a new class for mandolins and their specs. If you came up with using an Instrument interface or abstract class, all the better!

Those spec classes sure look a lot alike. How about we use an abstract base class here, too?

BRAIN POWER

What do you think about this design? Will it do what the customer wants it to do? How flexible is it? Do you think software designed like this will be easy to extend and maintain?

_____

_____

_____

—————— there are no
Dumb Questions ——————

Q: We made Instrument abstract because we abstracted the properties common to Guitar and Mandolin into it, right?

A: No, we made `Instrument` abstract because in Rick's system right now, there's no such thing as an actual "instrument." All it does is provide a common place to store properties that exist in both the `Guitar` and `Mandolin` classes. But since an instrument currently has no behavior outside of its subclasses, it's really just defining common attributes and properties that all instruments need to implement.

So while we did abstract out the properties common to both instrument types, that doesn't necessarily mean that `Instrument` *has* to be abstract. In fact, we might later make `Instrument` a concrete class, if that starts to make sense in our design...

Q: Couldn't we do the same thing with GuitarSpec and MandolinSpec? It looks like they share a lot of common attributes and operations, just like Guitar and Mandolin.

A: Good idea! We can create another abstract base class, called `InstrumentSpec`, and then have `GuitarSpec` and `MandolinSpec` inherit from that base class:

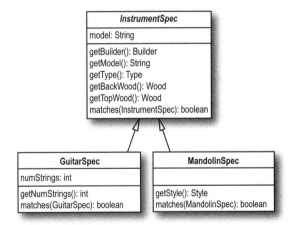

Let's put everything together...

Behold: Rick's new application

It looks like all that work on design back in Chapter 1 has paid off;
it took us less than 10 pages to add support for mandolins to Rick's
search tool. Here's the completed class diagram:

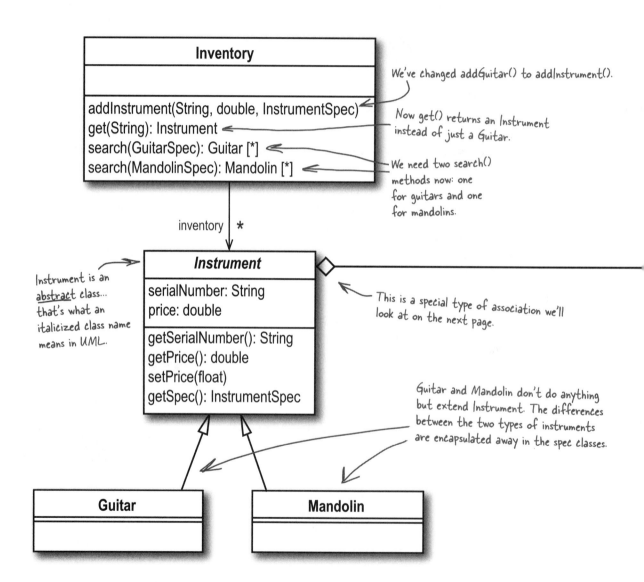

We've changed addGuitar() to addInstrument().

Now get() returns an Instrument instead of just a Guitar.

We need two search() methods now: one for guitars and one for mandolins.

Instrument is an abstract class... that's what an italicized class name means in UML.

This is a special type of association we'll look at on the next page.

Guitar and Mandolin don't do anything but extend Instrument. The differences between the two types of instruments are encapsulated away in the spec classes.

Inventory

addInstrument(String, double, InstrumentSpec)
get(String): Instrument
search(GuitarSpec): Guitar [*]
search(MandolinSpec): Mandolin [*]

inventory | *

Instrument

serialNumber: String
price: double

getSerialNumber(): String
getPrice(): double
setPrice(float)
getSpec(): InstrumentSpec

Guitar

Mandolin

Whenever you find common behavior in two or more places, look to abstract that behavior into a class, and then reuse that behavior in the common classes.

Here's the principle that led to us creating both the Instrument and InstrumentSpec abstract base classes.

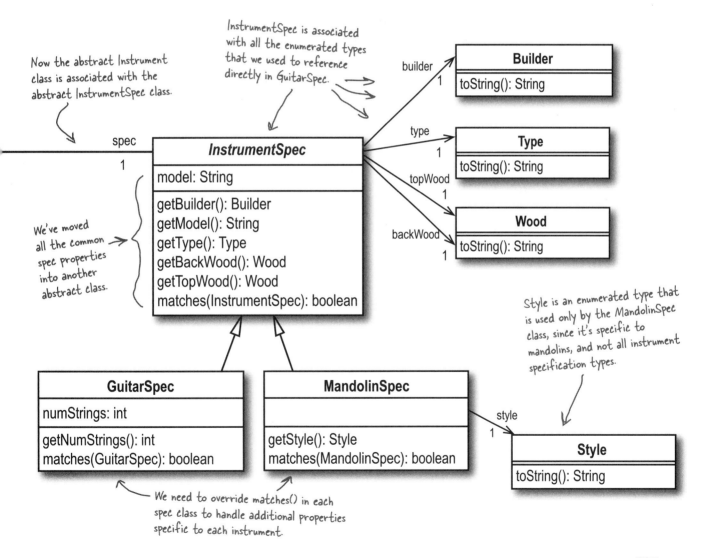

Now the abstract Instrument class is associated with the abstract InstrumentSpec class.

InstrumentSpec is associated with all the enumerated types that we used to reference directly in GuitarSpec.

We've moved all the common spec properties into another abstract class.

Style is an enumerated type that is used only by the MandolinSpec class, since it's specific to mandolins, and not all instrument specification types.

We need to override matches() in each spec class to handle additional properties specific to each instrument.

Class diagrams dissected (again)

Now that you've added abstract classes, subclasses, and a new kind of association, it's time to upgrade your UML and class diagram skills.

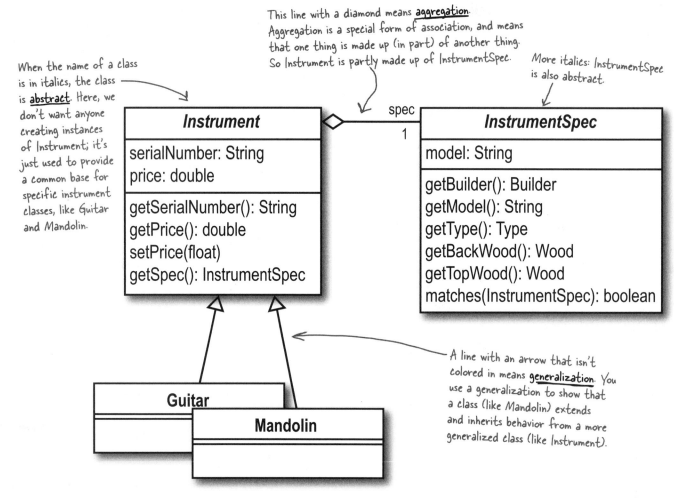

This line with a diamond means **aggregation**. Aggregation is a special form of association, and means that one thing is made up (in part) of another thing. So Instrument is partly made up of InstrumentSpec.

More italics: InstrumentSpec is also abstract.

When the name of a class is in italics, the class is **abstract**. Here, we don't want anyone creating instances of Instrument; it's just used to provide a common base for specific instrument classes, like Guitar and Mandolin.

Instrument

serialNumber: String
price: double

getSerialNumber(): String
getPrice(): double
setPrice(float)
getSpec(): InstrumentSpec

spec
1

InstrumentSpec

model: String

getBuilder(): Builder
getModel(): String
getType(): Type
getBackWood(): Wood
getTopWood(): Wood
matches(InstrumentSpec): boolean

Guitar

Mandolin

A line with an arrow that isn't colored in means **generalization**. You use a generalization to show that a class (like Mandolin) extends and inherits behavior from a more generalized class (like Instrument).

Fold this page down so you can refer back to it when you forget some of UML's notation and symbols.

UML Cheat Sheet

What we call it in Java	What we call it in UML	How we show it in UML
Abstract Class	Abstract Class	*Italicized Class Name*
Relationship	Association	⟶
Inheritance	Generalization	⟶▷
Aggregation	Aggregation	⟶◇

there are no Dumb Questions

Q: Are there lots more types of symbols and notations that I'm going to have to keep up with to use UML?

A: There are a lot more symbols and notations in UML, but it's up to you how many of them you use, let alone memorize. Many people use just the basics you've already learned, and are perfectly happy (as are their customers and managers). But other folks like to really get into UML, and use every trick in the UML toolbox. It's really up to you; as long as you can communicate your design, you've used UML the way it's intended.

Let's code Rick's new search tool

We can start off by creating a new class, **Instrument**, and making it
abstract. Then we put all the properties common to an instrument in this class:

We used the <u>aggregation</u>
form of association because
each Instrument is made up
of the serialNumber and
price member variables, <u>and</u>
an InstrumentSpec instance.

```
public abstract class Instrument {

    private String serialNumber;
    private double price;
    private InstrumentSpec spec;

    public Instrument(String serialNumber, double price,
                      InstrumentSpec spec) {
        this.serialNumber = serialNumber;
        this.price = price;
        this.spec = spec;
    }

    // Get and set methods for serial number and price

    public InstrumentSpec getSpec() {
        return spec;
    }
}
```

Instrument is abstract... you
have to instantiate subclasses of
this base class, like Guitar.

Most of this is pretty
simple, and looks a lot
like the old Guitar class
we had.

Instrument
serialNumber: String
price: double
getSerialNumber(): String
getPrice(): double
setPrice(float)
getSpec(): InstrumentSpec

Instrument.java

Next we need to rework **Guitar.java**, and create a class for mandolins.
These both extend **Instrument** to get the common instrument properties,
and then define their own constructors with the right type of spec class:

All each
instrument
class needs
is to extend
Instrument,
and provide
a constructor
that takes the
right kind of
spec object.

```
public class Mandolin extends Instrument {
```

```
public class Guitar extends Instrument {

    public Guitar(String serialNumber, double price,
                  GuitarSpec spec) {
        super(serialNumber, price, spec);
    }
}
```

Number, double price,
ec) {
spec);

Guitar

Guitar.java

Mandolin

Mandolin.java

Mandolin is almost identical
to Guitar; it just takes in a
MandolinSpec in the constructor,
instead of a GuitarSpec.

Create an abstract class for instrument specifications

With the instruments taken care of, we can move on to the spec classes. We need to create another abstract class, **InstrumentSpec**, since so many instruments have common specifications:

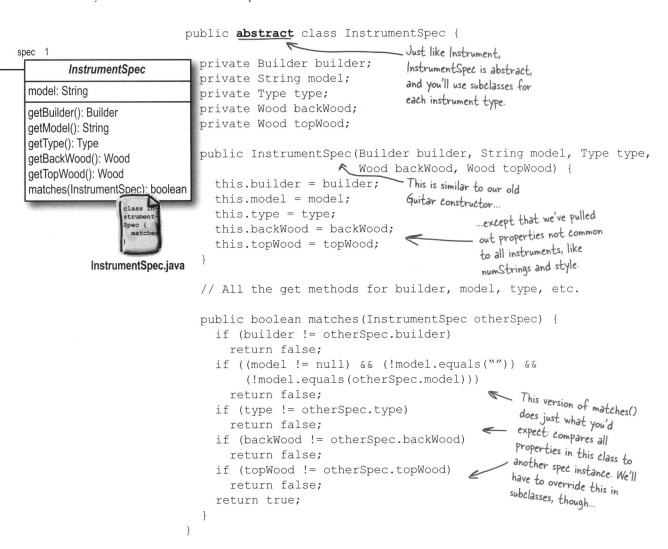

```
public abstract class InstrumentSpec {
```
Just like Instrument, InstrumentSpec is abstract, and you'll use subclasses for each instrument type.

spec   1

InstrumentSpec
model: String
getBuilder(): Builder
getModel(): String
getType(): Type
getBackWood(): Wood
getTopWood(): Wood
matches(InstrumentSpec): boolean

```
class In-
strument-
Spec {
    matches
}
```

InstrumentSpec.java

```
    private Builder builder;
    private String model;
    private Type type;
    private Wood backWood;
    private Wood topWood;

    public InstrumentSpec(Builder builder, String model, Type type,
                          Wood backWood, Wood topWood) {
        this.builder = builder;
        this.model = model;
        this.type = type;
        this.backWood = backWood;
        this.topWood = topWood;
    }

    // All the get methods for builder, model, type, etc.

    public boolean matches(InstrumentSpec otherSpec) {
        if (builder != otherSpec.builder)
            return false;
        if ((model != null) && (!model.equals("")) &&
            (!model.equals(otherSpec.model)))
            return false;
        if (type != otherSpec.type)
            return false;
        if (backWood != otherSpec.backWood)
            return false;
        if (topWood != otherSpec.topWood)
            return false;
        return true;
    }
}
```

This is similar to our old Guitar constructor...

...except that we've pulled out properties not common to all instruments, like numStrings and style.

This version of matches() does just what you'd expect: compares all properties in this class to another spec instance. We'll have to override this in subclasses, though...

Let's code GuitarSpec...

With **InstrumentSpec** coded up, it's pretty simple to write the **GuitarSpec** class:

> Just as Guitar extended Instrument, GuitarSpec extends InstrumentSpec.

```java
public class GuitarSpec extends InstrumentSpec {

  private int numStrings;

  public GuitarSpec(Builder builder, String model, Type type,
                    int numStrings, Wood backWood, Wood topWood) {
    super(builder, model, type, backWood, topWood);
    this.numStrings = numStrings;
  }

  public int getNumStrings() {
    return numStrings;
  }

  // Override the superclass matches()
  public boolean matches(InstrumentSpec otherSpec) {
    if (!super.matches(otherSpec))
      return false;
    if (!(otherSpec instanceof GuitarSpec))
      return false;
    GuitarSpec spec = (GuitarSpec)otherSpec;
    if (numStrings != spec.numStrings)
      return false;
    return true;
  }
}
```

> Only a guitar has a numStrings property; it's not in the Instrument superclass.

> This constructor just adds the guitar-specific properties to what's already stored in the base InstrumentSpec class.

> matches() uses the superclass's matches(), and then performs additional checks to make sure the spec is the right type, and matches the guitar-specific properties.

> GuitarSpec gets a lot of its behavior from InstrumentSpec now, so the code for GuitarSpec has slimmed down a lot from Chapter 1.

InstrumentSpec

model: String

getBuilder(): Builder
getModel(): String
getType(): Type
getBackWood(): Wood
getTopWood(): Wood
matches(InstrumentSpec): boolean

GuitarSpec

numStrings: int

getNumStrings(): int
matches(GuitarSpec): boolean

class
Guitar-
Spec {
  match-
es()

GuitarSpec.java

good design = flexible software

...and MandolinSpec, too

After seeing **GuitarSpec**, **MandolinSpec** is pretty simple.
It's very similar, with the addition of a member variable to
reference the mandolin's style (like "A" or "F" style), and a
slightly different **matches()** method:

```java
public class MandolinSpec extends InstrumentSpec {

    private Style style;          // Only mandolins have a Style, so this is not
                                  // pushed up into the InstrumentSpec base class.

    public MandolinSpec(Builder builder, String model, Type type,
                        Style style, Wood backWood, Wood topWood) {
      super(builder, model, type, backWood, topWood);
      this.style = style;
    }

    public Style getStyle() {
      return style;
    }

    // Override the superclass matches()
    public boolean matches(InstrumentSpec otherSpec) {
      if (!super.matches(otherSpec))              // Just like GuitarSpec, MandolinSpec
        return false;                             // uses its superclass to do basic
      if (!(otherSpec instanceof MandolinSpec))   // comparison, and then casts to
        return false;                             // MandolinSpec and compares the
      MandolinSpec spec = (MandolinSpec)otherSpec; // mandolin-specific properties.
      if (!style.equals(spec.style))
        return false;
      return true;
    }
}
```

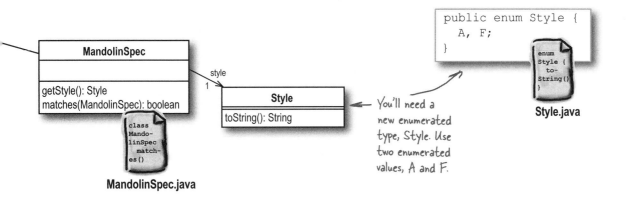

```java
public enum Style {
    A, F;
}
```

MandolinSpec

getStyle(): Style
matches(MandolinSpec): boolean

style
1

Style

toString(): String

You'll need a
new enumerated
type, Style. Use
two enumerated
values, A and F.

Style.java

MandolinSpec.java

Finishing up Rick's search tool

All that's left is to update the **Inventory** class to
work with multiple instrument types, instead of just the
Guitar class:

> The inventory list now holds multiple types of instruments, not just guitars.

Inventory
inventory: Instrument [*]
addInstrument(String, double, InstrumentSpec) get(String): Instrument search(GuitarSpec): Guitar [*] search(MandolinSpec): Mandolin [*]

class Inventory { search() }

Inventory.java

```java
public class Inventory {

  private List inventory;

  public Inventory() {
    inventory = new LinkedList();
  }

  public void addInstrument(String serialNumber, double price,
                      InstrumentSpec spec) {
    Instrument instrument = null;
    if (spec instanceof GuitarSpec) {
      instrument = new Guitar(serialNumber, price, (GuitarSpec)spec);
    } else if (spec instanceof MandolinSpec) {
      instrument = new Mandolin(serialNumber, price, (MandolinSpec)spec);
    }
    inventory.add(instrument);
  }

  public Instrument get(String serialNumber) {
    for (Iterator i = inventory.iterator(); i.hasNext(); ) {
      Instrument instrument = (Instrument)i.next();
      if (instrument.getSerialNumber().equals(serialNumber)) {
        return instrument;
      }
    }
    return null;
  }

  // search(GuitarSpec) works the same as before

  public List search(MandolinSpec searchSpec) {
    List matchingMandolins = new LinkedList();
    for (Iterator i = inventory.iterator(); i.hasNext(); ) {
      Mandolin mandolin = (Mandolin)i.next();
      if (mandolin.getSpec().matches(searchSpec))
        matchingMandolins.add(mandolin);
    }
    return matchingMandolins;
  }
}
```

> By using the Instrument and InstrumentSpec classes, we can turn addGuitar() into a more generic method, and create any kind of instrument.

> Hmmm... this isn't so great. Since Instrument is abstract, and we can't instantiate it directly, we have to do some extra work before creating an instrument.

> Here's another spot where using an abstract base class makes our design more flexible.

> We need another search() method to handle mandolins.

> At this point, you're ready to try out Rick's improved app. See if you can update FindGuitarTester on your own, and see how things are working with these design changes.

there are no
Dumb Questions

Q: Guitar and Mandolin only have a constructor. That seems sort of silly. Do we really need a subclass for each type of instrument just for that?

A: We do, at least for now. Otherwise, how could you tell a mandolin from a guitar? There's no other way to figure out what type of instrument you're working with than by checking the type of the class. Besides, those subclasses allow us to have constructors that ensure that the right type of spec is passed in. So you can't create a `Guitar`, and pass a `MandolinSpec` into its constructor.

Q: But with Instrument as an abstract class, the addInstrument() method in Inventory.java becomes a real pain!

A: You're talking about `addInstrument()` on page 212, aren't you? Yes, with `Instrument` as an abstract class, you do have some extra code to deal with. But it's still a fairly small price to pay to ensure that you can't create an `Instrument`, which really doesn't exist in the real world.

These are little indicators that we may have a design problem. When things just don't seem to make sense in your application, you may want to investigate a little further... which is exactly what we're about to do.

Q: Isn't there some middle ground, though? I mean, even if there's no such thing as an "instrument" that isn't a guitar or mandolin or whatever, it still seems like we must have a design problem somewhere. Right?

A: Well, you may be onto something. It does seem like parts of our code would benefit from a concrete `Instrument` class, while other parts wouldn't. Sometimes this means you have to make a decision one way or the other, and just accept the trade-off. But maybe there's more going on here that we're not thinking about...

Q: Why do we have two different versions of search()? Can't we combine those into a single method that takes an InstrumentSpec?

A: Since `InstrumentSpec` is an abstract class, like `Instrument`, Rick's clients will have to give either a `GuitarSpec` or a `MandolinSpec` to the `search()` method in `Inventory`. And since a spec will match only other specs of the same instrument type, there's never a case where both mandolins *and* guitars would be returned in the list of matching instruments. So even if you consolidated the two `search()` methods into one, you wouldn't get any functionality benefit—and even worse, it might *look* like the method would return both mandolins and guitars (since the return type of `search()` would be `Instrument [*]`), even though it never actually would.

Wow, this is really starting to look pretty good! Using those abstract classes helped us avoid any duplicate code, and we've got instrument properties encapsulated away into our spec classes.

You've made some <u>MAJOR</u> improvements to Rick's app

You've done a lot more than just add support for mandolins to Rick's application. By abstracting common properties and behavior into the **Instrument** and **InstrumentSpec** classes, you've made the classes in Rick's app more independent. That's a significant improvement in his design.

I don't know... it seems like we've still got a few problems, like the almost-empty Guitar and Mandolin classes, and addInstrument() with all that nasty instrument-specific code. Are we just supposed to ignore those?

Great software isn't built in a day

Along with some major design improvements, we've uncovered a few problems with the search tool. That's OK... you're almost always going to find a few new problems when you make big changes to your design.

So now our job is to take Rick's better-designed application, and see if we can improve it even further... to take it from good software to GREAT software.

3 steps to great software (revisited)

Is Rick's search tool **great software**?

Remember the three things we talked about that you can do to write great software? Let's review them to see how well we've done on the latest version of Rick's search tool.

1. Does the new search tool do what it's supposed to do?

_____

_____

_____

2. Have you used solid OO principles, like encapsulation, to avoid duplicate code and make your software easy to extend?

_____

_____

_____

3. How easy is it to reuse Rick's application? Do changes to one part of the app force you to make lots of changes in other parts of the app? Is his software loosely coupled?

_____

_____

_____

Be sure to answer these questions, and then turn the page to see what we wrote down.

> Great software *every time*? I can hardly **imagine** what that would be like!

Exercise Solutions

Is Rick's search tool **great software**?

Remember the three things we talked about that you can do to write great software? Let's review them to see how well we've done on the latest version of Rick's search tool.

1. Does the new search tool do what it's supposed to do?

   Absolutely. It finds guitars and mandolins, although not at the same time. So maybe it just mostly does what it's supposed to do. Better ask Rick to be sure...

2. Have you used solid OO principles, like encapsulation, to avoid duplicate code and make your software easy to extend?

   We used encapsulation when we came up with the InstrumentSpec classes, and inheritance when we developed an Instrument and InstrumentSpec abstract superclass. But it still takes a lot of work to add new instrument types...

3. How easy is it to reuse Rick's application? Do changes to one part of the app force you to make lots of changes in other parts of the app? Is his software loosely coupled?

   It's sort of hard to use just parts of Rick's application. Everything's pretty tightly connected, and InstrumentSpec is actually part of Instrument (remember when we talked about aggregation?).

Looks like there's still some work to do... but I'll bet this will be amazing by the time you're done.

It's OK if you got some different answers and had different ideas than we did on these questions... just make sure you thought things through, and that you understand why we answered how we did.

I'm loving what you're doing to my search tool! As long as you're here, I think I'd like to start carrying bass guitars, banjos, and dobros (you know, those guitars you play with a slide). And how about fiddles, too?

Let's put Rick's software to the test.

One of the best ways to see if software is well-designed is to try and **CHANGE** it.

If your software is hard to change, there's probably something you can improve about the design. Let's see how hard it is to add a couple of new instruments to Rick's app:

We'll have to change Inventory again, and add support for the four new instrument types. Not a pleasant experience....

Four new instrument types means four new classes, one for each instrument type.

We need four new spec objects, too, each one adding its own set of instrument-specific properties.

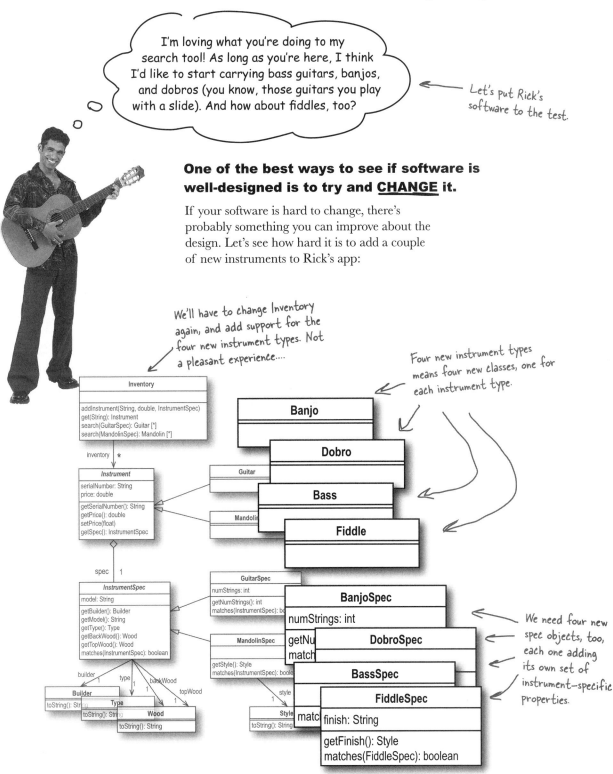

Uh oh... adding new instruments is **not** easy!

If ease of change is how we determine if our software is
well-designed, then we've got some real issues here. Every
time we need to add a new instrument, we have to add
another subclass of `Instrument`:

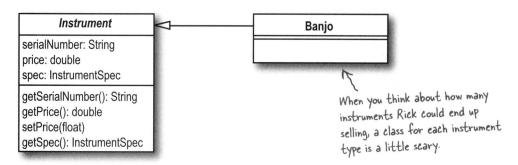

*When you think about how many
instruments Rick could end up
selling, a class for each instrument
type is a little scary.*

Then, we need a new subclass of
`InstrumentSpec`, too:

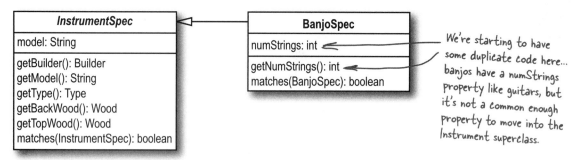

*We're starting to have
some duplicate code here...
banjos have a numStrings
property like guitars, but
it's not a common enough
property to move into the
Instrument superclass.*

Then things start to really get nasty when you
have to update the **Inventory** class's methods to
support the new instrument type:

*For a refresher on the
problems with addInstrument(),
flip back to page 212.*

*Remember all that
instanceof and if/else stuff
in addInstrument()? It
gets worse with every new
instrument type we support.*

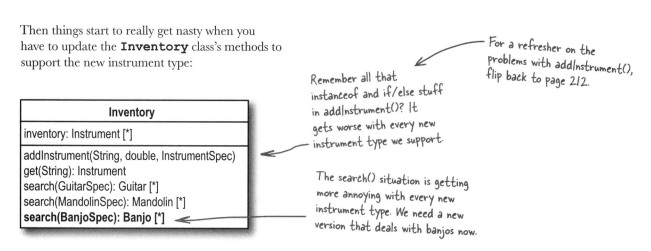

*The search() situation is getting
more annoying with every new
instrument type. We need a new
version that deals with banjos now.*

So what are we supposed to do now?

It looks like we've definitely still got some work to do to turn Rick's application into great software that's truly easy to change and extend. But that doesn't mean the work you've done isn't important... lots of times, you've got to improve your design to find some problems that weren't so apparent earlier on. Now that we've applied some of our OO principles to Rick's search tool, we've been able to locate some issues that we're going to have to resolve if we don't want to spend the next few years writing new **Banjo** and **Fiddle** classes (and who really wants to do that?).

Before you're ready to really tackle the next phase of Rick's app, though, there are a few things you need to know about. So, without further ado, let's take a quick break from Rick's software, and tune in to...

OO CATASTROPHE!
Objectville's Favorite Quiz Show

OO CATASTROPHE!

Objectville's Favorite Quiz Show

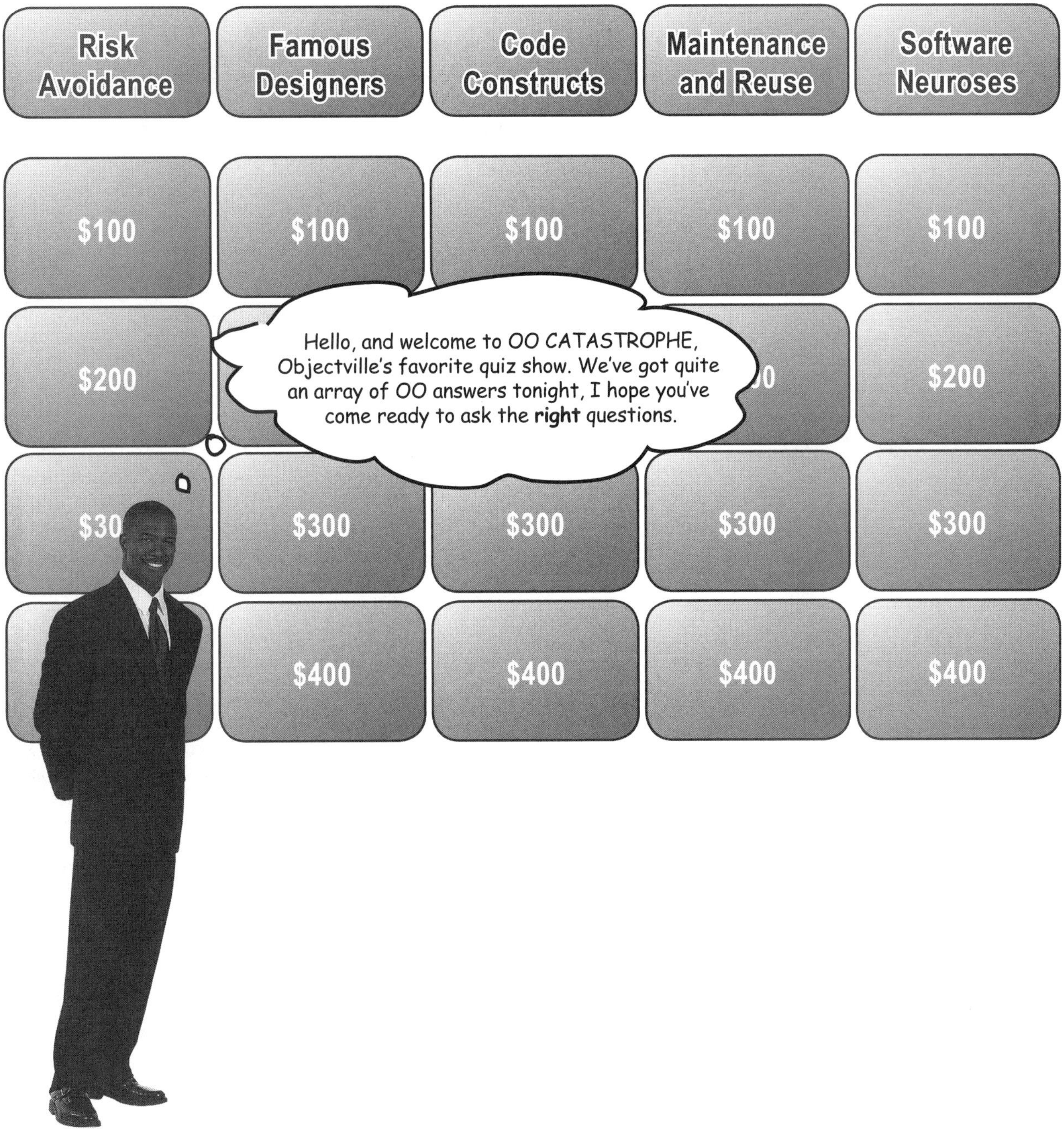

We've got some great OO categories today, so let's get started. Remember, I'll read off an answer, and it's your job to come up with the question that matches the answer. Good luck!

there are no
Dumb Answers

A: It might not seem like it, but we are working on Rick's search tool, in a manner of speaking. We're going to need some pretty advanced OO techniques to make his application flexible and reusable, and we wanted to give you a chance to get a handle on these principles before you had to start applying them to a pretty complicated problem.

Q: Why are we playing a game show? Shouldn't we be fixing Rick's search tool?

A: The questions that match up with the answers in this chapter aren't easy, but you should be able to reason them all out. Take your time; it's important that you come up with these questions on your own if at all possible, and only then turn the page to get a little more information on each question and the OO principle it involves. Besides, we think you're getting to be a pretty kick-ass developer, so we have lots of confidence in you.

Q: If these are new OO principles, how am I supposed to figure out what the questions are? That's asking a lot, isn't it?

OO CATASTROPHE!

Objectville's Favorite Quiz Show

Risk Avoidance	Famous Designers	Code Constructs	Maintenance and Reuse	Software Neuroses
$100	$100	$100	$100	$100
$200	$200		$200	$200
$300	$300			
$400	$400			

This code construct has the dual role of defining behavior that applies to multiple types, and also being the preferred focus of classes that use those types.

Write what you think the question is for the answer above.

"What is _____?"

Did you get this? You should have asked this as the question for the answer on page 223.

"What is an INTERFACE?"

Suppose you've got an application that has an interface, and then lots of subclasses that inherit common behavior from that interface:

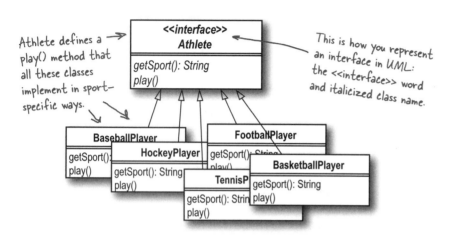

Athlete defines a play() method that all these classes implement in sport-specific ways.

This is how you represent an interface in UML: the <<interface>> word and italicized class name.

Anytime you're writing code that interacts with these classes, you have two choices. You can write code that interacts directly with a subclass, like **FootballPlayer**, or you can write code that interacts with the interface, **Athlete**. When you run into a choice like this, you should *always* favor **coding to the interface, not the implementation**.

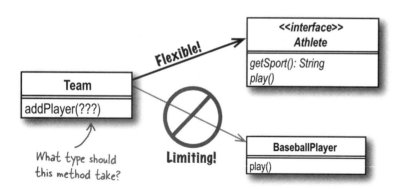

What type should this method take?

Why is this so important? Because it adds *flexibility* to your app. Instead of your code being able to work with only one specific subclass—like **BaseballPlayer**—you're able to work with the more generic **Athlete**. That means that your code will work with any subclass of **Athlete**, like **HockeyPlayer** or **TennisPlayer**, and even subclasses that haven't even been designed yet (anyone for **CricketPlayer**?).

Coding to an interface, rather than to an implementation, makes your software easier to extend.

By coding to an interface, your code will work with all of the interface's subclasses—even ones that haven't been created yet.

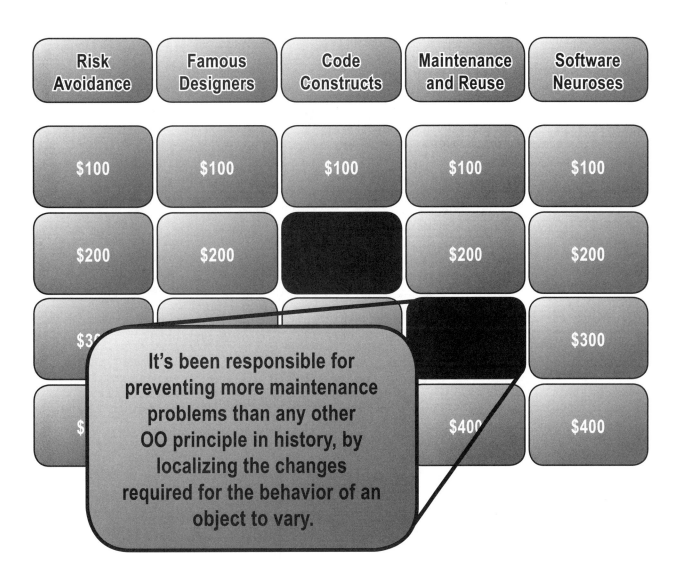

"What is _____?"

"What is <u>ENCAPSULATION?</u>"

We've talked a fair bit about encapsulation already, in terms of preventing duplicate code. But there's more to encapsulation than just avoiding lots of copy-and-paste. Encapsulation also helps you **protect your classes from unnecessary changes**.

Anytime you have behavior in an application that you think is likely to change, you want to move that behavior away from parts of your application that probably *won't* change very frequently. In other words, you should always try to **encapsulate what varies**.

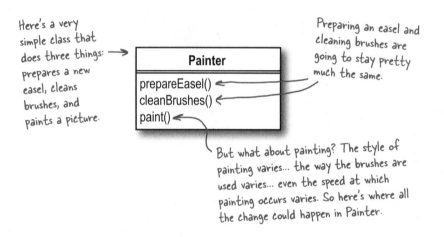

Here's a very simple class that does three things: prepares a new easel, cleans brushes, and paints a picture.

Preparing an easel and cleaning brushes are going to stay pretty much the same.

But what about painting? The style of painting varies... the way the brushes are used varies... even the speed at which painting occurs varies. So here's where all the change could happen in Painter.

It looks like **Painter** has two methods that are pretty stable, but that **paint()** method is going to vary a lot in its implementation. So let's encapsulate what varies, and move the implementation of how a painter paints out of the **Painter** class.

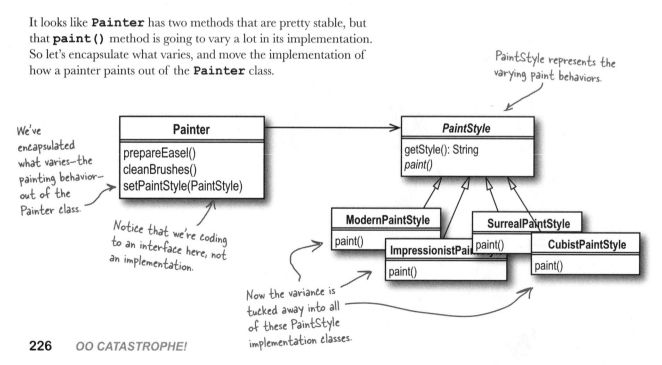

We've encapsulated what varies—the painting behavior—out of the Painter class.

Notice that we're coding to an interface here, not an implementation.

PaintStyle represents the varying paint behaviors.

Now the variance is tucked away into all of these PaintStyle implementation classes.

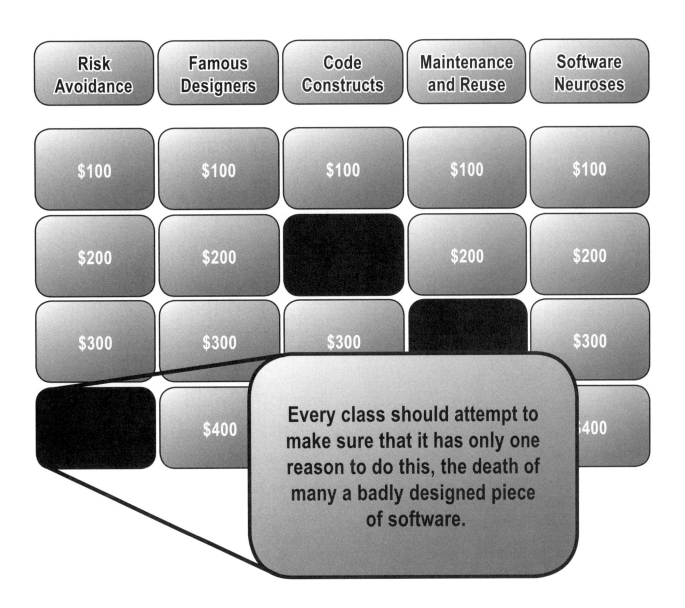

"What is _____?"

"What is <u>CHANGE?</u>"

You already know that the one constant in software is CHANGE. Software that isn't well-designed falls apart at the first sign of change, but great software can change easily.

The easiest way to make your software resilient to change is to make sure *each class has only one reason to change*. In other words, you're minimizing the chances that a class is going to have to change by reducing the number of things in that class that can *cause* it to change.

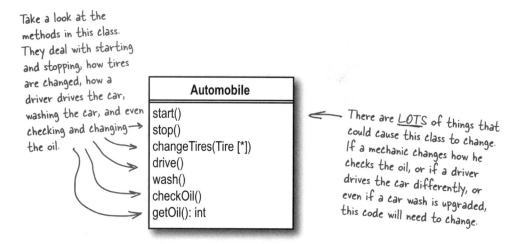

Take a look at the methods in this class. They deal with starting and stopping, how tires are changed, how a driver drives the car, washing the car, and even checking and changing the oil.

Automobile

start()
stop()
changeTires(Tire [*])
drive()
wash()
checkOil()
getOil(): int

There are <u>LOTS</u> of things that could cause this class to change. If a mechanic changes how he checks the oil, or if a driver drives the car differently, or even if a car wash is upgraded, this code will need to change.

When you see a class that has more than one reason to change, it is probably *trying to do too many things*. See if you can break up the functionality into multiple classes, where *each individual class does only one thing*—and therefore has only **one** reason to change.

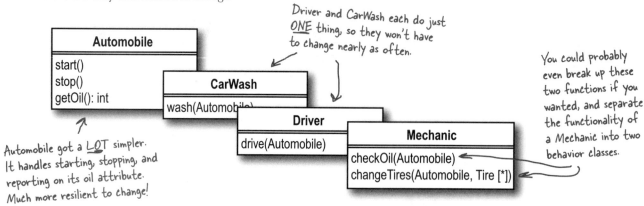

Driver and CarWash each do just <u>ONE</u> thing, so they won't have to change nearly as often.

Automobile

start()
stop()
getOil(): int

CarWash

wash(Automobile)

Driver

drive(Automobile)

Mechanic

checkOil(Automobile)
changeTires(Automobile, Tire [*])

Automobile got a <u>LOT</u> simpler. It handles starting, stopping, and reporting on its oil attribute. Much more resilient to change!

You could probably even break up these two functions if you wanted, and separate the functionality of a Mechanic into two behavior classes.

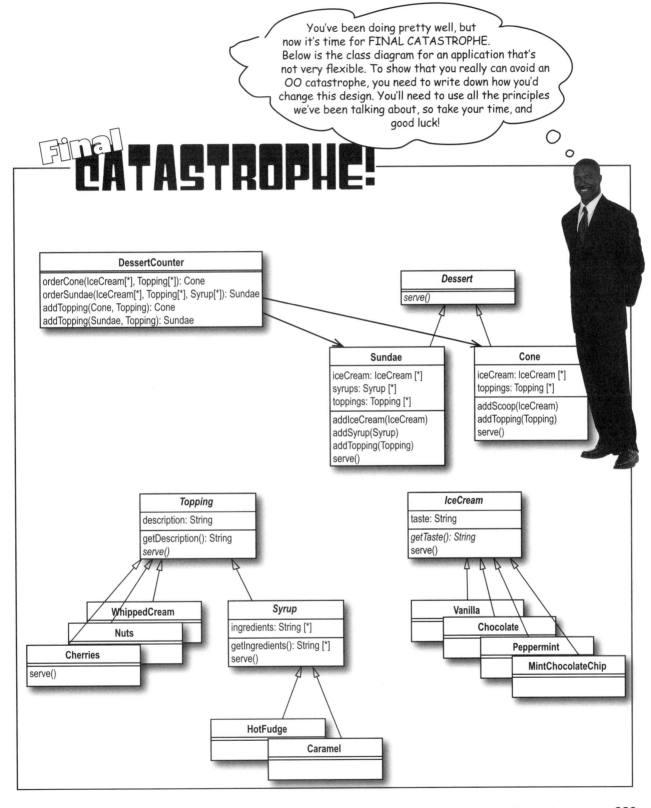

Final CATASTROPHE!
Answers

DessertCounter is coding to implementations of the Dessert interface. We can reduce these two order methods to one: orderDessert(), and then return the interface, Dessert.

DessertCounter

orderCone(IceCream[*], Topping[*]): Cone
orderSundae(IceCream[*], Topping[*], Syrup[*]): Sundae
addTopping(Cone, Topping): Cone
addTopping(Sundae, Topping): Sundae

Dessert

serve()

DessertCounter has **more than one reason to change**: if the ordering process changes, or if how the Cone and Sundae class adds toppings changes. Adding a topping should be done to the Dessert classes directly, not here.

Syrup is an implementation of Topping... we really don't need a method specifically to add a Topping. That's coding to an implementation.

Sundae

iceCream: IceCream [*]
syrups: Syrup [*]
toppings: Topping [*]

addIceCream(IceCream)
addSyrup(Syrup)
addTopping(Topping)
serve()

Cone

iceCream: IceCream [*]
toppings: Topping [*]

addScoop(IceCream)
addTopping(Topping)
serve()

There are a _LOT_ of serve() implementations floating around. We should try and **encapsulate what varies**, and put all the serving code in one place. That way, if the serving process changes, we don't need to change ALL these classes.

there are no Dumb Answers

A: You've seen several times already that when you see a potential for duplicate code, you should look to encapsulate. In this case, it's reasonable to assume that serving a **Sundae** probably isn't that different from serving a **Cone**.

So you could create a new class, called **DessertService**, and put the **serve()** method in that class. Then, all of your **Dessert**, **IceCream**, and **Topping** classes could simply refer to **DessertService.serve()**. If **serve()** changes, you've got to update code in only one place: **DessertService**.

So you're encapsulating what might vary—the code in the **serve()** method—and you're making sure that each class has only a single reason to change. That's a double win!

Q: How did you know to encapsulate the serve() methods out of all those different classes? I missed that.

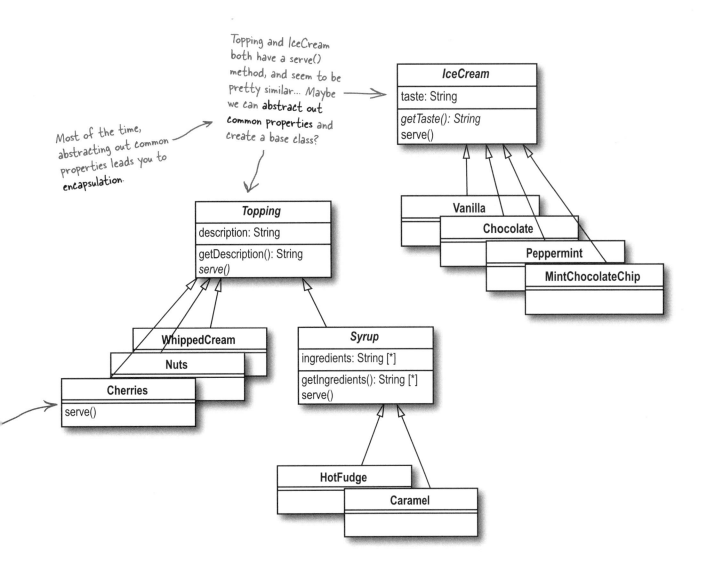

Topping and IceCream both have a serve() method, and seem to be pretty similar... Maybe we can **abstract out common** properties and create a base class?

Most of the time, abstracting out common properties leads you to **encapsulation.**

IceCream

taste: String

getTaste(): String
serve()

Vanilla

Chocolate

Peppermint

MintChocolateChip

Topping

description: String

getDescription(): String
serve()

WhippedCream

Nuts

Cherries

serve()

Syrup

ingredients: String [*]

getIngredients(): String [*]
serve()

HotFudge

Caramel

It's been great having you as a contestant, and we'd love to have you back next week, but we just received an urgent call from a "Rick"? Something about getting back to work on his search tool?

You're ready to tackle Rick's inflexible code now

With a few new OO tools and techniques under your belt, you're definitely ready to go back to Rick's software, and make it a lot more flexible. By the time you're done, you'll have used everything you've just learned on **OO Catastrophe**, and made it easy to change Rick's application, too.

OO Principles

Encapsulate what varies.

Code to an interface rather than to an implementation.

Each class in your application should have only one reason to change.

These three principles are HUGE! Take note of them, as we'll be using them a lot in the upcoming chapters.

5 (part 2) good design = flexible software

Give Your Software a 30-minute Workout

And stretch... 2... 3... 4...

Ever wished you were just a bit more flexible?

When you run into problems making changes to your application, it
probably means that your software needs to be **more flexible and
resilient**. To help stretch your application out, you're going to do some
analysis, a whole lot of design, and learn how OO principles can really
loosen up your application. And for the grand finale, you'll see how
higher cohesion can really help your coupling. Sound interesting? Turn
the page, and let's get back to fixing that inflexible application.

Back to Rick's search tool

Loaded up with some new OO principles, we're ready to tackle making Rick's application well-designed and flexible. Here's where we left off, and some of the problems we've discovered:

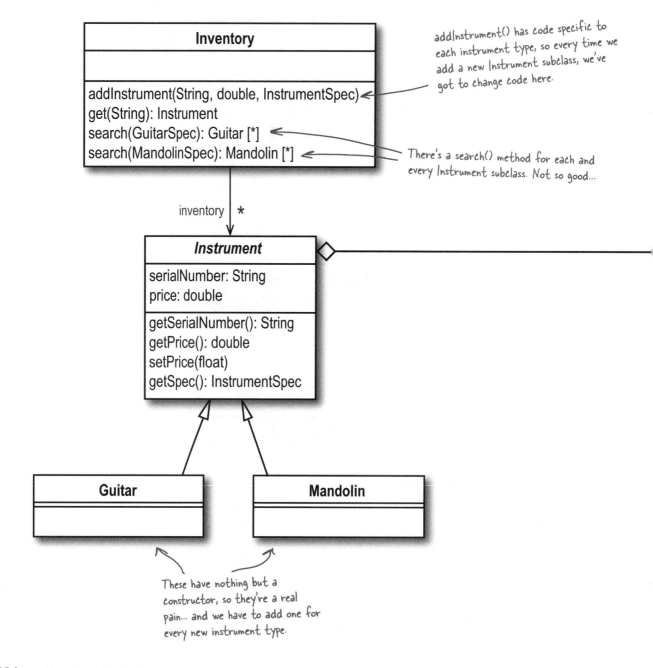

addInstrument() has code specific to each instrument type, so every time we add a new Instrument subclass, we've got to change code here.

There's a search() method for each and every Instrument subclass. Not so good...

These have nothing but a constructor, so they're a real pain... and we have to add one for every new instrument type.

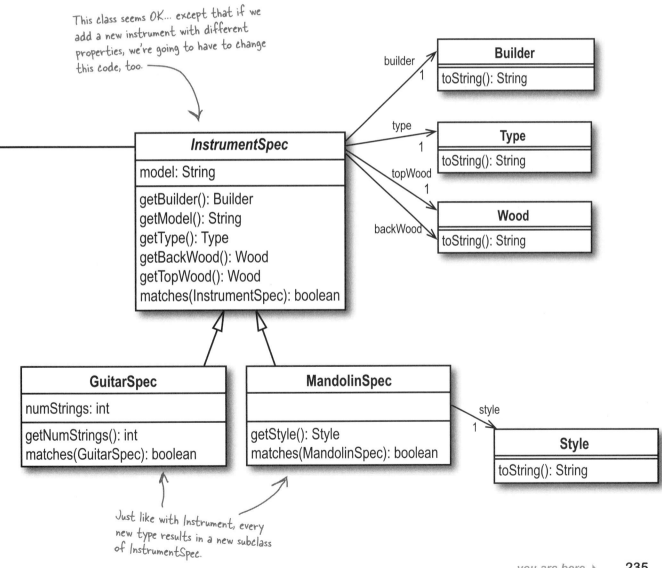

This class seems OK... except that if we add a new instrument with different properties, we're going to have to change this code, too.

Just like with Instrument, every new type results in a new subclass of InstrumentSpec.

Guys, I've been looking over this class diagram for Rick's application, and there's just got to be a better way to deal with this search() method thing.

Frank

Jim

Joe

Frank: Yeah, it's a pain, but I don't see any way to get around it. We have to let Rick's clients search for each different type of instrument somehow.

Jim: I still don't see why we can't have just one search() method that takes in an InstrumentSpec. Wouldn't that cut down on all those different versions of search()?

Joe: Well, it would, but we still don't have any way to return multiple types of instruments. If the client provides a GuitarSpec, it's never going to match a BanjoSpec or MandolinSpec. So the list returned from search() will always have only the type of instrument that the client's spec is for.

Jim: Because we can't instantiate InstrumentSpec, right? It's an abstract class, so we have to create a MandolinSpec, or a BanjoSpec, or whatever.

Frank: So maybe that's the problem... besides, shouldn't we be coding to an interface like InstrumentSpec, not an implementation like GuitarSpec or BanjoSpec?

Joe: Hmmm. I hadn't thought about that, but you're right; we really should be focusing on the interface, and not all those implementation classes.

A closer look at the search() method

It seems pretty clear that there's a problem with the way we're handling searches for Rick's clients. We could make **InstrumentSpec** a concrete class, but would that solve all our problems?

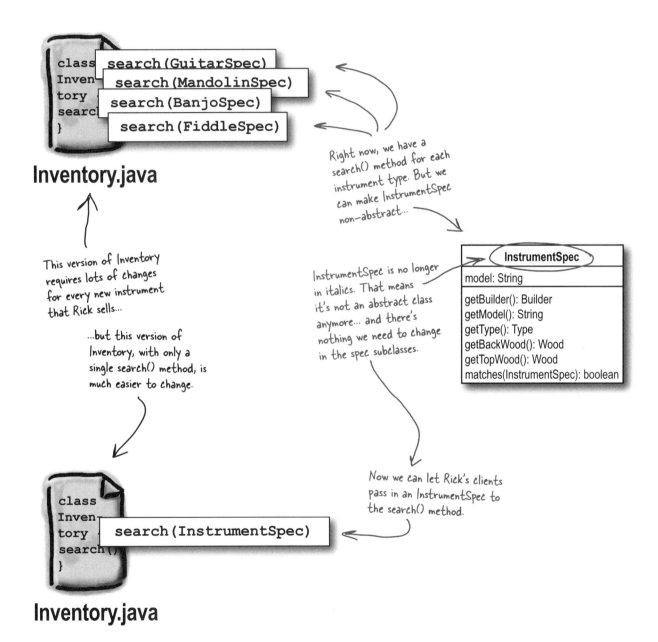

Inventory.java

class Inventory {

search(GuitarSpec)
search(MandolinSpec)
search(BanjoSpec)
search(FiddleSpec)

}

This version of Inventory requires lots of changes for every new instrument that Rick sells...

...but this version of Inventory, with only a single search() method, is much easier to change.

Right now, we have a search() method for each instrument type. But we can make InstrumentSpec non-abstract...

InstrumentSpec is no longer in italics. That means it's not an abstract class anymore... and there's nothing we need to change in the spec subclasses.

InstrumentSpec

model: String

getBuilder(): Builder
getModel(): String
getType(): Type
getBackWood(): Wood
getTopWood(): Wood
matches(InstrumentSpec): boolean

Now we can let Rick's clients pass in an InstrumentSpec to the search() method.

Inventory.java

class Inventory {
search()
}

search(InstrumentSpec)

The benefits of our analysis

Let's take what we've figured out about turning **InstrumentSpec** into a concrete class, and see if it makes the design of **Inventory** any better.

Inventory
inventory: Instrument [*]
addInstrument(String, double, InstrumentSpec) get(String): Instrument **search(InstrumentSpec): Instrument [*]**

Here's the big change that this page highlights.

Inventory.java

```java
public class Inventory {

  private List inventory;

  public Inventory() {
    inventory = new LinkedList();
  }

  public void addInstrument(String serialNumber, double price,
                            InstrumentSpec spec) {
    Instrument instrument = null;
    if (spec instanceof GuitarSpec) {
      instrument = new Guitar(serialNumber, price, (GuitarSpec)spec);
    } else if (spec instanceof MandolinSpec) {
      instrument = new Mandolin(serialNumber, price, (MandolinSpec)spec);
    }
    inventory.add(instrument);
  }

  public Instrument get(String serialNumber) {
    for (Iterator i = inventory.iterator(); i.hasNext(); ) {
      Instrument instrument = (Instrument)i.next();
      if (instrument.getSerialNumber().equals(serialNumber)) {
        return instrument;
      }
    }
    return null;
  }

  public List search(InstrumentSpec searchSpec) {
    List matchingInstruments = new LinkedList();
    for (Iterator i = inventory.iterator(); i.hasNext(); ) {
      Instrument instrument = (Instrument)i.next();
      if (instrument.getSpec().matches(searchSpec))
        matchingInstruments.add(instrument);
    }
    return matchingInstruments;
  }
}
```

We still have some issues here... this method gets bigger and more complicated every time we add a new type of instrument...

...and we're coding to the implementation classes, not the Instrument base class.

search() is looking much better! Only one version, and it takes in an InstrumentSpec now.

We're coding to the Instrument base type now, not the implementation classes like Guitar and Mandolin. This is a much better design.

On top of better design, now search() can return all instruments that match, even if that list contains different types of instruments, like two guitars and one mandolin.

One of these things is not like the other...
or is it?

The search() method isn't the only thing that makes adding new instruments to Rick's application difficult. You also have to add a new subclass of Instrument for each new instrument type. But why? Let's do a little more analysis.

Why is there a need for an Instrument class in Rick's application?

_____

_____

_____

What things are common to all instruments?

_____

_____

_____

What things are different between instruments?

_____

_____

_____

If you have any ideas for how you might change Rick's application so that you don't need all the instrument-specific subclasses, mark those changes on the class diagram below. Feel free to add or remove classes and properties; it's up to you to decide how you can improve Rick's design.

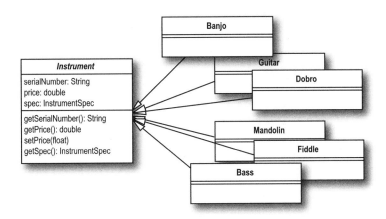

One of these things is not like the other...
or is it?

Sharpen your pencil
answers

The search() method isn't the only thing that makes adding new instruments to Rick's application difficult. You also have to add a new subclass of Instrument for each new instrument type. But why? Let's do a little more analysis.

Why is there a need for an Instrument class in Rick's application?
Most instruments have at least a few common properties, like serial number and price. Instrument stores the common properties, and then each specific instrument type can extend from Instrument.

You didn't need to write down exactly what we did, but you should be thinking along the same lines here.

What things are common to all instruments?
The serial number, the price, and some set of specifications (even though the details of those specs may be different for different instrument types).

What things are different between instruments?
The specifications: each type of instrument has a different set of properties that it can contain. And since each instrument has a different InstrumentSpec, each has a different constructor.

If you have any ideas for how you might change Rick's application so that you don't need all the instrument-specific subclasses, mark those changes on the class diagram below. Feel free to add or remove classes and properties; it's up to you how you can improve Rick's design.

Did you come up with any ideas for changing Rick's application?

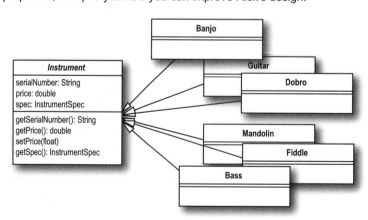

A closer look at the instrument classes

Even though **search()** is looking better, there are still some real problems with all the instrument subclasses, and the **addInstrument()** method in **Inventory**.

Remember, we originally made **Instrument** abstract because each instrument type was represented by its own subclass:

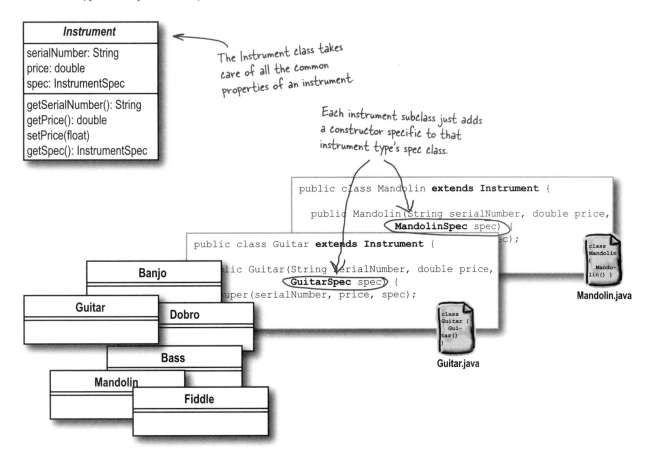

The Instrument class takes care of all the common properties of an instrument.

Each instrument subclass just adds a constructor specific to that instrument type's spec class.

```
public class Mandolin extends Instrument {

    public Mandolin(String serialNumber, double price,
        MandolinSpec spec) {
            ...c);
```

Mandolin.java

```
public class Guitar extends Instrument {

    ...lic Guitar(String serialNumber, double price,
        GuitarSpec spec) {
            ...uper(serialNumber, price, spec);
```

Guitar.java

Instrument

serialNumber: String
price: double
spec: InstrumentSpec

getSerialNumber(): String
getPrice(): double
setPrice(float)
getSpec(): InstrumentSpec

Banjo

Guitar

Dobro

Bass

Mandolin

Fiddle

But classes are really about <u>behavior</u>!

But the reason you usually create a subclass is because the **behavior** of the subclass is different than the superclass. In Rick's application, is the behavior of a **Guitar** different than that of an **Instrument**? Does it *function* differently in his application than a **Mandolin** or **Banjo**?

Guitar and Mandolin and the other instruments don't have different behavior. But they have different **properties**... so we have to have subclasses for each instrument, right?

All the instruments—at least from Rick's perspective—***behave the same***. So that leaves only two reasons to have subclasses for each instrument type:

If we were writing a system that represented how these instruments played, we might need subclasses to handle behavior like pluck(), strum(), or frail().

1. Because the **Instrument** class represents a concept, and not an actual object, it really should be abstract. So we have to have subclasses for each instrument type.

This is a good OO principle, but it sure is causing headaches with all the subclasses. We'll come back to this one in a moment.

2. Each different type of instrument has different properties, and uses a different subclass of **InstrumentSpec**, so we need an instrument-specific constructor for each type of instrument.

This looks like another case where we're coding to an implementation instead of an interface. So this isn't a good reason to keep Instrument abstract.

These seem like pretty good reasons (well, at least the first one does), but we're ending up with lots of extra classes that don't do much... and that makes our software inflexible and difficult to change. So what do we do?

Remember the second step in writing great software, from back in Chapter 1:

Since Rick's app already does what it needs to do (Step 1), we're ready to try and make his software more flexible.

Apply basic OO principles to add flexibility.

How can we take this step and apply it to the problems we're finding in Rick's app?

Sharpen your pencil

Object-Oriented Principles to the rescue!

There's definitely a problem with Rick's app, but we're not sure what it is. When you don't know what to do to solve a design problem, just run through the OO principles you know, and see if any of them might help improve your software's design.

For each principle, check the box if you think it could help us out. Then, if you checked the box for a principle, it's up to you to write down how you could use that principle to improve Rick's search tool design.

☐ Inheritance

_____
_____
_____
_____

☐ Polymorphism

_____
_____
_____
_____

☐ Abstraction

_____
_____
_____
_____

☐ Encapsulation

_____
_____
_____
_____

→ See what we thought on the next page.

Sharpen your pencil
answers

Object-Oriented Principles to the rescue!

There's definitely a problem with Rick's app, but we're not sure what it is. When you don't know what to do to solve a design problem, just run through the OO principles you know, and see if any of them might help improve your software's design.

☑ Inheritance

<u>We're using inheritance already with the Instrument and InstrumentSpec classes, and their subclasses. But it does seem like the instrument-specific subclasses don't actually do anything but inherit from Instrument... they just have slightly different constructors.</u>

☑ Polymorphism

<u>We use polymorphism in the search() method to treat all instruments as instances of Instrument, instead of worrying about whether they're a Guitar or a Mandolin. So searching is a lot easier... but it would be nice to be able to use this in addInstrument(), too, and cut down on some repetitive code.</u>

☑ Abstraction

<u>InstrumentSpec abstracts the details about each instruments specifications away from the Instrument class itself, so that we can add new instrument properties without affecting the basic Instrument class.</u>

☑ Encapsulation

<u>We're using encapsulation a lot, but maybe we can use it even more... remember, encapsulate what varies! Since the properties in each instrument type are what varies, can we somehow encapsulate those properties away from Instrument and InstrumentSpec completely?</u>

> Guys, we've been using inheritance, polymorphism, and abstraction in this design. But I'm beginning to think the key is encapsulation. Remember what we learned about separating what changes from what stays the same?

Joe: Yeah, you're talking about *encapsulating what varies*, right?

Frank: Exactly! And we know that the properties for each instrument are what varies in the application.

Jim: I thought we'd been over this; that's why we have all those subclasses of Instrument, like Guitar and Mandolin. So we can represent the differences between each instrument.

Frank: But that really didn't help... and besides, the *behavior* of each instrument doesn't vary, so do we really need subclasses for each one?

Joe: So you're saying we would make Instrument a concrete class, instead of being abstract, right? And then we can get rid of all those instrument-specific subclasses.

Jim: But... I'm totally confused. What about the properties that vary across each instrument?

Frank: What about them? The Instrument class has a reference to an InstrumentSpec, and all the property differences can be handled by those classes. Look:

We actually already have the properties encapsulated away from the rest of the application! We just weren't taking advantage of our good design decision.

Instrument isn't in italics anymore; it's a concrete class.

We made InstrumentSpec non-abstract, too.

Instrument

serialNumber: String
price: double

getSerialNumber(): String
getPrice(): double
setPrice(float)
getSpec(): InstrumentSpec

spec
1

InstrumentSpec

builder: Builder
model: String
type: Type
backWood: Wood
topWood: Wood

getBuilder(): Builder
getModel(): String
getType(): Type
getBackWood(): Wood
getTopWood(): Wood
matches(InstrumentSpec): boolean

GuitarSpec

numStrings: int

getNumStrings(): int
matches(GuitarSpec): boolean

MandolinSpec

getStyle(): Style
matches(MandolinSpec): boolean

There's really no reason to have instrument-specific subclasses! They just add complexity to our application.

Death of a design (decision)

One of the hardest things you will ever do is to let go of mistakes you made *in your own designs*. In Rick's search tool, it doesn't make sense to have separate `Instrument` subclasses for each type of instrument. But it took us almost 30 pages (and 2 parts of Chapter 5) to figure that out. Why?

Because <u>it seemed to make sense at the time</u>, and it's <u>HARD</u> to change something you thought was already working!

R. I. P.

Instrument-specific subclasses

You will be missed (well, not so much)

> ### Code once, look twice (or more!)
>
> *Keep looking over your designs when you run into problems. A decision you made earlier may be what's causing you headaches now.*

It's easy to rip apart someone else's code, but you've got to learn to look at your own code, and identify problems. This is also where peer review, having fellow programmers look at your code, can really be a lifesaver. Don't worry if you have to make changes; a better-designed application will save you tons of time in the long run.

Design is <u>iterative</u>... and you have to be willing to <u>change your own designs</u>, as well as those that you inherit from other programmers.

Let's kill our bad design decision to create instrument-specific subclasses once and for all, and get on with writing great software again.

> ### Pride kills good design
>
> *Never be afraid to examine your own design decisions, and improve on them, even if it means backtracking.*
>
> Watch it!

Let's turn some bad design decisions into good ones

Let's kill all those instrument-specific subclasses:

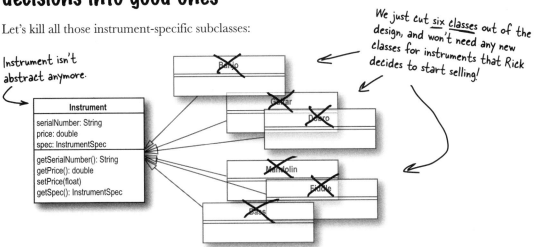

Instrument isn't abstract anymore.

Instrument

serialNumber: String
price: double
spec: InstrumentSpec

getSerialNumber(): String
getPrice(): double
setPrice(float)
getSpec(): InstrumentSpec

We just cut six classes out of the design, and won't need any new classes for instruments that Rick decides to start selling!

We also probably need a new property in each instrument to let us know what type of instrument it is:

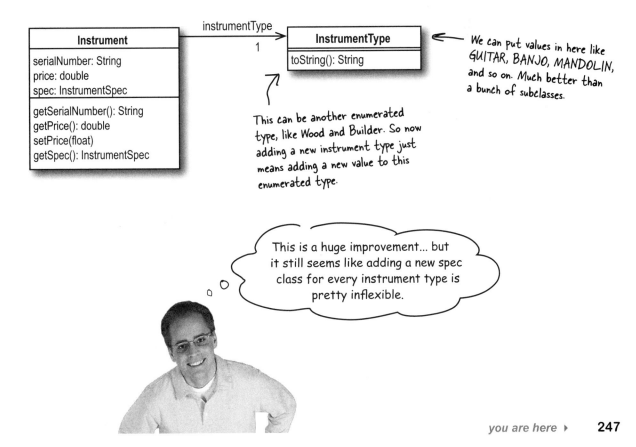

Instrument

serialNumber: String
price: double
spec: InstrumentSpec

getSerialNumber(): String
getPrice(): double
setPrice(float)
getSpec(): InstrumentSpec

instrumentType
1

InstrumentType

toString(): String

We can put values in here like GUITAR, BANJO, MANDOLIN, and so on. Much better than a bunch of subclasses.

This can be another enumerated type, like Wood and Builder. So now adding a new instrument type just means adding a new value to this enumerated type.

This is a huge improvement... but it still seems like adding a new spec class for every instrument type is pretty inflexible.

One more cubicle conversation
(and some help from Jill)

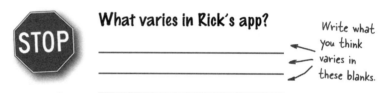

I hate to butt in, but I've been thinking about something you said earlier, Joe: **Encapsulate what varies**.

Jill's been listening in on the chapter, and has some ideas on how to improve Rick's app.

Joe: But we just did that... we made Instrument concrete, and got rid of all the instrument-specific subclasses.

Jill: Actually, I think that's really only the first step. What really varies in Rick's software?

What varies in Rick's app?

_____   Write what you think varies in these blanks.

_____

_____

Frank: We've gone through this already: the properties for each instrument are what vary.

Jill: So can we encapsulate them somehow?

Joe: We already have: we used the InstrumentSpec class for that.

Frank: Wait a second, Joe. We used InstrumentSpec because those properties were used by both clients and instruments. So that was more about duplicate code...

Jill: Yes! That's my point... the properties inside InstrumentSpec vary, too. So maybe we need to add *another* layer of encapsulation.

Joe: So since the properties of each instrument vary, we should pull those out of InstrumentSpec? It's almost like double-encapsulation or something.

Jill: Sort of... we encapsulate the specifications common across client requests and instruments from the Instrument class, and then we encapsulate the properties that vary from the InstrumentSpec class.

"Double encapsulation" in Rick's software

This really isn't an OOA&D term, so don't be surprised if your professor looks at you funny if you use it in class.

Let's look at the layer of encapsulation we already have, and then see how we can add a little more encapsulation to get those properties that vary out of the **InstrumentSpec** class.

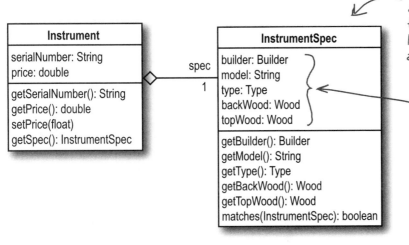

We realized in Chapter 1 that clients and instruments both needed to use these properties, so we created the InstrumentSpec class to abstract them away from the Instrument class.

The problem is that these properties vary across instruments, and so we're having to add a subclass for each type of instrument.

Since some of these properties vary, we want to move them out of the **InstrumentSpec** class. We need a way to refer to properties and their values, but not have those properties hardcoded into the **InstrumentSpec** class. Any ideas for how we could do that?

What type(s) do you think you could use to represent properties and access their values, but not have to change your InstrumentSpec class to support new properties?

_____

_____

_____

By encapsulating what varies, you make your application more flexible, and easier to change.

Getting dynamic with instrument properties

What did you come up with on the last page to store properties? We decided that using a **Map** would be a great way to handle various types of properties, and still be able to easily add new properties at any time:

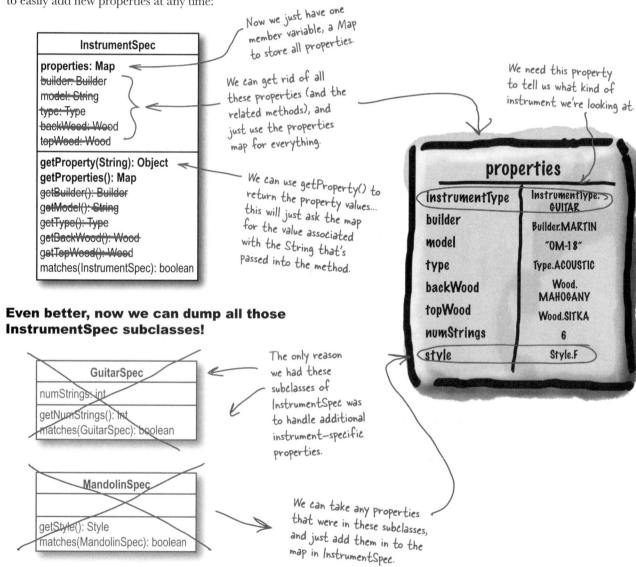

Now we just have one member variable, a Map to store all properties.

We can get rid of all these properties (and the related methods), and just use the properties map for everything.

We can use getProperty() to return the property values... this will just ask the map for the value associated with the String that's passed into the method.

We need this property to tell us what kind of instrument we're looking at.

InstrumentSpec

properties: Map
~~builder: Builder~~
~~model: String~~
~~type: Type~~
~~backWood: Wood~~
~~topWood: Wood~~

getProperty(String): Object
getProperties(): Map
~~getBuilder(): Builder~~
~~getModel(): String~~
~~getType(): Type~~
~~getBackWood(): Wood~~
~~getTopWood(): Wood~~
matches(InstrumentSpec): boolean

properties

instrumentType	InstrumentType.GUITAR
builder	Builder.MARTIN
model	"OM-18"
type	Type.ACOUSTIC
backWood	Wood.MAHOGANY
topWood	Wood.SITKA
numStrings	6
style	Style.F

Even better, now we can dump all those InstrumentSpec subclasses!

~~**GuitarSpec**~~

~~numStrings: int~~

~~getNumStrings(): int~~
~~matches(GuitarSpec): boolean~~

The only reason we had these subclasses of InstrumentSpec was to handle additional instrument-specific properties.

~~**MandolinSpec**~~

~~getStyle(): Style~~
~~matches(MandolinSpec): boolean~~

We can take any properties that were in these subclasses, and just add them in to the map in InstrumentSpec.

What we did: a closer look

Anytime you see something that varies, you should look for a way to encapsulate. In the case of **InstrumentSpec**, we realized that the properties of an instrument vary.

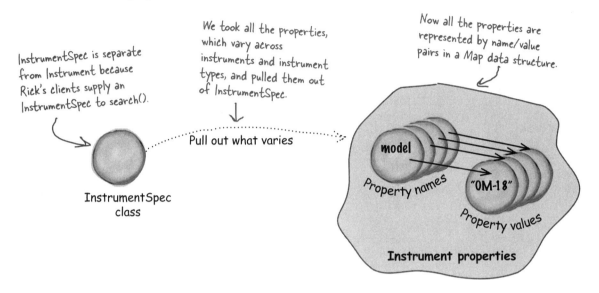

InstrumentSpec is separate from Instrument because Rick's clients supply an InstrumentSpec to search().

We took all the properties, which vary across instruments and instrument types, and pulled them out of InstrumentSpec.

Pull out what varies

Now all the properties are represented by name/value pairs in a Map data structure.

InstrumentSpec class

model

Property names

"OM-18"

Property values

Instrument properties

When you have a set of properties that vary across your objects, use a collection, like a Map, to store those properties dynamically.

You'll remove lots of methods from your classes, and avoid having to change your code when new properties are added to your app.

Using the new Instrument and InstrumentSpec classes

Let's take one last look at how our new **Instrument** and **InstrumentSpec** classes work in practice. Here's where we are with the design right now:

InstrumentSpec's Map uses these enumerated types.

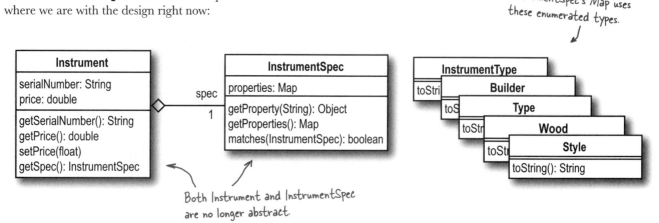

Both Instrument and InstrumentSpec are no longer abstract.

If you were accessing a guitar, and wanted to know who built it, here's how you could do that:

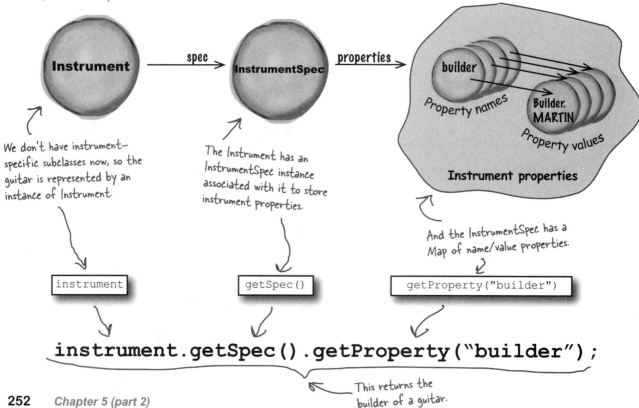

We don't have instrument-specific subclasses now, so the guitar is represented by an instance of Instrument.

The Instrument has an InstrumentSpec instance associated with it to store instrument properties.

And the InstrumentSpec has a Map of name/value properties.

```
instrument.getSpec().getProperty("builder");
```

This returns the builder of a guitar.

Code Magnets

Using a Map for storing properties seems like a good idea, but let's see how things look once we actually code up a new version of InstrumentSpec. Your job is to finish off the code below using the magnets at the bottom of the page.

```java
import java.util._____;
import java.util._____;
import java.util._____;

public class InstrumentSpec {

  private _____ properties;

  public InstrumentSpec(_____ _____) {
    if (properties == _____) {
      this.properties = new _____();
    } else {
      this.properties = new _____(_____);
    }
  }

  public _____ getProperty(String _____) {
    return properties.get(_____);
  }

  public _____ getProperties() {
    return _____;
  }

  public boolean matches(_____ otherSpec) {
    for (_____ i = otherSpec._____().keySet()._____();
        i._____(); ) {
      String _____ = (String)i._____();
      if (!properties.get(_____).equals(
          otherSpec.getProperty(_____))) {
        return _____;
      }
    }
    return _____;
  }
}
```

true   Iterator   Map   Map   propertyName   hasNext   getProperties   InstrumentSpec

true   List   Map   propertyName   propertyName   HashMap   null   Map   properties

Object   iterator   Map   false   false   iterator   properties

InstrumentSpec   HashMap   null   next   propertyName   properties

propertyName   getProperties   HashMap

Code Magnets Solutions

Using a Map for storing properties seems like a good idea, but let's see how things look once we actually code up a new version of InstrumentSpec. Your job was to finish off the code below:

```java
import java.util.Iterator;
import java.util.HashMap;
import java.util.Map;

public class InstrumentSpec {

    private Map properties;

    public InstrumentSpec(Map properties) {
        if (properties == null) {
            this.properties = new HashMap();
        } else {
            this.properties = new HashMap(properties);
        }
    }

    public Object getProperty(String propertyName) {
        return properties.get(propertyName);
    }

    public Map getProperties() {
        return properties;
    }

    public boolean matches(InstrumentSpec otherSpec) {
        for (Iterator i = otherSpec.getProperties().keySet().iterator();
             i.hasNext(); ) {
            String propertyName = (String)i.next();
            if (!properties.get(propertyName).equals(
                otherSpec.getProperty(propertyName))) {
                return false;
            }
        }
        return true;
    }
}
```

You could actually use any implementation of the Map interface you wanted here.

Be sure you got these two right; otherwise, matches() will always return the wrong result.

getProperties
false
null
true
InstrumentSpec
List

Q: So now both Instrument and InstrumentSpec are concrete classes?

A: Right. `Instrument` isn't just a concept anymore; it represents actual instruments in Rick's inventory. And `InstrumentSpec` is what clients use to pass in their specs when they're searching, and what `Instrument` uses to store properties for an instrument.

Q: So I can get rid of my Guitar and Mandolin subclasses?

A: Yup. As well as `Banjo`, `Dobro`, and any other instrument-specific subclasses of `Instrument` you may have created.

Q: And that's because we use the Instrument class directly now, right?

A: You got it! Remember, you typically subclass because *behavior* changes. In the `Instrument` subclasses, no behavior was changing; in fact, all we did for each instrument subclass was create a new constructor. That added a ton of classes, reduced the flexibility of our app, and really didn't give us any helpful functionality.

Q: I understood getting rid of Guitar and Mandolin, but I'm confused about why we don't need the different subclasses of InstrumentSpec anymore.

A: It's OK; that's one of the trickiest parts of the design of Rick's application. Remember, one of the key principles in any OO design is to encapsulate what varies. In Rick's app, the properties of each instrument varied. So we pulled those properties out of `InstrumentSpec`, and put them into a `Map`. Now, when you add another instrument with a new property, you can just add the new property as a name/value pair in the `properties Map`.

Q: And with less classes to deal with, our software is more flexible?

A: In this case, that's true. There are certainly times where adding classes will make your design more flexible, though. Remember, adding an `InstrumentSpec` class helped separate instruments from their properties, and that was good; but in this chapter, we've been removing classes, and that's made it easier to add new instruments to Rick's software.

Q: I never would have figured out that we didn't need subclasses for instruments or their specs. How am I supposed to ever get good at this?

A: The best way to get good at software design is to write software! In Rick's application, we had to go down some wrong paths—like adding `Guitar` and `Mandolin` classes—to figure out what the right thing to do was.

Most good designs come about through bad designs; almost nobody gets it all right the first time. So just do what makes sense, and then start applying your OO principles and patterns to see if you can make improvements to what you've got.

Most good designs come from analysis of bad designs.

Never be afraid to make mistakes and then change things around.

Finishing up Rick's app: the InstrumentType enum

We've almost got ourselves a great piece of software. Let's follow through on our new design ideas, starting with a new enumerated type for each instrument type:

So far, these are the types of instruments that Rick sells.

```java
public enum InstrumentType {

  GUITAR, BANJO, DOBRO, FIDDLE, BASS, MANDOLIN;

  public String toString() {
    switch(this) {
      case GUITAR:   return "Guitar";
      case BANJO:    return "Banjo";
      case DOBRO:    return "Dobro";
      case FIDDLE:   return "Fiddle";
      case BASS:     return "Bass";
      case MANDOLIN: return "Mandolin";
      default:       return "Unspecified";
    }
  }
}
```

InstrumentType
toString(): String

enum InstrumntType { toString() }

InstrumentType.java

toString() just makes it easier to print things out.

Let's update Inventory, too

With the changes to **Instrument** and **InstrumentSpec**, our **Inventory** class starts to get much simpler:

Inventory
inventory: Instrument [*]
addInstrument(String, double, InstrumentSpec) get(String): Instrument search(InstrumentSpec): Instrument [*]

```java
public class Inventory {

  public void addInstrument(String serialNumber, double price,
                            InstrumentSpec spec) {
    Instrument instrument = null;
    if (spec instanceof GuitarSpec) {
      instrument = new Guitar(serialNumber, price, (GuitarSpec)spec);
    } else if (spec instanceof MandolinSpec) {
      instrument = new Mandolin(serialNumber, price, (MandolinSpec)spec);
    }
    Instrument instrument = new Instrument(serialNumber, price, spec);
    inventory.add(instrument);
  }

  // etc
}
```

Adding an instrument just got a lot easier.

Now we're able to instantiate Instrument directly, since it's no longer abstract.

class Inventory { search() }

Inventory.java

Sharpen your pencil

Let's see what we've <u>really</u> done.

We've made a ton of changes to Rick's software, all in the name of "more flexibility." Let's see how things look now. Flip back to the class diagram of Rick's app on page 234, and recall what things looked like when we started. Then, below, draw a class diagram for how Rick's application looks now.

Answers on the next page!

Behold: Rick's <u>flexible</u> application

We've made a ton of changes to Rick's application... and it's easy to
forget what we've been working towards. Look at the class diagram below,
though, and see how much simpler Rick's application is now:

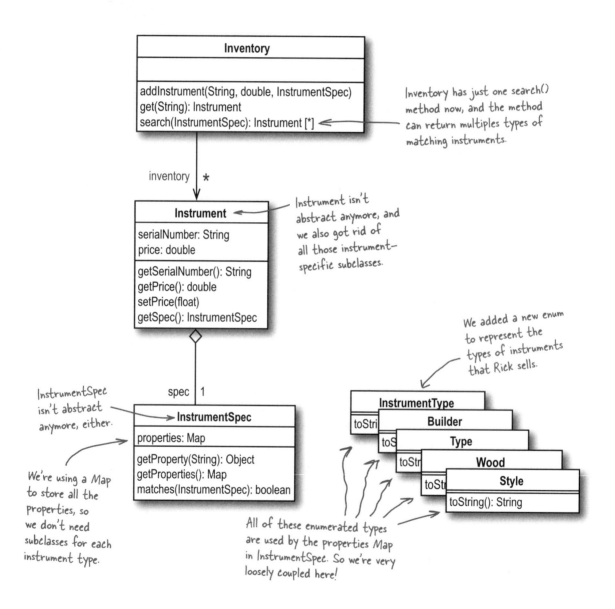

Inventory has just one search()
method now, and the method
can return multiples types of
matching instruments.

Instrument isn't
abstract anymore, and
we also got rid of
all those instrument-
specific subclasses.

We added a new enum
to represent the
types of instruments
that Rick sells.

InstrumentSpec
isn't abstract
anymore, either.

We're using a Map
to store all the
properties, so
we don't need
subclasses for each
instrument type.

All of these enumerated types
are used by the properties Map
in InstrumentSpec. So we're very
loosely coupled here!

But does the application actually work?

Rick's software looks a lot better than it did way back at the beginning of this chapter—and it sure looks better than when we added all those subclasses for banjos and mandolins. But we've still got to make sure his search tool actually works! So let's update our test class, and check out how searches work with the new version of Rick's software:

FindInstrument.java

```java
public class FindInstrument {

  public static void main(String[] args) {
    // Set up Rick's inventory
    Inventory inventory = new Inventory();
    initializeInventory(inventory);

    Map properties = new HashMap();
    properties.put("builder", Builder.GIBSON);
    properties.put("backWood", Wood.MAPLE);
    InstrumentSpec clientSpec = new InstrumentSpec(properties);

    List matchingInstruments = inventory.search(clientSpec);
    if (!matchingInstruments.isEmpty()) {
      System.out.println("You might like these instruments:");
      for (Iterator i = matchingInstruments.iterator(); i.hasNext(); ) {
        Instrument instrument = (Instrument)i.next();
        InstrumentSpec spec = instrument.getSpec();
        System.out.println("We have a " + spec.getProperty("instrumentType") +
          " with the following properties:");
        for (Iterator j = spec.getProperties().keySet().iterator();
            j.hasNext(); ) {
          String propertyName = (String)j.next();
          if (propertyName.equals("instrumentType"))
            continue;
          System.out.println("   " + propertyName + ": " +
            spec.getProperty(propertyName));
        }
        System.out.println("  You can have this " +
          spec.getProperty("instrumentType") + " for $" +
          instrument.getPrice() + "\n---");
      }
    } else {
      System.out.println("Sorry, we have nothing for you.");
    }
  }

  // initializeInventory() method here
}
```

Now clients fill out an InstrumentSpec. Since this test client didn't specify an instrument type, the search could bring back guitars, mandolins, or anything else that Rick sells.

We have to work a little more directly with the Map that InstrumentSpec uses, but it's easy now to just loop through each instrument's properties and print them out.

We want to skip over the instrumentType property, since we've already handled that before we start looping.

We also need to add some instruments to Rick's inventory so we can search for more than guitars... we'll do that on the next page.

Inventory Roundup

To see if the new version of Rick's software works, we need to run a search on more than just guitars. Your job is to write code for the initializeInventory() method in FindInstrument.java, and add several guitars, mandolins, and banjos to Rick's inventory. Below, we've listed the instruments Rick currently has, and even written code to add the first guitar to help you get started.

Guitars

Collings CJ 6-string acoustic, Indian Rosewood back and sides, Spruce top, Serial #11277, for $3999.95

Martin D-18 6-string acoustic, Mahogany back and sides, Adirondack top, Serial #122784, for $5495.95

Fender stratocastor 6-string electric, Alder back and sides and top, Serial #V95693, for $1499.95

Fender stratocastor 6-string electric, Alder back and sides and top, Serial #V9512, for $1549.95

Gibson SG '61 Reissue 6-string electric, Mahogany back, sides, and top, Serial #82765501, for $1890.95

Gibson Les Paul 6-string electric, Maple back, sides, and top, Serial #70108276, for $2295.95

Mandolins

Gibson F5-G acoustic mandolin, Maple back, sides, and top, Serial #9019920, for $5495.99

Remember, the numStrings attribute doesn't apply to mandolins.

Banjos

Banjos do not have a top wood.

Gibson RB-3 5-string acoustic banjo, Maple back and sides, Serial #8900231, for $2945.95

Banjos do <u>not</u> have a top wood.

Answers on page 262

Here's the beginning of initializeInventory(), where the first guitar shown above is added to Rick's inventory.

```
private static void initializeInventory(Inventory inventory) {
  Map properties = new HashMap();
  properties.put("instrumentType", InstrumentType.GUITAR);
  properties.put("builder", Builder.COLLINGS);
  properties.put("model", "CJ");
  properties.put("type", Type.ACOUSTIC);
  properties.put("numStrings", 6);
  properties.put("topWood", Wood.INDIAN_ROSEWOOD);
  properties.put("backWood", Wood.SITKA);
  inventory.addInstrument("11277", 3999.95,
    new InstrumentSpec(properties));
  // your code goes here
}
```

You should write code here to add the other instruments shown above.

FindInstrument.java

Test driving Rick's well-<u>designed</u> software

Be sure you've added all the instruments shown on the last page to your **initializeInventory()** method in **FindInstrument.java**, and then compile all your classes. Now you're ready to take Rick's software for a test drive...

...well, almost. First, you need to figure out what a search based on the current version of **FindInstrument** should return. Here's the set of preferences that Rick's current client has supplied:

Rick's client didn't specify an instrument type, but he wants something from Gibson with a maple back.

```
Map properties = new HashMap();
properties.put("builder", Builder.GIBSON);
properties.put("backWood", Wood.MAPLE);
InstrumentSpec clientSpec =
    new InstrumentSpec(properties);
```

```
class
FindIn-
stru-
ment {
main()}
```

FindInstrument.java

Based on those specs, look over the instruments shown on the last page, and write in which guitars, mandolins, and banjos you think Rick's search tool should return:

```
File Edit Window Help TheSearchIsOn
%java FindInstrument
You might like these instruments:
_____
_____
_____
_____
_____
_____
_____
_____
_____
```

Write in the instruments you think that running FindInstrument should return based on Rick's inventory.

<u>SPECIAL</u> <u>BONUS</u> <u>CREDIT</u>
Try and write the instruments that this program finds exactly as FindInstrument will output them.

Inventory Roundup Solutions

To see if the new version of Rick's software works, we need to run a search on more than just guitars. Your job was to write code for the initializeInventory() method in FindInstrument.java, and add several guitars, mandolins, and banjos to Rick's inventory.

```java
private static void initializeInventory(Inventory inventory) {
  Map properties = new HashMap();
  properties.put("instrumentType", InstrumentType.GUITAR);
  properties.put("builder", Builder.COLLINGS);
  properties.put("model", "CJ");
  properties.put("type", Type.ACOUSTIC);
  properties.put("numStrings", 6);
  properties.put("topWood", Wood.INDIAN_ROSEWOOD);
  properties.put("backWood", Wood.SITKA);
  inventory.addInstrument("11277", 3999.95,
    new InstrumentSpec(properties));

  properties.put("builder", Builder.MARTIN);
  properties.put("model", "D-18");
  properties.put("topWood", Wood.MAHOGANY);
  properties.put("backWood", Wood.ADIRONDACK);
  inventory.addInstrument("122784", 5495.95,
    new InstrumentSpec(properties));

  properties.put("builder", Builder.FENDER);
  properties.put("model", "Stratocaster");
  properties.put("type", Type.ELECTRIC);
  properties.put("topWood", Wood.ALDER);
  properties.put("backWood", Wood.ALDER);
  inventory.addInstrument("V95693", 1499.95,
    new InstrumentSpec(properties));
  inventory.addInstrument("V9512", 1549.95,
    new InstrumentSpec(properties));
```

This is a bit of a shortcut: we're just using the same Map over and over.

> Collings CJ 6-string acoustic, Indian Rosewood back and sides, Spruce top, Serial #11277, for $3999.95

> Martin D-18 6-string acoustic, Mahogany back and sides, Adirondack top, Serial #122784, for $5495.95

> Fender stratocastor 6-string electric, Alder back and sides and top, Serial #V95693, for $1499.95

> Fender stratocastor 6-string electric, Alder back and sides and top, Serial #V9512, for $1549.95

The specs for these two Strats are the same; only the properties in Instrument are different.

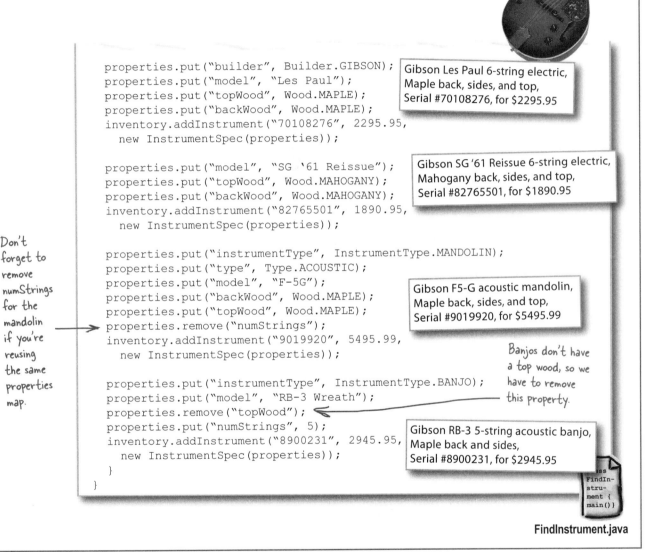

```
        properties.put("builder", Builder.GIBSON);
        properties.put("model", "Les Paul");
        properties.put("topWood", Wood.MAPLE);
        properties.put("backWood", Wood.MAPLE);
        inventory.addInstrument("70108276", 2295.95,
          new InstrumentSpec(properties));
```

Gibson Les Paul 6-string electric,
Maple back, sides, and top,
Serial #70108276, for $2295.95

```
        properties.put("model", "SG '61 Reissue");
        properties.put("topWood", Wood.MAHOGANY);
        properties.put("backWood", Wood.MAHOGANY);
        inventory.addInstrument("82765501", 1890.95,
          new InstrumentSpec(properties));
```

Gibson SG '61 Reissue 6-string electric,
Mahogany back, sides, and top,
Serial #82765501, for $1890.95

```
        properties.put("instrumentType", InstrumentType.MANDOLIN);
        properties.put("type", Type.ACOUSTIC);
        properties.put("model", "F-5G");
        properties.put("backWood", Wood.MAPLE);
        properties.put("topWood", Wood.MAPLE);
        properties.remove("numStrings");
        inventory.addInstrument("9019920", 5495.99,
          new InstrumentSpec(properties));
```

Don't forget to remove numStrings for the mandolin if you're reusing the same properties map.

Gibson F5-G acoustic mandolin,
Maple back, sides, and top,
Serial #9019920, for $5495.99

```
        properties.put("instrumentType", InstrumentType.BANJO);
        properties.put("model", "RB-3 Wreath");
        properties.remove("topWood");
        properties.put("numStrings", 5);
        inventory.addInstrument("8900231", 2945.95,
          new InstrumentSpec(properties));
      }
    }
```

Banjos don't have a top wood, so we have to remove this property.

Gibson RB-3 5-string acoustic banjo,
Maple back and sides,
Serial #8900231, for $2945.95

class FindInstrument { main() }

FindInstrument.java

Rick's got working software, his client has three choices:

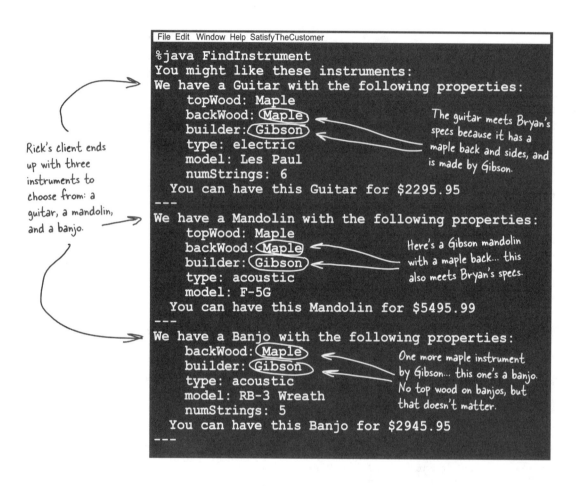

Rick's client ends up with three instruments to choose from: a guitar, a mandolin, and a banjo.

```
File Edit  Window Help  SatisfyTheCustomer
%java FindInstrument
You might like these instruments:
We have a Guitar with the following properties:
    topWood: Maple
    backWood: Maple
    builder: Gibson
    type: electric
    model: Les Paul
    numStrings: 6
  You can have this Guitar for $2295.95
---
We have a Mandolin with the following properties:
    topWood: Maple
    backWood: Maple
    builder: Gibson
    type: acoustic
    model: F-5G
  You can have this Mandolin for $5495.99
---
We have a Banjo with the following properties:
    backWood: Maple
    builder: Gibson
    type: acoustic
    model: RB-3 Wreath
    numStrings: 5
  You can have this Banjo for $2945.95
---
```

The guitar meets Bryan's specs because it has a maple back and sides, and is made by Gibson.

Here's a Gibson mandolin with a maple back... this also meets Bryan's specs.

One more maple instrument by Gibson... this one's a banjo. No top wood on banjos, but that doesn't matter.

---

there are no Dumb Questions

Q: My output isn't the same as yours. What did I do wrong?

A: If your version of Rick's tool returned different guitars, or output the same guitars but with different properties, then you should be sure you have the same instruments in your inventory as we do. Check the exercise on page 260, and the answers on page 261-262, and make sure the instruments you have in Rick's inventory match ours.

Q: Is this really a good test since we only have one banjo and one mandolin?

A: That's a great question, and you're right, it would be better to have a few more mandolins and banjos to really make sure Rick's search tool picks only matching mandolins and banjos. Go ahead and add a few non-matching banjos or mandolins, and try testing out Rick's search tool with the additional instruments.

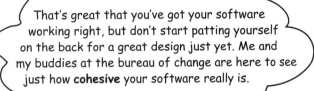

That's great that you've got your software working right, but don't start patting yourself on the back for a great design just yet. Me and my buddies at the bureau of change are here to see just how **cohesive** your software really is.

bureau de change

* How easy is it to <u>change</u> Rick's software?

* Is Rick's software really <u>well-designed</u>?

* And what the heck does <u>cohesive</u> mean?

The Great Ease-of-Change Challenge

How easy is it to change Rick's search tool?

Let's add support for dobros and fiddles back into Rick's application. We tried to do that earlier, back in the first part of Chapter 5, and it turned into a total mess. Things should be much easier this time, right? Below is the class diagram for the current version of Rick's software.

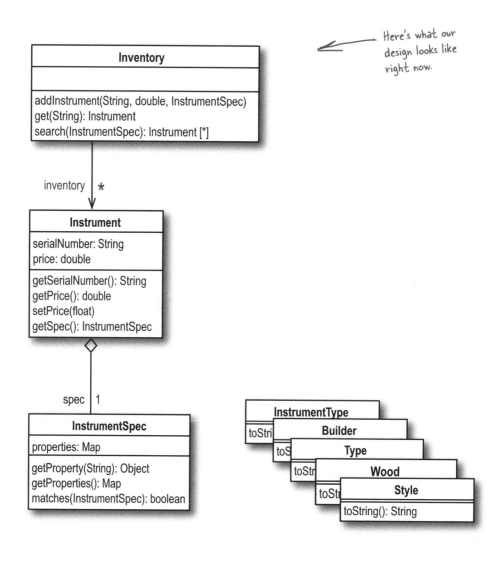

Here's what our design looks like right now.

good design = *flexible software*

bureau de change

↑
Seeing how easy it is to change your software is one of the best ways to figure out if you really have well-designed software.

Let's apply the **ease-of-change test** to our software:

1 How many classes did you have to **add** to support Rick's new instrument types?

_____

_____

2 How many classes did you have to **change** to support Rick's new instrument types?

_____

_____

3 Suppose that Rick decided that he wanted to start keeping up with what year an instrument was made in. How many classes would you need to change to support keeping up with this new information?

_____

_____

4 Rick also wants to add a new property, neckWood, that tracks what wood is used in the neck of an instrument. How many classes would you need to change to support this property?

_____

_____

⟶ Answers on page 268

The Great Ease-of-Change Challenge

How easy is it to change Rick's search tool?

Let's add support for dobros and fiddles back into Rick's application. We tried to do that earlier, and it turned into a total mess. Things should be much easier this time, right?

Let's apply the **ease-of-change test** to our software:

1 How many classes did you have to **add** to support Rick's new instrument types?

> *None! We got rid of all the instrument-specific*
> *subclasses of Instrument and InstrumentSpec.*

2 How many classes did you have to **change** to support Rick's new instrument types?

> *One: we need to add any new instrument types to the*
> *InstrumentType enumerated type.*

3 Suppose that Rick decided that he wanted to start keeping up with what year an instrument was made in. How many classes would you need to change to support keeping up with this new information?

> *None! You can just store the year that an instrument*
> *was made in the properties Map in InstrumentSpec.*

4 Rick also wants to add a new property, neckWood, that tracks what wood is used in the neck of an instrument. How many classes would you need to change to support this property?

> *One in the worst case, and maybe none! neckWood*
> *is just another property we can store in the*
> *InstrumentSpec map... but we might need to add new*
> *wood enumerated values to the Wood enum.*

Sweet! Our software is easy to change...
...but what about that "cohesive" thing?

A cohesive class does
one thing
really well and
does not try to
do
or be
something else.

The more cohesive your classes are, the higher the cohesion of your software.

Cohesive classes are focused on specific tasks. Our Inventory class worries about just Rick's inventory, not what woods can be used in a guitar, or how to compare two instrument specs.

Look through the methods of your classes—do they all relate to the name of your class? If you have a method that looks out of place, it might belong in another class.

Instrument doesn't try to handle searches, or keep up with what woods are available. It is focused on describing an instrument—and nothing else.

---

the Scholar's Corner

cohesion. Cohesion measures the degree of connectivity among the elements of a single module, class, or object. The higher the cohesion of your software is, the more well-defined and related the responsibilities of each individual class in your application. Each class has a very specific set of closely related actions it performs.

Cohesion, and one reason for a class to change

You may not realize it, but we've already talked about cohesion in this book. Remember this?

> **Every class should attempt to make sure that it has only one reason to do this, the death of many a badly designed piece of software.**

This was one of the answers from OO CATASTROPHE! Do you remember what the question was?

Cohesion is really just a measure of how closely related the functionality of the classes in an application are. If one class is made up of functionality that's all related, then it has only one reason to change... which is what we already talked about in **OO CATASTROPHE!**

Here are the classes we talked about when we made sure each class had only a single reason to change:

The function of each of these classes is well-defined. Each one is a highly cohesive class, and that makes it easy to change, <u>without</u> changing the other classes.

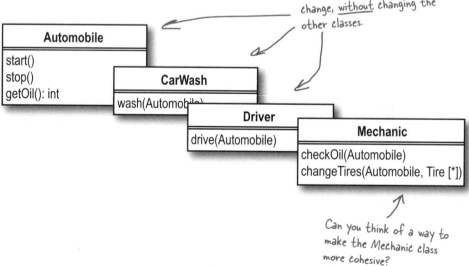

Automobile

start()
stop()
getOil(): int

CarWash

wash(Automobile)

Driver

drive(Automobile)

Mechanic

checkOil(Automobile)
changeTires(Automobile, Tire [*])

Can you think of a way to make the Mechanic class more cohesive?

Q: So cohesion is just a fancy word for how easy it is to change my application?

A: Not exactly. Cohesion focuses on how you've constructed each individual class, object, and package of your software. If each class does just a few things that are all grouped together, then it's probably a **highly cohesive** piece of software. But if you have one class doing all sorts of things that aren't that closely related, you've probably got **low cohesion**.

Q: So highly cohesive software is loosely coupled, right?

A: Exactly! In almost every situation, *the more cohesive your software is, the looser the coupling between classes*. In Rick's application, the `Inventory` class really worries just about managing inventory—and not about how instruments are compared or what properties are stored in an instrument spec. That means that `Inventory` is a highly cohesive class. That also means it's loosely coupled with the rest of the application—changes to `Instrument`, for example, don't have a lot of effect on the `Inventory` class.

Q: But all that means the software will be easier to change, doesn't it?

A: Most of the time, yes. But remember the version of Rick's application that we started with in this chapter? It only supported guitars, and we didn't even have `Instrument` or `InstrumentSpec` classes. That was pretty cohesive software— `Guitar` was very loosely coupled with `Inventory`. However, it took a lot of work and redesign to support mandolins.

When you fundamentally change what an application does—like going from selling only one type of instrument to multiple types—you may have to make lots of changes to a design that's already cohesive and loosely coupled. So cohesion isn't *always* a test of how easy it is to change software; but in cases where you're *not* dramatically changing how software works, highly cohesive software is usually easy to change.

Q: And high cohesion is better than low cohesion?

A: Right. Good OO design is when each class and module in your software does **one basic thing**, and that one thing really well. As soon as one class starts doing two or three different things, you're probably moving away from cohesion, and good OO design.

Q: Wouldn't software that's cohesive be easier to reuse, as well as change?

A: You got it. High cohesion and loose coupling adds up to software that can easily be extended, or even broken up and reused, because all the objects in the software aren't interdependent.

Think about it this way: the higher the cohesion in your application, the better defined each object's job is. And the better defined an object (and its job) is, the easier it is to pull that object out of one context, and have the object do the same job in another context. The object is happy to just keep on doing its very specific job, no matter where it's being used.

Q: And we've been making Rick's application more cohesive throughout his chapter, haven't we?

A: For the most part, yes. But let's look a little bit closer at that question...

Rick's software, in review

So have our changes to Rick's software resulted in high cohesion? Are our objects loosely coupled? And can we make changes easily? Let's take a look:

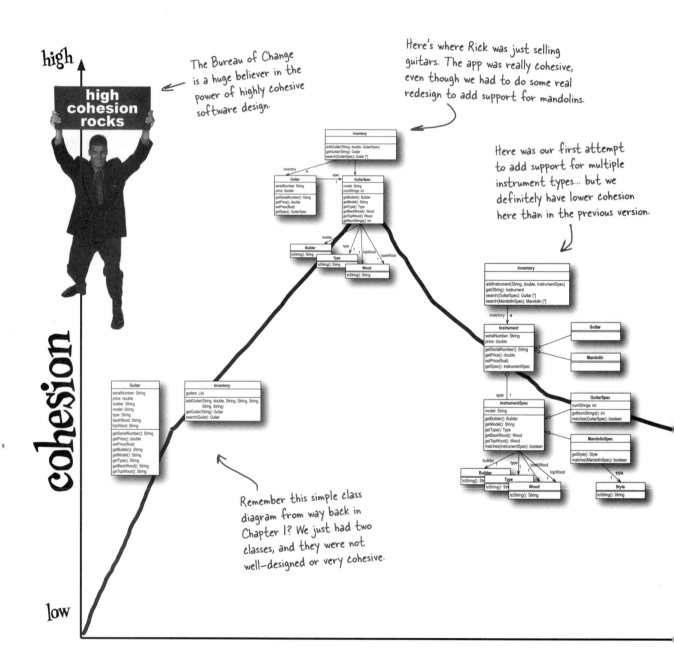

The Bureau of Change is a huge believer in the power of highly cohesive software design.

Here's where Rick was just selling guitars. The app was really cohesive, even though we had to do some real redesign to add support for mandolins.

Here was our first attempt to add support for multiple instrument types... but we definitely have lower cohesion here than in the previous version.

Remember this simple class diagram from way back in Chapter 1? We just had two classes, and they were not well-designed or very cohesive.

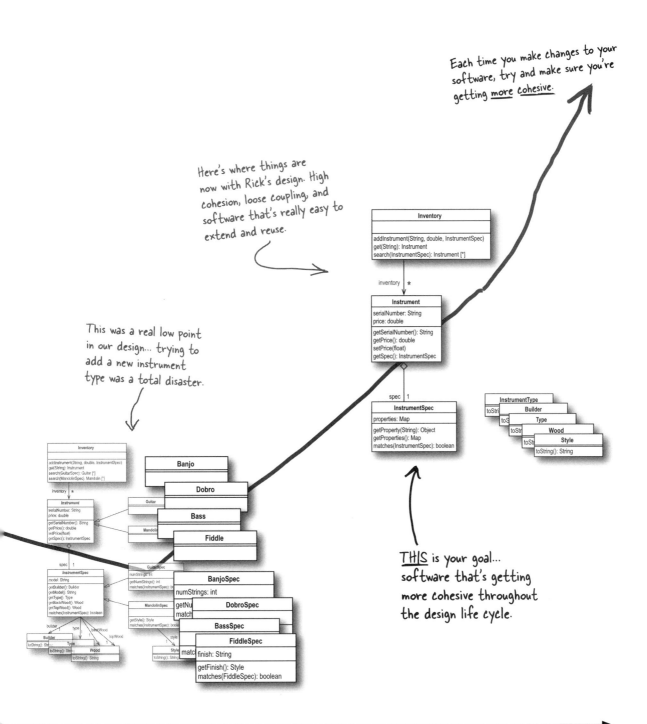

Each time you make changes to your software, try and make sure you're getting *more* cohesive.

Here's where things are now with Rick's design. High cohesion, loose coupling, and software that's really easy to extend and reuse.

This was a real low point in our design... trying to add a new instrument type was a total disaster.

THIS is your goal... software that's getting more cohesive throughout the design life cycle.

the design life cycle

This sounds great and all, but how do you know when you're done? I mean, is there some sort of scale of cohesion, and when I get to a "10" or whatever, it means that I'm finished?

Great software is usually about being <u>good</u> <u>enough.</u>

It's hard to know when to stop designing software. Sure, you can make sure that your software does what it's supposed to do, and then start working on increasing the flexibility and cohesion of your code. *But then what?*

Sometimes you just have to stop designing because you run out of time... or money... and sometimes you just have to recognize you've *done a good enough job to move on.*

If your software works, the customer is happy, and you've done your best to make sure things are designed well, then it just might be time to move on to the next project. Spending hours trying to write "perfect software" is a waste of time; spending lots of time writing great software and then moving on, is sure to win you **more work**, **big promotions**, and loads of **cash and accolades**.

Knowing when to say "It's good enough!"

> I love it! I can finally sell any kind of instrument I want, and help my clients find just what they're looking for.

Make sure the customer is happy

Before you ever leave a project, you always want to make sure your software does what it's supposed to do.

> Really nice design here. High cohesion, the classes are loosely coupled... I'll bet the next time Rick needs something changed, we won't have too much trouble at all.

Once you've got functionality down, move on to making good design decisions, using solid OO principles to add flexibility.

Make sure your design is flexible

If you've done <u>both</u> of these things, it may just be time to <u>move on</u>... to the next project, the next application, even the next chapter!

Tools for your OOA&D Toolbox

Wow, you've really come a long way since we started working with Rick way back in Chapter 1. You've learned a ton about design, so let's do a quick review of what you've added to your toolbox.

We did a ton of design in this chapter, so take a second to review everything we've learned.

Requirements

Good requirements ensure you[...] works like your customers exp[...]

Make sure your requirements [...] by developing use cases for y[...]

Use your use cases to find ou[...] things your customers forgot[...]

Your use cases will reveal any [...] or missing requirements that [...] have.

Your requirements will always [...] grow) over time.

Analysis and Design

Well-designed software is easy to change and extend.

Use basic OO principles like encapsulation and inheritance to make your software more flexible.

If a design isn't flexible, then <u>CHANGE IT</u>! Never settle on bad design, even if it's <u>your</u> bad design that has to change.

Make sure each of your classes is cohesive: each of your classes should focus on doing ONE THING really well.

Always strive for higher cohesion as you move through your software's design life cycle.

The goal of good design is highly cohesive, loosely coupled software.

OO Principles

Encapsulate what varies.

Code to an interface rather than to an implementation.

Each class in your application should have only one reason to change.

Classes are about behavior and functionality.

Between OO CATASTROPHE! and this chapter, we've added quite a few new OO principles to our toolbox.

OOA&D Cross

This one is a particularly tough puzzle: almost all the answers are more than one word, and they're spread across **both** parts of Chapter 5. Good luck, and keep that left brain working.

Across

3. Never code to this if you can help it.
8. Great software is easy to _____.
12. Software that's easy to change is _____.
13. Do this to what varies.
15. Never be afraid to do this to your designs.
17. This will kill good design.
18. Classes are about this.
19. When one thing is made up of another.

Down

1. Always code to this if possible.
2. Most good designs come from analysis of these.
4. Abstract classes are written this way in UML class diagrams.
5. When a class inherits behavior from another class.
6. This was the type of group ensuring your software was highly cohesive.
7. Apply these to add flexibility to your software.
9. Cohesive classes do this really well.
10. Don't be afraid to do this; it will help you find better solutions.
11. We used this test to see if Rick's application was cohesive.
14. Highly cohesive software is also almost always _____ coupled.
16. Great software must always do what it is _____ to do.

Exercise Solutions

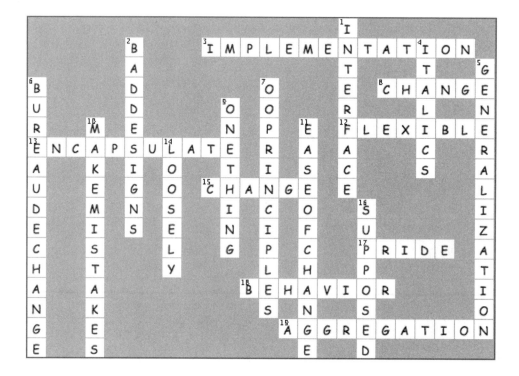

6 solving really big problems

"My Name is Art Vandelay... I am an Architect"

I was just thinking... do you remember if we ever tightened the bolts down on those basement girders? Oh well...

It's time to build something REALLY BIG. Are you ready?

You've got a ton of tools in your OOA&D toolbox, but how do you use those tools when you have to build something **really big**? Well, you may not realize it, but **you've got everything you need** to handle big problems. We'll learn about some new tools, like **domain analysis** and **use case diagrams**, but even these new tools are based on things you already know about—like listening to the customer and understanding what you're going to build before you start writing code. Get ready... it's time to start playing the architect.

Look, all this stuff about writing great software sounds terrific, but *real* applications have a lot more than five or ten classes. How am I supposed to turn **big applications** into great software?

You solve <u>big problems</u> the same way you solve <u>small problems</u>.

We've been working with fairly simple applications so far... Rick's guitar shop had less than fifteen classes in its worst state, and Doug's dog door never had more than five. But everything you've learned so far applies to working with big applications, too.

Remember these steps to writing great software? They all apply to working with huge, 1000+ class applications just as much as when you're working with just a couple of classes.

1. Make sure your software does what the customer wants it to do.

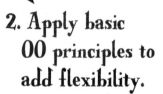

2. Apply basic OO principles to add flexibility.

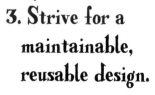

3. Strive for a maintainable, reusable design.

It's all in how you <u>look</u> <u>at</u> the big problem

Think about how you work on big problems, in big software applications. You usually look at the big picture, but then start working on just one part of the application's functionality.

The best way to look at a big <u>problem</u> is to see it as lots of individual pieces of functionality.

You can treat each of those pieces as an <u>individual</u> <u>problem</u> to solve, and apply the things you already know.

Once you get one part of an application working like you want it to, then you can move on to another piece of functionality within the app. At each step, though, you're applying the same basic principles we've been talking about for the last 250 pages or so.

You can solve a big problem by breaking it into lots of functional pieces, and then working on each of those pieces individually.

This BIG PROBLEM is really just a collection of functionalities, where each piece of functionality is really a smaller problem on its own.

Small Problem

Small Problem

Small Problem

Small Problem

Small Problem

Big Problem

The things you already know...

You've already learned a lot of things that will help you solve big software problems... you just may not have realized it. Let's take a quick look at some of the things we already know about how to write great (big) software:

Using encapsulation helps with big problems, too. The more you encapsulate things, the easier it will be for you to break a large app up into different pieces of functionality.

By encapsulating what varies, you make your application more flexible, and easier to change.

Coding to an interface, rather than to an implementation, makes your software easier to extend.

The best way to get good requirements is to understand what a system is supposed to do.

If you know what each small piece of your app's functionality should do, then it's easy to combine those parts into a big app that does what it's supposed to do.

This is even more important in big apps. By coding to an interface, you reduce dependencies between different parts of your application... and "loosely coupled" is always a good thing, remember?

Analysis helps you ensure your system works in a real-world context.

This sure doesn't change with bigger problems. In fact, the higher the cohesion of your app, the more independent each piece of functionality is, and the easier it is to work on those pieces one at a time.

Analysis is even more important with large software... and in most cases, you start by analyzing individual pieces of functionality, and then analyzing the interaction of those pieces.

Great software is easy to change and extend, and does what the customer wants it to do.

Got a big problem? Take a few of these little principles, and call me in the morning. I bet you'll have things under control in no time.

So let's solve a <u>BIG</u> problem!

Enough about what you already know; let's see how we can apply these things to a brand new, really big piece of software. Turn the page to learn a bit about Gary, his new game company, and a large software project.

Here's the big problem we're going to be working on for the next few chapters.

Gary's Games
Vision Statement

Gary's Games provides frameworks that game designers can use to create turn-based strategy games. Unlike arcade-style shoot-'em-up games and games that rely on audio and video features to engage the player, our games will focus on the technical details of strategy and tactics. Our framework provides the bookkeeping details to make building a particular game easy, while removing the burden of coding repetitive tasks from the game design.

The game system framework (GSF) will provide the core of all of Gary's Games. It will be delivered as a library of classes with a well-defined API that should be usable by all board game development project teams within the company. The framework will provide standard capabilities for:

- Defining and representing a board configuration
- Defining troops and configuring armies or other fighting units
- Moving units on the board
- Determining legal moves
- Conducting battles
- Providing unit information

The GSF will simplify the task of developing a turn-based strategic board game so that the users of the GSF can devote their time to implementing the actual games.

I'm not interested in one of those fancy, flashy Star Wars rip-off games... I want something with strategy, that makes you think! A cool turn-based war game, that's the ticket.

This is Gary. He looks pretty serious, but he's an absolute nut for strategy games.

Sharpen your pencil

What should we do first?

Below are several things that you might start out doing to get going on Gary's Games. Check the boxes next to the things *you think* we should start with.

☐ Talk to Gary.

☐ Gather requirements.

☐ Start a class diagram.

☐ Talk to people who might use the framework.

☐ Write use cases.

☐ Start a package diagram.

Hey, this is an easy one.
We start out by writing out the
requirements and use cases, like we did
with Doug's Dog Doors.

One of the
programmers on
your team.

Requirements and use cases are a good place to start...

Starting out working on a system by
building a requirements list and writing
use cases is a great idea. You can figure out
what a system is supposed to do, and just
go down your list adding functionality bit
by bit... solving lots of small problems to
solve one really big problem.

But I'm not sure we really
have enough information to figure out
the requirements or use cases yet... all
we've got is that fancy vision statement.
But that really doesn't tell us much about
what the system we're building is
supposed to do.

...but what do we **really** know about the system so far?

That vision statement seemed to have a
lot of information about what Gary wants,
but it leaves a lot open to interpretation.

What kind of board did Gary have in
mind? And who's the customer, really?
Game players or game designers? And
will all the games be historically based, or
do we have to support things like lasers
and spaceships? It sounds like there's a lot
more we need to know before we can write
a very good set of requirements.

We need a **lot** more information

All we've got to go on with Gary's system so far is a vision statement... and that didn't tell us very much at all. So now we've got to figure out what the system is supposed to do. So how do we do *that*?

This is called **commonality**... what things are <u>similar</u>?

What is the system **like?**

One way you can find out more about a system is to figure out what the system is <u>like</u>. In other words, are there some things that you <u>do</u> <u>know</u> <u>about</u> that the system functions or behaves like?

This is called **variability**... what things are <u>different</u>?

What is the system <u>not</u> **like?**

Another great way to find out what a system should do is to figure out what it's <u>not</u> like. This helps you determine what you <u>don't</u> <u>need</u> to worry about in your system.

So let's listen in on one of Gary's meetings, and see what we can find out...

Customer Conversation

We need to listen in a little more on what Gary and his team are planning before we can get started on the game system framework he wants us to build.

> Remember that old computer game, Zork? Everybody loved that thing, even though it was pure text.

We've already found some *commonality!* The system has an interface sort of like this Zork game.

Bob in marketing.

Bethany in design.

Susan and Tom in sales.

Tom: Yeah, Gary loves text-based games. And people are getting a little tired of all the fancy graphics in games like Star Wars episode 206 (or whatever the heck they're up to these days).

Here's some variability. The system is <u>not</u> a graphic-rich game.

Bethany: And we need all sorts of different time periods. We could have a Civil War version, with battles at Antietam and Vicksburg, and a World War I version over in Europe... players will love all the historical stuff, I'll bet.

Flexbililty is going to be key if we're going to support all these variations.

Susan: Nice idea, Beth! I'll bet we can let game designers create add-on packs, too, so you could buy a World War II: Allies game, and then buy an add-on for other forces that the core game didn't include.

Bob: That's a cool marketing point, too... if our system supports different time periods, unit types, uniforms, and offensives, we're going to be able to sell this to almost anyone developing games.

Bethany: Do you think we need to worry about battles that aren't historical? I mean, we could sell our system to the folks that make the fancy starship games, and let them create sci-fi battles, right?

Tom: Hmmm... I'll bet Gary would go for that, if they're still creating turn-based games. Why not clean up on that market as well as the history buffs?

Bob: Do you think we could market this as a system to create everything from online Risk to a modern-day Stratego? Those were both killer strategy board games back in the day... I'd love to sell our system to people that make those sorts of games.

A little more commonality... so we're really aiming at turn-based wargames.

Bethany: So let's talk details. We know we've got to sell this to lots of game designers, so we need it to be really flexible. I'm thinking we start with a nice square board, and fill it up with square tiles.

Tom: We can let the game designers pick how many tiles on the board, right? They can choose a height and width, or something like that?

OK, now we're starting to get some ideas about actual features of the game system.

Bethany: Yeah. And then we should support all different types of terrains: mountains, rivers, plains, grass...

Susan: ...maybe space or craters or asteroid or something for the space games...

Bob: Even underwater tiles, like seaweed or silt or something, right?

Bethany: Those are great ideas! So we just need a basic tile that can be customized and extended, and a board that we can fill with all the different tiles.

Susan: Do we have to worry about all those movement rules and things that these games usually have?

Tom: I think we have to, don't we? Don't most of these strategy games have all sorts of complicated rules, like a unit can only move so many tiles because he's carrying too much weight, or whatever?

Strategy games again... we definitely have some commonality with that type of game to pay attention to.

Bethany: I think most of the rules depend on the specific game, though. I think we should leave that up to the game designers who use our framework. All our framework should do is keep track of whose turn it is to move, and handle basic movement stuff.

Susan: This is great. We can build a framework for challenging, fun strategy games, and make a ton of money, too.

Bob: This is starting to sound pretty cool! Let's get this to Gary and those software guys he's hired, so they can get started.

> So did you get all that? You're ready to start working on my new game system now, right?

Figure out the features

You've learned a lot about what Gary and his team want the game system framework to do, so let's take that information and figure out the *features* of the system.

Bethany said the game system should support different time periods. That's a feature of the game system.

> **Bethany:** And we need all sorts of <u>different</u> <u>time</u> <u>periods</u>. We could have a Civil War version, with battles at Antietam and Vicksburg, and a World War I version over in Africa and Italy... players will love all the historical stuff, I'll bet.

Here's another feature: different types of terrain. This single feature will probably create several individual requirements.

> **Bethany:** Yeah. And then we should support all <u>different</u> <u>types</u> <u>of</u> terrains: mountains, rivers, plains, grass...
>
> **Susan:** ...maybe space or craters or asteroid or something for the space games...
>
> **Bob:** Even underwater tiles, like seaweed or silt or something, right?

But what is a feature, anyway?

A feature is just a *high-level description* of something a system needs to do. You usually get features from talking to your customers (or listening in on their conversations, like we just did on the last few pages).

A lot of times, you can take one feature, and come up with several different requirements that you can use to satisfy that feature. So figuring out a system's features is a great way to start to get a handle on your requirements.

Starting with the features of a system is really helpful in big projects—like Gary's game system—when you don't have tons of details, and just need to get a handle on where to start.

Feature (from customer)   **Requirement (for developer)**

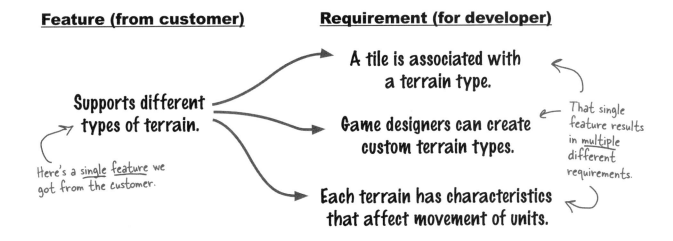

Supports different types of terrain.

Here's a single feature we got from the customer.

A tile is associated with a terrain type.

Game designers can create custom terrain types.

That single feature results in multiple different requirements.

Each terrain has characteristics that affect movement of units.

Get features from the customer, and then figure out the requirements you need to implement those features.

Sharpen your pencil

We need a list of features for Gary's game system.

You've got plenty of information from Gary and his team, and now you know how to turn that information into a set of features. Your job is to fill in the blanks below with some of the features you think Gary's game system framework should have.

_____   _____
_____   _____

_____   _____
_____   _____

_____   _____
_____   _____

Sharpen your pencil
answers

We need a list of features for Gary's game system.

You've got plenty of information from Gary and his team, and now you know how to turn that information into a set of features. Your job is to fill in the blanks below with some of the features you think Gary's game system framework should have.

Supports different types of terrain.

Supports multiple types of troops or units that are game-specific.

Each game has a board, made up of square tiles, each with a terrain type.

Supports different time periods, including fictional periods like sci-fi and fantasy.

Supports add-on modules for additional campaigns or battle scenarios.

The framework keeps up with whose turn it is and coordinates basic movement.

It's OK if these aren't the exact features you got, or if you had more detailed things in this list. These are just what we came up with.

> This all seems pretty arbitrary... some of those features look just like requirements. What's the big difference between calling something a feature, and calling something a requirement?

Don't get hung up on the "difference" between a feature and a requirement.

Lots of people use "feature" to mean different things, so it's not a term you should get too worked up about. For some people, a feature *is* a requirement; and you'll even hear some people say "feature requirement," which really can get confusing.

Others think of features as higher-level than requirement, which is how we've been talking about them. So it might take several requirements to satisfy one feature of a system.

The main thing is that if you're stuck on where to get started, especially with a big project, you can gather features (or requirements!) to get a handle on the high-level things you know you'll need to take care of in the system you're building.

Q: So there's no difference between a feature and a requirement?

A: Well, this really depends on who you ask. For some people, a feature is a "big" thing that a system does, like "support different types of terrain." But to put that feature into place, there are lots of "small" things that the system must do, like "define a base terrain type" and "allow developers to extend the base terrain type" and "allow each tile to contain multiple terrain types." All of these little things are considered requirements. So a single feature is satisfied by several requirements, like this:

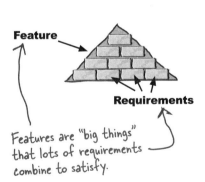

Features are "big things" that lots of requirements combine to satisfy.

Q: You said, "some people." So there are other ways to look at features and requirements?

A: Right. A lot of other people don't make such a distinction between a feature and a requirement. One feature might be "supports different time periods" (which is a pretty big thing), and another might be "allow for water as a type of terrain" (which is a pretty small, specific thing). In this approach, there's not really a big difference between what a feature is and what a requirement is. So these people see things a lot more like this:

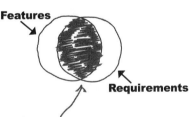

In this approach, there's a lot of overlap in what a feature is, and what a requirement is. The two terms are more or less interchangeable.

Q: So which is right?

A: Both! Or neither, if you prefer. There's no "one right way" to think about features and requirements, especially if you don't want to waste lots of time arguing over definitions with your programmer buddies. You're better off thinking about both features and requirements as the things your system needs to do. If you want to consider features the "big picture" things, and requirements the "smaller, more detailed" things, that's OK... just don't get into any barroom fights over it, alright?

Can't we all just get along?

OK, so we've got the feature and requirement thing figured out. **Now** we can write some use cases, right?

Use cases don't always help you see the <u>big picture</u>.

When you start to write use cases, you're really getting into a lot of detail about what the system should do. The problem is that can cause you to lose sight of the big picture. In Gary's game system, we're really not ready for a lot of detail... we're just trying to figure out what the framework actually is at this point.

So even though you *could* start writing use cases, that probably won't help you figure out exactly what you're trying to build, from the big-picture point of view. When you're working on a system, it's a good idea to <u>defer</u> <u>details</u> as long as you can... you won't get caught up in the *little things* when you should be working on the *big things*.

Always <u>defer</u> <u>details</u> as long as you can.

If we did write use cases for Gary's game system, who would the actors be?

So what **are** we supposed to do now? You've been telling us we need to know what the system is supposed to do for like 200 pages now, and suddenly use cases aren't a good idea? What gives?

You <u>still</u> need to know what your system is supposed to do... but you need a <u>BIG-PICTURE</u> view.

Even though use cases might be a little too focused on the details for where we are in designing the system right now, you still need to have a good understanding of what your system needs to do. So you need a way to focus on the big picture, and figure out what your system should do, while still avoiding getting into too much detail.

Ever hear that a picture is worth a thousand words?

Let's see if we can <u>show</u> what the system is supposed to do.

Use case diagrams

Sometimes you need to know what a system does,
but don't want to get into all the detail that use cases
require. When you're in a situation like this, a use case
diagram could be just what you need:

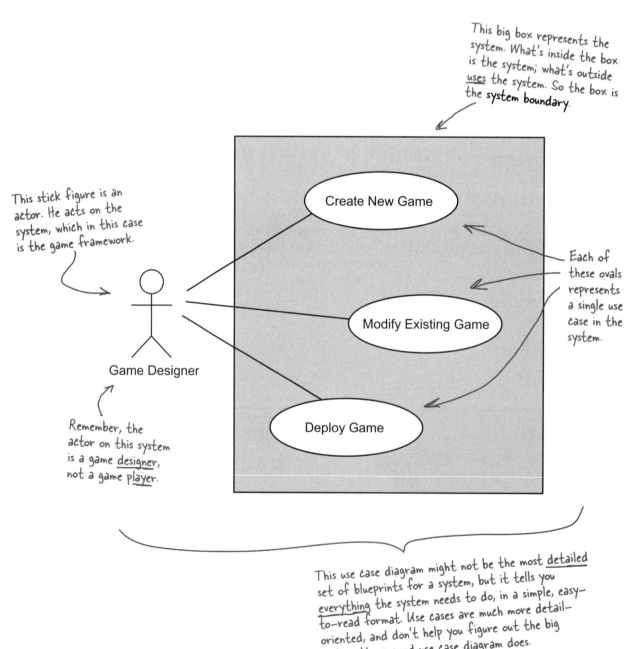

This big box represents the
system. What's inside the box
is the system; what's outside
<u>uses</u> the system. So the box is
the **system boundary**.

This stick figure is an
actor. He acts on the
system, which in this case
is the game framework.

Create New Game

Each of
these ovals
represents
a single use
case in the
system.

Modify Existing Game

Game Designer

Deploy Game

Remember, the
actor on this system
is a game <u>designer</u>,
not a game pl<u>ayer</u>.

This use case diagram might not be the most <u>detailed</u>
set of blueprints for a system, but it tells you
<u>everything</u> the system needs to do, in a simple, easy-
to-read format. Use cases are much more detail-
oriented, and don't help you figure out the big
picture like a good use case diagram does.

OK, this is just plain **stupid**. What good does that diagram do us? Do we really need to draw a picture to figure out that game designers are going to create and modify games?

Use case diagrams are the blueprints for your system.

Remember, our focus here is on the *big picture*. That use case diagram may seem sort of vague, but it does help you keep your eye on the fundamental things that your system *must* do. Without it, you could easily get so caught up in the details of how a designer creates a new game that you completely forget that they need to actually *deploy* that game. With a use case diagram, you'll never forget about the big picture.

But what about all those features we worked so hard to figure out? They don't even show up on the use case diagram!

Use your feature list to make sure your use case diagram is complete.

Once you have your features and a use case diagram, you can make sure you're building a system that will do everything it needs to. Take your use case diagram, and make sure that all the use cases you listed will cover all the features you got from the customer. Then you'll know that your diagram—the blueprints for your system—is complete, and you can start building the system.

Feature Magnets

It's time to match up the game framework's features to the use cases in your use case diagram. Place the magnet for each feature on the use case that will handle that feature. If your use case diagram is complete, then you should be able to attach each feature magnet to a use case on your diagram. Good luck!

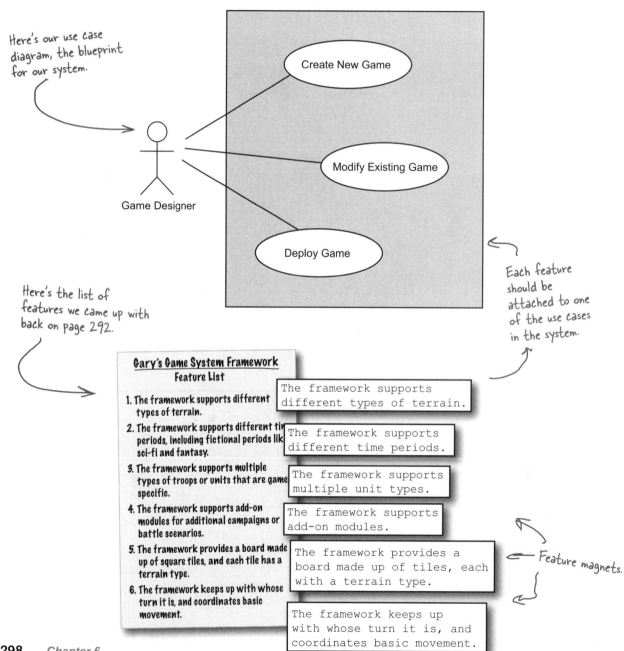

Here's our use case diagram, the blueprint for our system.

Game Designer

Create New Game

Modify Existing Game

Deploy Game

Each feature should be attached to one of the use cases in the system.

Here's the list of features we came up with back on page 292.

Gary's Game System Framework
Feature List

1. The framework supports different types of terrain.
2. The framework supports different time periods, including fictional periods like sci-fi and fantasy.
3. The framework supports multiple types of troops or units that are game specific.
4. The framework supports add-on modules for additional campaigns or battle scenarios.
5. The framework provides a board made up of square tiles, and each tile has a terrain type.
6. The framework keeps up with whose turn it is, and coordinates basic movement.

The framework supports different types of terrain.

The framework supports different time periods.

The framework supports multiple unit types.

The framework supports add-on modules.

The framework provides a board made up of tiles, each with a terrain type.

The framework keeps up with whose turn it is, and coordinates basic movement.

Feature magnets.

Q: **So an actor is a person that uses the system?**

A: An actor is actually any external entity (it doesn't have to be a person) that interacts with the system. So in a cash machine, you'd obviously have a person that uses the system as an actor, but you might also have the bank as an actor, because it deposits money in the system. If it's not part of the system but acts on the system, it's an actor.

Q: **What's the box around everything for? And why are the actors outside of the box?**

A: The box shows the boundaries of the system. So you have to code up everything *inside* the box, but you don't have to worry about the stuff *outside* the box. The actors—the game designers using your framework—are outside of the box because they use your system; they're not part of it.

Q: **And each circle is a use case?**

A: Right. That's part of why use case diagrams are great for getting a handle on the big picture: they can show you multiple use cases, and how all those use cases work together to do really big tasks. It also helps you avoid getting into details about a particular requirement too early (like now, when you should be worrying about the overall system design).

Q: **I've seen use case diagrams with lines marked with <<include>> and <<extend>>. What's that about?**

A: UML and use case diagrams do define ways to specify what kinds of relationships exist between use cases. So you could say that one use case includes another, or that one use case extends another. That's what the **<<include>>** and **<<extend>>** keywords mean.

However, it's easy to spend a lot of time arguing over whether a use case extends this use case, or includes that one. And suddenly, you're spending your time on how a tile can support mountains or units need to carry a backpack, instead of focusing on the bigger picture. You can use **<<include>>** and **<<extend>>**, but it's really not that big of a deal, and those keywords should <u>never</u> distract from the overall design process.

Q: **So use case diagrams are more about a general picture of the system than including lots of little details?**

A: Now you've got it! If you're worrying too much about what to call a use case, or whether you should use a particular relationship between use cases, you've lost sight of the big picture. Use your use case diagrams to get a clear 10,000-foot view of your system, nothing more.

Thanks for all the info, but can we get back to that Feature Magnets exercise? I'm stuck trying to match one of the features to a use case...

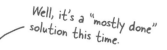

Well, it's a "mostly done" solution this time.

Feature Magnets Solutions

It's time to match up the game framework's features to the use cases in your use case diagram. Were you able to find a use case for each feature in the game framework?

Almost all of the features have to do with a game designer creating a new game.

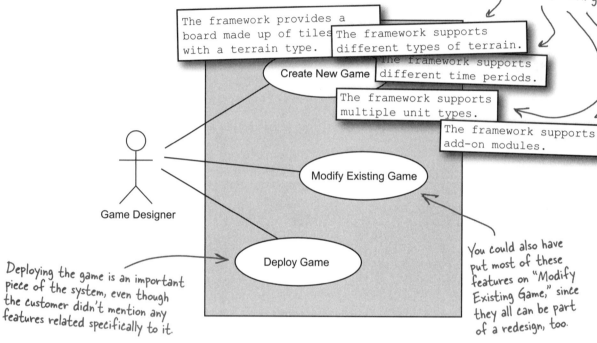

The framework provides a board made up of tiles with a terrain type.

The framework supports different types of terrain.

The framework supports different time periods.

The framework supports multiple unit types.

The framework supports add-on modules.

Create New Game

Modify Existing Game

Game Designer

Deploy Game

Deploying the game is an important piece of the system, even though the customer didn't mention any features related specifically to it.

You could also have put most of these features on "Modify Existing Game," since they all can be part of a redesign, too.

But there's one feature still left... what up with that?

The framework keeps up with whose turn it is, and coordinates basic movement.

There's probably one feature you had some trouble placing on the use case diagram. Think about this feature carefully: it's really *not* something the game designer directly interacts with or worries about, because the functionality is already taken care of.

So how is this feature related to the system? And what actors are involved? And are we missing some use cases in our diagram?

What do you think?

We know this is a feature, but why doesn't it have a place in our blueprints?

The Little Actor

A small Socratic exercise in the style of The Little Lisper

What system are you designing?	A game framework, duh!
So what is the point of the framework?	To let game designers build games.
So the game designer is an actor on the system?	Yes. I've got that in my use case diagram.
And what does the game designer do with the framework?	Design games. I thought we established that!
Is the game the same as the framework?	Well, no, I suppose not.
Why not?	The game is complete, and you can actually play it. All the framework provides is a foundation for the game to be built on.
So the framework is a set of tools for the game designer?	No, it's more than that. I mean, the feature I'm stuck on is something the framework handles for each individual game. So it's more than just tools for the designer.
Interesting. So the framework is part of the game, then?	Well, I guess so. But it's like a lower level, like it just provides some basic services to the game. The game sort of sits on top of the framework.
So the game actually uses the framework?	Yes, exactly.
Then the game actually uses the system you're building?	Right, that's just what I said. Oh, wait... then...
...if the game uses the system, what is it?	An actor! The game is an actor!

Actors are people, too
(well, not always)

It turns out that in addition to the game designer,
the game itself is an actor on the framework you're
building. Let's see how we can add a new actor to our
use case diagram:

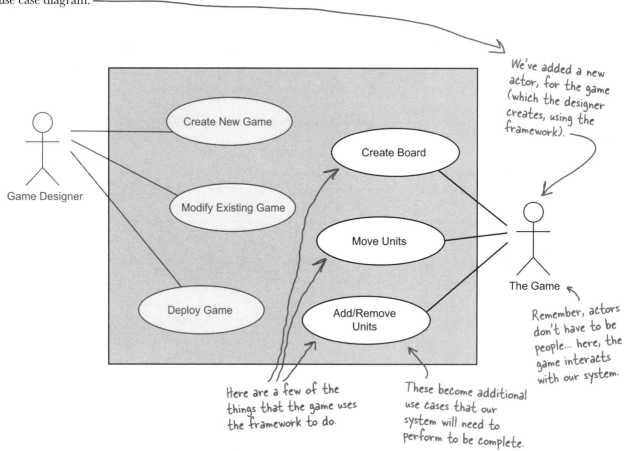

We've added a new
actor, for the game
(which the designer
creates, using the
framework).

Game Designer

Create New Game

Create Board

Modify Existing Game

Move Units

Deploy Game

Add/Remove
Units

The Game

Remember, actors
don't have to be
people... here, the
game interacts
with our system.

Here are a few of the
things that the game uses
the framework to do.

These become additional
use cases that our
system will need to
perform to be complete.

Do these new use cases
take care of the feature we
couldn't find a place for?

```
The framework keeps up
with whose turn it is, and
coordinates basic movement.
```

Use case diagram... check!
Features covered... check!

With a new actor in place, we can finally take our use
case diagrams and our features, and match them all up.

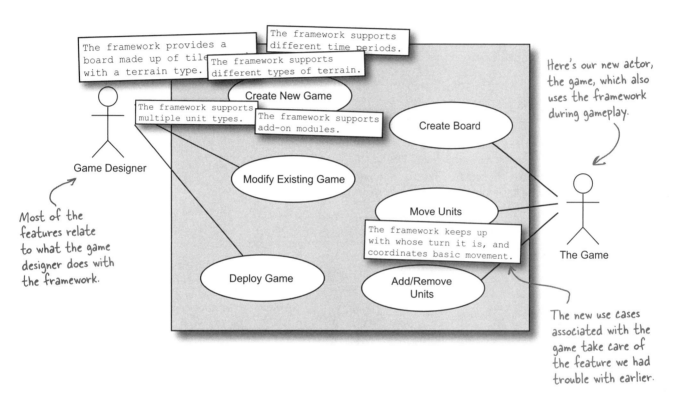

The framework provides a
board made up of tile
with a terrain type.

The framework supports
different time periods.

The framework supports
different types of terrain.

The framework supports
multiple unit types.

The framework supports
add-on modules.

Here's our new actor,
the game, which also
uses the framework
during gameplay.

Game Designer

Most of the
features relate
to what the game
designer does with
the framework.

Create New Game

Create Board

Modify Existing Game

Move Units

The framework keeps up
with whose turn it is, and
coordinates basic movement.

The Game

Deploy Game

Add/Remove
Units

The new use cases
associated with the
game take care of
the feature we had
trouble with earlier.

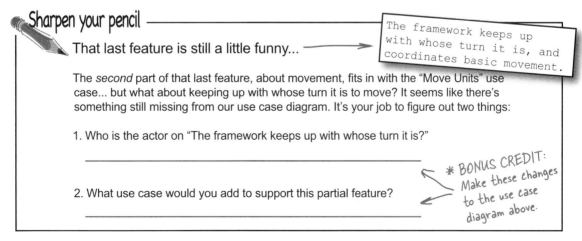

Sharpen your pencil

That last feature is still a little funny...

The framework keeps up
with whose turn it is, and
coordinates basic movement.

The *second* part of that last feature, about movement, fits in with the "Move Units" use
case... but what about keeping up with whose turn it is to move? It seems like there's
something still missing from our use case diagram. It's your job to figure out two things:

1. Who is the actor on "The framework keeps up with whose turn it is?"

_____

2. What use case would you add to support this partial feature?

_____

* BONUS CREDIT:
Make these changes
to the use case
diagram above.

Sharpen your pencil
answers

> The framework keeps up with whose turn it is, and coordinates basic movement.

That last feature is still a little funny...

The *second* part of that last feature, about movement, fits in with the "Move Units" use case... but what about keeping up with whose turn it is to move? It seems like there's something still missing on our use case diagram. It's your job to figure out two things:

1. Who is the actor on "The framework keeps up with whose turn it is?"

   The game is still the actor... it's using the framework to handle managing whose turn it is.

2. What use case would you add to support this partial feature?

   We need a use case for "Take Turn" where the framework handles basic turn duties, and lets the custom game handle the specifics of that process.

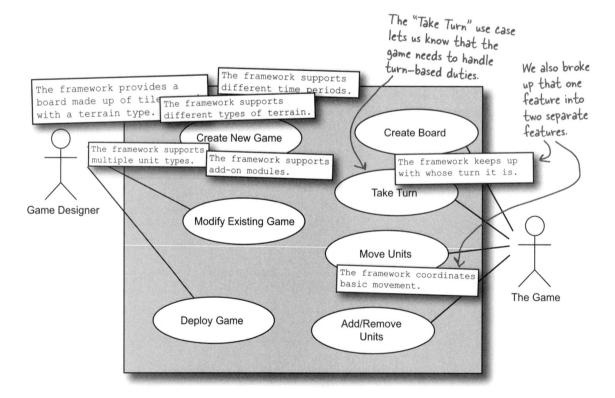

The "Take Turn" use case lets us know that the game needs to handle turn-based duties.

We also broke up that one feature into two separate features.

The framework provides a board made up of tiles with a terrain type.

The framework supports different time periods.

The framework supports different types of terrain.

Create New Game

The framework supports multiple unit types.

The framework supports add-on modules.

Create Board

The framework keeps up with whose turn it is.

Take Turn

Game Designer

Modify Existing Game

Move Units

The framework coordinates basic movement.

The Game

Deploy Game

Add/Remove Units

So what exactly have we done?

You've got a list of features that Gary's game system framework needs to support, and that tells you all the major pieces of the system you need to build. This is a lot like the requirements list you built way back in Chapter 2 for Todd and Gina's dog door... except it focuses on the big picture.

Use a feature or requirement list to capture the <u>BIG</u> <u>THINGS</u> that your system needs to do.

Once you've got your features and requirements mapped out, you need to get a basic idea of how the system is going to be put together. Use cases are often too detailed at this stage, so a use case diagram can help you see what a system is like at 10,000 feet... kind of like a blueprint for your application.

Draw a use case diagram to show what your system <u>IS</u> without getting into unnecessary detail.

Here's our feature list... the system <u>has</u> to do these things.

Gary's Game System Framework
Feature List

1. The framework supports different types of terrain.
2. The framework supports different time periods, including fictional periods like sci-fi and fantasy.
3. The framework supports multiple types of troops or units that are game-specific.
4. The framework supports add-on modules for additional campaigns or battle scenarios.
5. The framework provides a board made up of square tiles, and each tile has a terrain type.
6. The framework keeps up with whose turn it is.
7. The framework coordinates basic movement.

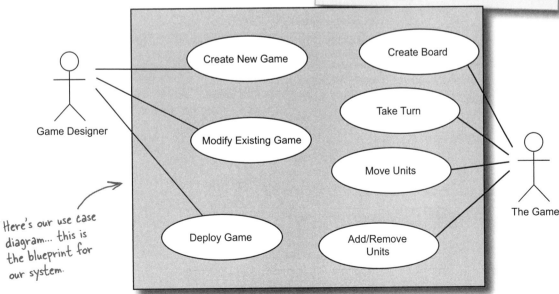

Here's our use case diagram... this is the blueprint for our system.

Cubicle Conversation

Jim

Frank

> Isn't it about time we started actually talking about code? I mean, I get that we need a feature list, and use case diagrams, and all that, but at some point we have to actually build something, you know?

Frank: I don't know, Jim. I think we *have* been talking about code.

Jim: How do you figure that? I mean, what line of code is "framework supports different types of terrain" really going to turn into?

Frank: You're talking about those features we figured out, right? Well, that's not just one line of code, but it certainly is a big chunk of code, right?

Jim: Sure... but when do we get to talk about what classes we need to write, and the packages we put those classes into?

Frank: We're getting to that, definitely. But the customer really doesn't understand what most of that stuff means... we'd never be sure we were building the right thing if we started talking about classes and variables.

Jim: What about class diagrams? We could use those to show what we're going to code, couldn't we?

Frank: Well, we could... but do you think the customer would understand that much better? That's really what domain analysis is all about. We can talk to the customer about their system, in terms that they understand. For Gary, that means talking about units, and terrain, and tiles, instead of classes, objects, and methods.

Domain analysis lets you check your designs, and still speak the customer's language.

Let's do a little <u>domain</u> <u>analysis</u>!

Let's put all these things we've figured out about the game system together, in a way that Gary, our customer, will actually understand. This is a process called **domain analysis**, and just means that we're describing a problem using terms the customer will understand.

The <u>domain</u> here is game systems.

These features are using terms that the <u>customer</u> understands.

Gary's Game System Framework
Feature List

1. The framework supports different types of terrain.
2. The framework supports different time periods, including fictional periods like sci-fi and fantasy.

1946

3. The framework supports multiple types of troops or units that are game-specific.
4. The framework supports add-on modules for additional campaigns or battle scenarios.
5. The framework provides a board made up of square tiles, and each tile has a terrain type.
6. The framework keeps up with whose turn it is.
7. The framework coordinates basic movement.

This whole feature list is a form of <u>analysis</u>, just like we've been doing in earlier chapters.

the Scholar's Corner

domain analysis. The process of <u>identifying</u>, <u>collecting</u>, <u>organizing</u>, and <u>representing</u> the <u>relevant</u> information of a <u>domain</u>, based upon the study of existing systems and their development histories, knowledge captured from domain experts, underlying theory, and emerging technology within a domain.

What <u>most</u> people give the customer...

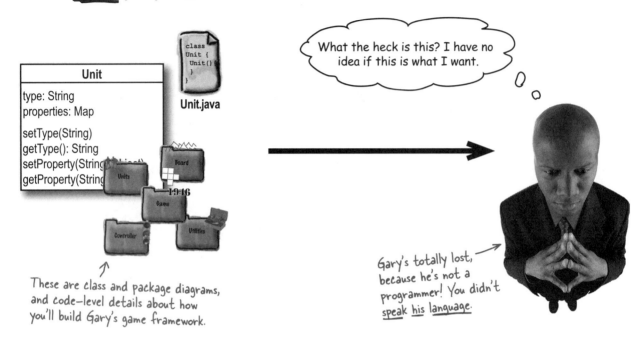

What the heck is this? I have no idea if this is what I want.

These are class and package diagrams, and code-level details about how you'll build Gary's game framework.

Gary's totally lost, because he's not a programmer! You didn't <u>speak</u> <u>his</u> <u>language</u>.

What <u>we're</u> giving the customer...

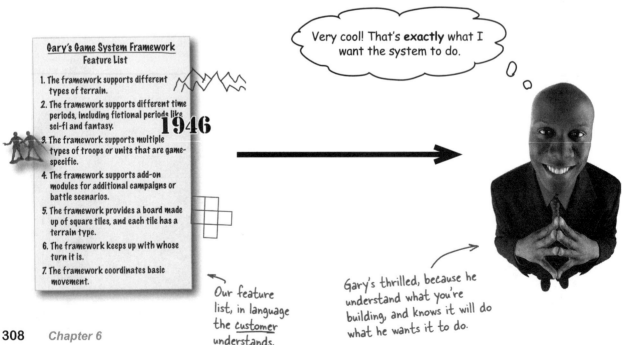

Very cool! That's **exactly** what I want the system to do.

Gary's Game System Framework
Feature List

1. The framework supports different types of terrain.
2. The framework supports different time periods, including fictional periods like sci-fi and fantasy.
3. The framework supports multiple types of troops or units that are game-specific.
4. The framework supports add-on modules for additional campaigns or battle scenarios.
5. The framework provides a board made up of square tiles, and each tile has a terrain type.
6. The framework keeps up with whose turn it is.
7. The framework coordinates basic movement.

1946

Our feature list, in language the <u>customer</u> understands.

Gary's thrilled, because he understand what you're building, and knows it will do what he wants it to do.

Now divide and conquer

With the customer onboard, and a nice completed set of blueprints, you're ready to start breaking up your big problem into different pieces of functionality—and then you can use what you've learned already to tackle each of those pieces of functionality, one at a time.

Here's a rough drawing of some of the core parts of the game framework.

Time Periods

We may not need to do much here... as long as we support different terrains, unit types, and weapons, this should come naturally.

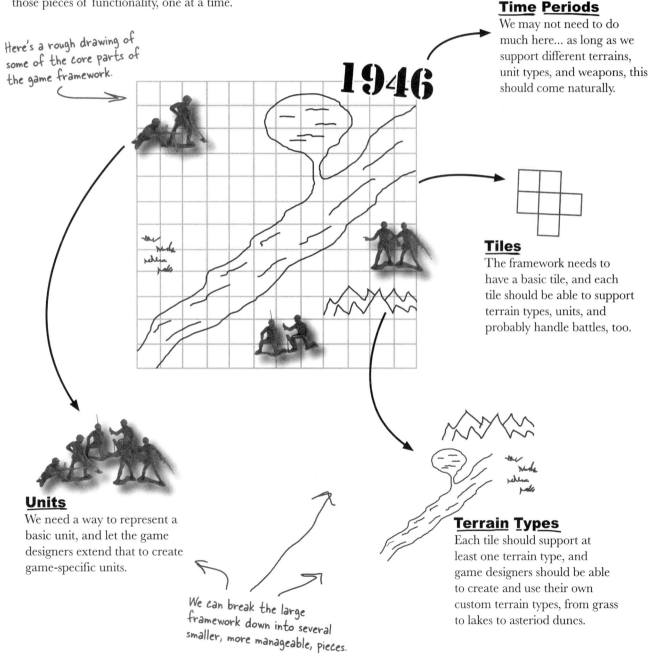

1946

Tiles

The framework needs to have a basic tile, and each tile should be able to support terrain types, units, and probably handle battles, too.

Units

We need a way to represent a basic unit, and let the game designers extend that to create game-specific units.

We can break the large framework down into several smaller, more manageable, pieces.

Terrain Types

Each tile should support at least one terrain type, and game designers should be able to create and use their own custom terrain types, from grass to lakes to asteriod dunes.

The Big Break-Up

It's time to break up our big problem—Gary's game framework—into lots of smaller pieces of functionality. You've already seen how we can divide the game and its features into some basic groups of functionality, so you're already well on your way.

Below are the features and diagrams we've been using throughout this chapter to show what Gary's system needs to do. You need to look at these, and figure out what modules you want to use to handle all this functionality, and how you want to split the features and requirements up. Make sure your modules cover everything you think the game framework will need to do!

Gary's Game System Framework
Feature List

1. The framework supports different types of terrain.
2. The framework supports different time periods, including fictional periods like sci-fi and fantasy.
3. The framework supports multiple types of troops or units that are game-specific.
4. The framework supports add-on modules for additional campaigns or battle scenarios.
5. The framework provides a board made up of square tiles, and each tile has a terrain type.
6. The framework keeps up with whose turn it is.
7. The framework coordinates basic movement.

Here's the game board to remind you of some of the major areas to focus on... but remember, this isn't everything!

You need to address all the features in the system...

...as well as the functionality laid out in your use case diagram.

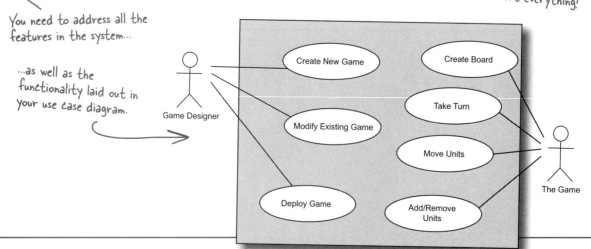

We've added a "Units" module to get you started. This would be where classes representing troops, armies, and related functionality would go.

Units

For each package/module, write in what you think that module should focus on.

You can add more modules if you need, or use less modules than we've provided. It's all up to you!

We have **BIG** problems, and I just can't handle them. It's time to break up.

Our Big Break-Up

Here's what we did to handle all the features of Gary's system, and to break the big problem up into several smaller, more manageable pieces of functionality.

Units

This takes care of troops, armies, and all the units used in a game.

1946

Game

We're using a Game module to store basic classes that can be extended by designers. These relate to the time period of the game, basic properties of the game, and anything else that sets up the basic structure of each game.

The board module handles the board itself, tiles, terrain, and other classes related to creating the actual board used in each game.

Board

We chose to NOT have a module just for terrain, or tiles, since there would only be one or two classes in those modules. Instead, we tied that all into the Board module.

Utilities

It's always a good idea to have a Utilities module, to store tools and helper classes that are shared across modules.

Controller

Here's where we can handle the turns of each player, basic movement, and anything else related to keeping a game actually going. This module is sort of the "traffic cop" for the games that designers create.

Relax

There's no single RIGHT answer to this exercise!

It's OK if your answers don't match up with ours exactly. There are lots of ways to design a system, and this is just the one we chose. What you do need to worry about is that you've covered all the features and use cases with your design, and that it makes sense... you don't want a module to have just one class in it, or one that will have one or two hundred.

Dude, this game is gonna **SUCK**! You don't even have a graphics package... even if it's not all fancy, I've gotta at least be able to see the freaking board and units.

Tony may know a lot about what makes for a killer game, but he's *not* your customer!

Don't forget who your customer **really** is

It might seem like Tony has a good point... until you remember who the customer for Gary's game system framework really is. Your job is to write a framework for game designers, not to create actual games. Every game's user interface will be different, so it's up to the game designer to take care of graphics, not you.

Domain analysis helps you avoid building parts of a system that <u>aren't</u> <u>your</u> job <u>to</u> <u>build</u>.

This is something that the game designer would create... it's not your responsibility.

Take a close look at the modules and groupings in the game system framework. Do you recognize a commonly used design pattern?

Here's a hint for you Head First Design Patterns readers.

You know, once the game designer adds in a Graphics module, this looks an awful lot like the Model-View-Controller pattern.

Most people refer to this as the MVC pattern.

It's the <u>M</u>odel-<u>V</u>iew-<u>C</u>ontroller Pattern!

Here's the game <u>controller</u> that we're going to write. It handles basic turns and figuring out what needs to happen with boards, units, etc.

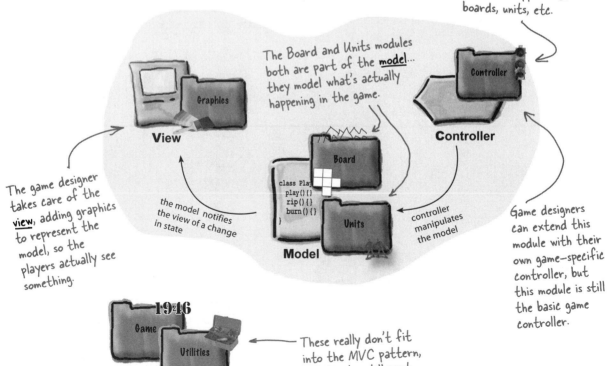

The Board and Units modules both are part of the **model**... they model what's actually happening in the game.

The game designer takes care of the <u>view</u>, adding graphics to represent the model, so the players actually see something.

the model notifies the view of a change in state

controller manipulates the model

View

Model

Controller

```
class Play
    play(){}
    rip(){}
    burn(){}
}
```

Game designers can extend this module with their own game-specific controller, but this module is still the basic game controller.

These really don't fit into the MVC pattern, but they're still part of the system.

What's a design pattern?
And how do I use one?

We've all used off-the-shelf libraries and frameworks. We take them, write some code against their APIs, compile them into our programs, and benefit from a lot of code someone else has written. Think about the Java APIs and all the functionality they give you: network, GUI, IO, etc. Libraries and frameworks go a long way towards a development model where we can just pick and choose components and plug them right in. But... they don't help us structure our own applications in ways that are easier to understand, more maintainable and flexible. That's where Design Patterns come in.

Design patterns don't go directly into your code, they first go into your BRAIN. A design pattern is just a way to design the solution for a particular type of problem. Once you've loaded your brain with a good working knowledge of patterns, you can then start to apply them to your new designs, and rework your old code when you find it's degrading into an inflexible mess of jungle spaghetti code.

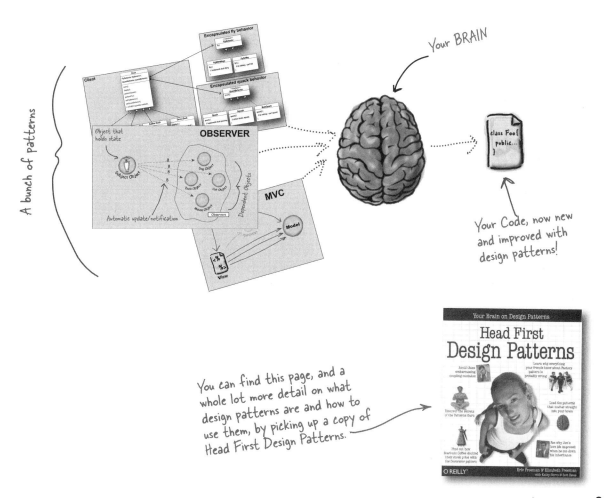

A bunch of patterns

Your BRAIN

class Foo{
public...
}

Your Code, now new and improved with design patterns!

You can find this page, and a whole lot more detail on what design patterns are and how to use them, by picking up a copy of Head First Design Patterns.

Head First Design Patterns

I haven't read Head First Design Patterns, and I'm still a bit fuzzy on exactly what a design pattern even is. What should I do?

Keep going! Design patterns are one of the la<u>st</u> steps of design.

It's OK if you're not familiar with design patterns. Design patterns help you take those last steps of design—once you've used OO principles like encapsulation and delegation to make your software flexible, a well-chosen design pattern can add just that extra bit of flexibility to your design, and save you some time, too.

But it's no big deal if you're not familiar with design patterns. You can still work through this book, and get a handle on really solid design. Then, we'd recommend you pick up Head First Design Patterns, and see how other people have been handling some classic design problems, and learn from them.

Feeling a little bit lost?

We've done a lot of things in this chapter, and some of them don't even seem to be related...

→ Gathering features

→ Domain analysis

→ Breaking Gary's system into modules

→ Figuring out Gary's system uses the MVC pattern.

But how does any of this really help us solve <u>BIG</u> problems?

Remember, the whole point of all this was to get a handle on how to deal with really large applications—like Gary's game system framework—that involve a lot more than some basic design and programming.

But here's the big secret: you've <u>already</u> done everything you need to handle Gary's BIG problem.

> OK, I must have missed that. Can you let me in on what I missed?

The power of OOA&D
(and a little common sense)

We started out with this rather vague, far-reaching vision statement. Now that's a BIG problem.

Once we knew what we were building, we created a use case diagram to help us understand the big picture.

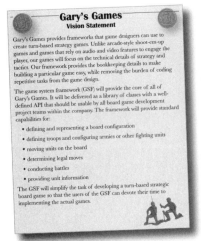

Gary's Games
Vision Statement

Gary's Games provides frameworks that game designers can use to create turn-based strategy games. Unlike arcade-style shoot-em-up games and games that rely on audio and video features to engage the player, our games will focus on the technical details of strategy and tactics. Our framework provides the bookkeeping details to make building a particular game easy, while removing the burden of coding repetitive tasks from the game design.

The game system framework (GSF) will provide the core of all of Gary's Games. It will be delivered as a library of classes with a well-defined API that should be usable by all board game development project teams within the company. The framework will provide standard capabilities for:

- defining and representing a board configuration
- defining troops and configuring armies or other fighting units
- moving units on the board
- determining legal moves
- conducting battles
- providing unit information

The GSF will simplify the task of developing a turn-based strategic board game so that the users of the GSF can devote their time to implementing the actual games.

❶ **We listened to the customer.**

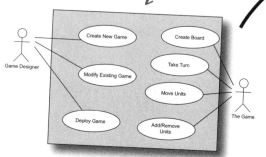

❸ **We drew up blueprints for the system we're building.**

Gary's Game System Framework
Feature List

1. The framework supports different types of terrain.
2. The framework supports different time periods, including fictional periods like sci-fi and fantasy.
3. The framework supports multiple types of troops or units that are game-specific.
4. The framework supports add-on modules for additional campaigns or battle scenarios.
5. The framework provides a board made up of square tiles, and each tile has a terrain type.
6. The framework keeps up with whose turn it is.
7. The framework coordinates basic movement.

Using domain analysis, we made sure we understand what Gary wanted his system to do.

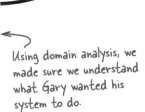

❷ **We made sure we understood the system.**

With a blueprint and feature list in hand, we were able to break up Gary's big app into lots of smaller pieces of individual functionality.

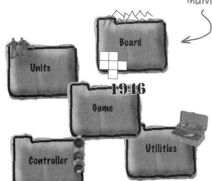

④ We broke the big problem up into smaller pieces of functionality.

Look! You already know how to solve these smaller problems, using everything you've already learned about analysis and design...

We even took a design pattern that we already understand, and applied it to our system.

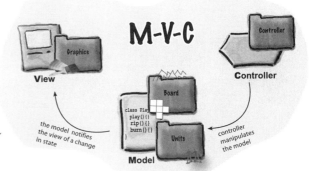

...and you can even figure out how to apply the MVC pattern from Head First Design Patterns.

⑤ We apply design patterns to help us solve the smaller problems.

Congratulations!

You've turned a **BIG PROBLEM** into a bunch of SMALLER PROBLEMS that you already know how to solve.

Tools for your OOA&D Toolbox

You've taken on a huge problem, and you're still standing! Review some of the things you've learned about handling big problems, and then you're ready for the return of the OOA&D crossword puzzle.

Requi~~rements~~

Good requi~~rements~~
works like

Make sure
by developi

Use your u
things your

Your use ca
or missing
have.

Your requir
grow) over

Analysi~~s~~

Well-designed
and extend.

Use basic OO
and inheritan
more flexible

If a design is
IT! Never se
it's your bad

Make sure ea
each of your
ONE THING

Always striv
move throug
lifecycle.

Solving Big Problems

Listen to the customer, and figure out what they want you to build.

Put together a feature list, in language the customer understands.

Make sure your features are what the customer actually wants.

Create blueprints of the system using use case diagrams (and use cases).

Break the big system up into lots of smaller sections.

Apply design patterns to the smaller sections of the system.

Use basic OOA&D principles to design an code each smaller section.

We've got a whole new category of techniques we learned about in this chapter.

OO Principles

Encapsulate what varies.

Code to an interface rather than to an implementation.

Each class in your application should have only one reason to change.

Classes are about behavior and functionality.

BULLET POINTS

- The best way to look at a big problem is to view it as a collection of smaller problems.

- Just like in small projects, start working on big projects by gathering features and requirements.

- Features are usually "big" things that a system does, but also can be used interchangeably with the term "requirements."

- Commonality and variability give you points of comparison between a new system and things you already know about.

- Use cases are detail-oriented; use case diagrams are focused more on the big picture.

- Your use case diagram should account for all the features in your system.

- Domain analysis is representing a system in language that the customer will understand.

- An actor is anything that interacts with your system, but isn't part of the system.

OOA&D Cross

It's time for another left-brain workout.
Below is a puzzle with lots of blank
squares; to the right are some clues. You
know what to do, so go for it!

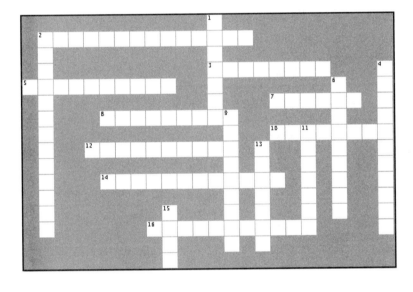

Across

2. This helps you speak to the customer in their language (2 words)
3. You can use your feature list to make sure your use case diagram is this.
5. Use cases don't always help you see this (2 words).
7. These aren't always people.
8. A feature is a ___ ___ description of something a system needs to do (2 words)
10. Art Vandelay's "real" last name
12. A use case diagram acts as this for your system.
14. You can figure out these based on your features.
16. This is the measure of how things are similar.

Down

1. An oval in a use case diagram represents one of these.
2. We applied ones of these to your Gary's framework.
4. The measure of how things are different.
6. You should solve a big problem by doing this to it (3 words)
9. You can figure out a system's features by _____ to the customer.
11. You solve big problems the ___ ___ you solve small problems (2 words).
13. Defer these as long as possible.
15. He wasn't the customer.

Exercise
Solutions

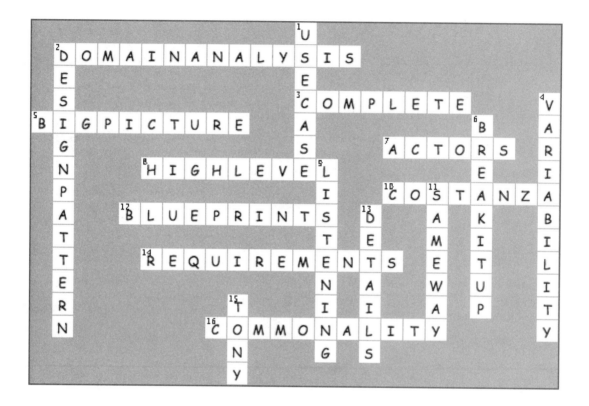

7 architecture

Bringing Order to Chaos

OK, I've got these blueprints now, but I'm still not sure how the whatchamacallit connects to the thingamajiggy.

You have to start somewhere, but you better pick the *right* somewhere! You know how to break your application up into lots of small problems, but all that means is that you have **LOTS** of small problems. In this chapter, we're going to help you figure out **where to start**, and make sure that you don't waste any time working on the wrong things. It's time to take all those **little pieces** laying around your workspace, and figure out how to turn them into a **well-ordered, well-designed application**. Along the way, you'll learn about the all-important **3 Qs of architecture**, and how **Risk** is a lot more than just a cool war game from the '80s.

Feeling a little overwhelmed?

So you've got lots of small pieces of functionality that you know how to take care of... but you've also got use case diagrams, feature lists, and a whole lot of other things to think about.

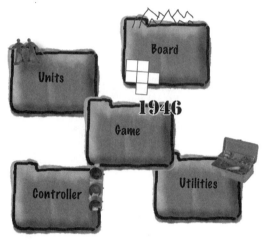

...individual modules to code...

> ### Gary's Game System Framework
> #### Feature List
>
> 1. The framework supports different types of terrain.
>
> 2. The framework supports different time periods, including fictional periods like sci-fi and fantasy.
>
> 3. The framework supports multiple types of troops or units that are game-specific.
>
> 4. The framework supports add-on modules for additional campaigns or battle scenarios.
>
> 5. The framework provides a board made up of square tiles, and each tile has a terrain type.
>
> 6. The framework keeps up with whose turn it is.
>
> 7. The framework coordinates basic movement.

We have feature lists...

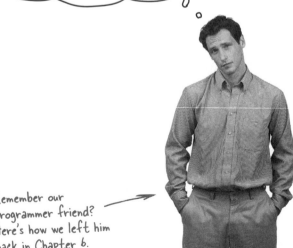

> OK, even if I do know how to handle all these individual pieces, where the heck am I supposed to start? Can you at least tell me what to do **FIRST**?

Remember our programmer friend? Here's how we left him back in Chapter 6.

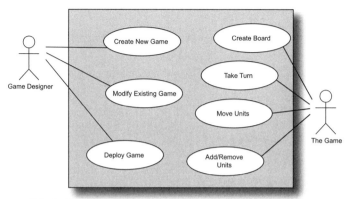

...high-level views of what we need to build...

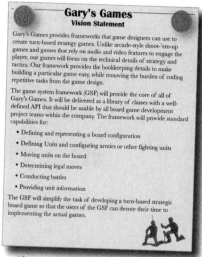

...the customer's vision...

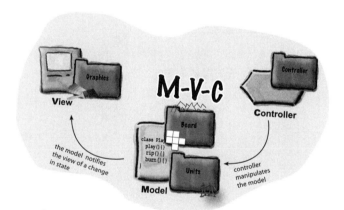

...and even some design patterns to apply.

Do you think it matters what you should try to do first? If you do, why? And what would *you* work on first?

We need an <u>architecture</u>

It's really not enough to just figure out the individual pieces of a big problem. You also need to know a little bit about how those pieces fit together, and which ones might be more important than others; that way, you'll know what you should work on *first*.

We already knew this...
architecture helps us
design these big systems.

Architecture is your
design structure,
and highlights the
most important
parts of your app, and the
relationships
between those parts.

Now <u>this</u> is
what we need...
how do we
figure out
what's most
important, so
we can build
those parts of
our app first?

Our use case
diagram was the
start of this, but
it's still pretty
unclear how all the
modules interact.

All this is particularly
important when you're working
with other programmers... you
have to all understand the
same architecture.

the Scholar's Corner

architecture. Architecture is the organizational structure of a system, including its decomposition into parts, their connectivity, interaction mechanisms, and the guiding principles and decisions that you use in the design of a system.

Architecture takes a big chaotic mess...

I have **no clue** what to do with all of this stuff.

Ever get this feeling? You've got lots of important diagrams and plans, but everything is just a huge mess.

These lists and patterns should help, but it's hard to know how it all fits together.

...and helps us turn it into a well-ordered application

This is what we want... to use all the information we have to create a nice, well-constructed application.

Wow... **now** I see how it all fits together!

All the diagrams and patterns are used to build the customer exactly what they want, all within a flexible, reusable design.

You write great software the same way, whether you're working on a small project, or a huge one. You can still apply the three steps we talked about way back in Chapter 1.

Remember this page from the first chapter? These 3 steps apply to building great <u>BIG</u> software, too.

We know that these three steps will help us tackle each of these individual pieces of the game system framework.

> **well-designed** apps rock
>
> # <u>Great</u> software in <u>3</u> <u>easy</u> <u>steps</u>
>
> It may not seem easy now, but we'll show you how OOA&D and some basic principles can change your software forever.
>
> **1. Make sure your software does what the customer wants it to do.**
>
> This step focuses on the customer. Make sure the app does what it supposed to do <u>FIRST</u>.
>
> **2. Apply basic OO principles to add flexibility.**
>
> Once your software works, you can start to remove duplicate code and use good OO practices
>
> **3. Strive for a maintainable, reusable design.**
>
> Got a good object-oriented app that does what it should? It's time to apply patterns and principles to make sure your software is ready to use for years to come.
>
> *you are here ▸* **11**

These three steps apply when you're working on really big applications, too. So we need to start with what the customer wants an app to do, before we get into details about the actual design of the app.

Really <u>BIG</u> application

Let's start with <u>functionality</u>

The first step is always to make sure an application does what it's supposed to do. In small projects, we used a requirements list to write down functionality; in big projects, we've been using a feature list to figure those things out:

> All of these features are about <u>functionality</u>... they focus on what the system has to <u>do</u>, not on what principles or patterns you use to build the system.

Gary's Game System Framework
Feature List

1. The framework supports different types of terrain.

2. The framework supports different time periods, including fictional periods like sci-fi and fantasy.

3. The framework supports multiple types of troops or units that are game-specific.

4. The framework supports add-on modules for additional campaigns or battle scenarios.

5. The framework provides a board made up of square tiles, and each tile has a terrain type.

6. The framework keeps up with whose turn it is.

7. The framework coordinates basic movement.

> We'll come back to these other diagrams and patterns later... but right now, we're focusing solely on the functionality of the system.

But which of these are the <u>most</u> impo<u>rtan</u>t?

Even if we know to start by focusing on functionality, we still need to figure out which pieces are the most important. *Those* are the pieces we want to focus on first.

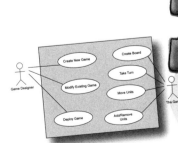

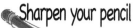

Sharpen your pencil

What do YOU think are the most important features?

Even though our feature list has only seven things on it, there's a lot of work in those seven features. It's your job to figure out which features you think are the most important, and then in what order you'd work on those things.

> **Gary's Game System Framework**
> **Feature List**
>
> 1. The framework supports different types of terrain.
> 2. The framework supports different time periods, including fictional periods like sci-fi and fantasy.
> 3. The framework supports multiple types of troops or units that are game-specific.
> 4. The framework supports add-on modules for additional campaigns or battle scenarios.
> 5. The framework provides a board made up of square tiles, and each tile has a terrain type.
> 6. The framework keeps up with whose turn it is.
> 7. The framework coordinates basic movement.

You've got to handle all of these features, but it's up to you to figure out the order you should tackle them in.

Write down the 4 things you'd do first, in order, in these blanks.

1. _____

2. _____

3. _____

4. _____

Wait a second... if architecture is about the **relationships** between the parts of an application, why are we talking about the individual parts? Shouldn't we be talking about how the parts work together?

The things in your application that are really important are <u>architecturally significant</u>, and you should focus on them <u>FIRST</u>.

You gotta start <u>somewhere!</u>

It's awfully hard to talk about the relationships between parts of a system if you don't have any of the parts themselves. So say you wanted to talk about how the Board module interacted with the Units module:

To figure out how these modules interact, you'd need to have at least the basics of the two modules in place first.

So architecture isn't just about the relationships between parts of your app; it's also about figuring out which parts are the *most* important, so you can start building those parts first.

The three Qs of architecture

When you're trying to figure out if something is architecturally significant, there are three questions you can ask:

1. Is it part of the <u>essence</u> of the system?

Is the feature really **core** to what a system actually is? Think about it this way: can you imagine the system without that feature? If not, then you've probably found a feature that is part of the **essence** of a system.

MEANING

2. What the ▆▆▆ does it mean?

Note from marketing: suggest replacing profanity with "heck."

If you're not sure what the description of a particular feature **really means**, it's probably pretty important that you pay attention to that feature. Anytime you're unsure about what something is, it could take lots of time, or create problems with the rest of the system. Spend time on these features early, rather than late.

3. How the "heck" do I <u>do</u> it?

Another place to focus your attention early on is on features that seem **really hard** to implement, or are **totally new** programming tasks for you. If you have no idea how you're going to tackle a particular problem, you better spend some time up front looking at that feature, so it doesn't create lots of problems down the road.

BE the Architect

To the right, you'll find the feature list we figured out in the last chapter. Your job is to play like you're the architect, and figure out what's architecturally significant by using the three Qs of architecture we just talked about.

Gary's Game System Framework
Feature List

1. The framework supports different types of terrain.

2. The framework supports different time periods, including fictional periods like sci-fi and fantasy.

3. The framework supports multiple types of troops or units that are game-specific.

4. The framework supports add-on modules for additional campaigns or battle scenarios.

5. The framework provides a board made up of square tiles, and each tile has a terrain type.

6. The framework keeps up with whose turn it is.

7. The framework coordinates basic movement.

What's significant?

_____

_____

_____

_____

_____

Check and see how close your answers here match up to what you wrote down on page 330.

Why?

_____

_____

_____

_____

Write down which of the three Qs applies (you can write more than one, if you need to)

BE the Architect Solutions

To the right, you'll find the feature list we figured out in the last chapter. Below are the things we thought were architecturally significant, and which of the three Qs we used to make our decisions.

Gary's Game System Framework
Feature List

1. The framework supports different types of terrain.

2. The framework supports different time periods, including fictional periods like sci-fi and fantasy.

3. The framework supports multiple types of troops or units that are game-specific.

4. The framework supports add-on modules for additional campaigns or battle scenarios.

5. The framework provides a board made up of square tiles, and each tile has a terrain type.

6. The framework keeps up with whose turn it is.

7. The framework coordinates basic movement.

We decided that the board was core to the game... without a board, there really isn't a game!

What's significant?

The board for the game

Game-specific units

The framework coordinates basic movement.

Why?

Q1

Q1, Q2

Q3 (and maybe Q2)

We thought that troops were essential to the game... and we're not sure what "game-specific" might really mean. So two Qs applied here.

This seems a little vague, but it's not something we're sure about how to do. Definitely worth spending some time up front figuring out what this means, and what we need to do.

there are no
Dumb Questions

Q: I'm a little confused about what you mean by the "essence" of the system. Can you say more about that?

A: The essence of a system is what it is at its most basic level. In other words, if you stripped away all the bells and whistles, all the "neat" things that marketing threw in, and all the cool ideas you had, what would the system *really* be about? That's the essence of a system.

When you're looking at a feature, ask yourself: "If this feature wasn't implemented, would the system still really be what it's supposed to be?" If the answer is no, you've found yourself an "essence feature." In Gary's system, we decided that the game wouldn't really be a game without a board and some units, and there are some more examples in the Brain Power at the bottom of the page.

Q: If you don't know what something means, isn't that a sign that you've got bad requirements?

A: No, but it is a sign that you might need to get some additional requirements, or at least some clarification. In the early stages, you can leave some details out to get a basic sense of a system. But at this stage, it's time to fill in some of those details, and that's what the second Q of architecture is all about.

Q: If I'm working on a new system, I probably won't know how to do anything on my feature list. So won't the 3rd Q of architecture about not knowing how to do something always apply?

A: No, not at all. For instance, even if you've never written code to decide whether a player typed in the letter "q" or the letter "x," you know how to write a basic `if`/`else` statement, and it's easy to grab keyboard input from a player. So a feature like getting keyboard input isn't something you don't know how to do, even if you've never written code specifically for that task before. It's just a few new details, really.

But if you had to write a multi-threaded chat server, and you're new to threads and network programming, then that would be something that you don't know how to do. Those are the things to look out for: particularly hard tasks that you're unsure about how to handle.

Q: Doesn't this all end up just being a judgment call, anyway?

A: In a lot of cases, yes. But as long as you choose to start working on the things that seem the most important to the system, you're going to get off to a good start.

What you *don't* want to do is see some things that look familiar—perhaps you've solved the same problem in another project—and start there. Start with the core pieces of the system, and the things that look like they might be particularly hard, and you'll be on the road to success.

The essence of a system is what that system is at its most <u>basic</u> level.

BRAIN POWER

What do you think the essence of each of these systems is:
- A weather-monitoring station?
- A home automation remote control?
- A beat-controlling, music-mixing DJ application?

We've got a lot less chaos now...

Using the three Qs of architecture, we've started to add some
order to all that confusion we started out with:

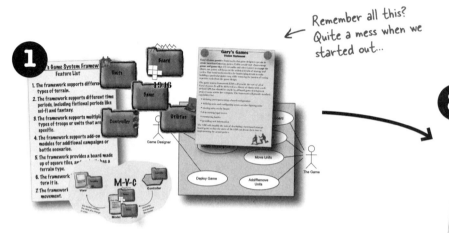

Remember all this? Quite a mess when we started out...

But then we focused on making the system do what it is supposed to do.

2

Gary's Game System Framework
Feature List

1. The framework supports different types of terrain.

2. The framework supports different time periods, including fictional periods like sci-fi and fantasy.

3. The framework supports multiple types of troops or units that are game-specific.

4. The framework supports add-on modules for additional campaigns or battle scenarios.

5. The framework provides a board made up of square tiles, and each tile has a terrain type.

6. The framework keeps up with whose turn it is.

7. The framework coordinates basic movement.

3

Gary's Game System Framework
KEY Features

1. The board for the game—essence of the system

2. Game-specific units—essence, and what does this mean?

3. Coordinating movement—what is it, and how do we do it?

Finally, we've narrowed that down to just a few key features to focus on.

> I know I love a man in uniform, but there are still choices to be made...

...but there's still plenty left to do

We've gotten Gary's system down to three key features, but the
big question remains: which one should you work on first?

Cubicle ~~Conversation~~ Argument

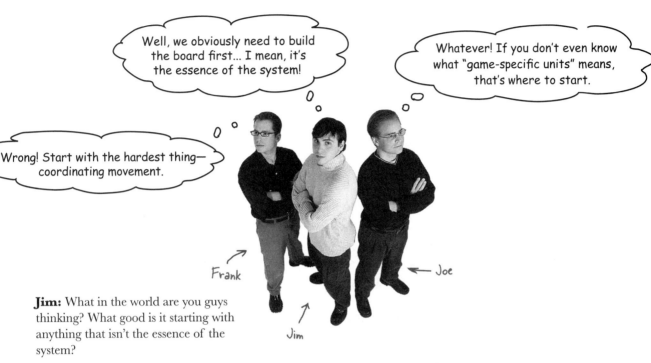

Well, we obviously need to build the board first... I mean, it's the essence of the system!

Whatever! If you don't even know what "game-specific units" means, that's where to start.

Wrong! Start with the hardest thing— coordinating movement.

Frank

Joe

Jim

Jim: What in the world are you guys thinking? What good is it starting with anything that isn't the essence of the system?

Joe: That's ridiculous. Even if that's the essence of the system, you've got to figure out what game-specific units are. That could take weeks to write if it's harder than we think!

Frank: Maybe... but we *know* that coordinating movement will be tough, because we don't have a clue how to do it! How can you possibly work on anything else when you *know* the movement deal is going to be difficult?

Joe: But the game-specific units might be difficult, too! We just don't know, and that's my point. We've got to figure out the parts of the system we don't know anything about, or they could be real trouble!

Jim: You guys go on and write movement engines and deal with units. Me, I'm gonna write a board, because... well... something tells me Gary will want to see a *board* for his *board game system*. And I'm not about to leave the board for later... I'm taking it on first.

Frank: You're both nuts. While you're putting off the hard tasks, I'm gonna make sure the things that I don't have any real idea about are taken care of, right away.

So who do *you* think is right? Do you agree with:

☐ **Jim (build the board)**   ☐ **Joe (build the game-specific units)**

☐ **Frank (build the movement engine)**

Check the box next to who you agree with.

Leave it to a bunch of boys to get into a big argument. I think they're **ALL** right... the problem isn't which feature to start with, the problem is **RISK**!

Jill works with Frank, Jim, and Joe, and is used to breaking up their arguments.

The reason that these features are architecturally significant is that they all introduce RISK to your project. It doesn't matter which one you start with—as long as you are working towards reducing the RISKS in succeeding.

Take another look at our key features:

Gary's Game System Framework
KEY Features

1. The board for the game—essence of the system
2. Game-specific units—essence, and what does this mean?
3. Coordinating movement—what is it, and how do we do it?

Since we don't know what this means, it could be a ton of work, and that's a RISK in meeting schedules and deadlines.

This is something we're not sure how to do, so there's a RISK that we won't figure it out, or it will take a really long time.

If the core features of the system aren't in place, there's a serious RISK that the customer won't like the system.

The point here is to REDUCE RISK, not to argue over which key feature you should start with first. You can start with ANY of these, as long as you're focused on building what you're supposed to be building.

> Well, I still think my risk is bigger than yours...

Sharpen your pencil

Find the risk in your own project.

Think about the project you're working on in your day job right now. Now write down the *first* thing you started working on when you started the project:

_____
_____
_____

Now think about the 3 Qs of architecture that we talked about back on page 332. If you applied those to your project, write down a few features that you think would be architecturally significant:

_____
_____
_____
_____

If you look at those features closely, you'll probably see that they all have a lot of **RISK** connected to them. They're the things that could cause you lots of problems, or delay you getting your project done. In the blanks below, write down which of those features you think you should have worked on first, and why. What risks did it create? What risks could you have reduced by working on it first?

_____
_____
_____
_____

 # Architecture Puzzle

For Gary's game system, let's start out by working on the board module. Your job is to write a **Board** interface that game designers can then use and extend to build their own games.

The problem:

You need a **Board** base type that game designers can use to create new games. The board's height and width are supplied by the game designers for their games. Additionally, the board can return the tile at a given position, add units to a tile, and return all the units at a given X-Y position.

Here are some detailed requirements that we got from Gary and his design team.

Your task:

1 Create a new class called **Board.java**.

2 Add a constructor to **Board** that takes in a width and height, and creates a new board with that height and width. The constructor also needs to fill the board with square tiles, one at each X-Y position.

3 Write a method that will return the tile at a given position, given that tile's X- and Y-position.

4 Write methods to add units to a tile based on that tile's X- and Y-position.

5 Write a method to return all the units on a tile, given the X- and Y-position of the tile.

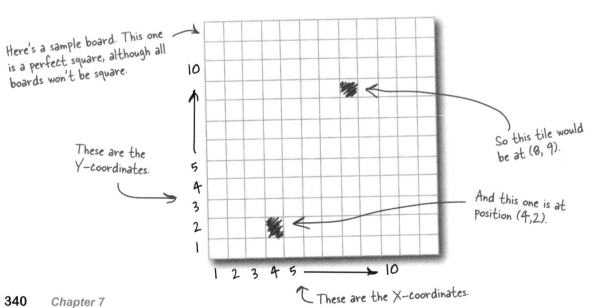

Here's a sample board. This one is a perfect square, although all boards won't be square.

These are the Y-coordinates.

So this tile would be at (8, 9).

And this one is at position (4,2).

These are the X-coordinates.

Answers on page 346

Use Cases Exposed

This week's interview:
Scenarios help reduce risk

HeadFirst: Hi there, Scenario, we appreciate you taking the time to talk with us today.

Scenario: I'm really happy to be here, especially in a chapter that isn't just about use cases.

HeadFirst: Well, yes, to tell the truth, I was rather surprised when I was told we'd be interviewing you. We're really focusing on architecture here, and working on features that would reduce risk.

Scenario: Absolutely! Well, that sounds like a very good way to approach big problems.

HeadFirst: Yes, well... ahem... then why are you here?

Scenario: Oh! I'm sorry, I just assumed you knew. I'm here to help reduce risk, also.

HeadFirst: But I thought you were just a particular path through a use case. We haven't even written any use cases yet!

Scenario: That's no problem, I can still be a real help. I mean, look, let's be honest, lots of developers just don't ever really take the time to sit down and write out use cases. Good grief, it took you something like four pages in Chapter 6 to convince people to even use a use case *diagram*, and that's much easier to draw than it is to write a use case!

HeadFirst: Well, that's true... there is a lot of resistance to writing out use cases. But they're really helpful, I thought they saved the day with Todd and Gina's dog door.

Scenario: Oh, I agree! But in cases where developers just don't have the time, or a use case is too formal for what's needed, I can really give you a lot of the advantages of a use case, without all the paperwork.

HeadFirst: Hmmm, that is appealing. So tell me how that works.

Scenario: Well, take that board you've been writing. Suppose you wanted to reduce the risks of Gary seeing it, and thinking of something important you forgot to add to it...

HeadFirst: Ahh, yes, forgetting an important requirement is always a risk!

Scenario: Well, you could come up with a simple scenario for how the board would be used— that's where I come in—and then make sure the board works with everything in your scenario.

HeadFirst: But there's no use case... what steps do we pick in the scenario we make up?

Scenario: It doesn't have to be that formal. You might say, "The game designer creates a new board 8 squares wide by 10 squares high," and "Player 1 kills Player 2's troops at (4, 5) so the board removes Player 2's troops from that tile."

HeadFirst: Oh, so just little descriptions of how the board is used?

Scenario: You've got it! Then you run through each description, and make sure your board handles those cases. It's not quite as thorough as a use case, but I really can help you make sure you don't forget any big requirements.

HeadFirst: This is fantastic! We'll be right back with more from Scenario.

Scenario Scramble

Write a scenario for the Board interface you just coded.

Reducing risk is the name of the game in this chapter. You've coded a Board interface based on a few requirements we gave you, but it's your job to figure out if we forgot anything—before Gary sees your work and finds a mistake.

This is the risk we're trying to reduce or eliminate using a scenario.

Your job is to take the fragments of a scenario from the bottom of this page, and put them into an order that makes sense on the bulletin board. The scenario should run through a realistic portion of a game. When you're done, see if you left out anything on the Board interface, and if you did, add the missing functionality into your code. You may not need all the scenario fragments; good luck!

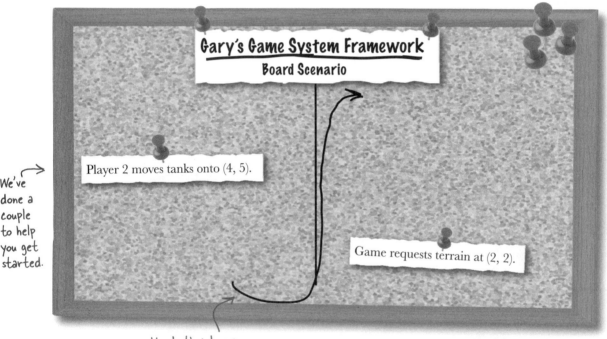

Gary's Game System Framework
Board Scenario

Player 2 moves tanks onto (4, 5).

Game requests terrain at (2, 2).

We've done a couple to help you get started.

Pin the scenario fragments onto this piece of paper.

Use both columns for the scenario.

Player 1 battles Player 2.

Player 1's units lose the battle.

Player 2 moves army onto (4, 5).

Game designer creates board with a height and width.

Game requests terrain at (4, 5).

Player 1's units are removed from (4, 5).

Player 2's units win the battle.

Game designer creates a new board.

Game requests units from (4, 5).

Player 1 moves artillery onto (4, 5).

Player 1 moves subs to (2, 2).

Game designer supplies height and width.

1946

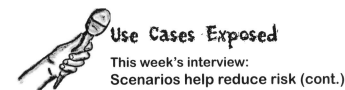

Use Cases Exposed

This week's interview:
Scenarios help reduce risk (cont.)

HeadFirst: We're back with Scenario, again. Scenario, we're getting quite a few calls. Would you mind taking some of our listener's questions?

Scenario: Sure, I'd be happy to.

HeadFirst: Great. First, here's one we're getting a lot. This is from Impatient in Idaho: "So you're saying I don't need to write use cases, anymore, right? I can just use scenarios?"

Scenario: Oh, thanks, Impatient, I actually get that question often. I firmly believe you should still write use cases whenever possible. I'm helpful for quick problems, and to find the most common requirements, but remember, I'm only *one* path through a use case. If there are lots of alternate paths, you might miss some important requirements if you used *just* a scenario for your requirements.

HeadFirst: That's right, we've actually had Happy Path and Alternate Path on our show before.

Scenario: Well, they're really just specialized versions of me, if you want the truth. We try not to talk much about our family relationships, we all wanted to make it in this world on our own. But we're really all part of the Scenario family. And you really need all of us to be sure you've got a system completely right. But if you're just getting started, and a use case seems like it might be premature, just using me is a good way to get started.

HeadFirst: OK, here's another question, from Nervous in Nebraska: "You said you would help me reduce risk, and I hate risk. Could you tell me exactly how you can help me avoid risk?"

Scenario: Another good question. Remember, when you're figuring out requirements, whether you're using a use case, a use case diagram, or a scenario, you're trying to make sure you are building just what the customer wants. Without good requirements, the risk is letting down or upsetting the customer by building the wrong thing.

HeadFirst: So you're reducing risk in the requirements phase?

Scenario: A lot of the time, yes. That's when you're writing use cases, putting together a requirements list, and using lots of scenarios to chart out all the paths through a use case.

HeadFirst: But you also help out in big project architecture, right? That's why we're interviewing you now?

Scenario: Exactly. Sometimes, you don't have a complete requirements list and a bunch of use cases, but you still need to get some basic work done to see how a system is going to work. That's what we've been doing here: using a scenario to get the basics of a module or piece of code down, so you can get the basic building blocks of your application in place.

HeadFirst: So you're really a handy guy, aren't you?

Scenario: I'd like to think so. I help in gathering requirements, in being sure your use cases are complete, but also in architecture, helping you reduce risk and reduce the chaos and confusion around what a particular module or piece of code does.

Scenario Scramble Solution

Write a scenario for the Board interface you just coded.

Below is the scenario we came up with. Yours might be a bit different, but you should at least have the game designer creating the board, a battle occuring between Player 1 and Player 2, and units being both added to and removed from

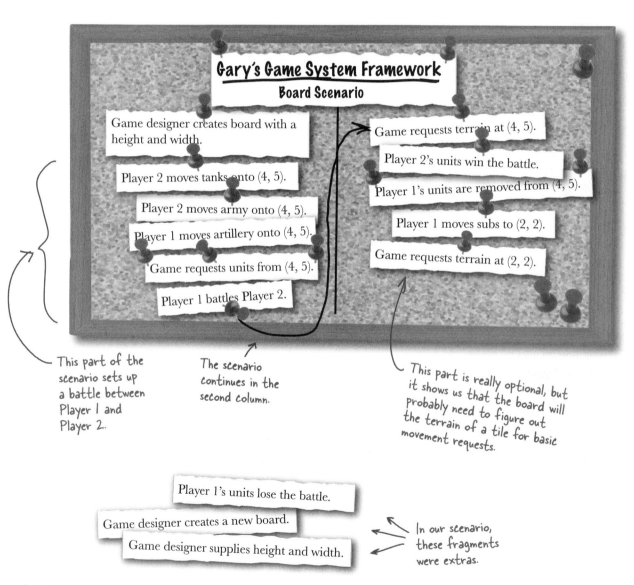

Gary's Game System Framework
Board Scenario

Game designer creates board with a height and width.

Player 2 moves tanks onto (4, 5).

Player 2 moves army onto (4, 5).

Player 1 moves artillery onto (4, 5).

Game requests units from (4, 5).

Player 1 battles Player 2.

Game requests terrain at (4, 5).

Player 2's units win the battle.

Player 1's units are removed from (4, 5).

Player 1 moves subs to (2, 2).

Game requests terrain at (2, 2).

This part of the scenario sets up a battle between Player 1 and Player 2.

The scenario continues in the second column.

This part is really optional, but it shows us that the board will probably need to figure out the terrain of a tile for basic movement requests.

Player 1's units lose the battle.

Game designer creates a new board.

Game designer supplies height and width.

In our scenario, these fragments were extras.

there are no
Dumb Questions

Q: Where did those requirements for the Architecture Puzzle on page 340 come from?

A: From Gary, with some common sense added in. If you think about what Gary's asked for, a game system framework, and then read back over the customer conversation in Chapter 6, you could probably come up with these requirements on your own. We did add a few specifics, like being able to add a unit to a specific tile, but that's really just thinking through the problem.

Q: But why didn't we write a use case to figure out the requirements?

A: We could have. But remember, we're not trying to complete the Board module, as much as get the basic pieces in place. That's all we need to reduce the risk of completing this piece of Gary's system. In fact, if we got into too much detail, we might actually *add* risk to the project, by working on details that really aren't important at this stage of things.

Q: Now you're telling me that use cases add risk? That can't be right!

A: No, use cases don't add risk when *used at the right time*. Right now, we've come up with some key features that could cause us headaches if we don't figure them out. But that doesn't mean we need to perfect the Board interface; we just need to get an understanding of how it works, so if there are any potential problem spots, we can catch them and avoid problems down the line. So at this point, the details you'd need to write a good use case are a bit of overkill.

But once we've got the key features sketched out, and handled the major risks, we'll go back to each module and really start to add detail in. At that point, a use case is very helpful.

Q: So that's why we used a scenario, right? To avoid getting into lots of unnecessary detail?

A: Exactly. A scenario gives us lots of the advantages of a use case, without forcing us to get into lots of detail that we don't need to worry about right now.

Architecture Puzzle (Revisited)

What's missing in Board.java?

Look closely at the scenario on the previous page. Did the requirements we used on page 340 cover everything in the completed scenario? If you think something is missing, write it in the blank below, and then add code to Board.java to handle the missing functionality.

_____

_____

Architecture Puzzle Solution

For Gary's game system, let's start out by working on the Board module. Below is the interface we wrote to handle what we thought the basic tasks of a board would be. See how your solution compares with ours.

```java
package headfirst.gsf.board;

import java.util.ArrayList;
import java.util.Iterator;
import java.util.List;

import headfirst.gsf.unit.Unit;

public class Board {

  private int width, height;
  private List tiles;

  public Board(int width, int height) {
    this.width = width;
    this.height = height;
    initialize();
  }

  private void initialize() {
    tiles = new ArrayList(width);
    for (int i=0; i<width; i++) {
      tiles.add(i, new ArrayList(height));
      for (int j=0; j<height; j++) {
        ((ArrayList)tiles.get(i)).add(j, new Tile());
      }
    }
  }
}
```

We put the Board class in a board-specific package. This lines up with the modules we decided on back in Chapter 6.

Here's a class we'll create in a minute, since we need it to finish up Board.

This constructor was laid out in the requirements. It takes the width and height in, and then calls initialize() to set up the board.

We represented the grid on the board as an array of arrays, using width and height as the dimensions.

Bonus Design Principle: Pull out setup code into its own method, so it doesn't make the rest of your code so confusing to read.

At each coordinate, we add a new instance of Tile. We'll have to write that class to make Board work as well... check the next page for how we defined Tile.

```
class
Board
{  ge-
tUnit()
}
```
Board.java

These methods are pretty self-explanatory, and were part of the requirements on page 340.

```
public Tile getTile(int x, int y) {
    return (Tile)((ArrayList)tiles.get(x-1)).get(y-1);
}

public void addUnit(Unit unit, int x, int y) {
    Tile tile = getTile(x, y);
    tile.addUnit(unit);
}
```

We decided to let the Tile class handle these operations, and just delegate adding and removing units to that class.

```
public void removeUnit(Unit unit, int x, int y) {
    Tile tile = getTile(x, y);
    tile.removeUnit(unit);
}
```

You should have figured out that we need a way to remove units from the scenario exercise on page 344. This is what was missing in our original requirements.

```
public void removeUnits(int x, int y) {
    Tile tile = getTile(x, y);
    tile.removeUnits();
}

public List getUnits(int x, int y) {
    return getTile(x, y).getUnits();
}
}
```

Here's another place where we delegate to the Tile class. Since a tile stores the units on it, it's really the tile's job to handle retrieving those units.

there are no Dumb Questions

Q: Doesn't using an array of arrays limit you to a square board?

A: No, although it does limit you to a board that uses (x, y) coordinates. For example, you can use (x, y) coordinates in a board made up of hexagon-shaped tiles, if you structure the hexagon tiles correctly. But for the most part, an array of arrays is more ideally suited to a square-tiled, rectangular board.

Q: So isn't that limiting? Why not use a graph, or even a Coordinate class, so you're not tied to (x, y) coordinates and a rectangular board?

A: If you wanted maximum flexibility, that might be a good idea. For this situation, though, our requirements (back on page 340) actually specified (x, y) coordinates. So we chose a solution that wasn't quite as flexible, but certainly was simpler. Remember, at this stage, we're trying to reduce risk, not increase it by going with a solution that is a lot more complex than we really need.

The Tile and Unit classes

To actually make **Board** compile and work, we need to create a **Tile** and **Unit** class. Here's how we wrote those classes:

```
package headfirst.gsf.unit;

public class Unit {

  public Unit() {
  }
}
```

Unit.java

We made Unit as <u>absolutely simple</u> as possible. There are lots of details to be added later, but we don't need those details to make Board work right now.

Tile is in the same package as the Board class... they're tightly related.

Tile has a list of the units on it at any given time.

These are the methods that Board uses to manipulate units. They're protected, so only classes in headfirst.gsf.board can access them.

```
package headfirst.gsf.board;

import java.util.LinkedList;
import java.util.List;

import headfirst.gsf.unit.Unit;

public class Tile {

  private List units;

  public Tile() {
    units = new LinkedList();
  }

  protected void addUnit(Unit unit) {
    units.add(unit);
  }

  protected void removeUnit(Unit unit) {
    units.remove(unit);
  }
}
```

Tile.java

Keep the right focus

You don't need to worry about everything that **Tile** and **Unit** will eventually need to do. Your focus is on making **Board** and its key features work, not on completing **Tile** or **Unit**. That's why we left **Unit** so bare, and added only a few methods to **Tile**.

Focus on one feature at a time to reduce risk in your project.

Don't get distracted with features that won't help reduce risk.

Q: If the Tile class handles adding and removing units, and you can get the tile at a coordinate from the Board using getTile(), why add those addUnit() and removeUnit() methods to Board. Couldn't you just call getTile(), and then use the Tile to do those things?

A: You could take that approach, and let all the **Unit**-related operations be handled directly through the **Tile** object returned from **getTile()**. We decided to add the **Unit**-related methods to **Board**, and have **Board** be the entry point for game designers. In fact, you'll see on the next page that we made **Tile**'s methods protected, so that only classes in the same package as **Tile**—like **Board**—could call **addUnit()** and **removeUnit()** directly. So we've really ensured that **Board** is the object used to work with tiles, units, and eventually terrain.

Q: I still think it would be easy to go ahead and add some more of the methods we know we'll need to Unit and Tile. Why not spend a little time on those classes now?

A: You're not trying to code the entire game system framework at this point; you're just trying to tackle a few key features, and reduce the major risks to your project. Spending time writing the **Unit** class, or fleshing out the **Tile** class, really isn't going to help you reduce risk. Instead, do just enough to get the **Board** class working, because it's the **Board** class that we decided was part of the essence of the system, and where we had a risk of failing if we didn't get that piece in place.

Once you've handled your key features, and reduced or eliminated the big risks to your project, then you'll have plenty of time to work on other features, like the **Unit** class. At this stage, though, you're trying to avoid spending time on anything that doesn't help you reduce the risks to your project succeeding.

 **GEt ONLiNE**

You can download these Board-related classes for Gary's framework at http://www.headfirstlabs.com. Just look for Head First OOA&D, and find "Gary's Game System - Board classes."

More order, less chaos

Our architecture and key feature list has helped us
get the basic **Board** in place, and make sure we're
capturing the essence of the system for the customer.
Let's look back at our key feature list:

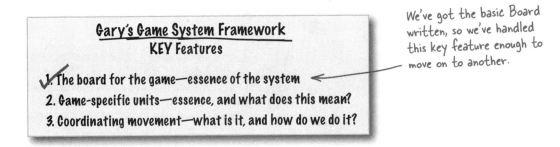

Gary's Game System Framework
KEY Features

1. The board for the game—essence of the system
2. Game-specific units—essence, and what does this mean?
3. Coordinating movement—what is it, and how do we do it?

*We've got the basic Board
written, so we've handled
this key feature enough to
move on to another.*

We've got structure now, too...

Even better, we've got some basic classes in place, and
we can start to think about our next key feature, and
how it fits into this structure.

*Even though Board doesn't
have any variables of type
Unit, it's still associated to
Unit because of its methods
that take in Unit instances.*

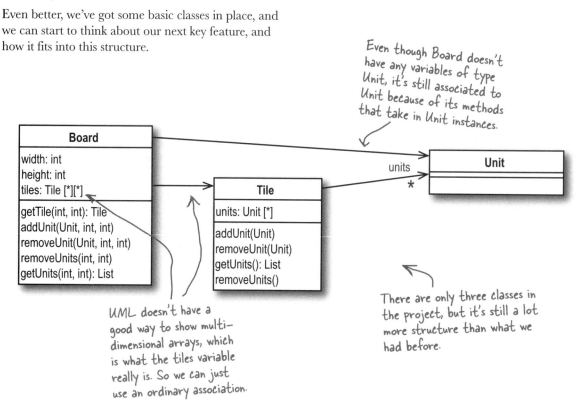

Board

width: int
height: int
tiles: Tile [*][*]

getTile(int, int): Tile
addUnit(Unit, int, int)
removeUnit(Unit, int, int)
removeUnits(int, int)
getUnits(int, int): List

Tile

units: Unit [*]

addUnit(Unit)
removeUnit(Unit)
getUnits(): List
removeUnits()

Unit

units

*

*UML doesn't have a
good way to show multi-
dimensional arrays, which
is what the tiles variable
really is. So we can just
use an ordinary association.*

*There are only three classes in
the project, but it's still a lot
more structure than what we
had before.*

Which feature should we work on next?

We've got a Unit class now, so why don't we tackle "game-specific units" next? Besides, we can also look at how Board and Unit interact.

Build on what you've already got done whenever possible.

When you've got nothing but requirements and diagrams, you've just got to pick a place to start. But now that we do have some code and classes, it's easiest to pick another key feature that relates to what we've already built. And remember our definition for architecture?

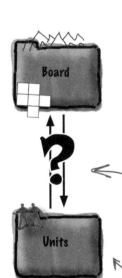

With some basic classes written, we can look at how classes interact, as well as begin to build on what we've already done.

Architecture is your **design structure,** and highlights the **most important** parts of your app, and the **relationships** between those parts.

You really can't talk about the relationships between parts if you don't have two parts that *have* a relationship. We know **Board** and **Unit** are related, and that "game-specific units" are a key feature, so that's the obvious thing to work on next.

Game-specific units... what does that mean?

The simplest way to understand a bit more about what "game-specific units" means is to talk to some of Gary's customers, the game designers who will be using his framework. Let's listen in on what they have to say:

Strategy is the key for our games. We use an advanced combat system where each unit has an attack strength, defense strength, and experience modifier.

I build sci-fi games, big huge space and planet battles. So I need to be able to have armies with lasers and create lots of spaceships.

Our customers are all about air battles, so we don't even need troops. I just want to be able to create a bunch of different types of planes, with different speeds, weapons, and that kind of thing.

Our games are realistic and long-term... we even keep up with the ages and relationships between characters in our games.

No good war game is good without weapons... lots of different types of weapons. And our units can hold two each, so it gets really fun fast.

Sharpen your pencil

What does "game-specific units" mean?

Now that you've heard from several of the game designers who want to use Gary's game system framework, you should have a good idea of what our second key feature is all about. Write down in the blanks below your idea of what you need to do to support "game-specific units."

_____

_____

_____

_____

When you're done, compare your answers with ours on the next page.

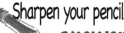

Sharpen your pencil

answers What does "game-specific units" mean?

Now that you've heard from several of the game designers who want to use Gary's game system framework, you should have a good idea of what our second key feature is all about. Write down in the blanks below your idea of what you need to do to support "game-specific units."

Each game based on the framework has different types of units,
with different attributes and capabilities. So we need to be able
to have properties for a unit that are different for each game,
and support multiple data types for those properties.

Some army-related games might have tanks and soldiers...

...and flight simulators might use planes, jets, and rockets.

...fantasy games might have rangers, magicians, and swordsmen...

Commonality revisited

We're starting to learn more about what "game-specific units" means, but we still need to figure out how to actually add support for this feature to our game system framework. Let's start by taking a look at the different types of units the customers mentioned, and figure out what's common between them.

We talked about commonality back on page 287 of Chapter 6, when we were trying to gather basic system requirements. It also applies to smaller problems, like the game-specific units.

```
attack = 12
experience = 22
defense = 9.5
```

Here are a few of the game-specific units, and their properties, mentioned on the last couple of pages.

```
weapon = Bazooka
name = "Simon"
```

```
speed = 110
gun = Gatling
model = "A-10 Thunderbolt II"
```

What is <u>common</u> among these different types of units? What <u>basic things</u> can we say that would apply to <u>any</u> game's units?

Design Puzzle

It's your job to figure out what's common, and should be a part of the basic Unit class, and what varies, and belongs in the game-specific subclasses of Unit. Write any properties and methods that you think belong in Unit in the class diagram for that class below, and then add properties and methods that you think belong in the game-specific subclasses to those diagrams.

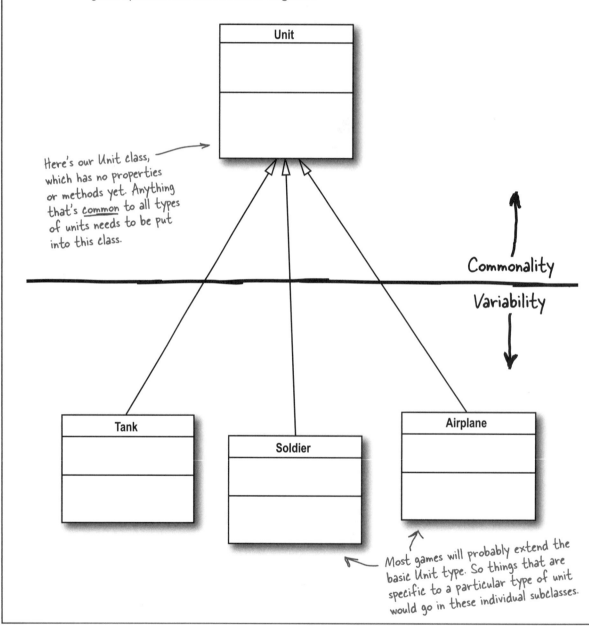

Here's our Unit class, which has no properties or methods yet. Anything that's _common_ to all types of units needs to be put into this class.

Commonality

Variability

Most games will probably extend the basic Unit type. So things that are specific to a particular type of unit would go in these individual subclasses.

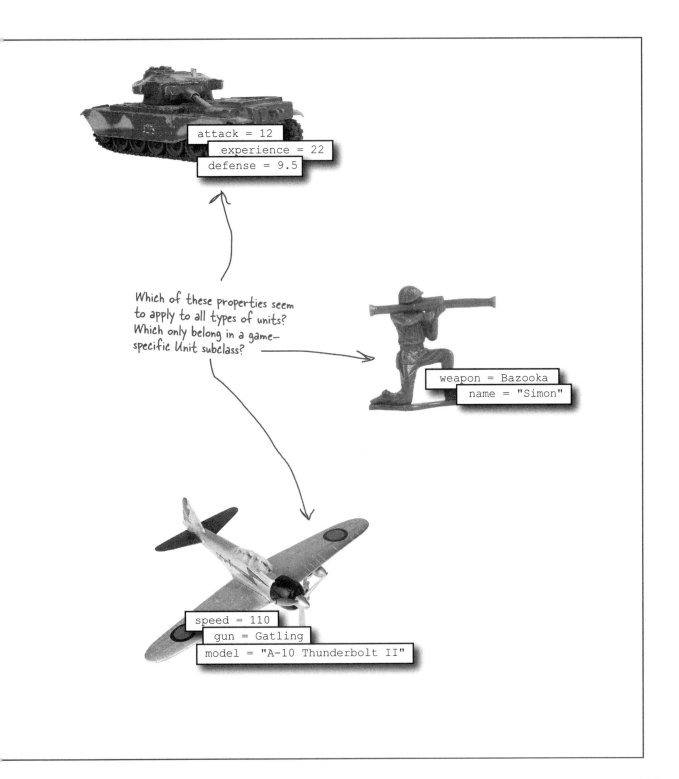

attack = 12
experience = 22
defense = 9.5

Which of these properties seem
to apply to all types of units?
Which only belong in a game-
specific Unit subclass?

weapon = Bazooka
name = "Simon"

speed = 110
gun = Gatling
model = "A-10 Thunderbolt II"

Solution #1: It's all different!

At first glance, you might have come up with a solution
that looks something like this:

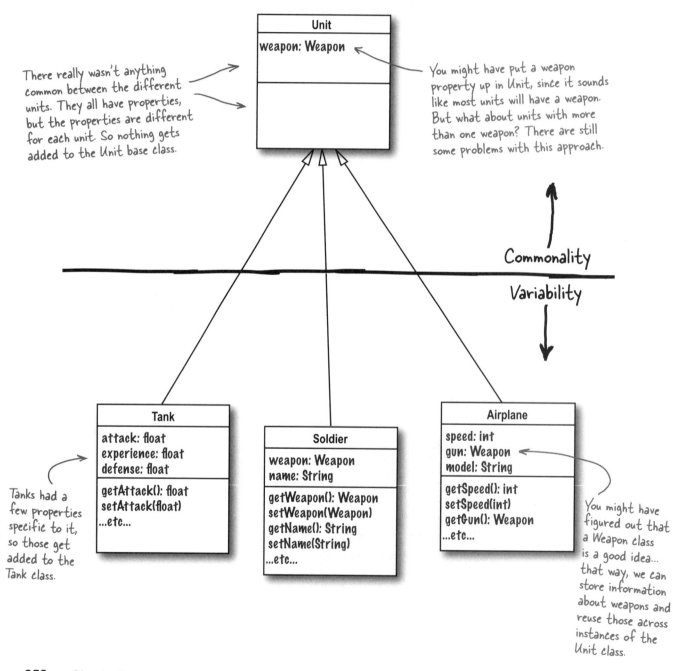

There really wasn't anything
common between the different
units. They all have properties,
but the properties are different
for each unit. So nothing gets
added to the Unit base class.

You might have put a weapon
property up in Unit, since it sounds
like most units will have a weapon.
But what about units with more
than one weapon? There are still
some problems with this approach.

Commonality

Variability

Tanks had a
few properties
specific to it,
so those get
added to the
Tank class.

You might have
figured out that
a Weapon class
is a good idea...
that way, we can
store information
about weapons and
reuse those across
instances of the
Unit class.

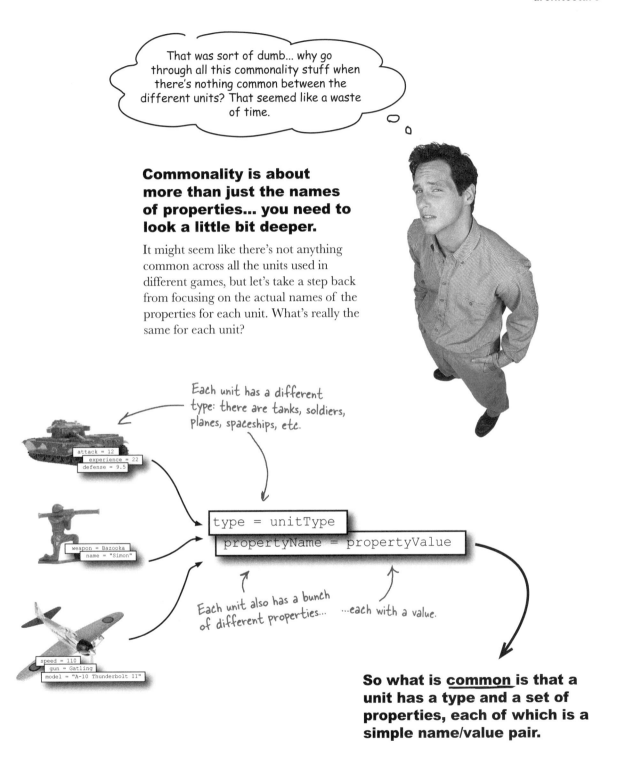

That was sort of dumb... why go through all this commonality stuff when there's nothing common between the different units? That seemed like a waste of time.

Commonality is about more than just the names of properties... you need to look a little bit deeper.

It might seem like there's not anything common across all the units used in different games, but let's take a step back from focusing on the actual names of the properties for each unit. What's really the same for each unit?

Each unit has a different type: there are tanks, soldiers, planes, spaceships, etc.

attack = 12
experience = 22
defense = 9.5

weapon = Bazooka
name = "Simon"

```
type = unitType
propertyName = propertyValue
```

Each unit also has a bunch of different properties...

...each with a value.

speed = 110
gun = Gatling
model = "A-10 Thunderbolt II"

So what is __common__ is that a unit has a type and a set of properties, each of which is a simple name/value pair.

Solution #2: It's all the same!

At first glance, you might have come up with a solution that looks something like this:

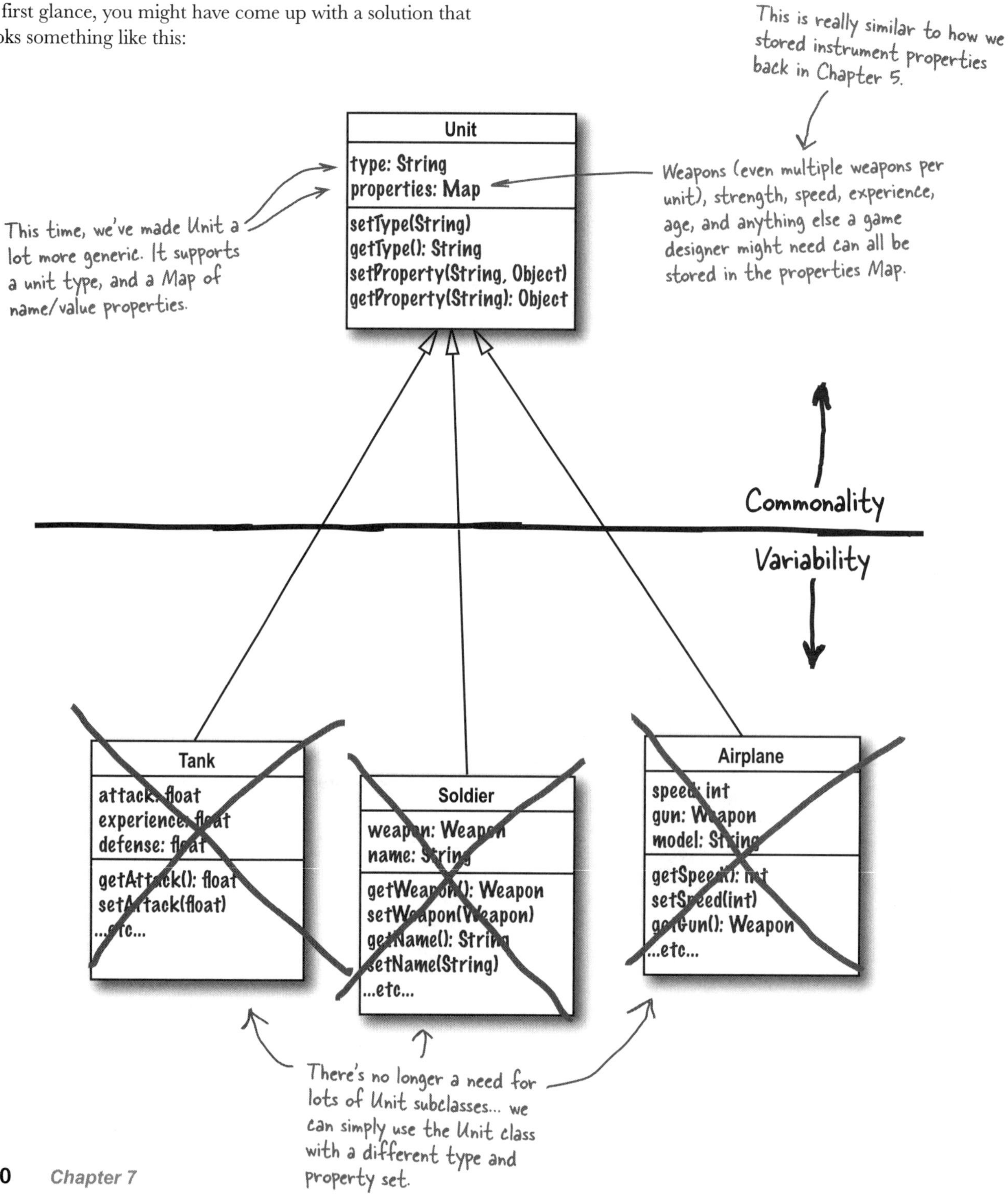

This is really similar to how we stored instrument properties back in Chapter 5.

Unit

type: String
properties: Map
setType(String)
getType(): String
setProperty(String, Object)
getProperty(String): Object

This time, we've made Unit a lot more generic. It supports a unit type, and a Map of name/value properties.

Weapons (even multiple weapons per unit), strength, speed, experience, age, and anything else a game designer might need can all be stored in the properties Map.

Commonality

Variability

Tank

attack: float
experience: float
defense: float
getAttack(): float
setAttack(float)
...etc...

Soldier

weapon: Weapon
name: String
getWeapon(): Weapon
setWeapon(Weapon)
getName(): String
setName(String)
...etc...

Airplane

speed: int
gun: Weapon
model: String
getSpeed(): int
setSpeed(int)
getGun(): Weapon
...etc...

There's no longer a need for lots of Unit subclasses... we can simply use the Unit class with a different type and property set.

OK, this is ludicrous. First, **nothing** was the same, and now **everything** is the same? How in the world is this helping me reduce risk or write better software?

Commonality analysis: the path to <u>flexible</u> <u>software</u>

Wondering why we spent all that time on commonality analysis? Look back at the first solution on page 358, and then again at the second solution, on the left, and then fill out the table below to see what commonality has really bought us in terms of our design:

This first row is what we've looked at so far: 3 different unit types.

100 may seem like a lot, but in massive war games, it's not so far-fetched.

Number of unit types	Number of unit classes – Solution #1	Number of unit classes – Solution #2
3		
5		
10		
25		
50		
100		

Which solution do you think is better? _____

Why? _____
_____
_____
_____

Number of unit types	Number of unit classes – Solution #1	Number of unit classes – Solution #2
3	4	1
5	6	1
10	11	1
25	26	1
50	51	1
100	101	1

With Solution #2, the single Unit class supported all types of units, with any number of different types of properties and attributes.

With Solution #1, you always had a Unit base class, and a subclass for each unit type.

We identified what was <u>common</u>, and put it in the Unit base class. The result was that game designers now only have to keep up with <u>ONE</u> unit class, instead of 25, 50, or 100!

```
            Unit
─────────────────────────────
type: String
properties: Map
─────────────────────────────
setType(String)
getType(): String
setProperty(String, Object)
getProperty(String): Object
```

With a single well-designed Unit class, we can support any number of different unit types.

Good design will <u>always</u> reduce risk.

there are no
Dumb Questions

Q: I can see how this would help me with my design, but what does any of this have to do with reducing risk?

A: Good design always reduces risk. By figuring out how best to design the **Unit** class, we can get it right the first time... before we're deep into working on the entire game system framework, and might have to make drastic changes to **Unit** that affect lots of other code.

Not only have we figured out what "game-specific units" means, but we've defined the basic **Unit** class, and now other classes like **Board** can relate to it without worrying about its design drastically changing in the middle or near the end of the project's development cycle.

And still more order...

We've figured out another key feature, reduced risk to our project even further, and only have one feature left to worry about.

> **Gary's Game System Framework**
> **KEY Features**
>
> ✓ 1. The board for the game—essence of the system
> ✓ 2. Game-specific units—essence, and what does this mean?
> 3. Coordinating movement—what is it, and how do we do it?

> Wait a second... we haven't written any code for the Unit class. Don't we need to do that before we go on to that last feature?

We're focusing on doing <u>just</u> the things that <u>reduce</u> risk.

Remember, the point of architecture is to **reduce risk**, and to **create order**. There are plenty of other things to work on in your application, but those are for after you've got a handle on how your application will be structured, and have the major risks reduced to the point where they are manageable.

We were trying to get a handle on the Unit class, and what "game-specific units" meant; at this point, we've done that:

Unit
type: String   properties: Map
setType(String)   getType(): String   setProperty(String, Object)   getProperty(String): Object

This class diagram is all you need at this point. It gives you the structure of the Unit class, and answers the question, "What does 'game-specific units' mean?"

Q: When we worked on the Board, we did code the Board class, but now you say we shouldn't code the Unit class. What gives?

A: The question you need to be always asking at this stage of a project is, "Will this reduce the risk to my project succeeding?" If the answer is yes, you should go ahead; if it's no, you probably can leave the task for a later stage of the project.

In the case of the **Board**, we needed to have a basic understanding of what the game board does, so we went ahead and coded a basic implementation. But for **Unit**, a class diagram and understanding its basic functionality was all we really needed to do. In both cases, we were reducing risk to our project, rather than focusing on coding or not coding a certain class or package.

Q: But couldn't we have just done a class diagram for Board, like we did for Unit, and stopped there?

A: You probably could have just done a class diagram. It's really a judgment call, and as long as you feel you're focusing on reducing the risk in your project, it's OK to stop with a class diagram, or take things a level or two deeper.

Q: Is it really good to ask the customer and users of a system about what it should do? Couldn't they lead us astray, or distract us?

A: It's usually a good idea to ask the customer, because it is *their* system that you're building. And really, the customer is only going to confuse you, or get you working on the wrong thing, if you're unsure of what you're supposed to be working on. As long as you go into a conversation clear on what your goals are, and you're listening for something specific, you should be able to filter out anything that might confuse or distract you.

Q: I'm still not sure I would have ever come up with using a Map for storing properties in the Unit class on my own.

A: That's OK; that's what tools like commonality and the three Qs of architecture are for. They help you get to solutions that you might not think of on your own, in a way that works on any type of project.

In the case of the **Unit** class, the point isn't that we used a **Map** to store properties. It's that we figured out that all units are basically just a unit type and a set of name/value pairs. Once we figured that out, the details about how we stored those name/value pairs were a piece of cake.

Q: So there's really not a lot of code involved in OOA&D, is there?

A: OOA&D is *all* about code—it's about writing great software, every time. But the way you get to good code isn't always by sitting down and writing it right away. Sometimes the best way to write great code is to hold off on writing code as long as you can. Plan, organize, architect, understand requirements, reduce risks... all these make the job of actually writing your code very simple.

Sometimes the best way to write great code is to hold off on writing code as long as you can.

BE the Author

All that's left is to handle coordinating game movement. But what would you do next to figure that out? Your job is to outline the next few pages of Head First OOA&D, and figure out how you'd take care of this last key feature.

366   Chapter 7

you are here ▸   367

368   Chapter 7

you are here ▸   369

✱Hint: check out what we did for the last key feature that we weren't clear on how to get started.

What does it mean?
Ask the customer.

Want to see the answers to the BE the Author exercise? Read the next four pages and see how close your pages are to what we did.

When you're not sure what a feature really means, one of the best things you can do is ask the customer. We did this with the game-specific units, so let's try the same thing for figuring out what coordinating movement means.

This looks pretty straightforward... it's a fairly simply calculation.

> Each unit has a movement property that says how many squares it can move, and the game checks the terrain to see if the move is legal.

> We hate games that aren't realistic... like when airplanes can fly through buildings! Our games check all the surrounding tiles for other units, and then apply a wind factor to the plane's speed property.

This is quite a bit more complicated... and totally different from the other game designer's requirements.

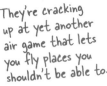

They're cracking up at yet another air game that lets you fly places you shouldn't be able to.

Do you know what "coordinating movement" means?

Listening to the customers should have given you a pretty good idea of what the third key feature of Gary's game system framework is all about. Write what you think that feature really means in the blanks below:

_____

_____

_____

_____

Now do some commonality analysis

Next you need to try and figure out what's common about the different movement scenarios that the customers on page 366 have been talking about. Are there some basic things that apply to all the different types of movement? If you think that there are, write those common things in the blanks below:

_____

_____

_____

_____

So now what would you do?

If you have an understanding of what "coordinating movement" means, and you know what things are common across all games, you should have an idea about what you need to do to the game framework to make this feature work. Write your ideas down in this final set of blanks:

_____

_____

_____

You can use these three basic steps anytime you're unsure about what a feature means, and how you need to implement that feature in your system.

1. Ask the customer

What does the feature mean?

2. Commonality analysis

How do I realize that feature in my system?

3. Implementation plan

Is there <u>anything</u> common here?

Here's what we thought we needed to do based on what Gary's customers were saying about movement:

Units should be able to move from one tile on the
board to another. Movement is based on a calculation or
algorithm specific to each game, and sometimes involves
the game-specific properties of a unit.

So what exactly is common among all the different possible movement scenarios? Remember what the customers said?

We hate games that aren't realistic... like when airplanes can fly through buildings! Our games check all the surrounding tiles for other units, and then apply a wind factor to the plane's speed property.

In this situation, there's an algorithm to see if a move is legal, and another algorithm to figure out how far a unit can go, based partly on that unit's properties.

Each unit has a movement property that says how many squares it can move, and the game checks the terrain to see if the move is legal.

In this case, there's a check to see if a move is legal, and another check of a unit's movement property.

What's common?	What's variable?
There's a check prior to a move to see if the move is legal.	The algorithm to check a move's legality is different for every game.
A unit's properties are used to see how far the unit can move.	The number and specific properties used are different for every game.
Factors other than the unit affect movement.	The factors that affect movement are different for every game.

See a recurring theme here?

This is where things like wind speed come into play.

It's "different for every game"

Did you see what kept showing up in our chart? Every time we found some commonality, the variability column had the same words: "different for every game."

When you find more things that are <u>different</u> about a feature than things that are the <u>same</u>, there may not be a good, generic solution.

In the case of Gary's system, if there's no generic solution, it really doesn't belong as part of the game framework.

Gary, we've thought it through, and we think we should let the game designers handle movement on their own. Anything we do in the framework would just make things a pain for them.

OK, it seems like you've thought things through, so I'm OK with that. Game designers love having more control, anyway.

---

there are no Dumb Questions

Q: How is this really that different from game-specific units?

A: With units, we did find some commonality: every unit had a type, and then name/value properties. With movement, every single game looked like it would handle things differently. So it made sense to leave movement to the game designers, rather than come up with a solution that was so generic that it was essentially useless.

Q: But there is some commonality, isn't there? A movement algorithm, and a check to see if a move is legal, right?

A: You're right. So, in theory, you could write a **Movement** interface, with a method like **move()** that took in a **MovementAlgorithm** and a **LegalMoveCheck**, or something similar. And then each game designer could extend **MovementAlgorithm** and **LegalMoveCheck**. If you thought of something like this, nice work! You're really ahead of the game.

But then ask yourself: what does this really gain? Game designers are going to have to learn your interfaces, and if they don't have a legality check, they might pass in **null** for the **LegalMoveCheck** parameter, and what would the interface for **MovementAlgorithm** look like, and... well, you're probably adding complexity, rather than really removing it.

Your job is to reduce risk and complexity, not increase it. We decided that it would be simpler to let game designers handle movement, and just change the position of units on the board (using methods on **Board**, which we *did* take care of for them).

Great. So we've got a little sheet of paper with some checkmarks, a few classes that we know aren't finished, and lots of UML diagrams. And I'm supposed to believe **this** is how you write great software?

Customers don't pay you for great code, they pay you for great software.

Absolutely! Remember, great <u>software</u> is more than just great <u>code</u>.

Great code is well-designed, and generally functions like it's supposed to. But great software not only is well-designed, it comes in on time and does what the customer really wants it to do.

That's what architecture is about: reducing the risks of you delivering your software late, or having it not work like the customer wants it to. Our key feature list, class diagrams, and those partially done classes all help make sure we're not just developing great *code*, but that we're developing great *software*.

Reducing risk helps you write great software

With all three key features figured out, we've got a handle on the major risks to our project succeeding. Look at how each step we've taken in this chapter has reduced the risks to our project:

Gary's Game System Framework
KEY Features

✓ 1. The board for the game—essence of the system

✓ 2. Game-specific units—essence, and what does this mean?

✓ 3. Coordinating movement—what is it, and how do we do it?

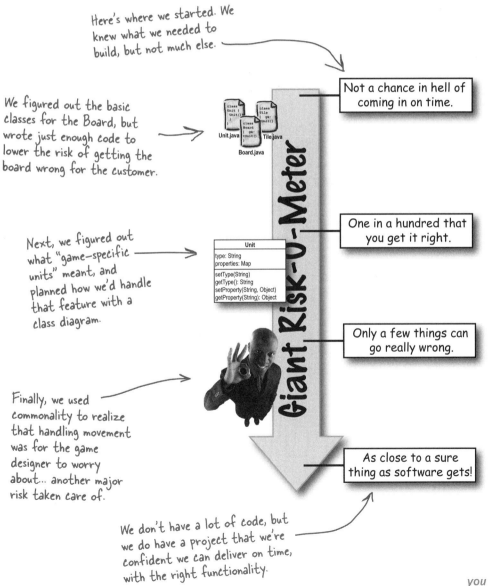

Here's where we started. We knew what we needed to build, but not much else.

Not a chance in hell of coming in on time.

We figured out the basic classes for the Board, but wrote just enough code to lower the risk of getting the board wrong for the customer.

Unit.java   Tile.java
Board.java

One in a hundred that you get it right.

Next, we figured out what "game-specific units" meant, and planned how we'd handle that feature with a class diagram.

Unit
type: String
properties: Map
setType(String)
getType(): String
setProperty(String, Object)
getProperty(String): Object

Only a few things can go really wrong.

Finally, we used commonality to realize that handling movement was for the game designer to worry about... another major risk taken care of.

As close to a sure thing as software gets!

We don't have a lot of code, but we do have a project that we're confident we can deliver on time, with the right functionality.

BULLET POINTS

- Architecture helps you turn all your diagrams, plans, and feature lists into a well-ordered application.

- The features in your system that are most important to the project are architecturally significant.

- Focus on features that are the essence of your system, that you're unsure about the meaning of, or unclear about how to implement first.

- Everything you do in the architectural stages of a project should reduce the risks of your project failing.

- If you don't need all the detail of a use case, writing a scenario detailing how your software could be used can help you gather requirements quickly.

- When you're not sure what a feature is, you should ask the customer, and then try and generalize the answers you get into a good understanding of the feature.

- Use commonality analysis to build software solutions that are flexible.

- Customers are a lot more interested in software that does what they want, and comes in on time, than they are in code that you think is really cool.

OOA&D Cross

The march of the crossword continues. Have you gotten every answer so far? Here's another set of clues to help you store all this architectural info in your brain for good.

Across

6. Focus on the things in your system that are architecturally _____ first.
9. These are the features that you should focus on first.
11. Use cases add risk when used at this time.
12. The essence of a system is what the system is at its most _____.
13. Focusing on more than one feature at a time does this to the risk in your project.
15. Use this type of analysis when you're not sure how to implement a confusing set of features.
16. Architecture highlights these parts of your application. (2 words)
17. Commonality analysis is one path to this type of software.

Down

1. Always start a project by focusing on this.
2. The second Q of architecture is about the _____ of a feature.
3. The first Q of architecture is about this.
4. You focus on key features to reduce this in your project.
5. These are a way to get basic requirements without the detail of a use case.
7. This is not the same as great code.
8. You usually trade off flexibility for this in your project's design.
10. You use architecture to turn a mess into this kind of application.
14. You write this type of software the same way, whether it's a big system or a small one.

Sharpen your pencil

answers   What's missing in Board.java?

Look closely at the scenario on the last page. Did the requirements
we used on page 340 cover everything in the completed scenario?
If you think something is missing, write it in the blank below, and
then add code to Board.java to handle the missing functionality.

We added a removeUnit()
and removeUnits() method
to Board.java to handle
this requirement.

The scenario talks about removing units, but there is no

requirement to remove units on page 340.

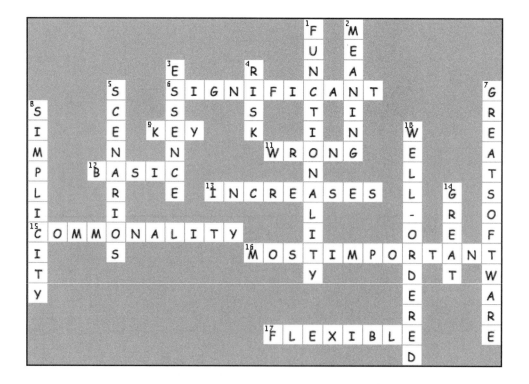

8 design principles

Originality is Overrated

Imitation is the sincerest form of not being stupid.

There's nothing as satisfying as coming up with a completely new and original solution to a problem that's been troubling you for days—until you find out someone else **solved the same problem**, long before you did, and did an even better job than you did! In this chapter, we're going to look at some **design principles** that people have come up with over the years, and how they can make you a better programmer. Lay aside your thoughts of "doing it your way"; this chapter is about **doing it the smarter, faster way**.

Design principle roundup

So far, we've really been concentrating on all the things that you do before you start coding your application. Gathering requirements, analysis, writing out feature lists, and drawing use case diagrams. Of course, at some point you actually are going to have to write some code. And that's where design principles really come into play.

 A **design principle** is a basic tool or technique that can be applied to designing or writing code to make that code more maintainable, flexible, or extensible.

You've already seen a few design principles in earlier chapters:

OO Principles

Encapsulate what varies.

Code to an interface rather than to an implementation.

Each class in your application should have only one reason to change.

Classes are about behavior and functionality.

In this chapter, we're going to look at several more key design principles, and how each one can improve the design and implementation of your code. We'll even see that sometimes you'll have to choose between two design principles... but we're getting ahead of ourselves. Let's begin by looking at the first of our design principles.

Using proven OO design principles results in more <u>maintainable</u>, <u>flexible</u>, and <u>extensible</u> software.

Principle #1: The Open-Closed Principle (OCP)

Our first design principle is the OCP, or the Open-Closed principle. The OCP is all about **allowing change**, but doing it **without requiring you to modify existing code**. Here's how we usually define the OCP:

Open-Closed Principle
Classes should be open for extension, and closed for modification.

You <u>close</u> classes by <u>not</u> allowing anyone to touch your working code.

Closed for modication...

Suppose you have a class with a particular behavior, and you've got that behavior coded up just the way you want it. Make sure that nobody can change your class's code, and you've made that particular piece of behavior **closed for modification**. In other words, nobody can change the behavior, because you've locked it up in a class that you're sure won't change.

...but open for extension

But then suppose someone else comes along, and they just have to change that behavior. You really don't want them messing with your perfect code, which works well in almost every situation... but you also want to make it possible for them to use your code, and extend it. So you let them subclass your class, and then they can override your method to work like they want it to. So even though they didn't mess with your working code, you still left your class **open for extension**.

You <u>open</u> classes by allowing them to be subclassed and extended.

Remember working on Rick's Stringed Instruments?

You probably didn't realize it, but we were using the Open-Closed Principle when we wrote those `InstrumentSpec` classes for Rick's Stringed Instruments, back in Chapter 5:

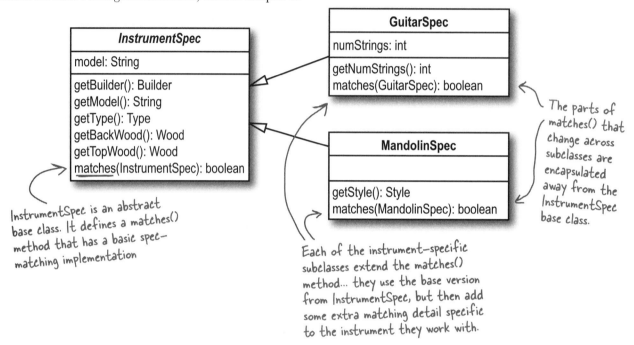

GuitarSpec

numStrings: int

getNumStrings(): int
matches(GuitarSpec): boolean

InstrumentSpec

model: String

getBuilder(): Builder
getModel(): String
getType(): Type
getBackWood(): Wood
getTopWood(): Wood
matches(InstrumentSpec): boolean

MandolinSpec

getStyle(): Style
matches(MandolinSpec): boolean

The parts of matches() that change across subclasses are encapsulated away from the InstrumentSpec base class.

InstrumentSpec is an abstract base class. It defines a matches() method that has a basic spec-matching implementation

Each of the instrument-specific subclasses extend the matches() method... they use the base version from InstrumentSpec, but then add some extra matching detail specific to the instrument they work with.

InstrumentSpec is <u>closed</u> for <u>modification</u>; the matches() method is defined in the base class and <u>doesn't change.</u>

But it's <u>open</u> for <u>extension</u>, because all of the subclasses can <u>change</u> the behavior of matches().

The OCP, step-by-step

Let's take what we did back in Chapter 5, and look at in terms of the OCP, one step at a time.

① **We coded matches() in InstrumentSpec. java, and <u>closed</u> it for modification.**

This version of `matches()` works just fine, and we don't want anyone messing with it. In other words, once we're done coding `InstrumentSpec` and this version of `matches()`, they shouldn't change.

InstrumentSpec
model: String
getBuilder(): Builder getModel(): String getType(): Type getBackWood(): Wood getTopWood(): Wood **matches(InstrumentSpec): boolean**

This method works fine, so we don't want anyone else touching it.

② **But we needed to <u>modify</u> matches() to work with instrument-specific spec classes.**

Even though `matches()` works great for other `InstrumentSpec` objects, it doesn't quite do what it should for guitars and mandolins. So even though `matches()` is closed for modification, we need a way to extend and change it... otherwise, `InstrumentSpec` isn't very flexible, which is a big problem.

③ **So we <u>extended</u> InstrumentSpec, and <u>overrode</u> matches() to change its behavior.**

We don't want to change the code in InstrumentSpec, but we can *extend* it, with `GuitarSpec` and `MandolinSpec`, and then *override* `matches()` in each of those classes to add instrument-specific behavior.

InstrumentSpec
model: String
getBuilder(): Builder getModel(): String getType(): Type getBackWood(): Wood getTopWood(): Wood matches(InstrumentSpec): boolean

GuitarSpec
numStrings: int
getNumStrings(): int **matches(GuitarSpec): boolean**

We don't <u>change</u> the original version of matches()...

...but we can <u>extend</u> InstrumentSpec, and still get new behavior.

> Gee, inheritance is powerful. Really, this is supposed to be some sort of great design principle? Come on.

The OCP is about <u>flexbility</u>, and goes beyond just inheritance.

It's certainly true that inheritance is a simple example of the open-closed principle, but there's a lot more to it than just subclassing and overriding a method. Anytime you write working code, you want to do your best to make sure that code *stays working*... and that means not letting other people change that code.

But there are going to be times when that code still needs to be changed, maybe for just one or two particular situations. Rather than just diving into your code and making a bunch of changes, the OCP lets you **extend** your working code, without **changing** that code.

There are lots of different ways to accomplish this, and while inheritance is often the easiest to implement, it's certainly not the only option. In fact, we'll talk about another great way to achieve this later in the chapter, when we talk about composition.

Sharpen your pencil

Find the OCP in your own project.

Think about the project you're currently working on. Can you find any places where you've used the OCP already? If so, write how you used the OCP in the blanks below:

_____

_____

_____

_____

Now think about a place in your project where you should be using the Open-Closed Principle, but you aren't yet. Write down in the blanks below what you think you need to do to put the OCP into place in your current project:

_____

_____

_____

_____

there are no Dumb Questions

Q: **What's the big deal about modifying code in a base class, or a class that you've already written?**

A: Once you have a class that works, and is being used, you really don't want to make changes to it unless you have to. But remember, CHANGE is the great constant in software development. With the OCP, we allow for change through extension, rather than having to go back and modify your existing code. Subclasses can add and extend the base class's behavior, without messing around with code that you already know is working and making the customer happy.

Q: **Isn't the OCP just another form of encapsulation?**

A: It's really a combination of *encapsulation* and *abstraction*. You're finding the behavior that stays the same, and abstracting that behavior away into a base class, and then locking that code up from modification. But then when you need new or different behavior, your subclasses handle the changes by extending the base class. That's where encapsulation comes in: you're encapsulating what varies (behavior in the subclasses) away from what stays the same (the common behavior in the base class).

Q: **So the only way to use the OCP is by extending another class?**

A: No, anytime your code is closed for modification but open for extension, you're using the OCP. So for example, if you had several private methods in a class, those are closed for modification—no other code can mess with them. But then you could add several public methods that invoked those private methods in different ways. You're extending the behavior of the private methods, without changing them. That's another example of the OCP in action.

Principle #2:
The Don't Repeat Yourself Principle (DRY)

Next up is the Don't Repeat Yourself principle, or DRY for short. This is another principle that looks pretty simple, but turns out to be critical in writing code that's easy to maintain and reuse.

Don't Repeat Yourself

Avoid duplicate code by abstracting out things that are common and placing those things in a single location.

A prime place to apply DRY...

You've seen the DRY principle in action, even if you didn't realize it. We used DRY back in Chapter 2, when Todd and Gina wanted us to close the dog door automatically after it had been opened.

Remember when we had code in the Remote class to automatically close the dog door once it had been opened?

```java
public void pressButton() {
  System.out.println(
    "Pressing the remote control button...");
  if (door.isOpen()) {
    door.close();
  } else {
    door.open();

    final Timer timer = new Timer();
    timer.schedule(new TimerTask() {
      public void run() {
        door.close();
        timer.cancel();
      }
    }, 5000);
  }
}
```

class
Remote {
    press-
Button()
}

Remote.java

```java
public void recognize(String bark) {
  System.out.println("   BarkRecognizer: " +
    "Heard a '" + bark + "'");
  door.open();

  final Timer timer = new Timer();
  timer.schedule(new TimerTask() {
    public void run() {
      door.close();
      timer.cancel();
    }
  }, 5000);
}
```

Doug suggested we put the same code in BarkRecognizer... but according to DRY, that's a BAD idea.

class
BarkRec-
ognizer
{
    update
}

BarkRecognizer.java

1. Let's abstract out the common code.

Using DRY, we first need to take the code that's common between **Remote** and **BarkRecognizer**, and put it in a single place. We figured out back in Chapter 2 the best place for it was in the **DogDoor** class:

Using DRY, we pull out all this code from Remote and BarkRecognizer, and put it in ONE place: the DogDoor class. So no more duplicate code, no more maintenance nightmares.

```java
public class DogDoor {
  public void open() {
    System.out.println("The dog door opens.");
    open = true;

    final Timer timer = new Timer();
    timer.schedule(new TimerTask() {
      public void run() {
        close();
        timer.cancel();
      }
    }, 5000);
  }
```

DogDoor.java

2. Now remove the code from other locations...

3. ...and reference the code from Step #1.

The next two steps happen at the same time. Remove all the code that you put in a single place in Step #1, and then reference the code you abstracted out explicitly if you need to:

First, we got rid of this code... it's all in DogDoor's open() method now.

We don't have to explicitly call the code we abstracted out... that's handled already by our call to door.open().

```java
public void recognize(String bark) {
  System.out.println("    BarkRecognizer: " +
    "Heard a '" + bark + "'");
  door.open();

  final Timer timer = new Timer();
  timer.schedule(new TimerTask() {
    public void run() {
      door.close();
      timer.cancel();
    }
  }, 5000);
}
```

BarkRecognizer.java

DRY is really about ONE requirement in ONE place

Abstracting out duplicate code is a good start to using DRY, but there's more to it than just that. When you're trying to avoid duplicate code, you're really trying to make sure that you only implement each feature and requirement in your application one single time.

In the dog door we just looked at, the feature we were trying to implement was automatically closing the door.

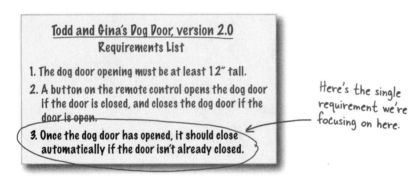

Todd and Gina's Dog Door, version 2.0
Requirements List

1. The dog door opening must be at least 12" tall.
2. A button on the remote control opens the dog door if the door is closed, and closes the dog door if the door is open.
3. Once the dog door has opened, it should close automatically if the door isn't already closed.

Here's the single requirement we're focusing on here.

Originally, though, we implemented that single feature in *two* places: **Remote.java** and **BarkRecognizer.java**.

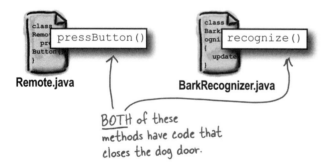

Remote.java — pressButton()

BarkRecognizer.java — recognize()

BOTH of these methods have code that closes the dog door.

By using DRY, we removed the duplicate code. But more importantly, we moved the implementation of this requirement, automatically closing the door, into *one* place, instead of *two* places:

DogDoor.java — open()

Now there is just ONE place we automatically close the door: open(), in DogDoor.

Q: So DRY *isn't* about duplicate code, and avoiding copy-and-paste?

A: DRY is about avoiding duplicate code, but it's also about doing it in a way that won't create more problems down the line. Rather than just tossing code that appears more than once into a single class, you need to make sure each piece of information and behavior in your system has a single, clear place where it exists. That way, your system always knows exactly where to go when it needs that information or behavior.

Q: If DRY is related to our features and requirements, then shouldn't we apply it to *gathering* those features and requirements as well as writing our code?

A: Absolutely, and that's a great idea! Whether you're writing requirements, developing use cases, or coding, you want to be sure that you don't duplicate things in your system. A requirement should be implemented one time, use cases shouldn't have overlap, and your code shouldn't repeat itself. DRY is about a lot more than just code.

Q: And this is all to avoid maintenance problems later, right?

A: Right. But it's more than just avoiding a need to update code in more than one place. Remember, DRY is about having a *single source* for a particular piece of information or behavior. But that single source has to make sense! You wouldn't want the bark recognizer to be the single source for closing the dog door, would you? Do you think the dog door should be asking the recognizer to close itself?

So DRY is not just removing duplication, it's also about making good decisions about how to break up your system's functionality.

DRY is about having each piece of information and behavior in your system in a single, <u>sensible place</u>.

Design Puzzle

DRY is about a lot more than just finding duplicate code in your system. It also applies to your features and requirements. It's time to put DRY into action on your own now, and to do it in more than just code.

The problem:

Todd and Gina have come up with yet more features for their dog door. It's your job to make sure the feature list we've assembled doesn't have any duplication issues, and that each feature is handled once and only once in the system you're designing for them.

Your task:

1 Read through the requirements and features list on the right. We've bolded the requirements and features that have been added since you last worked on the dog door.

2 Look through the new features and requirements, and see if you see any possible duplication in the new things you'd need to build.

3 Annotate the requirements and features list indicating what you think has been duplicated.

4 Rewrite the duplicate requirements at the bottom of the list so that there is no more duplication.

5 Write a new definition for the DRY principle in the space below, and make sure you talk about more than just duplicate code.

Write your own definition for DRY that includes what you've learned over the last few pages.

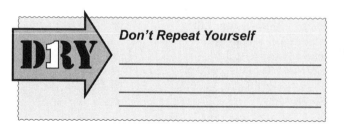

Don't Repeat Yourself

Todd and Gina's Dog Door, version 3.0
Requirements and Features List

These are the requirements you've already seen...

...and these are the new features and requirements.

1. The dog door opening must be at least 12" tall.

2. A button on the remote control opens the dog door if the door is closed, and closes the dog door if the door is open.

3. Once the dog door has opened, it should close automatically if the door isn't already closed.

4. A bark recognizer must be able to tell when a dog is barking.

5. The bark recognizer must open the dog door when it hears barking.

6. The dog door should alert the owner when something inside the house gets too close for the door to open without knocking it over.

7. The dog door will open during certain hours of the day.

8. The dog door can be integrated into the house's overall alarm system to ensure the alarm doesn't go off when the dog door opens and closes.

9. The dog door should make a noise if the door cannot open because of a blockage outside.

10. The dog door will track how many times the dog enters and leaves the inside of the house.

11. When the dog door closes, the household alarm system re-arms if it was active before the door opened.

Write any new or updated requirements, without duplication, here at the bottom of the list.

→ Solutions on the next page.

-Design Puzzle Solutions

DRY is about a lot more than just finding duplicate code in your system. It also applies to your features and requirements. Your job was to put DRY into action on your own, in the context of requirements rather than just code.

The problem:

> Todd and Gina have come up with yet more features for their dog door. It's your job to make sure the feature list we've assembled doesn't have any duplication issues, and that each feature is handled once and only once in the system you're designing for them.

Your task:

1 Read through the requirements and features list on the right. We've bolded the requirements and features that have been added since you last worked on the dog door.

2 Look through the new features and requirements, and see if you see any possible duplication in the new things you'd need to build.

3 Annotate the requirements and features list indicating what you think has been duplicated.

4 Rewrite the duplicate requirements at the bottom of the list so that there is no more duplication.

5 Write a new definition for the DRY principle in the space below, and make sure you talk about more than just duplicate code.

Here's what we wrote for our definition of DRY.

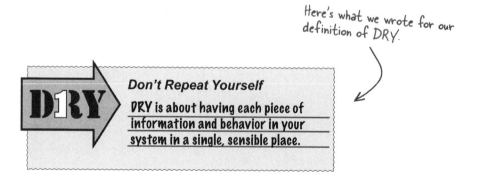

Don't Repeat Yourself

DRY is about having each piece of information and behavior in your system in a single, sensible place.

Todd and Gina's Dog Door, version 3.0
Requirements and Features List

1. The dog door opening must be at least 12" tall.

2. A button on the remote control opens the dog door if the door is closed, and closes the dog door if the door is open.

3. Once the dog door has opened, it should close automatically if the door isn't already closed.

4. A bark recognizer must be able to tell when a dog is barking.

5. The bark recognizer must open the dog door when it hears barking.

6. ~~The dog door should alert the owner when something inside the house gets too close for the door to open without knocking it over.~~

7. The dog door will open during certain hours of the day.

8. The dog door can be integrated into the house's overall alarm system to ensure the alarm doesn't go off when the dog door opens and closes.

9. ~~The dog door should make a noise if the door cannot open because of a blockage outside.~~

10. The dog door will track how many times the dog enters and leaves the inside of the house.

11. When the dog door closes, the household alarm system re-arms if it was active before the door opened.

The door alerts the owner if there is an obstacle inside or outside of the house that stops the door from operating.

When the door opens, the house alarm system will disarm, and when the door closes, the alarm system will re-arm (if the alarm system is turned on).

Here's what we did to the requirements list.

#6 and #9 are almost identical. One focuses on the inside, and the other on the outside, but the basic functinality is the same.

Requirements #7 and #10 were fine, and stayed the same.

Here's how we combined and re-wrote #6 and #9.

#8 and #11 both relate to the house alarm... they're really duplicates of the same basic functionality, too.

Here's our new requirement from #8 and #11.

Principle #3:
The Single Responsibility Principle (SRP)

The SRP is all about responsibility, and which objects in your system do what. You want each object that you design to have just one responsibility to focus on—and when something about that responsibility changes, you'll know exactly where to look to make those changes in your code.

Single Responsibility Principle

Every object in your system should have a single responsibility, and all the object's services should be focused on carrying out that single responsibility.

Hey, we've talked about this before... this is the same as a class having only one reason to change, isn't it?

You've implemented the Single Responsibility Principle correctly when each of your objects has <u>only</u> <u>one</u> <u>reason</u> <u>to</u> <u>change.</u>

Q: SRP sounded a lot like DRY to me. Aren't both about a class doing the one thing it's supposed to do?

A: They are related, and often appear together. DRY is about putting a piece of functionality in a single place, such as a class; SRP is about making sure that a class does only one thing, and that it does it well.

In good applications, one class does one thing, and does it well, *and* no other classes share that behavior.

Q: Isn't having each class do only one thing kind of limiting?

A: It's not, when you realize that the one thing a class does can be a pretty *big* thing. For example, the `Board` class in Gary's Games does a lot of different small tasks, but they're all related to a single big thing: handling the board in a game. It does that one thing, and that's all the Board class does, so it's a great example of using the SRP.

Q: And using SRP will help my classes stay smaller, since they're only doing one thing, right?

A: Actually, the SRP will often make your classes *bigger*. Since you're not spreading out functionality over a lot of classes—which is what many programmers not familiar with the SRP will do—you're often putting more things into a class.

But using the SRP will usually result in less classes, and that generally makes your overall application a lot simpler to manage and maintain.

Q: This sounds a lot like cohesion, are they the same thing?

A: Cohesion is actually just another name for the SRP. If you're writing highly cohesive software, then that means that you're correctly applying the SRP.

Spotting multiple responsibilities

Most of the time, you can spot classes that aren't using the
SRP with a simple test:

1 On a sheet of paper, write down a bunch of lines like this: The [blank]
[blanks] itself. You should have a line like this for every method in the class
you're testing for the SRP.

2 In the first blank of each line, write down the class name; in the second
blank, write down one of the methods in the class. Do this for each
method in the class.

3 Read each line out loud (you may have to add a letter or word to get it to
read normally). Does what you just said make any sense? Does your class
really have the responsibility that the method indicates it does?

> **If what you've just said <u>doesn't</u> <u>make</u> <u>sense</u>,
> then you're probably violating the SRP with
> that method. The method might belong on a
> <u>different</u> class... think about moving it.**

*Here's what your
SRP analysis sheet
should look like.*

SRP Analysis for _____

*Write the class name
in this blank, all the
way down the sheet.*

*Write each method
from the class in this
blank, one per line.*

The _____ _____ itself.
The _____ _____ itself.
The _____ _____ itself.

*Repeat this line for each
method in your class.*

Sharpen your pencil

Apply the SRP to the Automobile class.

Do an SRP analysis on the Automobile class shown below. Fill out the sheet with the class name methods in Automobile, like we've described on the last page. Then, decide if you think it makes sense for the Automobile class to have each method, and check the right box.

Automobile
start()
stop()
changeTires(Tire [*])
drive()
wash()
checkOil()
getOil(): int

We looked at this class in CATASTROPHE back in Chapter 5.

← Yes, we realize you can peek back at Chapter 5 and cheat here, but we're trusting you not to. Try the exercise on your own first, and only look back at what we did in Chapter 5 if you get stuck.

SRP Analysis for ___Automobile___

	Follows SRP	**Violates SRP**
The _____ _____ itself.	☐	☐
The _____ _____ itself.	☐	☐
The _____ _____ itself.	☐	☐
The _____ _____ itself.	☐	☐
The _____ _____ itself.	☐	☐
The _____ _____ itself.	☐	☐
The _____ _____ itself.	☐	☐

← If what you read doesn't make sense, then the method on that line is probably violating the SRP.

Sharpen your pencil
answers
Apply the SRP to the Automobile class.

Your job was to do an SRP analysis on the Automobile class shown below. You should have filled out the sheet with the class name methods in Automobile, and decided if you think it makes sense for the Automobile class to have each method.

It makes sense that the automobile is responsible for starting, and stopping. That's a function of the automobile.

An automobile is *NOT* responsible for changing its own tires, washing itself, or checking its own oil.

SRP Analysis for ___Automobile___

				Follows SRP	Violates SRP
The	Automobile	start[s]	itself.	☑	☐
The	Automobile	stop[s]	itself.	☑	☐
The	Automobile	changesTires	itself.	☐	☑
The	Automobile	drive[s]	itself.	☐	☑
The	Automobile	wash[es]	itself.	☐	☑
The	Automobile	check[s] oil	itself.	☐	☑
The	Automobile	get[s] oil	itself.	☑	☐

You may have to add an "s" or a word or two to make the sentence readable.

This one was a little tricky... we thought that while an automobile might start and stop itself, it's really the responsibilty of a *driver* to drive the car.

You should have thought carefully about this one, and what "get" means. This is a method that just returns the amount of oil in the automobile... and that *is* something that the automobile should do.

Cases like this are why SRP analysis is just a *guideline*. You still are going to have to make some judgment calls using common sense and your own experience.

Going from multiple responsibilities to a single responsibility

Once you've done an analysis, you can take all the methods that don't make sense on a class, and move those methods to classes that do make sense for that particular responsibility.

It's a driver's responsibility to drive the car, not the automobile itself.

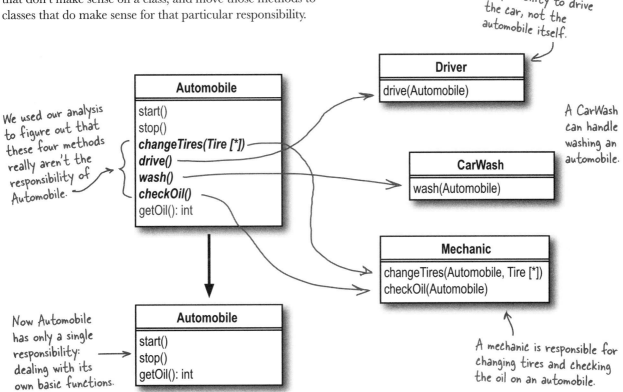

We used our analysis to figure out that these four methods really aren't the responsibility of Automobile.

A CarWash can handle washing an automobile.

Now Automobile has only a single responsibility: dealing with its own basic functions.

A mechanic is responsible for changing tires and checking the oil on an automobile.

---

there are no
Dumb Questions

Q: How does SRP analysis work when a method takes parameters, like wash(Automobile) on the CarWash class?

A: Good question! For your SRP analysis to make any sense, you need to include the parameter of the method in the method blank. So you would write "The <u>CarWash</u> washes [an] automobile itself." That method makes sense (with the **Automobile** parameter), so it would stay on the **CarWash** class.

Q: But what if CarWash took in an Automobile parameter as part of its constructor, and the method was just wash()? Wouldn't SRP analysis give you a wrong result?

A: It would. If a parameter that might cause a method to make sense, like an **Automobile** for the **wash()** method on **CarWash**, is passed into a class's constructor, your SRP analysis might be misleading. But that's why you always need to apply a good amount of your own common sense and knowledge of the system in addition to what you learn from the SRP analysis.

SRP Sightings

The SRP has already made a few appearances in our work so far; now that you're getting familiar with the SRP, it's time for you to figure out where and how it's been used. Your task is to look at the page below and figure out how SRP was used, and why.

This is from the dog door, back in Chapter 3.

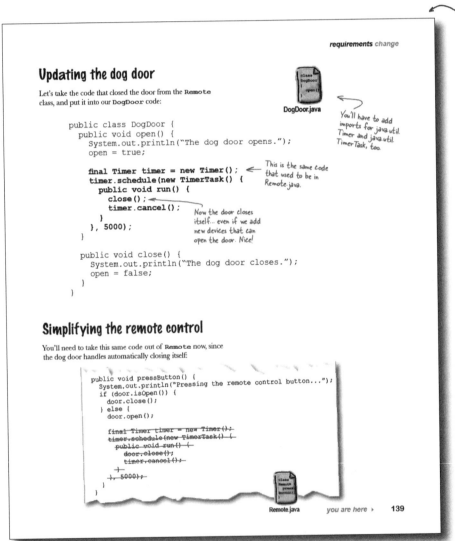

requirements change

Updating the dog door

Let's take the code that closed the door from the `Remote` class, and put it into our `DogDoor` code:

DogDoor.java

You'll have to add imports for java.util. Timer and java.util. TimerTask, too.

```
public class DogDoor {
  public void open() {
    System.out.println("The dog door opens.");
    open = true;

    final Timer timer = new Timer();
    timer.schedule(new TimerTask() {
      public void run() {
        close();
        timer.cancel();
      }
    }, 5000);
  }

  public void close() {
    System.out.println("The dog door closes.");
    open = false;
  }
}
```

This is the same code that used to be in Remote.java.

Now the door closes itself... even if we add new devices that can open the door. Nice!

Simplifying the remote control

You'll need to take this same code out of `Remote` now, since the dog door handles automatically closing itself:

```
public void pressButton() {
  System.out.println("Pressing the remote control button...");
  if (door.isOpen()) {
    door.close();
  } else {
    door.open();

    final Timer timer = new Timer();
    timer.schedule(new TimerTask() {
      public void run() {
        door.close();
        timer.cancel();
      }
    }, 5000);
  }
}
```

Remote.java

you are here ▸ **139**

How do you think the Single Responsibility Principle was used in Todd and Gina's dog door? Write your answer in the blanks below:

_____

_____

_____

_____

Now see if you can find two more instances in the book's examples so far where we've used the SRP to make our design better and more flexible. You can find the SRP in the dog door, Rick's instrument inventory searcher, or Gary's game framework. Write down each instance you found, and how you think the SRP is being used.

<u>First</u> <u>Instance</u>

Example application: ___ Rick's Instruments   ___ Doug's Dog Doors   ___ Gary's Games

How SRP is being used:

Check off which example application you found the SRP being used in.

_____

_____

_____

_____

Write in how you think the SRP was applied in this example.

There's the SRP!

<u>Second</u> <u>Instance</u>

Example application: ___ Rick's Instruments   ___ Doug's Dog Doors   ___ Gary's Games

How SRP is being used:

_____

_____

_____

_____

_____

_____

SRP Sightings Revealed!

Let's look back on the times that SRP has already shown up in our software. Here are the SRP sightings we came up with; see if your answers are similar.

This is from the dog door, back in Chapter 3.

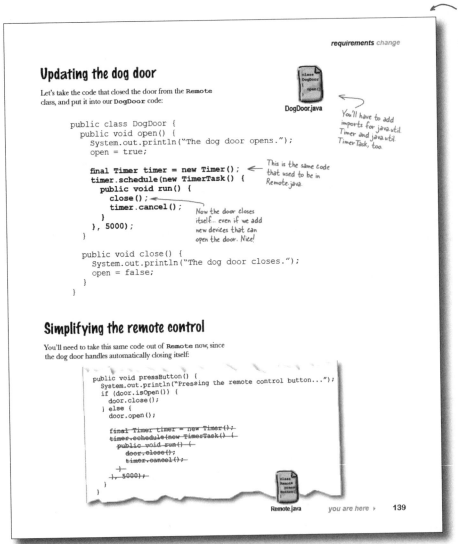

requirements change

Updating the dog door

Let's take the code that closed the door from the `Remote` class, and put it into our `DogDoor` code:

DogDoor.java

You'll have to add imports for java.util. Timer and java.util. TimerTask, too.

```java
public class DogDoor {
  public void open() {
    System.out.println("The dog door opens.");
    open = true;

    final Timer timer = new Timer();
    timer.schedule(new TimerTask() {
      public void run() {
        close();
        timer.cancel();
      }
    }, 5000);
  }

  public void close() {
    System.out.println("The dog door closes.");
    open = false;
  }
}
```

This is the same code that used to be in Remote.java.

Now the door closes itself... even if we add new devices that can open the door. Nice!

Simplifying the remote control

You'll need to take this same code out of `Remote` now, since the dog door handles automatically closing itself:

```java
public void pressButton() {
  System.out.println("Pressing the remote control button...");
  if (door.isOpen()) {
    door.close();
  } else {
    door.open();

    final Timer timer = new Timer();
    timer.schedule(new TimerTask() {
      public void run() {
        door.close();
        timer.cancel();
      }
    }, 5000);
  }
}
```

Remote.java

you are here ▸ 139

How do you think the Single Responsibility Principle was used in Todd and Gina's dog door? Write your answer in the blanks below:

> **We moved the code to close the dog door out of Remote.java, and avoided**
> **duplicating the same code in the BarkRecognizer (DRY in effect there!). We**
> **also made sure that the DogDoor class handled all tasks relating to the**
> **operation of the dog door—it has that single responsibility.**

Here's what we wrote about how SRP (and DRY) helped us out with the dog door.

Now see if you can find two more instances in the book's examples so far where we've used the SRP to make our design better and more flexible. You can find the SRP in the dog door, Rick's instrument inventory searcher, or Gary's game framework. Write down each instance you found, and how you think the SRP is being used.

First Instance

Example application: ✗ Rick's Instruments ___ Doug's Dog Doors ___ Gary's Games

How SRP is being used:

> **We created a matches() method on InstrumentSpec, rather than leaving**
> **the code to compare instruments in the search() method of Inventory. So an**
> **InstrumentSpec handles everything related to an instrument's properties—**
> **that code isn't spread out over other classes. That's SRP in action.**

You don't have to have the same examples that we found. Just make sure the SRP was applied in similar ways to the ones we wrote down here, and you've got it.

Second Instance

Example application: ___ Rick's Instruments ___ Doug's Dog Doors ✗ Gary's Games

How SRP is being used:

> **When we used a Map to store properties for all types of units in the Unit**
> **class, we were using the SRP. So instead of having game-specific Units have**
> **to deal with their properties, and still have the base Unit class dealing with**
> **a different set of properties, we moved all property-related functionality**
> **into the nit class. So handling the properties feature is taken care of in ONE**
> **single place—the Unit class.**

Contestant #4:
The Liskov Substitution Principle (LSP)

Next up in our design principle parade is the Liskov Substitution
Principle, or the LSP. It's definition is as simple as it gets:

Liskov Substitution Principle

*Subtypes must be substitutable for
their base types.*

> OK, earlier you convinced
> me that the OCP is more than just
> basic inheritance, but here you are
> with the subclassing thing again. We're
> programmers, we know how to use
> inheritance correctly by now.

**The LSP is all about <u>well</u>-<u>designed</u>
inheritance. When you inherit from
a base class, you must be able to
<u>substitute</u> <u>your</u> <u>subclass</u> for that
base class without things going
terribly <u>wrong</u>. Otherwise, you've
used inheritance incorrectly!**

Misusing subclassing: a case study in misusing inheritance

Suppose that Gary's Games has a new client who wants to use their game system framework to create World War II air battles. They need to take the basic **Board** base type, and extend it to support a 3-dimensional board to represent the sky. Here's what they've done:

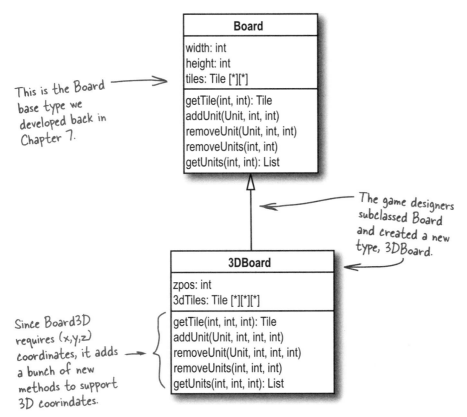

This is the Board base type we developed back in Chapter 7.

The game designers subclassed Board and created a new type, 3DBoard.

Since Board3D requires (x,y,z) coordinates, it adds a bunch of new methods to support 3D coorindates.

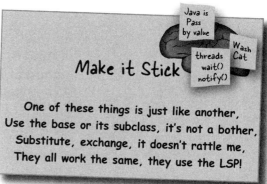

Make it Stick

Java is Pass by value

threads wait() notify()

Wash Cat

One of these things is just like another,
Use the base or its subclass, it's not a bother,
Substitute, exchange, it doesn't rattle me,
They all work the same, they use the LSP!

LSP reveals hidden problems with your inheritance structure

At first glance, it may seem like subclassing **Board** and using inheritance is a great idea. But look closer, there are lots of problems that this approach creates:

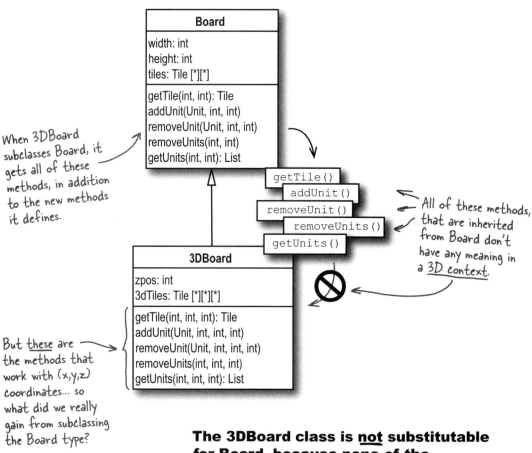

When 3DBoard subclasses Board, it gets all of these methods, in addition to the new methods it defines.

All of these methods, that are inherited from Board don't have any meaning in a 3D context.

But _these_ are the methods that work with (x,y,z) coordinates... so what did we really gain from subclassing the Board type?

The 3DBoard class is <u>not</u> substitutable for Board, because none of the methods on Board work correctly in a 3D environment. Calling a method like getUnits(2, 5) <u>doesn't</u> <u>make</u> <u>sense</u> for 3DBoard. So this design violates the LSP.

Even worse, we don't know what passing a coordinate like (2,5) even <u>means</u> to 3DBoard. This is <u>not</u> a good use of inheritance.

"Subtypes must be substitutable for their base types"

We already said that LSP states that a subtype must be substitutable for its base type. But what does that really mean? Technically, it doesn't seem to be a problem:

```
Board board = new 3DBoard();
```

From the compiler's point of view, 3DBoard can be used in place of a Board here.

But when you start to actually *use* that instance of **3DBoard** like a **Board**, things can get confusing very fast:

```
Unit unit = board.getUnits(8, 4);
```

Remember, board here is actually an instance of the subtype, 3DBoard.

But what does this method mean on 3DBoard?

So even though **3DBoard** is a subclass of **Board**, it's not substitutable for **Board**... the methods that **3DBoard** inherited don't have the same meaning as they do on the superclass. Even worse, it's not clear what meaning those methods *do* have!

Inheritance (and the LSP) indicate that any method on Board should be able to be used on 3DBoard... that 3DBoard can stand in for Board without any problems.

Some bit of code calls a method from Board, but on an instance of 3DBoard.

```
Unit unit = removeUnits(8, 4);
```

Board
width: int
height: int
tiles: Tile [*][*]
getTile(int, int): Tile
addUnit(Unit, int, int)
removeUnit(Unit, int, int)
removeUnits(int, int)
getUnits(int, int): List

3DBoard
zpos: int
3dTiles: Tile [*][*][*]
getTile(int, int, int): Tile
addUnit(Unit, int, int, int)
removeUnit(Unit, int, int, int)
removeUnits(int, int, int)
getUnits(int, int, int): List

But what do these methods mean for 3DBoard? They probably don't mean anything!

Violating the LSP makes for confusing code

It might seem like this isn't such a big deal, but code that violates LSP can be confusing, and a real nightmare to debug. Let's think a bit about someone who comes to use the badly designed **3DBoard** for the first time.

They probably start out by checking out the class's methods:

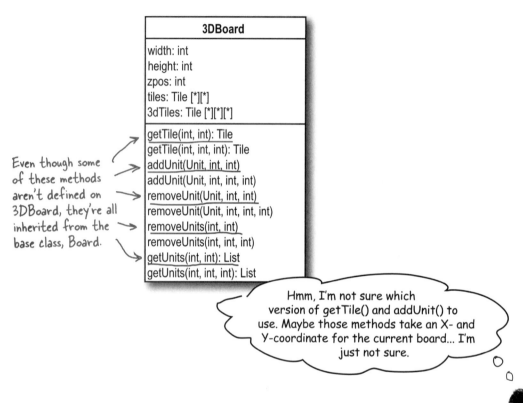

3DBoard
width: int
height: int
zpos: int
tiles: Tile [*][*]
3dTiles: Tile [*][*][*]
getTile(int, int): Tile
getTile(int, int, int): Tile
addUnit(Unit, int, int)
addUnit(Unit, int, int, int)
removeUnit(Unit, int, int)
removeUnit(Unit, int, int, int)
removeUnits(int, int)
removeUnits(int, int, int)
getUnits(int, int): List
getUnits(int, int, int): List

Even though some of these methods aren't defined on 3DBoard, they're all inherited from the base class, Board.

Hmm, I'm not sure which version of getTile() and addUnit() to use. Maybe those methods take an X- and Y-coordinate for the current board... I'm just not sure.

It's <u>hard</u> <u>to</u> <u>understand</u> code that misuses inheritance.

When you use inheritance, your subclass gets all the methods from its superclass, even if you don't want those methods. And if you've used inheritance badly, then you're going to end up with a lot of methods that you don't want, because they probably don't make sense on your subclass.

So what can you do to avoid this? First, be sure your subclasses can substitute for their base types, which is just following the LSP. Second, learn about some *alternatives* to using inheritance in your code...

Solving the 3DBoard problem <u>without</u> using inheritance

It's not enough to just know that inheritance isn't the answer... now we've got to figure out what we *should* have done. Let's look at the **Board** and **3DBoard** classes again, and see how we can create a 3-dimensional board without using inheritance.

The Board class has functionality that 3DBoard needs, but it's <u>not</u> the base type for 3DBoard.

```
┌─────────────────────────────┐
│           Board             │
├─────────────────────────────┤
│ width: int                  │
│ height: int                 │
│ tiles: Tile [*][*]          │
├─────────────────────────────┤
│ getTile(int, int): Tile     │
│ addUnit(Unit, int, int)     │
│ removeUnit(Unit, int, int)  │
│ removeUnits(int, int)       │
│ getUnits(int, int): List    │
└─────────────────────────────┘
```

boards ↑ *

Instead of extension, we're using an association. So 3DBoard can use the behavior of Board, without having to extend from it and violate the LSP.

3DBoard can store an array of Board objects, and end up with a 3D collection of boards.

The 3DBoard methods use the zpos coordinate to figure out which Board instance in the array to use, and then delegates the (x,y) coords to that Board's functions.

```
┌──────────────────────────────────┐
│             3DBoard               │
├──────────────────────────────────┤
│ zpos: int                         │
│ 3dTiles: Tile [*][*][*]           │
├──────────────────────────────────┤
│ getTile(int, int, int): Tile      │
│ addUnit(Unit, int, int, int)      │
│ removeUnit(Unit, int, int, int)   │
│ removeUnits(int, int, int)        │
│ getUnits(int, int, int): List     │
└──────────────────────────────────┘
```

This is a form of <u>delegation</u>. The 3DBoard class delegates a lot of its functionality to the individual Board instances.

These methods look a lot like the methods in Board, but they need to <u>use</u> the functionality in Board, rather than <u>extend</u> it. So inheritance isn't a good option here.

So what options are there besides inheritance?

<u>Delegate</u> functionality to another class

You've already seen that delegation is when one class hands off the task of doing something to another class. It's also just one of several alternatives to inheritance.

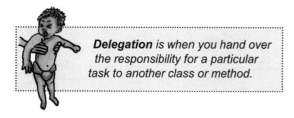

> **Delegation** is when you hand over the responsibility for a particular task to another class or method.

Delegation was what we used to solve the **3DBoard** problem we've been looking at, without resorting to inheritance:

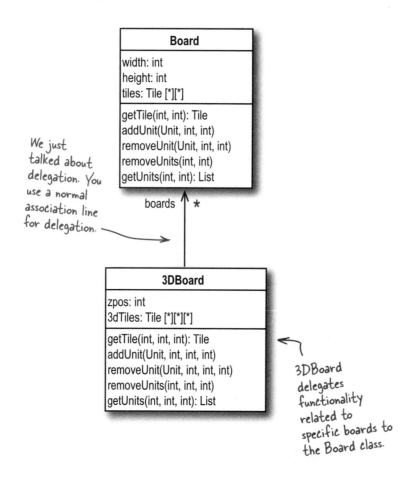

Board

width: int
height: int
tiles: Tile [*][*]

getTile(int, int): Tile
addUnit(Unit, int, int)
removeUnit(Unit, int, int)
removeUnits(int, int)
getUnits(int, int): List

We just talked about delegation. You use a normal association line for delegation.

boards ↑ *

3DBoard

zpos: int
3dTiles: Tile [*][*][*]

getTile(int, int, int): Tile
addUnit(Unit, int, int, int)
removeUnit(Unit, int, int, int)
removeUnits(int, int, int)
getUnits(int, int, int): List

3DBoard delegates functionality related to specific boards to the Board class.

When to use delegation

Delegation is best used when you want to use another class's functionality, as is, without changing that behavior at all. In the case of **3DBoard**, we wanted to use the various methods in the **Board** class:

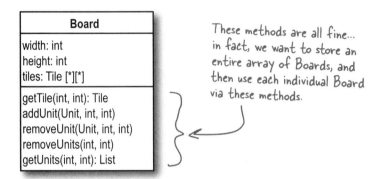

These methods are all fine... in fact, we want to store an entire array of Boards, and then use each individual Board via these methods.

Since we don't want to change the existing behavior, but we do want to use it, we can simply create a delegation relationship between **3DBoard** and **Board**. **3DBoard** stores multiple instances of **Board** objects, and delegates handling each individual board-related task.

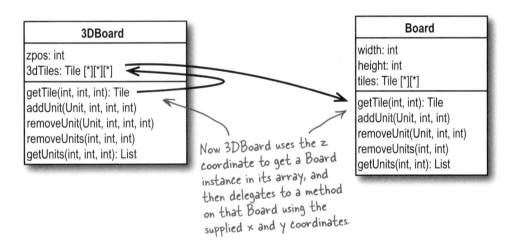

Now 3DBoard uses the z coordinate to get a Board instance in its array, and then delegates to a method on that Board using the supplied x and y coordinates.

If you need to use functionality in another class, but you <u>don't want to change</u> that functionality, consider using delegation instead of inheritance.

Use <u>composition</u> to assemble behaviors from other classes

Sometimes delegation isn't quite what you need; in delegation, the behavior of the object you're delegating behavior to never changes. **3DBoard** *always* uses instances of **Board**, and the behavior of the **Board** methods *always* stay the same.

But in some cases, you need to have more than one single behavior to choose from. For example, suppose we wanted to develop a **Weapon** interface, and then create several implementations of that interface that all behave differently:

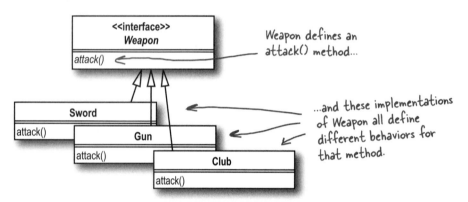

Weapon defines an attack() method...

...and these implementations of Weapon all define different behaviors for that method.

Now we need to use the behavior from these classes in our **Unit** class. One of the properties in our **properties Map** will be "weapon", and the value for that property needs to be an implementation of the **Weapon** class. But a **Unit** might change weapons, so we don't want to tie the weapon property to a specific implementation of **Weapon**; instead, we just want each **Unit** to be able to reference a **Weapon**, regardless of which implementation of **Weapon** we want to use.

We don't want to be stuck with one particular weapon... instead, we want to <u>choose</u> between the available weapon types.

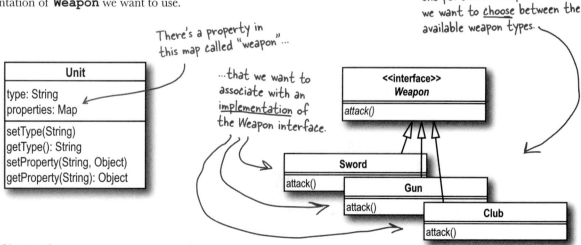

There's a property in this map called "weapon"...

...that we want to associate with an <u>implementation</u> of the Weapon interface.

When to use composition

When we reference a whole family of behaviors like in the Unit
class, we're using **composition**. The **Unit**'s weapons property is
composed of a particular **Weapon** implementation's behavior. We
can show this in UML like this:

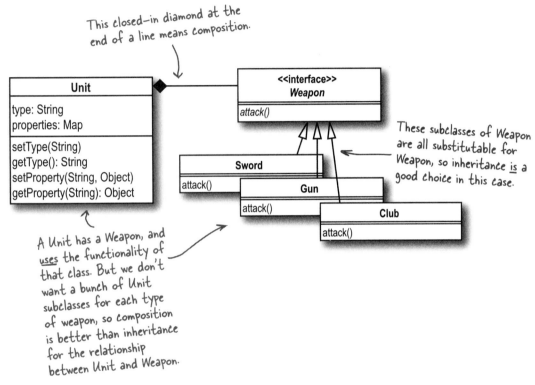

This closed-in diamond at the end of a line means composition.

These subclasses of Weapon are all substitutable for Weapon, so inheritance is a good choice in this case.

A Unit has a Weapon, and uses the functionality of that class. But we don't want a bunch of Unit subclasses for each type of weapon, so composition is better than inheritance for the relationship between Unit and Weapon.

Composition is most powerful when you want to use behavior defined
in an interface, and then <u>choose</u> from a variety of implementations
of that interface, at both compile time and run time.

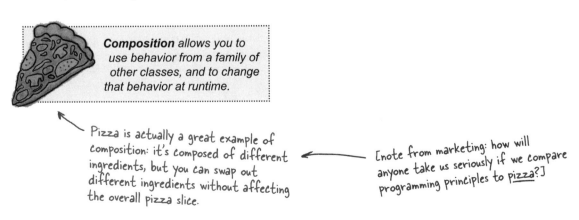

> **Composition** allows you to
> use behavior from a family of
> other classes, and to change
> that behavior at runtime.

Pizza is actually a great example of composition: it's composed of different ingredients, but you can swap out different ingredients without affecting the overall pizza slice.

[note from marketing: how will anyone take us seriously if we compare programming principles to pizza?]

When the pizza is gone, so are the ingredients...

There's one important point we haven't mentioned so far about composition. When an object is composed of other objects, and the owning object is destroyed, *the objects that are part of the composition go away, too.* That's a little confusing, so let's take a closer look at what that actually means.

Here's our **Unit** class again, which has a composition relationship to the **Weapon** interface and its implementations:

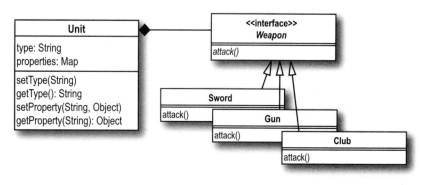

Suppose we create a new **Unit**, and assign its weapon property to an instance of **Sword**:

```
Unit pirate = new Unit();
pirate.setProperty("weapon", new Sword());
```

This Unit is composed with an instance of Sword.

What happens if this **Unit** is destroyed? Obviously, the **pirate** variable is trashed, but the instance of **Sword** referenced by pirate is also thrown away. It doesn't exist *outside of* the **pirate** object.

This Sword object does <u>not exist</u> outside of the context of this particular Unit.

If you get rid of the pirate Unit object...

...then you're automatically getting rid of the Sword object associated with pirate, too.

In composition, the object composed of other behaviors <u>owns</u> those behaviors. When the object is destroyed, <u>so</u> <u>are</u> <u>all</u> <u>of</u> <u>its</u> <u>behaviors</u>.

The behaviors in a composition <u>do</u> <u>not</u> <u>exist</u> outside of the composition itself.

> I get it... composition is really about ownership. The main object owns the composed behavior, so if that object goes away, all the behavior does, too.

Can you think of an example where the ownership aspect of composition would be a negative in your application? When might you want the composed objects to exist outside of the composing class?

Aggregation: composition, without the abrupt ending

What happens when you want all the benefits of composition—flexibility in choosing a behavior, and adhering to the LSP—but your composed objects need to exist *outside* of your main object? That's where aggregation comes in.

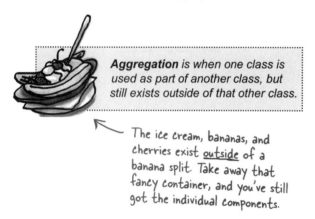

Aggregation *is when one class is used as part of another class, but still exists outside of that other class.*

The ice cream, bananas, and cherries exist <u>outside</u> of a banana split. Take away that fancy container, and you've still got the individual components.

You've already used aggregation...

We've been using aggregation already, in Rick's Stringed Instruments, from Chapter 5:

A line with an open diamond at the end means aggregation.

InstrumentSpec is used as part of an Instrument, but the spec can also exist <u>outside</u> of an Instrument (like when it's supplied by a customer for searching).

Instrument
serialNumber: String price: double
getSerialNumber(): String getPrice(): double setPrice(float) getSpec(): InstrumentSpec

spec
1

InstrumentSpec
properties: Map
getProperty(String): Object getProperties(): Map matches(InstrumentSpec): boolean

We were able to avoid all those instrument-specific subclasses by using aggregation here.

Aggregation versus composition

It's easy to get confused about when you should use composition, and when you should use aggregation. The easiest way to figure this out is to ask yourself, *Does the object whose behavior I want to use exist outside of the object that uses its behavior?*

If the object does make sense existing on its own, then you should use aggregation; if not, then go with composition. But be careful! Sometimes the slightest change in the usage of your objects can make all the difference.

Five-Minute Mystery

Joel leaned back in his seat, arched his back, and thought again about buying that new Aeron chair once his stock options came in. Being a game programmer was hard work, and Joel was the last coder in the office yet again.

"People are gonna go nuts over Cows Gone Wild," he thought. He pulled up the user guide for Gary's Game System Framework, and started to think about how he was going to implement the cowboys, one of the last features he had to deal with. Suddenly, his eyes lit upon the Unit class, and he realized that he could use Units for cowboys, and the Weapon interface for lassos, revolvers, and even branding irons.

Joel created Lasso, Revolver, and BrandingIron classes, and made sure they all implemented the Weapon interface. He even added a Weapon property to his Building class, so the cowboys could hang their gear up at the end of long days chasing the cows.

"This is so money... a little bit of composition, and I'll bet boss-man Brad will put me as the lead designer in the game credits." He quickly drew up a class diagram of what he had done for the morning shift, colored in his composition diamond between the Unit and Weapon classes, and headed for Taco Bell on the way back to his apartment.

Little did Joel know that when he got back into work the next day, Brad would be yelling at him, instead of congratulating him...

What did Joel do wrong?

Answer on page 421

Inheritance is just one option

We started out this section talking about the LSP, and the basic idea that subclasses must be substitutable for their base classes. More importantly, though, now you have several ways to reuse behavior from other classes, beyond inheritance.

Let's take a quick look back at our options for reusing behavior from other classes, without resorting to subclassing.

Delegation

Delegate behavior to another class when you don't want to change the behavior, but it's not your object's responsibility to implement that behavior on its own.

Composition

You can reuse behavior from one or more classes, and in particular from a family of classes, with **composition**. Your object completely owns the composed objects, and they do not exist outside of their usage in your object.

Aggregation

When you want the benefits of composition, but you're using behavior from an object that does exist outside of your object, use **aggregation**.

> All three of these OO techniques allow you to reuse behavior **without** violating the LSP.

If you favor delegation, composition, and aggregation <u>over</u> inheritance, your software will usually be more flexible, and easier to maintain, extend, and reuse.

Q: I thought subclassing was a good thing. Now you're saying it's a *bad* thing?

A: No, subclassing and inheritance are key to any good OO programming language. The LSP is not about subclassing, though; it's about *when* to subclass. If your subclass really is substitutable for its base type, then you've probably done a good job using inheritance. If your subclass is *not* substitutable for its base type, then you might look at other OO solutions like aggregation or delegation.

Q: But it is OK to use delegation, composition, or aggregation in a class that really shouldn't extend another class?

A: Sure. In fact, the LSP doesn't apply at all to aggregate or delegate classes, because those are two great ways to fix an inheritance tree that doesn't conform to the LSP. You might even say that good use of the LSP goes hand-in-hand with more delegation, composition, and aggregation.

Q: Do we really need to apply the LSP all the time to figure this out? Isn't this just writing good OO software?

A: Lots of times, you don't need to worry about the formal name of a design principle to write good code. For example, look back at the **Board** example on page 401; to make **3DBoard** extend **Board**, all of the methods had to be changed! That should be a real tip-off that you're got some inheritance problems.

Q: There were a lot of weird UML symbols in there. How am I supposed to remember what they all mean?

A: You really don't need to memorize these symbols at all. While UML provides specific notation for aggregation and composition, they are all just different forms of association. So just like we did with delegation, you can use a normal line with an arrow, a normal association, for composition and aggregation.

Q: But won't that be confusing to developers if they don't know what type of association should be used?

A: That's possible, but it also allows for a lot more flexibility. Suppose that you decide later on that when an army is destroyed, you don't want the individual units destroyed as well. So you might change the relationship between army and unit from composition to aggregation.

If you're using a basic association arrow, you won't need to change your class diagram at all. It also gives the developer freedom to come up with their own ideas about how to implement the association.

There's nothing wrong with using the aggregation and composition symbols, but you shouldn't get too hung up on it, especially if you're early on in the development cycle. You never know what might change later, and flexibility is always better than rigidity in your design.

Who Am I?

A bunch of classes involved in OO principles, all in full costume, are playing a party game, "Who Am I?" They give a clue, and you try to guess who they are, based on what they say. Assume they always tell the truth about themselves. If they happen to say something that could be true for more than one of them, choose all for whom that sentence can apply. Fill in the blanks next to the sentence with the names of one or more attendees. The first one's on us.

Tonight's attendees:

Subclass   Delegated Class   Aggregated Class
Delegating Class   Composite Class

I'm substitutable for my base type.   _____

I let someone else do things for me.   _____

My behavior is used as part of
another class's behavior.   _____

I change the behavior of
another class.   _____

I don't change the behavior
of another class.   _____

I can combine the behavior of
other classes together.   _____

I'm not gonna go away, even
if other related classes do.   _____

I get my behavior and
functionality from my base type.   _____

———▶ Unmask the principles on page 420

BULLET POINTS

- The Open-Closed Principle keeps your software reusable, but still flexible, by keeping classes open for extension, but closed for modification.

- With classes doing one single thing through the Single Responsibility Principle, it's even easier to apply the OCP to your code.

- When you're trying to determine if a method is the responsibility of a class, ask yourself, *Is it this class's job to do this particular thing?* If not, move the method to another class.

- Once you have your OO code nearly complete, be sure that you Don't Repeat Yourself. You'll avoid duplicate code, and ensure that each behavior in your code is in a single place.

- DRY applies to requirements as well as your code: you should have each feature and requirement in your software implemented in a single place.

- The Liskov Substitution Principle ensures that you use inheritance correctly, by requiring that subtypes be substitutable for their base types.

- When you find code that violates the LSP, consider using delegation, composition, or aggregation to use behavior from other classes without resorting to inheritance.

- If you need behavior from another class but don't need to change or modify that behavior, you can simply delegate to that class to use the desired behavior.

- Composition lets you choose a behavior from a family of behaviors, often via several implementations of an interface.

- When you use composition, the composing object owns the behaviors it uses, and they stop existing as soon as the composing object does.

- Aggregation allows you to use behaviors from another class without limiting the lifetime to those behaviors.

- Aggregated behaviors continue to exist even after the aggregating object is destroyed.

Tools for your OOA&D Toolbox

We've got a lot more OO principles to add to the toolbox. Let's add what we've learned to our notes—and remember: these principles are best used together, not separately!

Requirements

Good requireme
works like your

Make sure your
by developing u

Use your
things you

Your use
or missing
have.

Your requ
grow) ove

Analysis and Design

Well-designed software is easy to cha
and extend.

Use basic OO principles like encapsula

OO Principles

Encapsulate what varies.

Code to an interface rather than to an implementation.

Each class in your application should have only one reason to change.

Classes are about behavior and functionality.

Classes should be open for extension, but closed for modification (the OCP)

Avoid duplicate code by abstracting out things that are common and placing them in a single location (the DRY principle)

Every object in your system should have a single responsibility, and all the object's services should be focused on carrying out that single responsibility (the SRP)

Subclasses should be suitable for their base classes (the LSP)

Solving Big Problems

Listen to the customer, and figure out what they want you to build.

Put together a feature list, in language the customer understands.

e your features are what the
actually wants.

eprints of the system using use
ams (and use cases).

big system up into lots of
tions.

n patterns to the smaller
the system.

OA&D principles to design and
aller section.

OOA&D Cross

This one is a particularly tough puzzle: almost all the answers are more than one word. Good luck, and keep that left brain working.

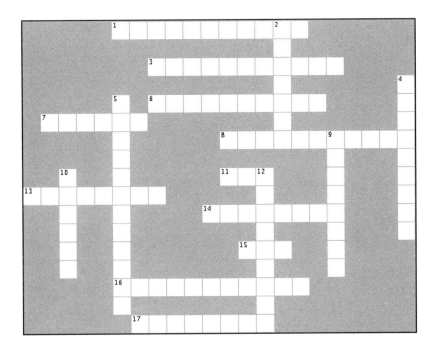

Across

1. A variation on composition.
3. This is when one object owns behaviors from other objects.
6. This is when you hand over responsibility for a particular behavior.
7. He was all about substitution.
8. The LSP reveals problems related to this.
11. You should keep a single piece of code in this many places.
13. You should have each piece of your information and this in a single, sensible place.
14. _____ out things that are common in your code.
15. Each object in your system should have this many responsibilities.
16. This is overrated in good OO software design.
17. Another term for SRP is this.

Down

2. Aggregated objects exist _____ of the classes that use them.
4. Subtypes must be substitutable for these.
5. Classes should be closed for this.
9. OO principles work best when used this way.
10. A well-designed class has only one reason to do this.
12. Classes should be open for this.

Who Am I? Solutions

A bunch of classes involved in OO principles, all in full costume, are playing a party game, "Who Am I?" They give a clue, and you try to guess who they are, based on what they say. Assume they always tell the truth about themselves. If they happen to say something that could be true for more than one of them, choose all for whom that sentence can apply. Fill in the blanks next to the sentence with the names of one or more attendees. The first one's on us.

Tonight's attendees:

Subclass   Delegated Class   Aggregated Class

Delegating Class   Composite Class

I'm substitutable for my base type.   ____subclass____

I let someone else do things for me.   ____delegating class, composite class____ ← This is a basic delegation definition, but a class that uses composition uses other classes for behavior, also.

My behavior is used as part of another class's behavior.   ____aggregated class____

I change the behavior of another class.   ____subclass____

I don't change the behavior of another class.   ____delegated class, aggregated class, delegating class, composite class____ ← A subclass is the only class that <u>changes</u> another class's behavior.

I can combine the behavior of other classes together.   ____composite class, delegating class____

I'm not gonna go away, even if other related classes do.   ____aggregated class, delegated class____ ←

I get my behavior and functionality from my base type.   ____subclass____

In aggregation and delegation, object instances are tied together, but not dependent on each other for their existence.

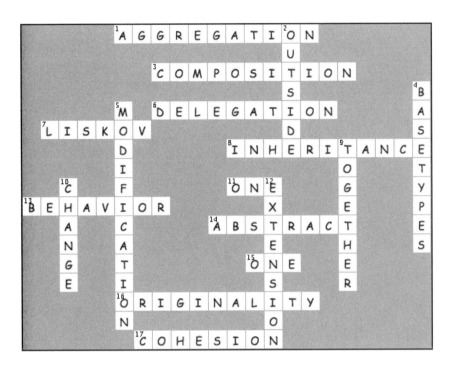

Exercise
Solutions

The crossword puzzle solution:

1. (across) AGGREGATION
2. (down) OUSD
3. (across) COMPOSITION
4. (down) BASETYPES
5. (down) MODIFICATION
6. (across) DELEGATION
7. (across) LISKOV
8. (across) INHERITANCE
9. (down) TOGGETHER
10. (down) CHANGE
11. (across) ONE
12. (down) EXTENSE
13. (across) BEHAVIOR
14. (across) ABSTRACT
15. (across) ONE
16. (across) ORIGINALITY
17. (across) COHESION

Five-Minute Mystery Solved

Joel's big mistake was revealed in this line:

He even added a Weapon property to his Building class, so the cowboys could hang their gear up at the end of long days chasing the cows.

When Joel decided that cowboys could hang up their weapons, he committed to the Lasso, Revolver, and BrandingIron classes existing *outside* of any individual Unit instance. No cowboy owned the gear; they just used the behavior of the gear for a time.

Since the Weapon implementations exist outside of a specific cowboy, Joel should have used aggregation instead of composition. Different cowboys could use the same Weapon implementation at different times, and those weapons should stay in existence, even if the cowboy using them was trampled by a mad cow.

9 iterating and testing

The Software is Still
for the Customer

I spent forever wondering what I could give you to show how much I think of your ideas, and then I had it: a beautiful new set of tests!

Oh, Jim! You really do care about what I want, don't you?

It's time to show the customer how much you really care. Nagging bosses? Worried clients? Stakeholders that keep asking, "Will it be done on time?" No amount of well-designed code will please your customers; you've got to **show them something working**. And now that you've got a solid OO programming toolkit, it's time to learn how you can **prove to the customer** that your software works. In this chapter, we learn about two ways to **dive deeper** into your software's functionality, and give the customer that warm feeling in their chest that makes them say, *Yes, you're definitely the right developer for this job!*

Your toolbox is filling up

We've learned quite a bit so far, and our toolbox of analysis and design tools is getting pretty full. We even added some OO programming techniques in the last chapter:

In Chapters 6 and 7, we used use case diagrams and a key feature list to turn a simple vision statement into an application architecture.

Our OO principles from Chapter 8 help us write well-designed, flexible OO software.

We've got a whole slew of principles and techniques to gather requirements, analyze and design, and solve all types of software problems.

Requirements

Good requi works like

Make sure by developi

Use your u things you

Your use ca or missing have.

Your requi grow) over

Analysis and Design

Well-designed software is easy to change and extend.

Use basic OO principles like encapsulation and inheritance to make your software more flexible.

If a design is IT! Never set it's your bad

Make sure ea each of your ONE THING

Always strive move through lifecycle.

OO Principles

Encapsulate what varies.

Code to an interface rather than an implementation.

Classes are about behavior and functionality.

Classes should be open for extension, but closed for modification (the OCP).

Avoid duplicate code by abstracting out things that are common and placing them in a single location (the DRY principle).

Every object in your system should have a single responsibility, and all the object's services should be focused on carrying out that single responsibility (the SRP).

Subclasses should be suitable for their base classes (the LSP).

Solving Big Problems

Listen to the customer, and figure out what th... nt you to build.

... a feature list, in language understands.

... features are what the ...ly wants.

...ts of the system using use ...nd use cases).

...tem up into lots of

...rns to the smaller ...stem.

...inciples to design and ...ection.

1. Make sure your software does what the customer wants it to do.

2. Apply basic OO principles to add flexibility.

The 3 steps to writing great software showed up back in Chapter 1, but we've been using them throughout every chapter.

3. Strive for a maintainable, reusable design.

That's great, really, you're an amazing developer, I'm sure. But I really don't care about any of that...
where's my application?

But you're still writing your software for the **CUSTOMER!**

All the tools and techniques you've been learning are terrific... but none of them matter if you don't use them to produce great software that makes your customer happy.

And most of the time, your customer won't care about all the OO principles and diagrams you create. They just want the software to work the way that it's supposed to.

Gary, from Gary's Games, is ready to see his game system framework in action.

We really don't have anything to show Gary yet. All we've done is start on a few of these key features, like the Board class and the Unit class diagram.

Frank

Jill

Joe

You write great software iteratively.

Work on the big picture, and then iterate over pieces of the app until it's complete.

Joe: Yeah, maybe we shouldn't have spent all this time on so many diagrams, and all this architecture stuff. We've got nothing to show Gary except a bunch of ovals with things like "Play Game" written inside them.

Frank: Come on guys, we've got a lot more done than that. It's going to be simple to finish up the Board class, because we've already got a start on writing a lot of that functionality.

Jill: Well, sure, but that's the only class we've written any code for. How are we supposed to show *that* to Gary?

Joe: Well, I guess we could write the Unit class pretty easily, since we did that class diagram. So it wouldn't take a lot more time to write the code for that class.

Frank: Exactly. And, really, we know how to write all of these classes. We can just take each class, or even an entire package, and apply all those OO principles and analysis and design techniques to each chunk of functionality.

Jill: But we've got to work on functionality now. We don't have time for a bunch more big-picture analysis and design.

Frank: But that's just the thing, Jill: we don't need to change what we're doing, we just need to iterate deeper.

Joe: Iterate deeper? What does that mean?

Frank: It just means we keep doing analysis and design, but now on each individual part of Gary's game system framework.

Jill: And as we build up the application, we'll have lots of pieces working that we can show to Gary, right?

Joe: And we get to use all these tools we've got to make sure the software is well-designed, too, right?

Frank: Exactly. But first, we've got a choice to make...

Iterating deeper:
two basic choices

When it comes to developing software, there is more than one way to iterate into specific parts of your application. You've got to take on smaller pieces of functionality, but there are two basic approaches to figuring out which small pieces to work on—and even what a "small piece" means in terms of your application.

You can choose to focus on <u>specific</u> <u>features</u> of the application. This approach is all about taking <u>one</u> <u>piece</u> <u>of</u> <u>functionality</u> that the customer wants, and working on that functionality until it's complete.

> **Feature driven development**
>
> *...is when you pick a specific feature in your app, and plan, analyze, and develop that feature to completion.*

You can also choose to focus on <u>specific</u> <u>flows</u> through the application. This approach takes a <u>complete</u> <u>path</u> through the application, with a <u>clear</u> <u>start</u> <u>and</u> <u>end</u>, and implements that path in your code.

> **Use case driven development**
>
> *...is when you pick a scenario through a use case, and write code to support that complete <u>scenario</u> through the use case.*

You'll often see the terms "flow" and "scenario" used interchangeably.

Both approaches to iterating are **driven** by <u>good</u> <u>requirements</u>.

Because requirements come from the customer, **both** approaches focus on delivering what the <u>**customer wants**</u>.

Feature driven development

When you're using **feature driven development**,
you work on a single feature at a time, and then
iterate, knocking off features one at a time until
you've finished up the functionality of an application.

With feature driven development, you pick a single feature, and the focus is on the feature list of your app.

Gary's Game System Framework
Feature List

1. The framework supports different types of terrain.

2. The framework supports different time periods, including fictional periods like sci-fi and fantasy.

3. The framework supports multiple types of troops or units that are game-specific.

4. The framework supports add-on modules for additional campaigns or battle scenarios.

5. The framework provides a board made up of square tiles, and each tile has a terrain type.

6. The framework keeps up with whose turn it is.

7. The framework coordinates basic movement.

So we might take feature #1, and work on the Terrain class, as well as the Tile class, to support different types of terrain.

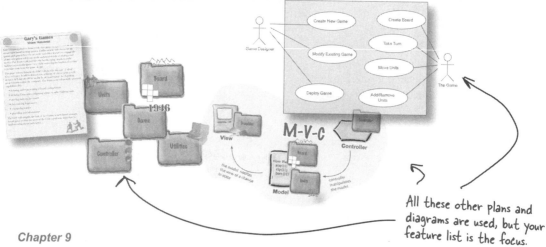

All these other plans and diagrams are used, but your feature list is the focus.

Use case driven development

With **use case driven development**, you work on completing
a single scenario through a use case. Then you take another
scenario and work through it, until all of the use case's scenarios
are complete. Then you iterate to the next use case, until all your
use cases are working.

With use case driven
development, you work from
the use case diagram, which
lists the different use
cases in your system.

Here, you could take the
Create Board use case, and
figure out all the scenarios
for that use case, and write
code to handle all of them.

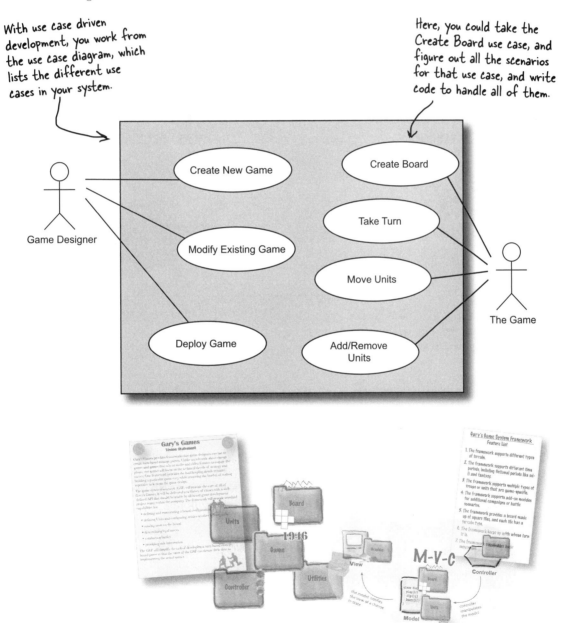

Two approaches to development

There's just one basic way to write code, isn't there? Well, there are actually a ton of different ways to go about iterating deeper and finishing up parts of your application. Most of these different approaches fall into the two basic categories we've been looking at, though. So how do you decide which to use?

What's the difference between feature driven and use case driven development?

Feature driven development is more granular

A single feature is often pretty small, and every application has a lot of them.

Use case driven development is more "big picture"

You'll be working on pretty major chunks of code at a time, since a single scenario often involves a lot of functionality.

Works well when you have a lot of different features that don't interconnect a whole lot.	Works well when your app has lots of processes and scenarios rather than individual pieces of functionality.
Allows you to show the customer working code faster.	Allows you to show the customer bigger pieces of functionality at each stage of development.
Is very functionality-driven. You're not going to forget about any features using feature driven development.	Is very user-centric. You'll code for all the different ways a user can use your system with use case driven development.
Works particularly well on systems with lots of disconnected pieces of functionality.	Works particularly well on transactional systems, where the system is largely defined by lengthy, complicated processes.

NAME THAT APPROACH!

Welcome to "Name That Approach!" Below are several statements, and each one is about a particular approach to iterating over parts of your system. Your job is to figure out which approach each statement refers to. Note that sometimes, a statement might apply to both approaches.

	Use Case Driven	Feature Driven
This approach deals with really small pieces of your application at a time.	☐	☐
This approach lets you focus on just a part of your application at a time.	☐	☐
This approach is all about a complete process in your application.	☐	☐
Using this approach, you can always test to see if you've completed the part of the application you're working on.	☐	☐
When you use this approach, your focus is on a diagram, not a list.	☐	☐

Welcome to "Name That Approach!" Below are several statements, and each one is about a particular approach to iterating over parts of your system. Your job is to figure out which approach each statement refers to. Note that sometimes, a statement might apply to both approaches.

	Use Case Driven	Feature Driven
This approach deals with really small pieces of your application at a time.	☐	☑
This approach lets you focus on just a part of your application at a time.	☑	☑
This approach is all about a complete process in your application.	☑	☐
Using this approach, you can always test to see if you've completed the part of the application you're working on.	☑	☑
When you use this approach, your focus is on a diagram, not a list.	☑	☐

Let's use feature driven development

Since Gary's losing patience, let's go with feature driven development. We can take just a single feature and work it through to completion, and it shouldn't take as much time as it would to write the code to support an entire use case.

Anytime you've got a customer impatient to see results, you should consider feature driven development, and starting with a feature you've already done some work on.

We go back to our feature list, from Chapters 6 and 7.

> ## Gary's Game System Framework
> ### Feature List
>
> 1. The framework supports different types of terrain.
> 2. The framework supports different time periods, including fictional periods like sci-fi and fantasy.
> 3. The framework supports multiple types of troops or units that are game-specific.
> 4. The framework supports add-on modules for additional campaigns or battle scenarios.
> 5. The framework provides a board made up of square tiles, and each tile has a terrain type.
> 6. The framework keeps up with whose turn it is.
> 7. The framework coordinates basic movement.

We already have the class diagram for Unit, so let's write the code for that class, and knock off feature #3.

Unit
type: String
properties: Map
setType(String)
getType(): String
setProperty(String, Object)
getProperty(String): Object

We also know that most of our other features depend on this class, so that makes it an even better candidate to start with.

BRAIN POWER

If you decided to go with use case driven development, what would you start working on first?

Analysis of a feature

Once you've decided on a feature to start with, you've got to do some more analysis. Let's start with what we had written down on the feature list:

3. The framework supports multiple types of troops or units that are game-specific.

Here's what we've got so far... but this is still a pretty generic description of what we need to code.

We also have the start of a class diagram, from Chapter 7:

Unit
type: String properties: Map
setType(String) getType(): String setProperty(String, Object) getProperty(String): Object

This looks like the blueprint for a good Unit class. So is anything missing?

It looks like we've got everything we need to start coding, right? To help us make sure we haven't forgotten anything, let's go back to using some textual analysis.

We don't have a use case to analyze, but we can revisit the vision statement for Gary's games, and see if we're covering everything that Gary wanted his units to do.

Here's Gary's vision statement, from way back in Chapter 6.

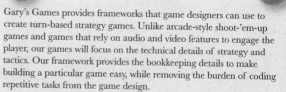

Gary's Games
Vision Statement

Gary's Games provides frameworks that game designers can use to create turn-based strategy games. Unlike arcade-style shoot-'em-up games and games that rely on audio and video features to engage the player, our games will focus on the technical details of strategy and tactics. Our framework provides the bookkeeping details to make building a particular game easy, while removing the burden of coding repetitive tasks from the game design.

The game system framework (GSF) will provide the core of all of Gary's Games. It will be delivered as a library of classes with a well-defined API that should be usable by all board game development project teams within the company. The framework will provide standard capabilities for:

* Defining and representing a board configuration
* Defining troops and configuring armies or other fighting units
* Moving units on the board
* Determining legal moves
* Conducting battles
* Providing unit information

The GSF will simplify the task of developing a turn-based strategic board game so that the users of the GSF can devote their time to implementing the actual games.

Compare the class diagram for Unit with this vision statement. Are there things missing from our class diagram?

What else might Gary expect to see when you say, "I'm done with writing code for the units in your framework?"

Fleshing out the Unit class

In our class diagram, all we've really figured out is how to represent the properties of a unit. But in Gary's vision statement, he's expecting his game system framework to support a lot more than just those game-specific properties.

This makes sense, because the key feature we were focusing on in Chapter 7 was not the entire Unit class, but just game-specific properties of a Unit.

Here are the things we came up with that Gary is expecting units in his framework to do:

1 **Each unit should have properties, and game designers can add new properties to unit types in their own games.**

Our class diagram is focused on this particular aspect of the Unit class right now.

2 **Units have to be able to move from one tile on a board to another.**

You should have some ideas about how to handle this from our work on a related key feature back in Chapter 7.

3 **Units can be grouped together into armies.**

These new features are all pulled straight from Gary's vision statement.

> Wow, great. **Another** list of things you're going to do. Look, I trust you and all, but I need to see something more than scraps of paper to believe your code is working.

Gary isn't satisfied with your use cases and lists... what do you think would make Gary believe that what you're working on will satisfy his requirements?

Showing off the Unit class

We worked on supporting game-specific units, and how to store the properties of a **Unit**, back in Chapter 7. But Gary wants more than a class diagram before he's convinced you're getting any work done.

Unit
type: String properties: Map
setType(String) getType(): String setProperty(String, Object) getProperty(String): Object

This may be what you need to start coding the Unit class, but it doesn't do anything to prove to Gary that you've got working units in the game system framework.

How about a test? Can't you come up with a way to show me the unit has properties, and can move around, and that you've got support for armies? I want to see your code actually running.

Your customers want to see something that makes sense to <u>them</u>

Your customers are used to seeing computer programs run on a computer. All those diagrams and lists may help you get on the same page with them in terms of requirements and what you're supposed to build, but you're going to need more than that before they think you've built anything useful.

You need to come up with some test scenarios that you can show to your customer, which will prove that your code works, and that it behaves like your customer expects it to.

Writing test scenarios

Be careful... this "scenario" isn't the same as the "scenario" we've been talking about in a use case scenario.

Test cases don't have to be very complex; they just provide a way to show your customer that the functionality in your classes is working correctly.

For the properties of a unit, we can start out with a simple test scenario that creates a new **Unit**, and adds a property to the unit. We could just show our customer a running program that displays output like this:

This test, although simple, lets your customer "see" that the code you're writing really works.

We start out by creating the Unit...

...then we set some properties...

...and finally get the properties and make sure the values match up with what we set.

```
File Edit  Window Help ItWorks
%java UnitTester
Testing the Unit class...
...Created a new unit
...Set "type" to "infantry"
...Set "hitPoints" to 25
...Getting unit type: "infantry"
...Getting unit hitPoints: 25

Test complete.
```

BE the Customer

We've already got one test scenario. It's your job to play Gary, and think of two more test scenarios that we can use to prove that the Unit class is working like it should. Write the output of each scenario in the code windows on the right.

Write the output you want Gary to see in these blanks.

```
File Edit  Window Help Scenario2
%java UnitTester
Testing the Unit class...
_____
_____
_____
_____
Test complete.
```

```
File Edit  Window Help Scenario3
%java UnitTester
Testing the Unit class...
_____
_____
_____
_____
_____
Test complete.
```

BE the Customer Solutions

Your job was to think of two more test scenarios that we can use to prove that the Unit class is working like it should. Here are the two scenarios we came up with:

```
File  Edit  Window  Help  ItWorks
%java UnitTester
Testing the Unit class...
...Created a new unit
...Set "type" to "infantry"
...Set "hitPoints" to 25
...Getting unit type: "infantry"
...Getting unit hitPoints: 25

Test complete.
```

Here's the first test scenario, which tests setting and getting property values.

Scenario #2: Changing property values

We decided to test setting, and then changing, the value of a property. If the **hitPoints** property is set, for example, and then set again, getting the value of **hitPoints** should return the most recent value for that property:

This is pretty similar-looking to the first scenario, above, but it tests changing a property value, rather than just setting and retrieving a property.

We always begin by creating a new Unit, so we can test things out.

Next we set the value of hitPoints, and then reset it to a new value.

```
File  Edit  Window  Help  Scenario2
%java UnitTester
Testing the Unit class...
...Created a new unit
...Set "hitPoints" to 25
...Set "hitPoints" to 15
...Getting unit hitPoints: 15


Test complete.
```

Finally, we make sure hitPoints has the most current value, and not the original value of 25.

Scenario #3: Getting non-existent property values

For our third scenario, we decided to test what would happen when you tried to retrieve the value of a property that had never been set. Error conditions like this crop up all the time, and we don't want our program crashing every time a game designer makes a small typo or mistake in their code. Here's what we did to test this:

This test shows the customer that you're not just dealing with happy paths... you're thinking about how to deal with uses of the software that are outside of the norm.

Start out by creating a new Unit again.

Next, we set a hitPoints property, which is the normal Unit usage.

Now let's try and access a property that has no value.

Finally, make sure the Unit still behaves when you ask for a property that does have a value.

```
File Edit  Window  Help  Scenario3
%java UnitTester
Testing the Unit class...
...Created a new unit
...Set "hitPoints" to 25
...Getting unit strength: [no value]
...Getting unit hitPoints: 25


Test complete.
```

You should test your software for <u>every</u> <u>possible</u> usage you can think of. <u>Be</u> <u>creative!</u>

Don't forget to test for <u>incorrect</u> <u>usage</u> of the software, too. You'll <u>catch</u> <u>errors</u> <u>early</u>, and make your customers very happy.

there are no
Dumb Questions

Q: We don't have any code written yet. Aren't we doing things a bit backwards by worrying about tests right now?

A: Not at all. In fact, if you know what tests you're going to use before you write your code, it's easy to figure out what code you're going to need to pass those tests. With the three test scenarios we just developed, it should be pretty simple to write the **Unit** class, and the tests tell us exactly how our code should behave.

Q: Isn't this just test driven development?

A: For the most part, yes. Formally, test driven development focuses on automated tests, and usually involves a testing framework like JUnit. But the idea of writing test cases, and then writing the code that will pass the test, is the core idea behind test driven development.

Q: So are we using test driven development or feature driven development? I'm confused...

A: Both. In fact, most good software analysis and design mixes lots of different approaches. You might start with a use case (use case driven development), and then choose just a small feature in that use case to start working on (which is really a form of feature driven development). Finally, you might use tests to figure out how to implement that feature (feature driven development).

Q: Why are the tests so simple? I expected something a little fancier.

A: You want to keep your tests simple, and have them test just a small piece of functionality at a time. If you start testing multiple things at once, it's hard to tell what might have caused a particular test to fail. You may need a lot more tests, but keep each one focused on a very specific piece of functionality.

Q: And each test makes sure a single method in the class works correctly, right?

A: No, each test really focuses on a single piece of *functionality*. That might involve one method, or several methods. For example, you can't test setting a property's value (which uses **setProperty()**) without getting that property's value as well (using **getProperty()**). So it's one piece of functionality—setting a property—but it takes two methods.

Q: Can you explain why you tested getting a property that you didn't set? Isn't that testing the wrong way to use the Unit class?

A: Testing incorrect usage of your software is usually at least as important as testing it when it's used properly. Game designers could easily mistype a property name, or write code that expects some other piece of a game to set a property and asks for a property that doesn't exist. It's your job to know what will happen in these situations.

Q: Now that we've got our tests planned out, we can finally start coding the Unit class, right?

A: Well, there's one more bit of design we need to think about first...

Test driven development focuses on getting the behavior of your classes right.

Guys, I've been looking at our class diagram for Unit, and I'm not sure that this is the best way to handle things. I think our commonality analysis might have been a little off.

Frank   Jill   Joe

Joe: What do you mean? We figured out that all properties in a Unit have a name and a value. So we decided to use a Map to store them all.

Frank: And game designers can add any new properties they want by just creating new property names, and sticking name/value pairs in the Map with the setProperty() method.

Jill: Right. But then, we also added a type property, since all units will have a type. And that's something common for all units...

Joe: Sure. See, we did do the commonality analysis right.

Jill: ...but we also now know that units can be assembled into groups, like armies or fleets or whatever. So what happens if we have two units of the same type in the same group... how can we tell the difference between them?

Frank: You think we need some sort of ID, don't you?

Jill: Yeah, maybe. Or at least a name... but even then, you can't really prevent duplication with a name property, can you?

Joe: OK, but that still doesn't mean we need to change our design. We can just add the ID property into our property Map. So we've got a nice, uniform way to access all those properties, using the getProperty() method.

Frank: He's right, Jill. And since we encapsulate away the details about property names into the properties Map, we could even change from using an ID to a name, or something totally different, and code using the Unit class wouldn't have to change much... you'd just need to use the new property name in getProperty(). That's a pretty slick design!

Jill: But what about commonality? If ID is really common to all types of Unit, shouldn't it be moved out of the Map, sort of like we did with the type property?

Joe: Whoa... encapsulation *or* commonality. That's tough... it seems like we can't do one without screwing up the other.

Unit
type: String properties: Map
setType(String) getType(): String setProperty(String, Object) getProperty(String): Object

Here's the current class diagram for Unit that Frank, Jill, and Joe are discussing.

Sharpen your pencil

Refine your commonality analysis.

Before we close the book on dealing with Unit properties, there are a few things you still need to think through. Below are several properties that different units might have, and two sheets of paper. Write down on the Commonality sheet the properties that you think all units, regardless of their type, would have; on the Variability sheet, write down properties you think only specific types of units might have.

Potential Unit Properties

name	weapon	allegiance	gear
type	hitPoints	wingspan	lastName
strength	weight	landSpeed	id
speed	intelligence	experience	groundSpeed
stamina	firstName	weapons	hunger

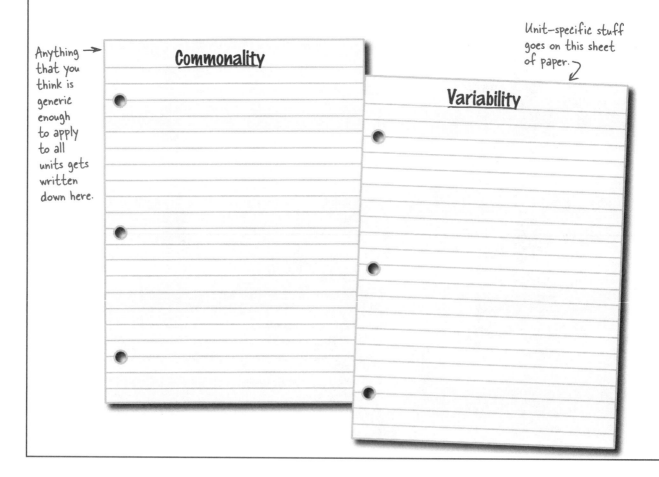

Anything → that you think is generic enough to apply to all units gets written down here.

Commonality

Unit–specific stuff goes on this sheet of paper. ↘

Variability

Now update the Unit class diagram.

With the details from your revised commonality analysis on page 442, you (might) need to update the Unit class diagram, shown below. Make any changes that might improve the design of the Unit class below, and add notes to remind yourself what the purpose of any additions you've made are going to be used for.

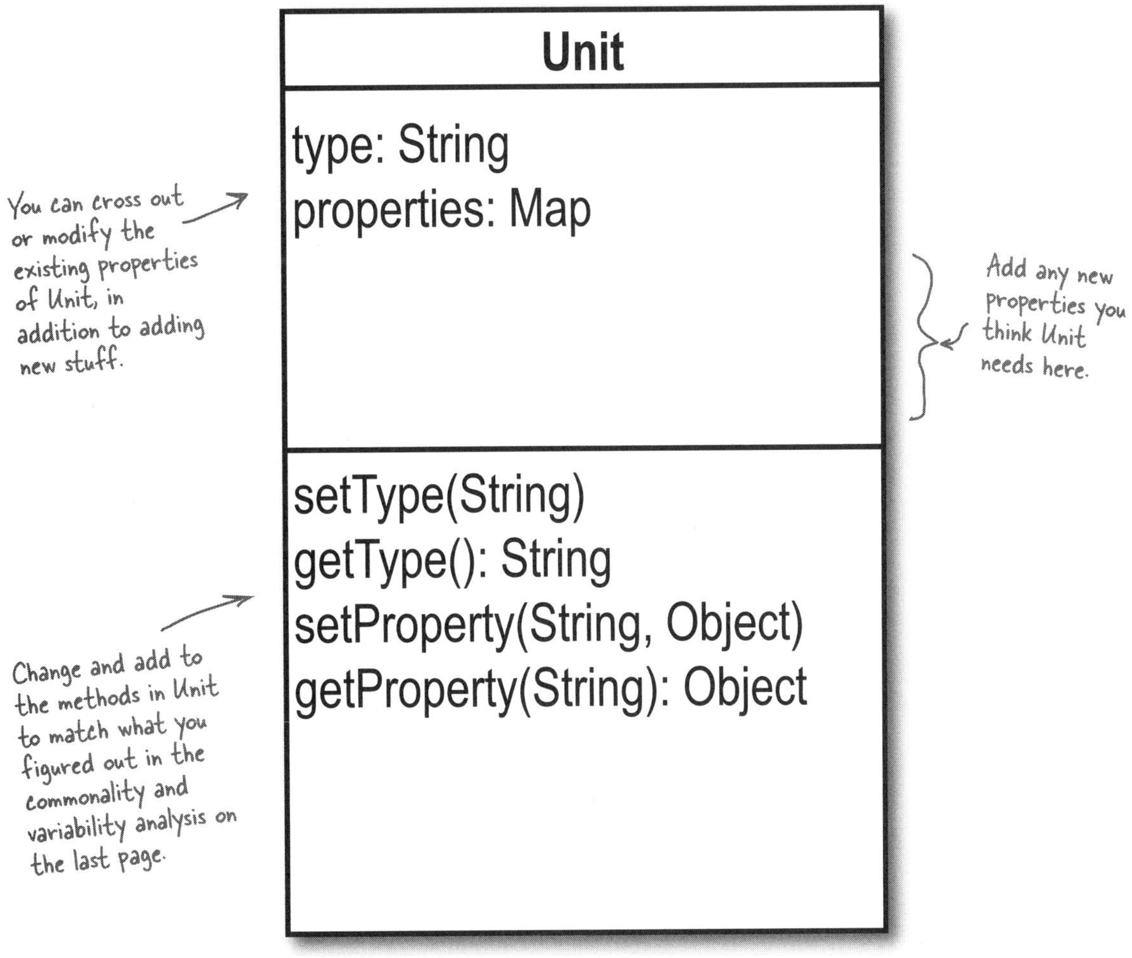

You can cross out or modify the existing properties of Unit, in addition to adding new stuff.

Add any new properties you think Unit needs here.

Unit
type: String properties: Map
setType(String) getType(): String setProperty(String, Object) getProperty(String): Object

Change and add to the methods in Unit to match what you figured out in the commonality and variability analysis on the last page.

Sharpen your pencil
answers

Refine your commonality analysis.

On page 442, we showed you several properties that different units might have. Your job was to write down on the Commonality sheet the properties that you think all units, regardless of their type, would have; on the Variability sheet, you should have written down properties you think only specific types of units might have.

You should definitely have written down "type", since we figured out that was common to all units back in Chapter 7.

"name" and "id" are pretty basic, and we thought that all units would probably have both properties.

We didn't find a lot of properties that could apply to any type of unit, so our commonality page is pretty thin.

Commonality

- type
- name
- id
- weapons

"weapons" might be a bit of a controversial decision. We figured that since these are war games, all units would have at least one weapon, but that some might have more than one. So a generic "weapons" property seemed a good fit for all unit types.

We also decided that we would never need just a single "weapon" property... units with one weapon would have just a single weapon in the "weapons" property. So we ditched this property.

⟶ ~~weapon~~

You may have a different idea about what makes a good game.

Relax

You might have played different games than we have, and come up with different common properties. That's OK—just focus on *how* and *why* you made your own decisions. We're going to use our choices in the rest of the chapter, so you should be comfortable with how we made our choices, too.

We moved most of the properties onto the Variability list, since they only apply to certain types of units.

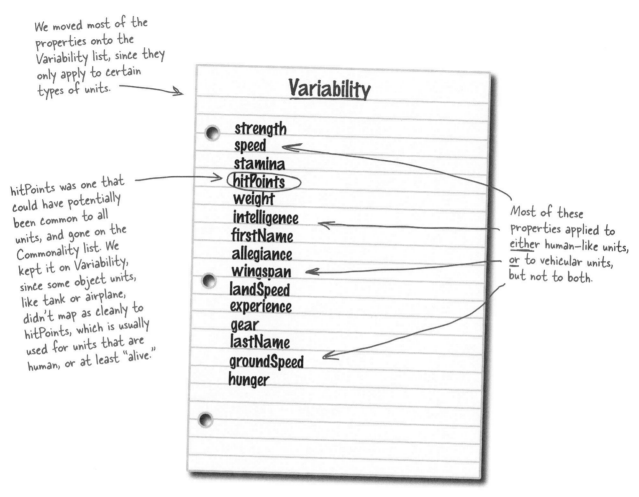

Variability

○ strength
speed
stamina
(hitPoints)
weight
intelligence
firstName
allegiance
○ wingspan
landSpeed
experience
gear
lastName
groundSpeed
hunger

○

hitPoints was one that could have potentially been common to all units, and gone on the Commonality list. We kept it on Variability, since some object units, like tank or airplane, didn't map as cleanly to hitPoints, which is usually used for units that are human, or at least "alive."

Most of these properties applied to either human–like units, or to vehicular units, but not to both.

there are no
Dumb Questions

Q: **I didn't have anything on the Commonality list except for "type". Where did I go wrong?**

A: You didn't go wrong at all. Analysis and design are all about making choices, and sometimes you're going to make a different choice than another programmer. There's nothing wrong with that, as long as you have good, well thought out reasons for the decision you made.

Q: **But won't different choices at least result in different code and design implementations?**

A: Yes, they sure will. But OOA&D, and software development, aren't about making a particular decision, since many times there isn't an exactly "right" or exactly "wrong" choice. They're about writing well-designed software, and that can happen in a lot of different ways.

In fact, even if two programmers made the *same* decision about commonality and variability in this exercise, it can lead to totally different design decisions when it comes to actually writing your classes. Let's assume for a moment that two developers both came up with the answers for commonality and variability shown here, and then tried to revise the **Unit** class to reflect what they figured out...

Solution #1: Emphasizing Commonality

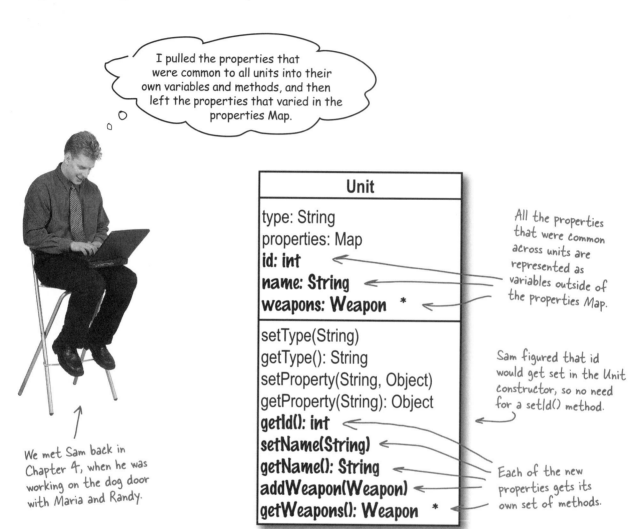

> I pulled the properties that were common to all units into their own variables and methods, and then left the properties that varied in the properties Map.

Unit

type: String
properties: Map
id: int
name: String
weapons: Weapon *

setType(String)
getType(): String
setProperty(String, Object)
getProperty(String): Object
getId(): int
setName(String)
getName(): String
addWeapon(Weapon)
getWeapons(): Weapon *

All the properties that were common across units are represented as variables outside of the properties Map.

Sam figured that id would get set in the Unit constructor, so no need for a setId() method.

Each of the new properties gets its own set of methods.

We met Sam back in Chapter 4, when he was working on the dog door with Maria and Randy.

In this solution, all game designers can directly access the **id**, **name**, and **weapons** properties, instead of having to use **getProperty()** and work through the more generic properties **Map**.

The emphasis is on keeping the **_common_** properties of a **Unit** **_outside_** of the **properties Map**, and leaving properties that **_vary_** **_inside_** the **properties Map**.

> You defintely found some commonality between different unit types, but what about good encapsulation? That Unit class doesn't seem very resistant to change, if you ask me.

Randy's learned a lot about OO design since we saw him last in Chapter 4.

Design decisions are always a tradeoff

Sam chose to emphasize the things that are common across all types of **Unit**s. But there are some negatives to Sam's design, too:

DRY

We're repeating ourselves

Now there are two different ways to access properties: through the **getId()**, **getName()**, and property-specific methods, and the **getProperty()** method. Two ways to access properties is almost certainly going to mean duplicate code somewhere.

When you see the potential for duplicate code, you'll almost always find maintenance and flexibility issues, as well.

Maintenance is a problem

Now you've got property names, like **id** and **name**, hard-coded into the **Unit** class. If a game designer doesn't want to use those, or wants to change them, it's going to be a real hassle, and require changes to the **Unit** class. This is usually where encapsulation would help, and that leads us to Randy's design choice...

Solution #2:
Emphasizing Encapsulation

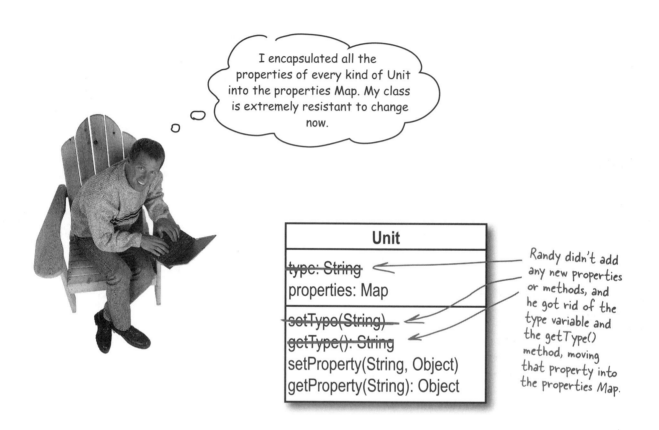

I encapsulated all the properties of every kind of Unit into the properties Map. My class is extremely resistant to change now.

Unit
~~type: String~~
properties: Map
~~setType(String)~~
~~getType(): String~~
setProperty(String, Object)
getProperty(String): Object

Randy didn't add any new properties or methods, and he got rid of the type variable and the getType() method, moving that property into the properties Map.

This solution focuses on encapsulating <u>all</u> the properties for a **Unit** into the **properties Map**, and providing a standard interface—the **getProperty()** method—for accessing all properties. Even properties that apply to all units, like **type** and **id**, are accessed through the **properties Map** in this solution.

The emphasis is on ***encapsulation***, and a ***flexible design***. Even if the names of common properties change, the **Unit** class can stay the same, since no property names are hardcoded into the class itself.

> But you're totally ignoring what's common across Units. And how are game designers going to know that we intended name, type, id, and weapons to be standard properties?

Tradeoffs with this decision, too...

Randy's solution is more resistant to changes, and uses a lot more encapsulation, but there are tradeoffs with this design, as well. Here are a few of the downsides to Randy's design:

We're ignoring commonality
Randy encapsulated all of the properties into the **properties Map**, but now there's nothing to indicate that **type**, **name**, **id**, and **weapons** are intended to be properties common to all **Unit** types.

Lots of work at runtime
getProperty() returns an **Object**, and you're going to have to cast that into the right value type for each different property, all at runtime. That's a lot of casting, and a lot of extra work that your code has to do at runtime, even for the properties that are common to all **Unit** types.

Which developer's solution do you think is best? Are there times where you think one solution might be the best choice, and other times where the other might work better?

you have to make a choice

Let's go with the commonality-focused solution

For Gary's game system framework, let's use Sam's solution, which pulls the common properties of a **Unit** out into their own properties and methods, and leaves unit-specific properties in a separate **Map**.

Unit properties	Unit movement	Unit groups

This is all still part of dealing with the properties of a unit.

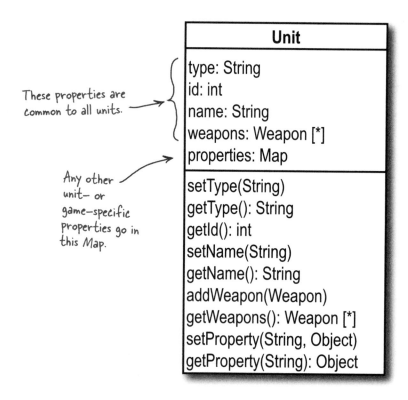

These properties are common to all units.

Any other unit- or game-specific properties go in this Map.

Unit
type: String id: int name: String weapons: Weapon [*] properties: Map
setType(String) getType(): String getId(): int setName(String) getName(): String addWeapon(Weapon) getWeapons(): Weapon [*] setProperty(String, Object) getProperty(String): Object

there are no Dumb Questions

Q: I thought the other design, that focused on encapsulation, was better. Is that OK?

A: Absolutely. Both design choices have positives, and either one might work well. The only thing you **cannot** do is be unwilling to change your design—whichever one you start with—if it turns out to not work well down the line. At each stage of iterating through your app, you need to reevaluate your design decisions, and make sure they're still solid.

Q: So how do I know when I need to change my design? My code won't just stop working, so what should I look out for?

A: Iteration is really the key point here. Lots of design decisions look great at one stage of your development, but then turn out to be a problem as you get deeper into a particular part of your app. So once you make a decision, stick with it, and iterate deeper into your application. As long as your design is working, and you're able to use good OO principles and apply design patterns, you're in good shape. If you start running into trouble with a decision, though, don't ever be afraid to change designs and rework things.

Q: What happens when I can't decide between a couple of good design choices?

A: You always have to make a choice, even if you're not 100% sure if it's the right one. It's always better to take your best guess, and see how things work out, rather than spend endless hours debating one choice or another. That's called *analysis paralysis*, and it's a sure way to not get anything done. It's much better to start down one path, even if you're not totally sure it's the right one, and get some work done, than to not make a choice at all.

Good software is built **iteratively**. Analyze, design, and then **iterate** **again**, working on smaller and smaller parts of your app.

Each time you iterate, **reevaluate** your design decisions, and don't be afraid to **CHANGE** something if it makes sense for your design.

Match your tests to your design

We've got test scenarios we want to show Gary, and a design for the **Unit** class. The last thing we need to do before coding is to make sure our design for **Unit** will allow us to code a solution that passes all the tests.

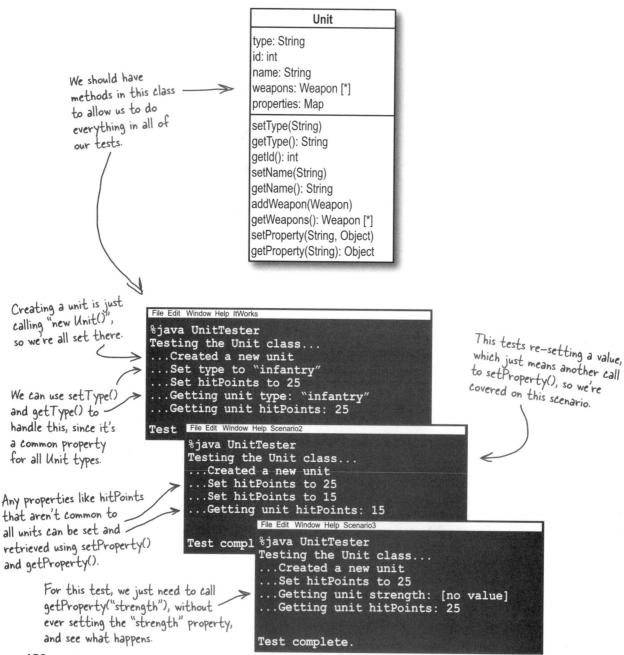

We should have methods in this class to allow us to do everything in all of our tests.

Unit
type: String id: int name: String weapons: Weapon [*] properties: Map
setType(String) getType(): String getId(): int setName(String) getName(): String addWeapon(Weapon) getWeapons(): Weapon [*] setProperty(String, Object) getProperty(String): Object

Creating a unit is just calling "new Unit()", so we're all set there.

We can use setType() and getType() to handle this, since it's a common property for all Unit types.

```
File Edit Window Help ItWorks
%java UnitTester
Testing the Unit class...
...Created a new unit
...Set type to "infantry"
...Set hitPoints to 25
...Getting unit type: "infantry"
...Getting unit hitPoints: 25
```

This tests re-setting a value, which just means another call to setProperty(), so we're covered on this scenario.

```
Test  File Edit Window Help Scenario2
%java UnitTester
Testing the Unit class...
...Created a new unit
...Set hitPoints to 25
...Set hitPoints to 15
...Getting unit hitPoints: 15
```

Any properties like hitPoints that aren't common to all units can be set and retrieved using setProperty() and getProperty().

```
Test compl %java UnitTester
Testing the Unit class...
...Created a new unit
...Set hitPoints to 25
...Getting unit strength: [no value]
...Getting unit hitPoints: 25

Test complete.
```

For this test, we just need to call getProperty("strength"), without ever setting the "strength" property, and see what happens.

Let's write the Unit class

It's been two chapters in coming, but we're finally ready to
write the code for the **Unit** class. Here's how we did it:

Unit.java

```java
package headfirst.gsf.unit;

public class Unit {
  private String type;
  private int id;
  private String name;
  private List weapons;
  private Map properties;

  public Unit(int id) {
    this.id = id;
  }

  public int getId() {
    return id;
  }

  // getName() and setName() methods
  // getType() and setType() methods

  public void addWeapon(Weapon weapon) {
    if (weapons == null) {
      weapons = new LinkedList();
    }
    weapons.add(weapon);
  }

  public List getWeapons() {
    return weapons;
  }

  public void setProperty(String property, Object value) {
    if (properties == null) {
      properties = new HashMap();
    }
    properties.put(property, value);
  }

  public Object getProperty(String property) {
    if (properties == null) {
      return null;
    }
    return properties.get(property);
  }
}
```

We take the ID of the Unit
in through the constructor...

...so we only need a getId(),
and not a setId() as well.

We didn't list the code for
these simple getters and
setters to save a little space.

You'll need a simple Weapon
class to make this code
compile. We created an
empty Weapon.java, with no
methods, for testing.

We wait until there's a
need for a weapons list to
instantiate a new List. That
saves a little bit of memory,
especially when there may be
thousands of units.

Just like the weapons List, we
don't create a HashMap for
properties until it's needed.

Since properties might not be
initialized, there's an extra
check here before looking up a
property's value.

Test cases dissected...

We've talked a lot about test cases, but so far, you haven't seen how to actually write one. Let's examine a test case up close, and see exactly what makes up a good test.

❶ Each test case should have an ID and a name.

The names of your test cases should describe what is being tested. Test names with nothing but a number at the end aren't nearly as helpful as names like **testProperty()** or **testCreation()**. You should also use a numeric ID, so you can easily list your tests cases out (something we'll do on the next page).

Try not to refer to tests as test1, test2, etc. Use descriptive names whenever possible.

❷ Each test case should have <u>one</u> <u>specific thing</u> that it tests.

Each of your test cases should be *atomic*: each should test only one piece of functionality at time. This allows you to isolate exactly what piece of functionality might not be working in your application.

One piece of functionality may involve one method, two methods, or even multiple classes... but to start with, focus on very simple pieces of functionality, one at a time.

❸ Each test case should have an input you supply.

You're going to give the test case a value, or a set of values, that it uses as the test data. This data is usually then used to execute some specific piece of functionality or behavior.

If you're setting hitPoints to 15, then "15" becomes the input you supply to your test case.

❹ Each test case should have an output that you expect.

Given your input, what should the program, class, or method output? You'll compare the actual output of the program with your expected output, and if they match, then you've got a successful test, and your software works.

This is what you want the program to output. So if you set type to "infantry", and then call getType(), your exepcted output is "infantry".

❺ Most test cases have a starting state.

Do you need to open a database connection, or create a certain object, or set some values before running your test? If so, that's all part of the starting state of the test case, and needs to be handled before you run the actual test.

There's not much starting state for the Unit class. We do need to create a new Unit, but that's about it.

Sharpen your pencil

Design your test cases.

Below is a table with 5 columns, one for each of the 5 important parts of a test case. Your job is to fill in the table with information for the test cases we've laid out in this chapter already. We've even done the first one to help get you started, and filled in a few empty spots on the rest of the tests.

This test sets the "type" property to a value of "infantry."

Remember, there's a difference between a common property like type, and unit-specific properties.

ID	What we're testing	Input	Expected Output	Starting State
1	Setting/Getting the type property	"type", "infantry"	"type", "infantry"	Existing Unit object
		"hitPoints", 25		
				Existing Unit object with hitPoints set to 25
4				

There are actually 4 individual things being tested in these three scenarios.

The first scenario tests getting and setting the "type" property, as shown here.

```
File Edit Window Help ItWorks
%java UnitTester
Testing the Unit class...
...Created a new unit
...Set type to "infantry"
...Set hitPoints to 25
...Getting unit type: "infantry"
...Getting unit hitPoints: 25

Test complete.
```

```
File Edit Window Help Scenario2
%java UnitTester
Testing the Unit class...
...Created a new unit
...Set hitPoints to 25
...Set hitPoints to 15
...Getting unit hitPoints: 15
```

```
File Edit Window Help Scenario3
%java UnitTester
Testing the Unit class...
...Created a new unit
...Set hitPoints to 25
...Getting unit strength: [no value]
...Getting unit hitPoints: 25


Test complete.
```

Sharpen your pencil

answers   Design your test cases.

Below is a table with 5 columns, one for each of the 5 important parts of a test case. Your job was to fill in the table with information for the test cases we've laid out in this chapter already.

In most of our tests, we want as output exactly what we supplied as input.

ID	What we're testing	Input	Expected Output	Starting State
1	Setting/Getting a common property	"type", "infantry"	"type", "infantry"	Existing Unit object
2	Setting/Getting a unit-specific property	"hitPoints", 25	"hitPoints", 25	Existing Unit object
3	Changing an existing property's value	"hitPoints", 15	"hitPoints", 15	Existing Unit object with hitPoints set to 25
4	Getting a non-existent property's value	N/A	"strength", no value	Existing Unit object without strength value

You should have one test case for working with common properties, and one for working with unit-specific ones.

The entire point of this test is to <u>not</u> supply a value for a property, and then try and retrieve that property's value.

Did you figure out that you needed to make sure there was no property with a previous value for this test case?

---

there are no
Dumb Questions

Q: How did our three test scenarios turn into four test cases?

A: Because the first test case really tested *two* things: setting and retrieving a common property, which has its own variable and access method (like `getType()`), and setting a retrieving a unit- or game-specific property, which is accessed through `getProperty()` (like `hitPoints`). That's two pieces of functionality, so two different test cases are required.

Q: And all these tests will let us know that our software works like it should, right?

A: It's a good start on that, yes, but remember, we started out writing the tests so that we could prove to the customer that the software we've been writing actually will work. Our test cases let the customer see some code actually running, as well as help us find bugs in our code before we get too far along in our development cycle.

Test Puzzle

Now that you know what test cases are, and have several written up in table form, you're ready to code a test class to show your customer that your software works, and prove to yourself that there aren't any bugs in the code that you've written.

The problem:

Gary wants to know that you're making progress on supporting units in his game system framework, and you want to be sure that the code you've written for **Unit.java** works properly.

Your task:

1 Create a new class called **UnitTester.java**, and import the **Unit** class and any related classes into it.

2 Add a new method for each test case you figured out from the table on page 456. Be sure to use descriptive names for the test methods.

3 Each test method should take in an instance of **Unit** with any starting state already set, and any other parameters you think you'll need to run the test and compare an input value with an expected output value.

4 The test method should set the supplied property name and property value on the provided **Unit**, and then retrieve the expected output property value using the expected output property name.

5 If the provided input value and expected output value match, the method should print out "Test passed"; if they don't match, the method should print "Test failed", along with the mismatched values.

6 Write a **main()** method that sets up the starting state for each test, and then runs each test.

Bonus Credit:

1 There are several things in **Unit.java** that are not being tested by the scenarios on page 456. Identify what each of these are, and create a test method for each.

2 Run these tests from your **main()** method as well.

 **Test Puzzle Solutions**

Here's the class we wrote to test the Unit class.

```java
public class UnitTester {

  public void testType(Unit unit, String type, String expectedOutputType) {
    System.out.println("\nTesting setting/getting the type property.");
    unit.setType(type);
    String outputType = unit.getType();
    if (expectedOutputType.equals(outputType)) {
      System.out.println("Test passed");
    } else {
      System.out.println("Test failed: " + outputType + " didn't match " +
        expectedOutputType);
    }
  }

  public void testUnitSpecificProperty(Unit unit, String propertyName,
              Object inputValue, Object expectedOutputValue) {
    System.out.println("\nTesting setting/getting a unit-specific property.");
    unit.setProperty(propertyName, inputValue);
    Object outputValue = unit.getProperty(propertyName);
    if (expectedOutputValue.equals(outputValue)) {
      System.out.println("Test passed");
    } else {
      System.out.println("Test failed: " + outputValue + " didn't match " +
        expectedOutputValue);
    }
  }

  public void testChangeProperty(Unit unit, String propertyName,
              Object inputValue, Object expectedOutputValue) {
    System.out.println("\nTesting changing an existing property's value.");
    unit.setProperty(propertyName, inputValue);
    Object outputValue = unit.getProperty(propertyName);
    if (expectedOutputValue.equals(outputValue)) {
      System.out.println("Test passed");
    } else {
      System.out.println("Test failed: " + outputValue + " didn't match " +
        expectedOutputValue);
    }
  }
```

Each test method has different parameters, since each method is testing different things in the Unit class.

Most tests end with a comparison of the expected output and the actual output.

Properties stored in the Map take Objects as input and output values.

This test is almost identical to test2(), because the starting state takes care of pre-setting the property to another value.

This test assumes you've set the starting state correctly... otherwise, it will ALWAYS fail.

```
class
Unit-
Tester {
test()
}
```

UnitTester.java

This last test doesn't need an input value, because that's what is being tested for: a property *without* a preset value. →

```java
public void testNonExistentProperty(Unit unit, String propertyName) {
    System.out.println("\nTesting getting a non-existent property's value.");
    Object outputValue = unit.getProperty(propertyName);
    if (outputValue == null) {
        System.out.println("Test passed");
    } else {
        System.out.println("Test failed with value of " + outputValue);
    }
}
```

hitPoints is set to 25 in testUnitSpecificProperty(), so we can call testChangeProperty() knowing that the value will be reset in that test case. ⟶

All our main() method needs to do is create a new Unit, and then run through the tests.

```java
public static void main(String args[]) {
    UnitTester tester = new UnitTester();
    Unit unit = new Unit(1000);
    tester.testType(unit, "infantry", "infantry");
    tester.testUnitSpecificProperty(unit, "hitPoints",
                            new Integer(25), new Integer(25));
    tester.testChangeProperty(unit, "hitPoints",
                            new Integer(15), new Integer(15));
    tester.testNonExistentProperty(unit, "strength");
}
}
```

And now for some bonus credit...

We added three new test cases to our table, to handle the three properties common to all units that aren't tested in UnitTester. You should be able to write three additional test methods based on this table. Did you figure these out on your own?

This test case doesn't test *all* common properties; it just tests the type property.

We need to test all three of the other common properties, since each uses its own specific methods.

ID	What we're testing	Input	Expected Output	Starting State
1	Setting/Getting the type property	"type", "infantry"	"type", "infantry"	Existing Unit object
2	Setting/Getting a unit-specific property	"hitPoints", 25	"hitPoints", 25	Existing Unit object
3	Changing an existing property's value	"hitPoints", 15	"hitPoints", 15	Existing Unit object with hitPoints set to 25
4	Getting a non-existent property's value	N/A	"strength", no value	Existing Unit object without strength value
5	Getting the id property	N/A	1000	Existing Unit object with an id of 1000
6	Setting/getting the name property	"name", "Damon"	"name", "Damon"	Existing Unit object
7	Adding/getting weapons	Axe object	Axe object	Existing Unit object

Prove yourself to the customer

With a **Unit** class and a set of test cases, you're ready to
show Gary some working code, and prove that you're on the
right track to building his game system framework just the
way he wants it. Let's show him the test class running:

Test classes aren't
supposed to be exciting
or sexy... they just
need to prove that your
software does what it's
supposed to do.

```
File Edit Window Help ProveToMe
%java UnitTester

Testing setting/getting the type property.
Test passed

Testing setting/getting a unit-specific
property.
Test passed

Testing changing an existing property's
value.
Test passed

Testing getting a non-existent property's
value.
Test passed
```

> This is great! You really do
> know what you're doing. I'll put a check
> in the mail, and you just keep on with
> the Unit class. Do you have units moving
> around the board yet?

Customers that see <u>running code</u> tend
to get happy, and keep paying you.
Customers that only see diagrams get
impatient and frustrated, so don't
expect much support or cash.

> It's not perfect for **me**—I don't need your framework returning null all the time, and my guys having to check for it. We'll write our code correctly, so if your framework gets asked for a property that doesn't exist, just throw an exception, OK?

Let's change the <u>programming contract</u> for the game system

When you're writing software, you're also creating a contract between that software and the people that use it. The contract details how the software will work when certain actions are taken—like requesting a non-existent property on a unit.

If the customer wants an action to result in different behavior, then you're changing the contract. So if Gary's framework should throw an exception when a non-existent property is queried, that's fine; it just means that the contract between game designers and the framework has changed.

Meet Sue. She manages a team of top-notch game developers, and they're interested in using Gary's game framework.

When you <u>program</u> <u>by</u> <u>contract</u>, <u>you</u> and your <u>software's users</u> are agreeing that your software will <u>behave</u> in a certain way.

Want to know more about what this means? Turn the page to find out more...

We've been <u>programming by contract</u> so far

The decisions we're making now affect the Unit class and how we handle non-existent properties, so we're still on this first bit of Unit functionality.

You probably didn't notice, but we've been doing something called **programming by contract** in the **Unit** class so far. In the **Unit** class, if someone asks for a property that doesn't exist, we've just returned null. We've been doing the same thing in **getWeapons()**; if the **weapons** list isn't initialized, we just return null there, too:

This list might not be initialized, so this could return null if there aren't any weapons for this unit.

If there aren't any properties, we return null...

...and if there isn't a value for the requested property, this will return null.

```java
public List getWeapons() {
    return weapons;
}

// other methods

public Object getProperty(String property) {
    if (properties == null) {
        return null;
    }
    return properties.get(property);
}
```

Even though you didn't know it, this code is defining a contract for what happens when a property doesn't exist.

Unit.java

This is the <u>contract</u> for Unit

The **Unit** class assumes that people using it are competent programmers, and that they can handle null return values. So our contract states something like this:

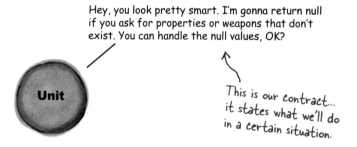

Hey, you look pretty smart. I'm gonna return null if you ask for properties or weapons that don't exist. You can handle the null values, OK?

Unit

This is our contract... it states what we'll do in a certain situation.

Programming by contract is really all about <u>trust</u>

When you return null, you're **trusting** programmers to be able to deal with null return values. Programmers are basically saying that they've coded things well enough that they won't ask for non-existent properties or weapons, so their code just doesn't worry about getting null values back from the **Unit** class:

> Hey, you look pretty smart. I'm gonna return null if you ask for properties or weapons that don't exist. You can handle the null values, OK?

Unit

> Look, we know what we're doing. Our code will only ask you for properties that exist. So just return null... trust us to do the right thing, OK?

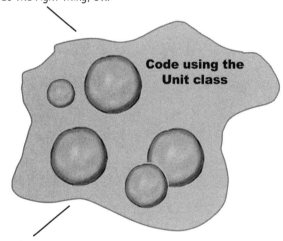
Code using the Unit class

And we can always <u>change</u> the contract if we need to...

Back on page 461, we were asked to stop returning null, and throw an exception instead. This really isn't a big change to the contract; it just means that now game designers are going to have big problems if they ask for non-existent properties or weapons.

> You know what? We're really confident we're not going to ask you for non-existent properties. In fact, if we do, just throw an exception, and it will crash the program, and we'll hunt down the bug. Trust us... throwing an exception is no problem.

> Sure. As long as you know I'm going to start throwing an Exception, we're good to go. I'll just change my code, and we'll start using this new contract.

Unit

But if you don't trust your users...

But what happens if you don't think your code will be used correctly? Or if you think that certain actions are such a bad idea that you don't want to let users deal with them in their own way? In these cases, you may want to consider **defensive programming**.

Suppose you were really worried that game designers using the Unit class, and asking for non-existent properties, were getting null values and not handling them properly. You might rewrite the `getProperty()` method like this:

```java
public Object getProperty(String property)
  throws IllegalAccessException {

  if (properties == null) {
    return null;
    throw new IllegalAccessException(
      "What are you doing? No properties!");
  }
  return properties.get(property);
  Object value = properties.get(property);
  if (value == null) {
    throw new IllegalAccessException(
      "You're screwing up! No property value.");
  } else {
    return value;
  }
}
```

This version of getProperty() can throw a CHECKED exception, so code using Unit will have to catch this exception.

We don't return null anymore... we make a BIG deal about asking for a non-existent property.

```
class
Unit {
  Unit()
}
```

Unit.java

This is a *defensive* version of Unit.java.

> I'm sure you're great code and all, but I just don't trust you. I could send you null, and you could totally blow up. So let's just be safe, and I'll send you a checked exception that you'll have to catch, to make sure you don't get a null value back and do something stupid with it.

Unit

Defensive programming assumes the worst, and tries to protect itself (and you) against misuse or bad data.

-or if they don't trust you...

Of course, when programmers use your code, they might not trust you either... they can program defensively as well. What if they don't believe that you'll only return non-null values from **getProperty()**? Then they're going to protect their code, and use defensive programming, as well:

Here's a sample of code that uses the Unit class.

```
// Some method goes out and gets a unit
Unit unit = getUnit();

// Now let's use the unit...
String name = unit.getName();
if ((name != null) && (name.length() > 0)) {
    System.out.println("Unit name: " + name);
}
Object value = unit.getProperty("hitPoints");
if (value != null) {
    try {
        Integer hitPoints = (Integer)value;
    } catch (ClassCastException e) {
        // Handle the potential error
    }
}
// etc...
```

This code does a LOT of error checking... it doesn't ever trust Unit to return valid data.

This code is written extremely defensively.

Defensive Programming taught here

there are no Dumb Questions

Q: You said on page 463 that we could change the contract to throw an exception, but then you said here that throwing an exception is defensive programming. I'm confused...

A: It's really not that important what kind of exception is thrown. What's important is how your customers and clients are *involved* in that decision. In programming by contract, you work with the client to agree on how you're going to handle problems; in defensive programming, you make that decision in a way that ensures your code doesn't crash, regardless of what the client wants to have happen.

When we decided to switch from returning null to throwing an exception, we did that by listening to the client, and agreeing on that particular action as a response to a request for non-existent properties. And we made the exception a **RuntimeException**, again because the client didn't want to add lots of **try/catch** blocks to their code. They could have just as easily asked for a checked exception, and we could have agreed—and *still* been programming by contract.

Compare that to defensive programming, where we're not really that interested in what the client wants. In defensive programming, we're making sure that we aren't responsible for crashing a program, and we even go out of our way to try and prevent the client from crashing their program.

Fireside Chats

Tonight's talk: **Programming by Contract and Defensive Programming duke it out over trust issues with programmers.**

Programming by Contract

It's nice to sit down with you and meet face to face, we really don't see each other like this very often.

What do you mean?

Well, sure, I guess... but you can't live your whole life in fear of bad code. At some point, you have to just commit to how you're going to behave, and trust other programmers to use you right.

Boy, it sounds like you have trust issues.

No. I trust programmers understand the contract that I provide them.

Defensive Programming

Yeah, I really don't like to get out much. There's just so much that can go wrong.

Well, I could be crossing the street, and slip on some Banana.peel() that hadn't been garbage collected, or some for loop without a good termination condition could come screaming through the intersection... there's a lot of bad code out there, you know?

Are you kidding me? Have you met most of the programmers writing the code you're talking about trusting? They're too busy watching *Lost* to worry about checking for bugs in their software. If they'd stop gawking at that Kate and her freckles, maybe I wouldn't have to double-check their work so much.

And you don't?

Contract? Oh, you still think that if you explain what you'll do in a certain situation, that a "good" programmer will use you correctly? Boy, what naivete!

Programming by Contract

Look, my contract explicitly states what I have to do, and what people that use me have to do.

Look, if programmers and users don't keep their end of the bargain, I can't be held responsible for that. If they violate the contract, they deserve what they get. I can't be held liable.

With tons of extra code, little "if (value == null)" checks everywhere? What a beating. Sounds like you slow things down more than anything.

Superman? You did **not** just say that...

But that's the point! I may not be great for lazy programmers, but I'm *terrific* for programmers who do check their work. They get a performance bump, and their code is shorter when they use me.

And that's what I provide, just without all the trust issues and baggage you bring along...

I'll show you safe code, you little...

Defensive Programming

Haven't you heard? Over 50% of contracts today end in divorce... or maybe that was a different stat, I'm not sure... anyway, do you really think programmers are paying attention to your little contract?

Sounds pretty callous to me. I try and help my users, and even protect them from themselves.

Sure, sometimes I'm not the best performer, but I sure keep everyone safe from disaster. I often like to think of myself... a bit like Superman.

It's true! Besides, how many times has your code gone up in smoke because of a lazy programmer who ignored your contract?

Short code, humph. I'd much rather have good code. Code that keeps programmers and users safe.

Hey, I've got a trust issue for you right here...

...transmission ended... Veuillez nous aider! ... 4 8 15 ...

Who Am I?

Feature Driven Development, Use Case Driven Development, Programming by Contract, and Defensive Programming have all showed up for a masquerade party, but none of them bothered to wear name tags. They're all a chatty bunch, though, so it's up to you to listen to what they're saying, and try and figure out who's behind the masks. Be careful.... sometimes more than one masked guest could be saying the same thing.

I'm very well-ordered. I prefer to take things one step at a time, until I've made it from start to finish.

_____

Well, sure, she said she would call, but how can you really believe anyone anymore?

_____

Oh, absolutely, requirements really get me motivated.

_____

I'm very well-behaved. In fact, I've been focusing on all of my own behavior before moving on to anything else.

_____

Really, it's all about my customer. I just want to satisfy them, after all.

_____

Hey, you're a big boy. You can deal with that on your own... it's really not my problem anymore, is it?

_____

As long as you're good with it, so am I. Who am I to tell you what to do, so long as you know what you can expect from me.

_____

→ Figure out who is who on page 481.

Sharpen your pencil

Change the programming contract for Unit.

Gary's clients want Unit to assume they're using it correctly. That means that if a non-existent property is being queried, then something has truly gone wrong in the game, and an exception needs to be thrown. Your job is to:

1. Update Unit.java so that requests for a non-existent property result in an exception being thrown. Figuring out the type of exception to use is up to you.

2. Update UnitTester and the test cases that this contract change affects to reflect this new contract.

3. Re-run UnitTester and make sure Unit.java still passes all of the tests.

Our answers are on the next page.

changing the contract

Sharpen your pencil
answers

Change the programming contract for Unit.

Gary's clients want Unit to assume they're using it correctly. That means that if a non-existent property is being queried, then something has truly gone wrong in the game, and an exception needs to be thrown.

The only method in Unit.java that you needed to change was getProperty().

Asking for a property when the properties Map is null is still asking for a non-existent property.

We throw a RuntimeException anytime a property that doesn't exist is queried.

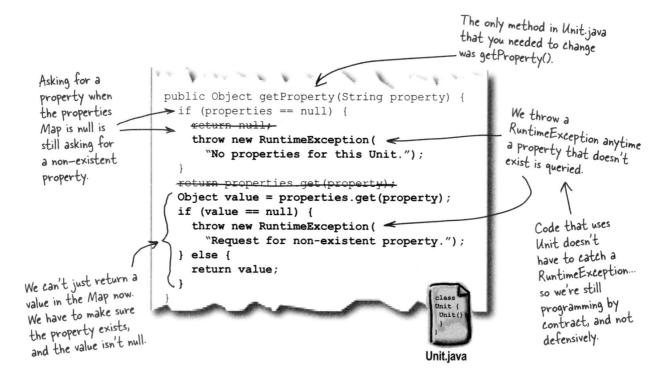

```
public Object getProperty(String property) {
    if (properties == null) {
        return null;
        throw new RuntimeException(
            "No properties for this Unit.");
    }
    return properties.get(property);
    Object value = properties.get(property);
    if (value == null) {
        throw new RuntimeException(
            "Request for non-existent property.");
    } else {
        return value;
    }
}
```

We can't just return a value in the Map now. We have to make sure the property exists, and the value isn't null.

Code that uses Unit doesn't have to catch a RuntimeException... so we're still programming by contract, and not defensively.

class Unit {
Unit()
}

Unit.java

there are no
Dumb Questions

Q: Why are you throwing a RuntimeException, and not a checked exception, like IllegalAccessException?

A: If you used a checked exception, code that calls **getProperty()** would have to check for that exception, in **try/catch** blocks. That's not what the client wanted; we agreed to a contract that would let them code without having to catch for any exceptions. So by using a **RuntimeException**, no extra worked is required for their client code to use the **Unit** class.

Q: What about the get methods for other properties, like weapons, name, and id?

A: **id** and **name** are an **int** and **String**, respectively, so those aren't a problem (**id** is required to create a new **Unit**, and name will either be null or a **String** with a value). The **weapons** property is a **List**, so if you call **getWeapons()** when there aren't any it's going to result in a null list being returned. You could change that method to throw an exception if the weapons list was empty, although that wasn't specifically asked for by the clients.

When you are <u>programming</u> **by** <u>contract</u>, you're working with client code to <u>agree</u> on how you'll handle problem situations.

When you're **programming** <u>defensively</u>, you're making sure the client gets a "safe" response, <u>no matter what</u> the client wants to have happen.

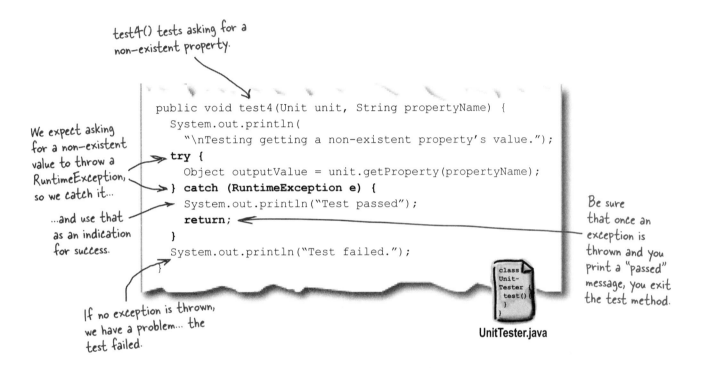

test4() tests asking for a non-existent property.

We expect asking for a non-existent value to throw a RuntimeException, so we catch it...

...and use that as an indication for success.

If no exception is thrown, we have a problem... the test failed.

```java
public void test4(Unit unit, String propertyName) {
    System.out.println(
        "\nTesting getting a non-existent property's value.");
    try {
        Object outputValue = unit.getProperty(propertyName);
    } catch (RuntimeException e) {
        System.out.println("Test passed");
        return;
    }
    System.out.println("Test failed.");
}
```

Be sure that once an exception is thrown and you print a "passed" message, you exit the test method.

UnitTester.java

Q: You said that programming by contract resulted in less code, but it seems like we just added a lot of code to Unit.java.

A: That's because instead of directly returning null, we throw a new **RuntimeException**. But that's more of a special case here than the rule. Most of the time, you'll not have much extra code on the service side, because you're simply returning objects and values without checking to see if they're non-null, or within a particular data range.

Q: I still don't see why we're switching to programming by contract here. Why is it so much better?

A: It's not a matter of being better or worse; it's a matter of what your customer wants. In fact, you'll rarely decide on your own if you want to do programming by contract or defensive programming. That's something that's usually determined by what your customer wants, and the types of users that will be using the software that you're writing.

Moving units

We've finally finished up unit properties, and can
move on to the next item on our list:

It took a while, but we're
finally on to the next piece of
functionality in the Unit class.

1 ✓ **Each unit should have properties, and
game designers can add new properties
to unit types in their own games.**

We're on to
dealing with
movement, now.

2 **Units have to be able to move from one
tile on a board to another.**

3 **Units can be grouped together into armies.**

Haven't we been here before?

This should sound pretty familiar... we already dealt
with movement in Chapter 7:

Back in Chapter 7, we
decided that handling
movement was different
for every game.

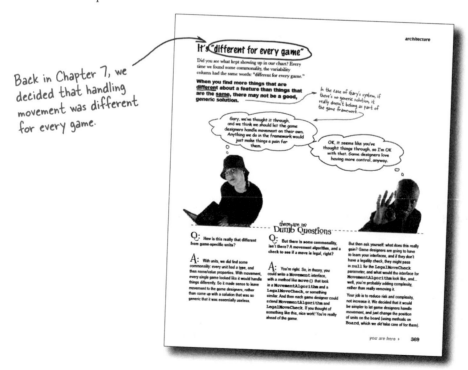

Break your apps up into smaller chunks of functionality

We've been talking a lot about iterating deeper into your application, and at each stage, doing more analysis and design. So you're taking each problem, and then breaking it up (either into use cases or features), and then solving a part of the problem, over and over. This is what we've been doing in this chapter: taking a single feature, and working on that feature until it's complete.

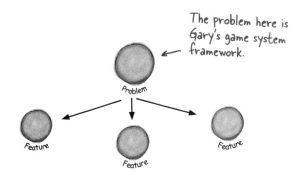

The problem here is Gary's game system framework.

But you can still break things up further...

But once you choose a single feature or use case, you can usually break that feature up into even smaller pieces of behavior. For example, a unit has properties and we have to deal with unit movement. And we also need to support groupings of units. So each of these individual pieces of behavior has to be dealt with.

Just like when you broke your app up and began to iterate, you'll have to do more analysis and design at each step. Always make sure your earlier decisions make sense, and change or rework those decisions if they don't.

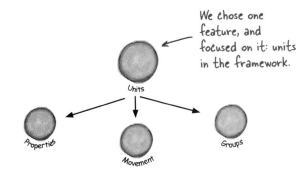

We chose one feature, and focused on it: units in the framework.

Your decisions can iterate down, too

Lots of times you'll find that decisions you made earlier save you work down the line. In Gary's system, we decided that game designers would deal with movement on their own. So now that we're talking about how to handle unit movement, we can take that decision we made earlier, and apply it here. Since it still seems sensible—there's no reason to change that decision—we can have game designers worry about handling unit movement, and move on to the next piece of behavior.

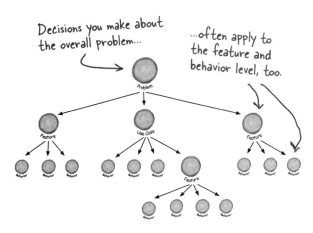

Decisions you make about the overall problem...

...often apply to the feature and behavior level, too.

Just add a note to your docs for the game designers that movement is up to them.

2 **Units have to be able to move from one tile on a board to another.**

We can check off this next bit of behavior in the Unit class.

Feature Puzzle

↑
Solve this puzzle,
and you've
completed the
behavior for the
Unit feature.

By now, you should have feature driven development, iteration, analysis, and design down pretty solid. We're going to leave it up to you to handle the last bit of behavior and finish off the **Unit** feature of Gary's game system framework.

The problem:

Gary's framework needs to support groups of units.

Your task:

1 Create a new class that can group units together, and both add and remove units to the group.

2 Fill out the table below with test case scenarios that will test your software, and prove to Gary that the grouping of units works.

3 Add methods to **UnitTester** to implement the test scenarios in the table, and make sure all your tests pass.

There's no
guarantee that
you'll use all these
rows... or that
you won't need
more rows.

ID	What we're testing	Input	Expected Output	Starting State

———→ See how we solved the puzzle on page 476.

BULLET POINTS

- The first step in writing good software is to make sure your application works like the customer expects and wants it to.

- Customers don't usually care about diagrams and lists; they want to see your software actually do something.

- Use case driven development focuses on one scenario in a use case in your application at a time.

- In use case driven development, you focus on a single scenario at a time, but you also usually code all the scenarios in a single use case before moving on to any other scenarios, in other use cases.

- Feature driven development allows you to code a complete feature before moving on to anything else.

- You can choose to work on either big or small features in feature-driven development, as long as you take each feature one at a time.

- Software development is always iterative. You look at the big picture, and then iterate down to smaller pieces of functionality.

- You have to do analysis and design at each step of your development cycle, including when you start working on a new feature or use case.

- Tests allow you to make sure your software doesn't have any bugs, and let you prove to your customer that your software works.

- A good test case only tests one specific piece of functionality.

- Test cases may involve only one, or several, methods in a single class, or may involve multiple classes.

- Test driven development is based on the idea that you write your tests first, and then develop software that passes those tests. The result is fully functional, working software.

- Programming by contract assumes both sides in a transaction understand what actions generate what behavior, and will abide by that contract.

- Methods usually return null or unchecked exceptions when errors occur in programming by contract environments.

- Defensive programming looks for things to go wrong, and tests extensively to avoid problem situations.

- Methods usually return "empty" objects or throw checked exceptions in defensive programming environments.

Feature Puzzle Solutions

Gary's framework needs to support groups of units, and
should also allow groups of those groups (in as many
nestings as the game designer wants to allow).

We decided to use a
Map, storing the ID
of a unit as the key,
and the Unit object
itself as the value of
an entry.

You create a new UnitGroup by
passing in a List of the units to add
to the group initially.

```java
public class UnitGroup {
  private Map units;

  public UnitGroup(List unitList) {
    units = new HashMap();
    for (Iterator i = unitList.iterator(); i.hasNext(); ) {
      Unit unit = (Unit)i.next();
      units.put(unit.getId(), unit);
    }
  }
```

The constructor just adds all the units
to its units Map, setting the key of
each entry to the ID of each unit.

```java
  public UnitGroup() {
    this(new LinkedList());
  }

  public void addUnit(Unit unit) {
    units.put(unit.getId(), unit);
  }
```

Here's the class diagram for
UnitGroup, to give you an overview
of what we did.

```java
  public void removeUnit(int id) {
    units.remove(id);
  }
```

By using a Map
of units, we can
retrieve and
remove units by
their ID, which
is a nice bit of
functionality.

```java
  public void removeUnit(Unit unit) {
    removeUnit(unit.getId());
  }

  public Unit getUnit(int id) {
    return (Unit)units.get(id);
  }

  public List getUnits() {
    List unitList = new LinkedList();
    for (Iterator i = units.entrySet().iterator(); i.hasNext(); )
    {
      Unit unit = (Unit)i.next();
      unitList.add(unit);
    }
    return unitList;
  }
}
```

UnitGroup
units: Map
addUnit(Unit)
removeUnit(int)
removeUnit(Unit)
getUnit(int): Unit
getUnits(): Unit [*]

There's a little bit of work
in returning a list of all units,
since we store the units in a
Map, but we thought it was
worth having units stored by ID.

And now for the test cases:

We started the IDs higher, so they wouldn't conflict with the IDs of the test cases we already have.

ID	What we're testing	Input	Expected Output	Starting State
10	Creating a new UnitGroup from a list of units	List of units	Same list of units	No existing instance of UnitGroup
11	Adding a unit to a group	Unit with ID of 100	Unit with ID of 100	UnitGroup with no entries
12	Getting a unit by its ID	100	Unit with ID of 100	UnitGroup with no entries
13	Getting all the units in a group	N/A	List of units that matches initial list	UnitGroup with a known list of units
14	Removing a unit by the ID of the unit	100	List of units (none with ID of 100)	UnitGroup with no entries
15	Removing a unit by the Unit instance	Unit with ID of 100	List of units (none with ID of 100)	UnitGroup with no entries

Here are the test cases for UnitGroup that we came up with. Did you think of any others?

We like to start with an empty UnitGroup, to make sure the units we're working with don't already appear in the UnitGroup.

 GET ONLINE

You should be able to write the code for UnitTester using the test case table shown here. If you want to see how your code compares with ours, visit http://www.headfirstlabs.com, click on Head First OOA&D, and look for "UnitGroup Test Cases."

Tools for your OOA&D Toolbox

We learned about several approaches to iterating through your project, and even a bit about two common programming practices in this chapter. Add all these to your toolbox:

Requirements

Good requireme
works like your

Make sure your

Analysis and Design

Well-designed software is easy to cha
and extend.

ke encapsula
your softwa

then CHA

Solving Big Problems

Listen to the customer, and figure out what they want you to build.

Put together a feature list, in language the customer understands.

Make sure your features are what the customer actually wants.

Create blueprints of the system using use

OO Principles

Encapsulate what varies.

Code to an interface rather than an implementation.

Each class in your application should have only one reason to change.

Classes

Classes
for me

Avoid
that a
locatio

Every

single
should
respons

Subclas
classes

Programming Practices

Programming by contract sets up an agreement about how your software behaves that you and users of your software agree to abide by.

Defensive programming doesn't trust other software, and does extensive error and data checking to ensure the other software doesn't give you bad or unsafe information.

Development Approaches

<u>Use case driven development</u> takes a single use case in your system, and focuses on completing the code to implement that entire use case, including all of its scenarios, before moving on to anything else in the application.

<u>Feature driven development</u> focuses on a single feature, and codes all the behavior of that feature, before moving on to anything else in the application.

<u>Test driven development</u> writes test scenarios for a piece of functionality before writing the code for that functionality. Then you write software to pass all the tests.

Good software development usually incorporates <u>all</u> of these development models at different stages of the development cycle.

OOA&D Cross

Lots of new terms in this chapter, so lots of little square boxes to fill in for this chapter's crossword. Review the chapter and see if you can get them all!

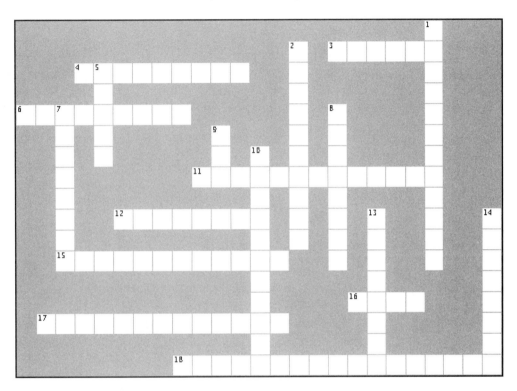

Across

3. Never be afraid to do this in design.
4. This type of programming protects you and focuses on preventing errors and invalid data.
6. You should test your software for this kind of usage.
11. Iterating your development based on specific pieces of functionality.
12. Feature driven development is very

_____.
15. Good development is driven by these.
16. Customers just want their software to do this.
17. Developing your software based on scenarios through a system.
18. Getting stuck trying to decide on one design decision or another.

Down

1. This is what you use to prove to the customer that your software works.
2. Program this way when you trust your users, and they trust you.
5. Testing weird and strange usages of your code will help you catch errors _____.
7. Use case diagrams and feature lists don't make sense to the _____.
8. Design decisions are always a _____.
9. A single test case can focus on this many pieces of functionality.
10. Great software is written like this.
13. You write software for the _____.
14. Once you choose a feature or use case, you need to do this again.

Exercise
Solutions

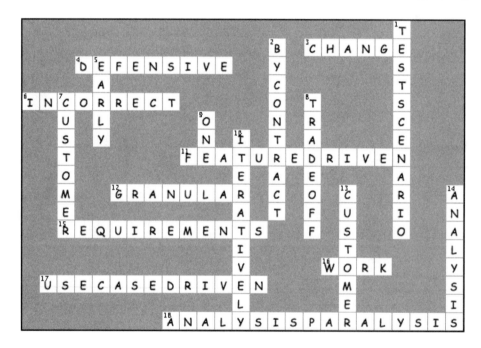

Who Am I? Solutions

Feature Driven Development, Use Case Driven Development, Programming by Contract, and Defensive Programming have all showed up for a masquerade party, but none of them bothered to wear name tags. They're all a chatty bunch, though, so it's up to you to listen to what they're saying, and try and figure out who's behind the masks. Be careful.... sometimes more than one masked guest could be saying the same thing.

I'm very well-ordered. I prefer to take things one step at a time, until I've made it from start to finish.

__Use Case Driven Development__

Well, sure, she said she would call, but how can you really believe anyone anymore?

__Defensive Programming__

Oh, absolutely, requirements really get me motivated.

__Feature Driven Development, Use Case Driven Development__

> You might have added Programming by Contract here, since a contract is really a form of requirements.

I'm very well-behaved. In fact, I've been focusing on all of my own behavior before moving on to anything else.

__Feature Driven Development__

Really, it's all about my customer. I just want to satisfy them, after all.

__All of them!__

> All of these techniques and tools are really about getting the customer the software that they want.

Hey, you're a big boy. You can deal with that on your own... it's really not my problem anymore, is it?

__Programming by Contract__

As long as you're good with it, so am I. Who am I to tell you what to do, so long as you know what you can expect from me.

__Programming by Contract__

Putting It All Together

Honey, I think you're a great programmer, but I just don't see how you're going to combine all those little bits and pieces into anything that makes sense.

You may not see it yet, Walter, but I'm going to take all these pieces and turn them into one big beautiful cake of OO goodness. Just you wait and see...

Are we there yet? We've been working on lots of individual ways to improve your software, but now it's time to **put it all together**. This is it, what you've been waiting for: we're going to take **everything** you've been learning, and show you how it's all really part of **a single process** that you can use over and over again to **write great software**.

Developing software, OOA&D style

You've got a lot of new tools, techniques, and ideas about how to develop great software by now... but we still haven't really put it all together.

That's what this chapter is all about: taking all the individual things you know how to do—like figuring out requirements, writing up use cases, and applying design patterns—and turning it into a reusable process that you can use to tackle even your trickiest software problems, over and over again.

So what does that process look like?

Break Up the Problem
Break your application up into modules of functionality, and then decide on an order in which to tackle each of your modules.

Requirements
Figure out the individual requirements for each module, and make sure those fit in with the big picture.

Use Case Diagrams
Nail down the big processes that your app performs, and any external forces that are involved.

Feature List
Figure out what your app is supposed to do at a high level

The Object-Oriented Analysi

1. Make sure your software does what the customer wants it to do

Does it seem like you spend a LOT of time worrying about functionality? That's because you do... if the customer isn't happy with what your software does, you won't succeed.

This entire section applies to each smaller problem.... so you'll solve a problem using these phases, iterate to another problem, and use these phases again.

Iterative Development

Domain Analysis
Figure out how your use cases map to objects in your app, and make sure your customer is on the same page as you are.

Preliminary Design
Fill in details about your objects, define relationships between the objects, and apply principles and patterns.

Implementation
Write code, test it, and make sure it works. Do this for each behavior, each feature, each use case, each problem, until you're done.

Delivery
You're done! Release your software, submit your invoices, and get paid.

Design Project Lifecycle

2. Apply basic OO principles to add flexibility.

3. Strive for a maintainable, reusable design.

These may seem like small parts of the process, but you'll spend most of your development time in the design and implementation phases.

> Look, I love your pretty arrows and all those labels, but I'm not convinced. We've used parts of that process, but how am I supposed to know using all those steps together like that really works?

Let's build a software project, from start to finish, using this process.

We've used all of the different parts of this process to work on software projects throughout the book, but we haven't yet really put it all together. But that's all about to change... we're going to let you build a pretty complex piece of software in this chapter, from feature list to implementation and delivery.

Along the way, you'll see for yourself how all the things you've been learning really do help you build great software. Get ready, this will be your final test.

OOA&D GENERAL'S WARNING: Answers to this exercise do NOT appear on the next page. Go ahead and work through this chapter, and we'll come back to these answers at the end of the chapter.

OOA&D Magnets

Before we dive into the problem we're going to be solving in this chapter, you need to make sure you see where all the things you've been learning fit in the big OOA&D Project Lifecycle. At the bottom of this page are OOA&D magnets for lots of the things you've learned about already; your job is to try and put those magnets on the right phase of the OOA&D lifecycle, shown again below.

You can put more than one magnet on each phase, and there are some magnets you may want to use more than once, so take your time, and good luck.

We've started a list for the Requirements phase to help you out.

Feature List	Use Case Diagrams	Break Up the Problem	Requirements	Domain Analysis	Preliminary Design	Implementation	Delivery

Requirements List
Textual Analysis

OO Principles
Scenario
Encapsulation
Architecture
Test Scenario
Analysis
Test Driven Development
Design Pattern
Requirements List
Textual Analysis
External Initiator
Commonality
Alternate Path
Alternate Path
Key Feature List
Class Diagram
Design Principles
Iteration
Architecture
Feature Driven Development
Cohesion
Variability
Delegation
Talk to the Customer

You can use each of these magnets as many times as you like.

The problem

Here's the project we're going to work through in
this chapter, from beginning to end:

Objectville Travel, Inc.
210 Tourist Ave.
Objectville, HF 90210

Statement of Work

Congratulations! Based on your amazing work for Rick's Stringed
Instruments and Doug's Dog Doors, we'd like to commission you
to program our brand new Objectville Travel RouteFinder.

With the recent increase in travel to Objectville, we want to
provide tourists an easy way to see the wonderful sights that make
Objectville so unique. The RouteFinder should be able to store
Objectville's complete network of subway lines, as well as all the
stations along each line. Objectville's subways are state-of-the-art,
and can go backwards and forwards between stations, so you don't
need to worry about the direction of any of the lines.

The RouteFinder should also be able to take a starting station, and a
destination station, and figure out a route to travel. Our travel agents
should be able to print out the route, indicating which lines to take,
which stations are passed on a line, and when travelers may need to
get off one line and get on another at a connecting station.

We pride ourselves on flexibility and extensibility in Objectville,
so we expect the RouteFinder to be easy to extend as we come up
with new ways to provide our tourists the best experience around in
object-based travel.

We look forward to seeing your design and a working RouteFinder
soon. We're all counting on you!

Sincerely,

Orbin Traveloctic, CEO

P.S. To help you get started, we've provided a map of Objectville's
subway lines, and a file with all of the stations and lines.

This page left intentionally blank,
so you can cut out the cool
Objectville Map on the next page ⟶
and hang it up on your cubicle wall.

[note from marketing: What are you thinking? Can't we
sell the poster as an add-on and charge extra?]

Objectville Subway Map

Legend

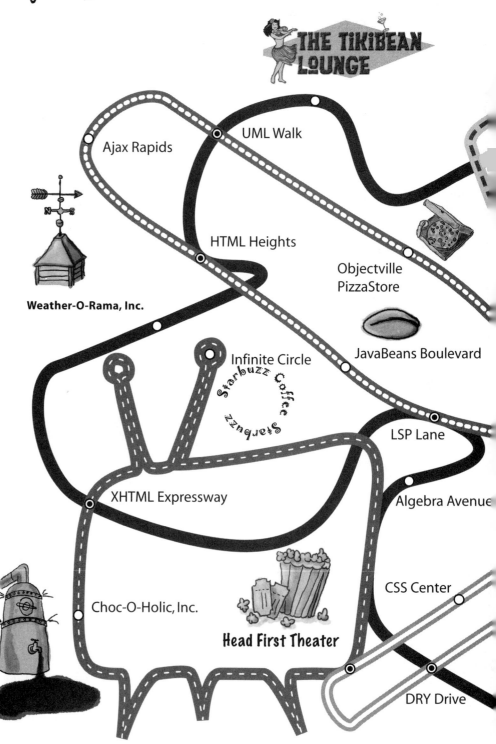

○ Local train station

◉ Interchange with other lines

•••••••• Booch Line

▬ ▬ ▬ Gamma Line

■ ■ ■ ■ Jacobson Line

▬▬▬ Liskov Line

═══ Meyer Line

▬ ▬ ▬ Rumbaugh Line

▬▬▬ Wirfs-Brock Line

THE TIKIBEAN LOUNGE

Ajax Rapids

UML Walk

HTML Heights

Weather-O-Rama, Inc.

Objectville PizzaStore

JavaBeans Boulevard

Infinite Circle

Starbuzz Coffee

LSP Lane

XHTML Expressway

Algebra Avenue

CSS Center

Choc-O-Holic, Inc.

Head First Theater

DRY Drive

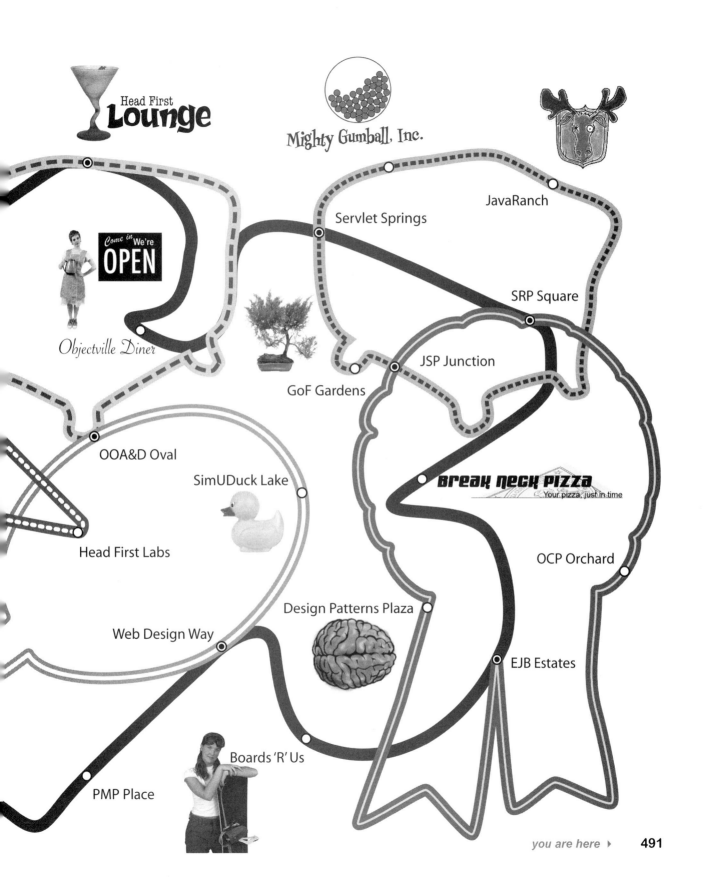

Head First **Lounge**

Mighty Gumball, Inc.

Come in We're **OPEN**

Objectville Diner

Servlet Springs

JavaRanch

SRP Square

JSP Junction

GoF Gardens

OOA&D Oval

SimUDuck Lake

BREAK NECK PIZZA
Your pizza, just in time

Head First Labs

OCP Orchard

Design Patterns Plaza

Web Design Way

EJB Estates

Boards 'R' Us

PMP Place

This page left intentionally blank, so
you can cut out the cool Objectville
Map on the previous page and hang
it up on your cubicle wall.

←─────────────────

Sharpen your pencil

Write the feature list for the RouteFinder app.

We're throwing you right into things. Your job is to take the Statement of Work on page 488, and use it to develop a feature list. You can refer back to Chapter 6 if you need help on what features are, and what a typical feature list looks like.

Objectville RouteFinder
Feature List

1. _____
   _____

2. _____
   _____

3. _____
   _____

4. _____
   _____

5. _____
   _____

6. _____
   _____

7. _____
   _____

You don't have to use all of these blanks if you don't think you need them all.

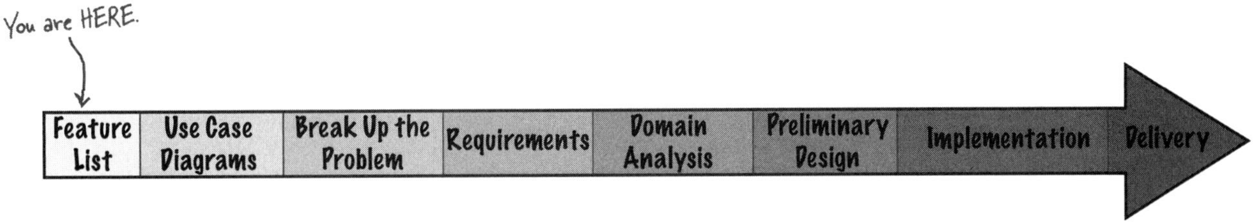

You are HERE.

| Feature List | Use Case Diagrams | Break Up the Problem | Requirements | Domain Analysis | Preliminary Design | Implementation | Delivery |

Sharpen your pencil
answers

Write the feature list for the RouteFinder app.

Your job was to take the Statement of Work on page 488, and use it to develop a feature list for the RouteFinder we're going to build.

Here's what we came up with. Your answers may not match ours exactly, but they should be pretty close, and cover these same basic four features.

Objectville RouteFinder
Feature List

1. **We have to be able to represent a subway line, and the stations along that line.**

2. **We must be able to load multiple subway lines into the program, including overlapping lines.**

   Lines overlap when they both share the same station.

3. **We need to be able to figure out a valid path between any two stations on any lines.**

   A "valid route" might be all on one line, or involve several different line.

4. **We need to be able to print out a route between two stations as a set of directions.**

   Printing is a separate feature... be sure you have this in your feature list.

---

there are no Dumb Questions

Q: Why aren't we gathering requirements? I'm still not clear on how a feature is really that different from a requirement, anyway.

A: Features and requirements are often used almost interchangeably. Most of the time, though, people say "feature" when they're talking about BIG things that an application needs to do. So it might take several requirements to satisfy one feature. And since features are usually a little bigger-picture than requirements, it's a good idea to start any new project by writing out a feature list, like we've done with the RouteFinder.

Q: Why did you list printing out the route as a separate feature? That's pretty easy once you've got a valid route between two stations, isn't it?

A: It probably will be, yes. But the feature list isn't just a list of hard problems you have to solve—it's a list of *all* the things your application has to be able to do. So even if a feature seems easy or trivial, put it on your feature list anyway.

Now you should really know what you're supposed to do

At this point, you've finished up that first phase.

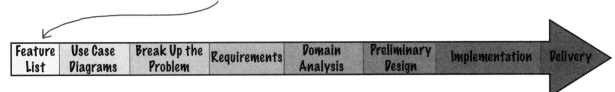

| Feature List | Use Case Diagrams | Break Up the Problem | Requirements | Domain Analysis | Preliminary Design | Implementation | Delivery |

With a feature list in hand, you should have a good understanding of the things that your app needs to do. You probably even can begin to think about the structure of your application, although we'll spend a lot more time on that in just a bit.

Once you've got your feature list down, you should move on to use case diagrams. Those will help you connect what your app *does* to how it will be *used*— and that's what customers really are interested in.

Your **feature lists** are all about understanding what your software is **supposed to <u>do</u>.**

Your **use case diagrams** let you start thinking about how your software **will be <u>used</u>,** without getting into a bunch of unnecessary details.

Sharpen your pencil

Decide on the structure for the RouteFinder code.

With feature lists in hand, let's look at how our app is going to be used. Below, we've started a use case diagram for the RouteFinder app. For this project, there are two actors, and just two use cases (sounds sort of simple, doesn't it?).

It's up to you to figure out who (or what) the two actors are, and to label the two use cases. If you need help, refer back to Chapter 6 for more on use case diagrams.

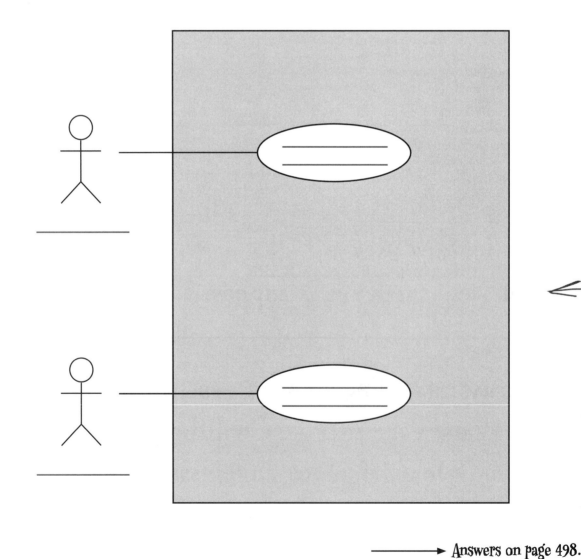

Answers on page 498.

Feature Magnets

Once you've got your use case diagrams figured out, you need to make sure that your use cases match up with the features you have to deliver to the customer. Below is the feature list for RouteFinder, as well as magnets for each feature. Place each magnet below on one of the use cases you filled in on page 496. Make sure you have each feature covered before turning the page.

Objectville RouteFinder
Feature List

1. **We have to be able to represent a subway line, and the stations along that line.**

2. **We must be able to load multiple subway lines into the program, including overlapping lines.**

3. **We need to be able to figure out a valid path between any two stations on any lines.**

4. **We need to be able to print out a route between two stations as a set of directions.**

> Represent subway lines, and stations along each line.

> Load multiple subway lines into the program.

> Figure out a valid route between two stops.

> Print directions for a particular route.

Each one of these magnets should go on one of the use cases over here.

You are HERE.

Feature List	Use Case Diagrams	Break Up the Problem	Requirements	Domain Analysis	Preliminary Design	Implementation	Delivery

Exercise Solutions

Decide on the structure for the RouteFinder code, and map your use cases back to your feature list.

You had a Sharpen Your Pencil, and a Feature Magnets to solve. You were supposed to figure out the actors and use cases for your system, and then make sure those use cases covered all the features we decided RouteFinder had to support.

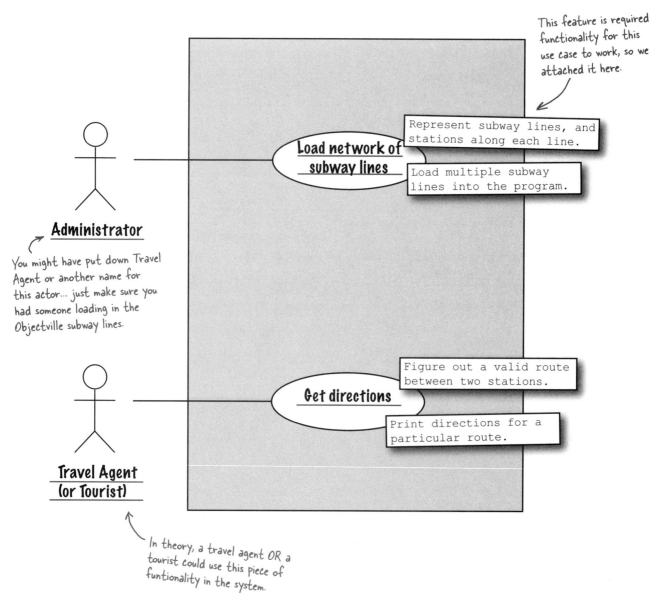

This feature is required functionality for this use case to work, so we attached it here.

Load network of subway lines

Represent subway lines, and stations along each line.

Load multiple subway lines into the program.

Administrator

You might have put down Travel Agent or another name for this actor... just make sure you had someone loading in the Objectville subway lines.

Get directions

Figure out a valid route between two stations.

Print directions for a particular route.

Travel Agent (or Tourist)

In theory, a travel agent OR a tourist could use this piece of funtionality in the system.

Use cases reflect <u>usage</u>, features reflect <u>functionality</u>

Let's look more closely at one of the feature-use case matches we showed you on the last page:

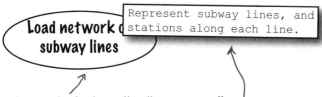

Represent subway lines, and stations along each line.

The "Load network of subway lines" use case really does not directly use our feature that deals with representing the subway. Obviously, we have to be able to represent the subway for this use case to work, but it's a stretch to tie the two together like this.

That's not a mistake, though; when we're writing use cases, we're dealing with just the **interactions** between actors and a system. We're just talking about the ways that your system is **used** (which is where the term "use case" came from).

This is something the RouteFinder must do for a use case to work, but it's not actually an interaction on its own. It's <u>NOT</u> part of any use case.

These are ways that our RouteFinder is used.

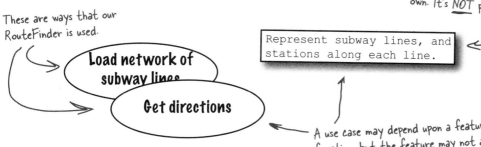

Represent subway lines, and stations along each line.

A use case may depend upon a feature to function, but the feature may not actually be part of the steps in the use case itself.

"Load network of subway lines" depends on a representation of the subway, but only uses that feature indirectly.

The features in your system reflect your system's <u>functionality</u>. Your system <u>must</u> do those things in order for the use cases to actually work, even though the functionality isn't always an explicit part of any particular use case.

You are (still) HERE.

Feature List	Use Case Diagrams	Break Up the Problem	Requirements	Domain Analysis	Preliminary Design	Implementation	Delivery

Q: Didn't you say that I should be able to match up every feature to a use case in my system?

A: Yes, and that's still true. Every feature in your system will be at least a part of addressing one or more uses cases in your use case diagram. But that doesn't mean that the use case has to actually directly use that feature. Lots of times, a feature makes it possible for a use case to function without being directly used by the use case itself.

In our RouteFinder, there would be no way to load a network of subway lines into the system (one of our use cases) without having a representation of a subway in the first place (one of our features). But the "Load Network" use case doesn't have any steps that match up directly with that feature... the steps in the use case just assume that a representation of the subway exists. So the use case indirectly uses the feature, without explicitly referring to it.

Q: So is a use case a requirement, or is a feature a requirement?

A: Both! Use cases are requirements for how people and things (actors) interact with your system, and features are requirements about things that your system must do. They're related, but they are not the same. Still, to implement a system's use cases, you're going to need the functionality in the system's features. That's why you should always be able to map your features to the use cases that they enable and are used by.

Q: What happens if I find a feature that I can't match up to a use case, even indirectly?

A: You should take a hard look at the feature, and make sure it really is a required part of your system. Your customer—and her customers—only interact with your system through the use cases. So if a feature doesn't at least indirectly make a use case possible, you're customer really isn't going to see a benefit. If you think you've got a feature that doesn't really affect how your system is used or performs, talk it over with the customer, but don't be afraid to cut something if it's not going to improve your system.

The features in your system are what the system does, and are not always reflected in your use cases, which show how the system is used.

Features and use cases work together, but they are not the same thing.

The Big Break-Up

We're starting to pick up some steam. With use case diagrams in place, you're ready to break this problem up into some smaller pieces of functionality. There are several ways to do this in any application, but our goal here is to keep the RouteFinder system very modular. That means keeping different pieces of functionality separate—each module should have a single responsibility.

Go ahead and break up the RouteFinder system into four different "modules". Think carefully about the best way to break up your system... it isn't necessarily going to line up with your four features (although it might!).

Write the name of what this module does in the blank.

HINT: Remember, you need to handle the system's functionality, but you also need to prove to the customer that your system works.

We're really moving along.

Feature List	Use Case Diagrams	Break Up the Problem	Requirements	Domain Analysis	Preliminary Design	Implementation	Delivery

The Big Break-Up, Solved

We're starting to pick up some steam. With use case diagrams in place, you're ready to break this problem up into some smaller pieces of functionality.

These three modules make up the system... they form a "black box" that is used by tourists and travel agents to get directions.

We added a Testing module, because we need some code that actually proves to our customer that the system works... not only in our "perfect world", but also in the real world.

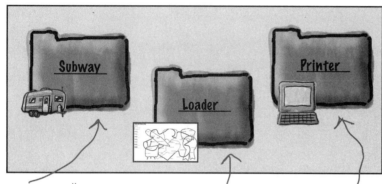

The Subway module has all the code that represents stations, connections between those stations, and the entire subway system itself. It also knows how to get directions from one station to another on its connections and lines.

We could have several different ways to load a subway: from a file, or with user input, or even from a database. Loading is really separate from the subway representation itself, so it gets its own module.

Printing is a lot like loading; it's separate from the subway system itself. This module handles printing the subway to any device or format that we might need.

Test is outside the system... it interacts with the system, but isn't part of the system itself.

✏️ **Sharpen your pencil**

Which OO principles are we using?

Check the box next to the OO principles you think we're using to break up the RouteFinder functionality in this manner.

Answers on page 504.

- ☐ Single Responsibility Principle
- ☐ Don't Repeat Yourself
- ☐ Encapsulation
- ☐ Delegation
- ☐ Polymorphism
- ☐ Liskov Substitution Principle

Now start to iterate

Once you've broken up your software into several individual pieces
of functionality, you're ready to start iterating over each piece of
functionality, until the application is complete.

At this point, we need to take our big-picture view of the system,
from our use case diagram, and refine that into requirements that
we can begin to tackle, one by one. For this first iteration, let's take
the "Load network of subway lines" use case, and turn that into a
set of requirements that isn't so big-picture. Then we can take care
of that use case, and iterate again, working on the next use case.

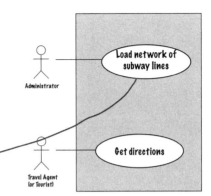

We're taking the
first use case from
our diagram, and
starting with it.

Sharpen your pencil

What approach to development are we using?

_____

_____

Sharpen your pencil

Write the use case for loading subway lines.

Turn that little oval into a full-blown use case. Write the steps
that RouteFinder needs to take to implement the "Load network
of subway lines" use case.

Load network of subway lines
Use Case

1. _____
2. _____
3. _____
4. _____
5. _____
6. _____

You can use
more room, or
more steps, if
you need them.

Not too sure about this use case? It's OK... turn the page for some help...

> How am I supposed to write this use case? I'm not totally sure I know what a subway line even is yet. And what about that file that Objectville travel said they were going to send over to us? Won't that affect how we write our use case?

You'll often have to do some extra work between breaking up the problem and writing your use cases.

You've just uncovered a "secret step" in our process for writing software the OOA&D way:

Here's the "extra step" that we sometimes need to take. → **Understand the Problem**

We really don't understand our problem well enough to write better requirements yet.

Feature List	Use Case Diagrams	Break Up the Problem	Requirements	Domain Analysis	Preliminary Design	Implementation	Delivery

If you get stuck writing a use case, there's nothing wrong with taking a step back, and examining the problem you're trying to solve a bit. Then, you can go back to your use case, and have a better chance of getting it written correctly.

By breaking up printing, loading, and representing the subway into three modules, we're making sure each module has only one reason to change.

We've encapsulated printing and loading, which might vary, away from the subway, which should stay the same.

Sharpen your pencil
answers   Which OO principles are we using?

Check the box next to the OO principles you think we used to break up the RouteFinder functionality into separate modules.

It's not clear if we're using delegation yet, although with SRP and encapsulation, we probably will at some point.

☑ Single Responsibility Principle   ☑ Delegation ←

☐ Don't Repeat Yourself   ☐ Polymorphism

☑ Encapsulation   ☐ Liskov Substitution Principle

A closer look at representing a subway

Before we can figure out how to load a subway line, there are two
things we need to get a good grasp of:

1 Understanding the basics of what a subway system is.

2 Understanding the information an administrator would have
when they're loading a set of subway stations and lines.

> We're on Iteration 1, trying to handle the first use case: loading a network of subway lines.

What is a station?

A subway system has stations, and connections between those stations,
and lines that are groups of connections. So let's begin by figuring out
exactly what a station is.

A station is just a point on the map, with a name. → ⊙ OOA&D Oval

And a connection between two stations?

As soon as you start adding several stations, you've got to deal with the
connections between those stations:

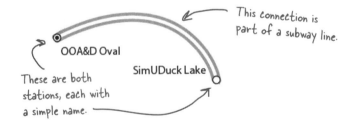

This connection is part of a subway line.

These are both stations, each with a simple name.

OOA&D Oval

SimUDuck Lake

Then a line is just a series of connections...

If you put several connections together, then you've got a subway line.

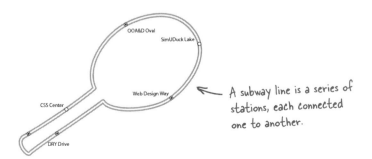

OOA&D Oval

SimUDuck Lake

Web Design Way

CSS Center

DRY Drive

A subway line is a series of stations, each connected one to another.

Sharpen your pencil
answers

What approach to development are
we using in this chapter?

Use-case driven development

Let's take a look at that subway file

We've got a basic idea now of what a subway is, so let's see what kind of data we've got to work with. Remember, Objectville Travel said they would send us a file with all the stations and lines, so this should give us an idea of what an administrator will use to load the lines into the subway system.

ObjectvilleSubway.txt, → the file that Objectville Travel sent us to load the subway lines from.

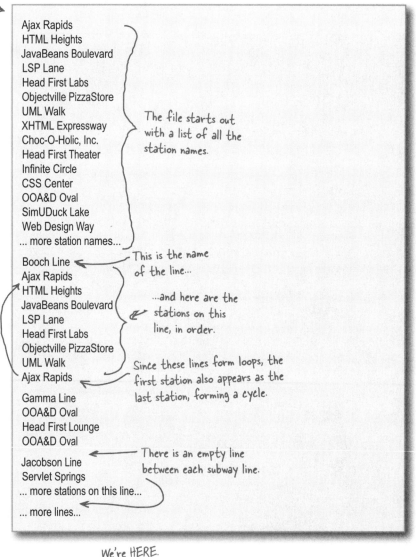

Ajax Rapids
HTML Heights
JavaBeans Boulevard
LSP Lane
Head First Labs
Objectville PizzaStore
UML Walk
XHTML Expressway
Choc-O-Holic, Inc.
Head First Theater
Infinite Circle
CSS Center
OOA&D Oval
SimUDuck Lake
Web Design Way
... more station names...

The file starts out with a list of all the station names.

Booch Line
Ajax Rapids
HTML Heights
JavaBeans Boulevard
LSP Lane
Head First Labs
Objectville PizzaStore
UML Walk
Ajax Rapids

This is the name of the line...

...and here are the stations on this line, in order.

Since these lines form loops, the first station also appears as the last station, forming a cycle.

Gamma Line
OOA&D Oval
Head First Lounge
OOA&D Oval

Jacobson Line
Servlet Springs
... more stations on this line...

... more lines...

There is an empty line between each subway line.

We're HERE.
↓

| Feature List | Use Case Diagrams | Break Up the Problem | Requirements | Domain Analysis | Preliminary Design | Implementation | Delivery |

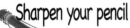 Sharpen your pencil

Write the use case for loading subway lines.

You should have enough understanding of what a subway system is, and the format of the Objectville Subway input file, to write this use case now.

Load network of subway lines
Use Case

1. _____
2. _____
3. _____
4. _____
5. _____
6. _____
7. _____
8. _____
9. _____

You can use more room, or more steps, if you need them.

Write the use case for loading subway lines.

You should have enough understanding of what a subway system is, and the format of the Objectville Subway input file, to write this use case now.

The first step is the start condition: the loader gets a new file to load from.

Did you get this step? We really don't want our system to have duplicate stations... that could be a real problem later on.

Here's another step where we validate input, to make sure the connection is valid for the current subway.

Steps like this, which indicate repeating other steps, help make your use cases a little more readable and concise.

Load network of subway lines
Use Case

1. **The administrator supplies a file of stations and lines.**

2. **The system reads in the name of a station.**

3. **The system validates that the station doesn't already exist.**

4. **The system adds the new station to the subway.**

5. **The system repeats steps 2-4 until all stations are added.**

6. **The system reads in the name of a line to add.**

7. **The system reads in two stations that are connected.**

8. **The system validates that the stations exist.**

9. **The system creates a new connection between the two stations, going in both directions, on the current line.**

10. **The system repeats steps 7-9 until the line is complete.**

11. **The system repeats steps 6-10 until all lines are entered.**

This is really only one possible way to write the use case. Instead of creating a "SubwayLine" object, we decided to just give the subway each connection, and associate the connection with a particular subway line.

You didn't have to write this down, but we thought it was important to remember that subways in Objectville can go in EITHER direction.

there are no
Dumb Questions

Q: My use case looks totally different. Is your use case the only solution to the puzzle?

A: No, not at all. By now you realize that there are lots of decisions you have to make to solve any problem, and our use case simply reflects the decisions we made. We're going to work with this particular use case throughout the rest of this chapter, so make sure you understand our reasoning behind it, but it's perfectly OK if you came up with your own use case that solves the same problem of loading a network of subway stations and lines.

Q: I didn't add any steps about validation to my use case. Is that OK?

A: Validation is something that you *should* add to your use case if you left it out. Making sure the stations for a connection actually exist is a lot like not having a dog door automatically close. It seems innocent enough, until the real world creeps in, and someone misspells a station name. Suddenly, you have the equivalent of software rodents: a connection that goes to a non-existent station. So if you left out validation, be sure to add it in to your own use case.

Let's see if our use case works

The use case for loading a network is a little tricky, and has several
groups of steps that repeat. Let's check the flow of things against our
text file before we go on to analyzing the use case, and starting to
design the classes in our system.

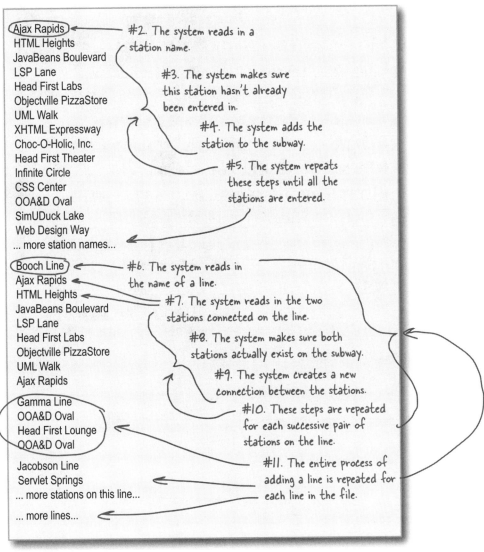

#1. The administrator supplies a file like this to the system loader.

Ajax Rapids
HTML Heights
JavaBeans Boulevard
LSP Lane
Head First Labs
Objectville PizzaStore
UML Walk
XHTML Expressway
Choc-O-Holic, Inc.
Head First Theater
Infinite Circle
CSS Center
OOA&D Oval
SimUDuck Lake
Web Design Way
... more station names...

#2. The system reads in a station name.

#3. The system makes sure this station hasn't already been entered in.

#4. The system adds the station to the subway.

#5. The system repeats these steps until all the stations are entered.

Booch Line
Ajax Rapids
HTML Heights
JavaBeans Boulevard
LSP Lane
Head First Labs
Objectville PizzaStore
UML Walk
Ajax Rapids

Gamma Line
OOA&D Oval
Head First Lounge
OOA&D Oval

Jacobson Line
Servlet Springs
... more stations on this line...

... more lines...

#6. The system reads in the name of a line.

#7. The system reads in the two stations connected on the line.

#8. The system makes sure both stations actually exist on the subway.

#9. The system creates a new connection between the stations.

#10. These steps are repeated for each successive pair of stations on the line.

#11. The entire process of adding a line is repeated for each line in the file.

Analysis and Design Puzzle

This time, it's your job to take on two phases of the OOA&D process at once. First, you need to perform textual analysis on the use case below, and figure out the nouns that are candidate classes, and the verbs that are candidate operations. Write the nouns and verbs in the blanks provided below the use case.

Load network of subway lines
Use Case

1. The administrator supplies a file of stations and lines.
2. The system reads in the name of a station.
3. The system validates that the station doesn't already exist.
4. The system adds the new station to the subway.
5. The system repeats steps 2-4 until all stations are added.
6. The system reads in the name of a line to add.
7. The system reads in two stations that are connected.
8. The system validates that the stations exist.
9. The system creates a new connection between the two stations, going in both directions, on the current line.
10. The system repeats steps 7-9 until the line is complete.
11. The system repeats steps 6-10 until all lines are entered.

Nouns (candidate classes):

_____   _____   _____

_____   _____   _____

Verbs (candidate operations):

_____   _____   _____

_____   _____   _____

It's on to preliminary design. Using the candidate nouns and verbs you got from the use case, draw a class diagram below of what you think the subway system might look like modeled in code. Use associations and any other UML notation you think will help make your design clear and understandable.

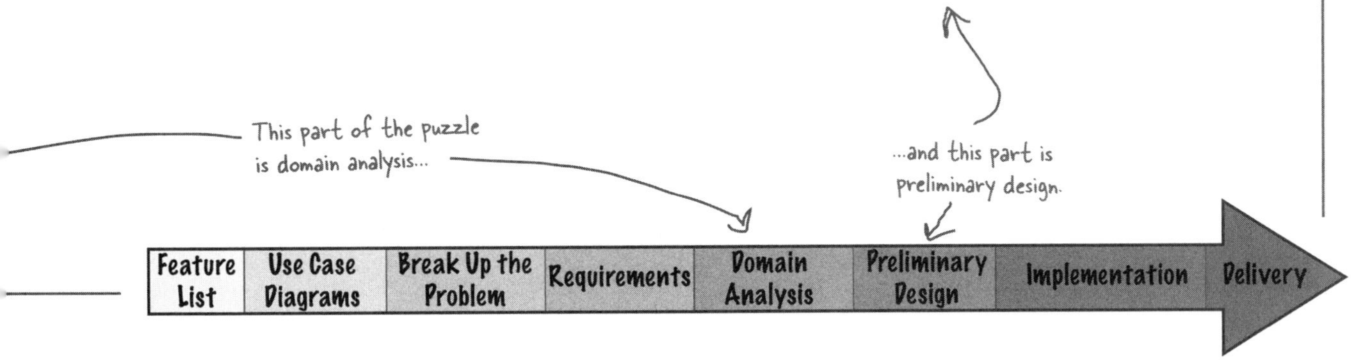

This part of the puzzle
is domain analysis...

...and this part is
preliminary design.

| Feature List | Use Case Diagrams | Break Up the Problem | Requirements | Domain Analysis | Preliminary Design | Implementation | Delivery |

 # Analysis and Design Puzzle Solutions

Load network of subway lines
Use Case

1. The administrator supplies a file of stations and lines.
2. The system reads in the name of a station.
3. The system validates that the station doesn't already exist.
4. The system adds the new station to the subway.
5. The system repeats steps 2-4 until all stations are added.
6. The system reads in the name of a line to add.
7. The system reads in two stations that are connected.
8. The system validates that the stations exist.
9. The system creates a new connection between the two stations, going in both directions, on the current line.
10. The system repeats steps 7-9 until the line is complete.
11. The system repeats steps 6-10 until all lines are entered.

These are easy... they all appear on our class diagram.

Nouns (candidate classes):

We know that actors are outside the system, so no class needed here.

~~administrator~~   ~~system~~

~~file~~   station

subway   line

connection

This is an input to our system, not something we model in our system.

We decided not to create a Line class... more on that when you turn the page.

Verbs (candidate operations):

We can use Java's I/O operations to handle this.

supplies a file
~~reads in~~

validates station
adds a station

~~repeats~~
adds a connection

Most of these directly map to methods on our classes.

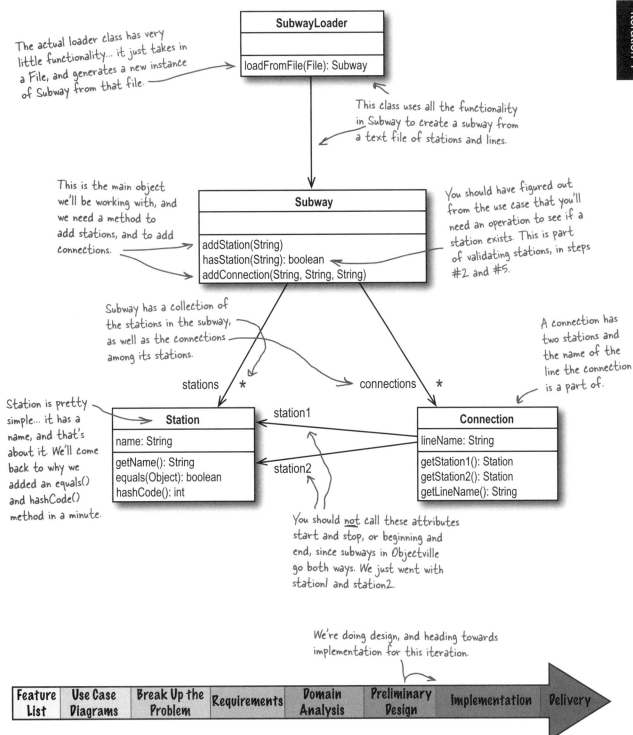

The actual loader class has very little functionality... it just takes in a File, and generates a new instance of Subway from that file.

SubwayLoader

loadFromFile(File): Subway

This class uses all the functionality in Subway to create a subway from a text file of stations and lines.

This is the main object we'll be working with, and we need a method to add stations, and to add connections.

Subway

addStation(String)
hasStation(String): boolean
addConnection(String, String, String)

You should have figured out from the use case that you'll need an operation to see if a station exists. This is part of validating stations, in steps #2 and #5.

Subway has a collection of the stations in the subway, as well as the connections among its stations.

stations   *   connections   *

A connection has two stations and the name of the line the connection is a part of.

Station is pretty simple... it has a name, and that's about it. We'll come back to why we added an equals() and hashCode() method in a minute.

Station

name: String

getName(): String
equals(Object): boolean
hashCode(): int

station1

station2

Connection

lineName: String

getStation1(): Station
getStation2(): Station
getLineName(): String

You should **not** call these attributes start and stop, or beginning and end, since subways in Objectville go both ways. We just went with station1 and station2.

We're doing design, and heading towards implementation for this iteration.

| Feature List | Use Case Diagrams | Break Up the Problem | Requirements | Domain Analysis | Preliminary Design | Implementation | Delivery |

To use a Line class or not to use a Line class... that is the question

It was pretty easy to look at our use case and figure out that we need a **Station**, **Connection**, and **Subway** class—those are fundamental to our system. But then we decided to *not* create a **Line** class. Instead, we just assigned a line name to each connection:

Lines only exist as String names attached to a particular Connection. →

Connection
station1: Station station2: Station lineName: String
getStation1(): Station getStation2(): Station getLineName(): String

We made this decision based on one thing: *we know how the system is going to be used*. In the original Statement of Work (back on page 488) from Objectville Travel, we were told we needed to represent a subway, and get directions between one station and another. Once we have those directions, we can simply ask each connection for its line; there doesn't seem to be a need for an actual **Line** class.

> **Your design decisions should be based on how your system will be used, as well as good OO principles.**

Even if it turns out we need to add a Line class later, that's no big deal. This is a **preliminary** design, and we can change it if we need to once we start writing our code.

there are no
Dumb Questions

Q: **I found the "validates that a station exists" verb, but where does that operation appear on any of the classes in your design?**

A: We modeled that operation as `hasStation()` on the **Subway** class. You could have called that operation `validate()` or `validateStation()`, but those aren't as descriptive as `hasStation()`, and you should always try and make your code as readable as possible.

Q: **Could you talk a little more about how you showed those repeated steps in the use case?**

A: Lots of times a use case has a set of steps that need to be repeated, but there's not a standard way to show that in use cases. So we just made one up! The point of a use case is to provide you with a clear set of steps that detail what your system should do, and we thought the clearest way to show those repeated steps was to write down "Repeat Steps 7-9."

Q: **I've been thinking about that subway representation, and it looks a lot like a graph data structure to me. Why aren't we using a graph?**

A: Wow, you must have taken a data structures or algorithms class recently! Yes, you can use a graph to represent the subway. In that case, each station would be a node, and each connection would be a labeled edge.

Q: **So then why aren't we using a graph structure in this example?**

A: We think it's really overkill in this situation. If you already know about graphs and nodes and edges, and you happen to have code for that sort of data structure lying around, then go ahead and use them. But from our point of view, we'd do more work adapting a graph to our needs than just coming up with a few simple classes for **Station** and **Connection**. Like almost everything else in the design stage, there are several ways to solve a problem, and you need to choose a solution that works well for you.

Q: **You lost me on the whole graph thing... what's all this about edges and nodes?**

A: It's OK; you don't need to know about graphs in order to understand and solve this particular problem. It's nothing to worry about, at least until we come up with a Head First Data Structures book (anyone? anyone?).

Our design decisions here...   ...have a lot of impact here.

Feature List	Use Case Diagrams	Break Up the Problem	Requirements	Domain Analysis	Preliminary Design	Implementation	Delivery

Code the Station class

We've got requirements in the form of a use case, a class diagram, and we know the **Station** class will fit into our **Subway** model. Now we're ready to start writing code:

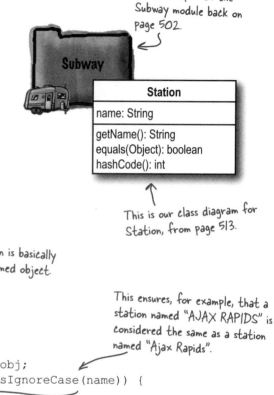

We came up with the Subway module back on page 502.

This is our class diagram for Station, from page 513.

If you want, you can put Station in a package like objectville.subway. It's up to you if you want to break up your modules by package.

```java
public class Station {
    private String name;

    public Station(String name) {
        this.name = name;
    }

    public String getName() {
        return name;
    }

    public boolean equals(Object obj) {
        if (obj instanceof Station) {
            Station otherStation = (Station)obj;
            if (otherStation.getName().equalsIgnoreCase(name)) {
                return true;
            }
        }
        return false;
    }

    public int hashCode() {
        return name.toLowerCase().hashCode();
    }
}
```

A Station is basically just a named object.

This ensures, for example, that a station named "AJAX RAPIDS" is considered the same as a station named "Ajax Rapids".

We figured there's going to be a lot of comparisons between stations, so we made sure we defined equals(). In this version, two Station objects are equal if they have the same name.

We base the hash code of a Station on the same property that comparisons are based on: the name of the station.

Watch it!

When you override equals() in Java, you should usually also override hashCode() to ensure correct comparisons.

The Java specification recommends that if two objects are equal, they should have the same hash code. So if you're deciding on equality based on a property, it's a good idea to also override hashCode() and return a hash code based on that same property. This is particularly important if you're using your object in a Hashtable or HashMap, which both make heavy use of the hashCode() method.

For a lot more on equals() and hashCode(), check out Chapter 16 of Head First Java.

Sharpen your pencil

Write the Connection class.

Using the class diagram on the right, complete the
Connection class by filling in the blanks with the correct lines
of code. Be sure your class will compile before you turn the
page and see our answers.

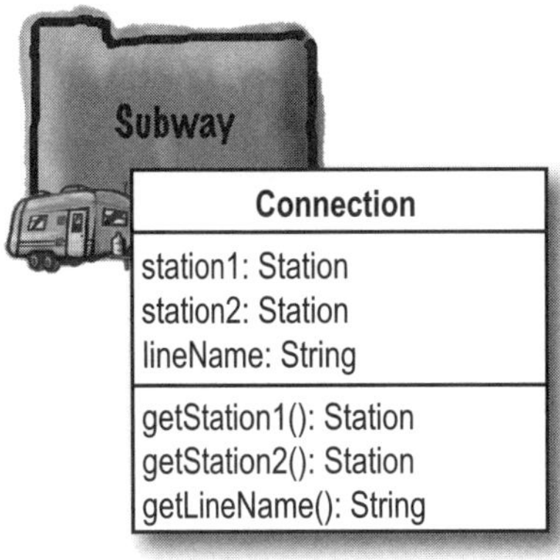

Subway

Connection
station1: Station
station2: Station
lineName: String
getStation1(): Station
getStation2(): Station
getLineName(): String

```
public class Connection {

    private _____ _____, _____;
    private _____ _____;

    public Connection(_____ _____, _____ _____,
                      _____ _____) {
        this._____ = station1;
        this._____ = station2;
        this._____ = lineName;
    }

    public _____ _____() {
        _____ station1;
    }

    public _____ _____() {
        _____ station2;
    }

    public _____ _____() {
        _____ lineName;
    }
}
```

We're well into the
implementation phase of our
first iteration, now.

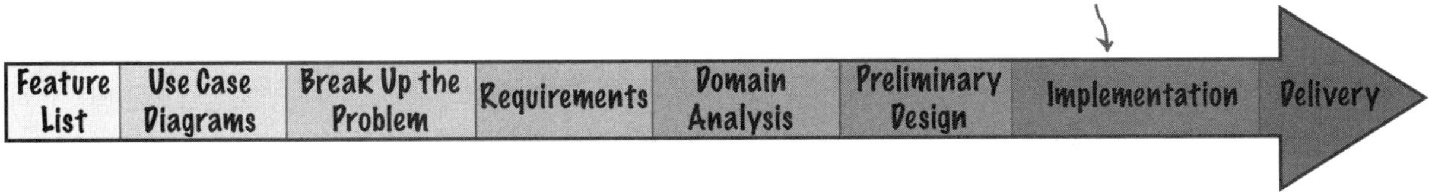

Feature List	Use Case Diagrams	Break Up the Problem	Requirements	Domain Analysis	Preliminary Design	Implementation	Delivery

 Sharpen your pencil

answers   Write the Connection class.

Using the class diagram on the right, your job was to fill in
the blanks and complete the Connection class.

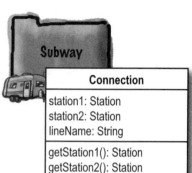

Subway

Connection
station1: Station
station2: Station
lineName: String
getStation1(): Station
getStation2(): Station
getLineName(): String

```
public class Connection {

    private  Station     station1  ,  station2  ;
    private  String      lineName  ;

    public Connection(  Station     station1  ,  Station     station2  ,
                        String      lineName  ) {
        this.  station1  = station1;
        this.  station2  = station2;
        this.  lineName  = lineName;
    }

    public  Station     getStation1  () {
        return  station1;
    }

    public  Station     getStation2  () {
        return  station2;
    }

    public  String      getLineName  () {
        return  lineName;
    }
}
```

You are HERE.

Feature List	Use Case Diagrams	Break Up the Problem	Requirements	Domain Analysis	Preliminary Design	Implementation	Delivery

Code the Subway class

Next up is the **Subway** class itself. With **Station** and **Connection** done, and a good class diagram, nothing here should be a surprise:

Subway
stations: Station [*] connections: Connection [*]
addStation(String): Station hasStation(String): boolean addConnection(String, String, String): Connection

```java
public class Subway {

  private List stations;
  private List connections;

  public Subway() {
    this.stations = new LinkedList();
    this.connections = new LinkedList();
  }

  public void addStation(String stationName) {
    if (!this.hasStation(station)) {
      Station station = new Station(stationName);
      stations.add(station);
    }
  }

  public boolean hasStation(String stationName) {
    return stations.contains(new Station(stationName));
  }

  public void addConnection(String station1Name, String station2Name,
                            String lineName) {
    if ((this.hasStation(station1Name)) &&
        (this.hasStation(station2Name))) {
      Station station1 = new Station(station1Name);
      Station station2 = new Station(station2Name);
      Connection connection = new Connection(station1, station2, lineName);
      connections.add(connection);
      connections.add(new Connection(station2, station1,
                                 connection.getLineName()));
    } else {
      throw new RuntimeException("Invalid connection!");
    }
  }
}
```

These will store all the stations, and the connections between those stations.

First, we validate the name, and make sure we don't already have this station.

If not, we create a new Station instance, and add it to the subway.

This method checks to see if a station is already in the subway's stations List.

Like addStation(), we begin with some validation: this time, we make sure both stations exist in the subway.

This is VERY important. Since Objectville subways run in both directions, we add two connections: one connection for both directions.

This is pretty rough in terms of error handling... see if you can come up with a better way to handle the case where one of the stations in the connection doesn't exist.

Points of interest on the Objectville Subway (class)

We threw a couple of new things into the **Subway** class; first, you'll see this line of code quite a bit:

```
Station station = new Station(stationName);
```

For example, when we create a new **Connection**, we have code like this:

```
Station station1 = new Station(station1Name);
Station station2 = new Station(station2Name);
Connection connection =
    new Connection(station1, station2, lineName);
```

Lots of programmers would take **station1Name**, and iterate through the list of stations in the **Subway** class to find the **Station** object that has a name of **station1Name**. But that takes a lot of time, and there's a better way. Remember how we defined an **equals()** and **hashCode()** method on our **Station** class?

Station
name: String
getName(): String equals(Object): boolean hashCode(): int

These methods allowed us to tell Java that when it compares two **Station** objects, just see if their name is the same. If the names are equal, *even if the objects don't refer to the same location in memory*, they should be treated as the same. So instead of looking for a particular Station object in the Subway class's list of station, it's much easier to just create a new Station and use it.

> Normally, equals() in Java just checks to see if two objects actually are the SAME object... in other words, it looks to see if they are actually both references to the same place in memory. But that's NOT what we want to use for comparison of two Station objects.

Because we overrode equals() and hashCode(), we can save <u>search time</u> and <u>complexity</u> in our code. Your design decisions should always make your implementation better, not more complicated or harder to understand.

What Java's <u>default</u> equals() implementation does...

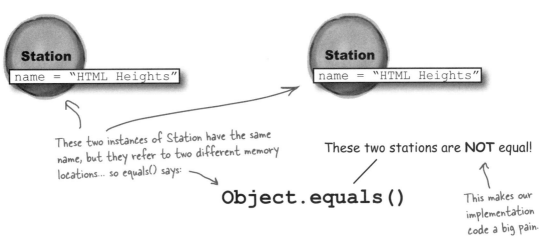

These two instances of Station have the same name, but they refer to two different memory locations... so equals() says:

Object.equals()

These two stations are **NOT** equal!

This makes our implementation code a big pain.

What <u>our</u> equals() implementation does...

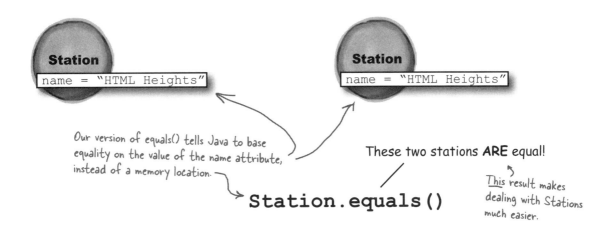

Our version of equals() tells Java to base equality on the value of the name attribute, instead of a memory location.

Station.equals()

These two stations **ARE** equal!

This result makes dealing with Stations much easier.

there are no Dumb Questions

Q: What does any of this have to do with OOA&D?

A: This is the very core of what makes OOA&D useful: because we understand our system, we realize that two stations should be considered identical if they have the same name. And, our design is improved by being able to compare stations based on their name, rather than their location in memory.

So the time we spent on requirements and getting a good grasp of our system made our design better, which in turn made implementing that design a lot simpler. That's the power of OOA&D: you can turn knowledge of your system into a flexible design, and even end up with cleaner code—all because you spent time up front listening to the customer and gathering requirements, rather than diving right into an IDE and typing in source code.

> Why aren't we just taking in a Station object in addStation(), and a Connection object in addConnection()? Wouldn't that make sense?

Frank: That's true. So we could change our Subway class to look more like this:

Subway
stations: Station [*] connections: Connection [*]
addStation(**Station**) hasStation(String): boolean addConnection(**Connection**)

Joe and Frank are suggesting taking in objects for these methods, rather than the strings that are the property values for those objects.

Jill: But then you're exposing the internals of your application!

Joe: Whoa... not sure what that means, but it sure doesn't sound like something I want to do. What are you talking about?

Jill: Well, look at our code right now. You don't have to work with a Station or Connection at all to load up the subway. You can just call methods on our new Subway class.

Frank: How is that any different from what we're suggesting?

Jill: If we went with your ideas, people that use the Subway class would have to also work with Station and Connection. In our version right now, they just work with Strings: the name of a station, and the name of a line.

Joe: And that's bad because...

Frank: Wait, I think I get it. Their code is getting tied in to how we implement the Station and Connection classes, since they're having to work with those classes directly.

Jill: Exactly! But with our version, we could change up Connection or Station, and we'd only have to change our Subway class. Their code would stay the same, since they're abstracted away from our implementations of Connection and Station.

Protecting your classes (and your client's classes, too)

Frank, Joe, and Jill are really talking about just one more form of abstraction. Let's take a closer look:

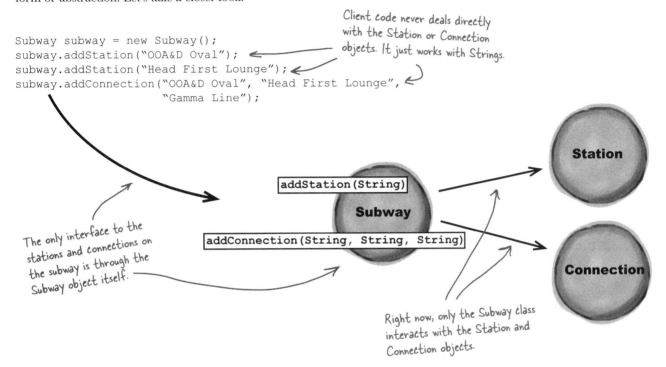

Client code never deals directly with the Station or Connection objects. It just works with Strings.

```
Subway subway = new Subway();
subway.addStation("OOA&D Oval");
subway.addStation("Head First Lounge");
subway.addConnection("OOA&D Oval", "Head First Lounge",
                     "Gamma Line");
```

The only interface to the stations and connections on the subway is through the Subway object itself.

`addStation(String)`

Subway

`addConnection(String, String, String)`

Station

Connection

Right now, only the Subway class interacts with the Station and Connection objects.

You should only expose clients of your code to the classes that they **NEED** to interact with.

Classes that the clients don't interact with can be changed with minimal client code being affected.

In this application, we could change how Station and Connection work, and it wouldn't affect code that only uses our Subway object; they're <u>protected</u> from changes to our implementation.

The SubwayLoader class

We're almost done with our first iteration, and our first use case. All that's left is to code the class that loads a subway based on the test file we got from Objectville Travel, Inc.

We're working on the Loader module now (see page 502).

Loader

SubwayLoader

loadFromFile(File): Subway

```java
public class SubwayLoader {
  private Subway subway;

  public SubwayLoader() {
    this.subway = new Subway();
  }

  public Subway loadFromFile(File subwayFile) throws IOException {
    BufferedReader reader = new BufferedReader(
      new FileReader(subwayFile));

    loadStations(subway, reader);
    String lineName = reader.readLine();
    while ((lineName != null) && (lineName.length() > 0)) {
      loadLine(subway, reader, lineName);
      lineName = reader.readLine();
    }

    return subway;
  }

  private void loadStations(Subway subway, BufferedReader reader)
      throws IOException {
    String currentLine;
    currentLine = reader.readLine();
    while (currentLine.length() > 0) {
      subway.addStation(currentLine);
      currentLine = reader.readLine();
    }
  }

  private void loadLine(Subway subway, BufferedReader reader,
                        String lineName)
      throws IOException {
    String station1Name, station2Name;
    station1Name = reader.readLine();
    station2Name = reader.readLine();
    while ((station2Name != null) && (station2Name.length() > 0)) {
      subway.addConnection(station1Name, station2Name, lineName);
      station1Name = station2Name;
      station2Name = reader.readLine();
    }
  }
}
```

We start out by loading all the stations.

Once we've got the stations, we need to get the next line, which should be a line name, and add the stations underneath that line into the subway.

Loading stations just involves reading a line, adding that line into the subway as a new station name, and then repeating, until we hit a blank line.

We read the first station, and the station after that...

...and then add a new connection using the current line name.

We take the current second station, bump it up to the first, and then read another line to get the new second station.

Method Magnets

Let's see exactly what happens when you call loadFromFile() in SubwayLoader, and give it the text file we got from Objectville Travel. Your job is to place the magnets from the bottom of this page—which match up to methods on the SubwayLoader and Subway classes—next to the lines in the text file where they'll be called.

ObjectvilleSubway.txt

Ajax Rapids
HTML Heights
JavaBeans Boulevard
LSP Lane
Head First Labs
Objectville PizzaStore
UML Walk
XHTML Expressway
Choc-O-Holic, Inc.
Head First Theater
Infinite Circle
CSS Center
OOA&D Oval
SimUDuck Lake
Web Design Way
... more station names...

Booch Line
Ajax Rapids
HTML Heights
JavaBeans Boulevard
LSP Lane
Head First Labs
Objectville PizzaStore
UML Walk
Ajax Rapids

Gamma Line
OOA&D Oval
Head First Lounge
OOA&D Oval

Jacobson Line
Servlet Springs
... more stations on this line...

... more lines...

There are only 5 methods that are involved here, but you'll need to use most of these magnets several times each.

`loadLine()` `loadStations()` `addStation()` `new Subway()` `addConnection()`

Method Magnet Solutions

Let's see exactly what happens when you call loadFromFile() in SubwayLoader, and give it the text file we got from Objectville Travel. Your job was to place the magnets from the bottom of this page next to the lines in the text file where they'll be called.

ObjectvilleSubway.txt

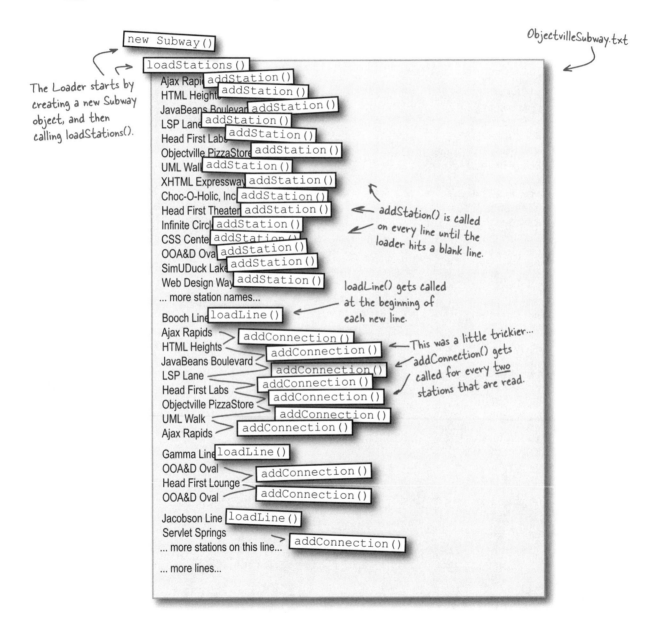

`new Subway()`

`loadStations()`

The Loader starts by creating a new Subway object, and then calling loadStations().

Ajax Rapids `addStation()`
HTML Heights `addStation()`
JavaBeans Boulevard `addStation()`
LSP Lane `addStation()`
Head First Labs `addStation()`
Objectville PizzaStore `addStation()`
UML Walk `addStation()`
XHTML Expressway `addStation()`
Choc-O-Holic, Inc `addStation()`
Head First Theater `addStation()`
Infinite Circle `addStation()`
CSS Center `addStation()`
OOA&D Oval `addStation()`
SimUDuck Lake `addStation()`
Web Design Way `addStation()`
... more station names...

addStation() is called on every line until the loader hits a blank line.

Booch Line `loadLine()`

loadLine() gets called at the beginning of each new line.

Ajax Rapids `addConnection()`
HTML Heights `addConnection()`
JavaBeans Boulevard `addConnection()`
LSP Lane `addConnection()`
Head First Labs `addConnection()`
Objectville PizzaStore `addConnection()`
UML Walk `addConnection()`
Ajax Rapids `addConnection()`

This was a little trickier... addConnection() gets called for every two stations that are read.

Gamma Line `loadLine()`
OOA&D Oval `addConnection()`
Head First Lounge `addConnection()`
OOA&D Oval

Jacobson Line `loadLine()`
Servlet Springs `addConnection()`
... more stations on this line...

... more lines...

Test Puzzle

You're almost done with the first use case, and our first iteration! All that's left is to test out our solution, and make sure it actually works.

The problem:

You need to test loading the **ObjectvilleSubway.txt** file, and make sure that **SubwayLoader** correctly loads in all stations and connections in the file.

Your task:

1 Add a method to **Subway** to check if a particular connection exists, given the two station names and the line name for that connection.

2 Write a test class, called **LoadTester**, with a **main()** method that loads the Objectville Subway system from the text file we got from Objectville Travel, Inc.

3 Write code in **LoadTester** that checks a few of the stations and connections from the text file against the **Subway** object returned from **SubwayLoader**'s **loadFromFile()** method. You should check to make sure that at least three stations and three connections on three different lines were all entered correctly.

4 Run your test program, and verify that we're really done with Iteration 1.

Here's the use case we're testing in this puzzle.

> **Load network of subway lines**
> **Use Case**
> 1. The administrator supplies a file of stations and lines.
> 2. The system reads in the name of a station.
> 3. The system validates that the station doesn't already exist.
> 4. The system adds the new station to the subway.
> 5. The system repeats steps 2-4 until all stations are added.
> 6. The system reads in the name of a line to add.
> 7. The system reads in two stations that are connected.
> 8. The system validates that the stations exist.
> 9. The system creates a new connection between the two stations, going in both directions, on the current line.
> 10. The system repeats steps 7-9 until the line is complete.
> 11. The system repeats steps 6-10 until all lines are entered.

Testing is really part of the implementation phase. Code isn't complete until it's tested.

Feature List	Use Case Diagrams	Break Up the Problem	Requirements	Domain Analysis	Preliminary Design	Implementation	Delivery

Test Puzzle Solution

Your job was to test the **SubwayLoader** and our subway representation to make sure you can load a subway system from a text file.

1 Add a method to **Subway** to check if a particular connection exists, given the two station names and the line name for that connection.

This is pretty straightforward... it iterates through each connection in the subway, and just compares the line name and stations to see if we've got a match.

```
public boolean hasConnection(String station1Name, String station2Name,
                             String lineName) {
  Station station1 = new Station(station1Name);
  Station station2 = new Station(station2Name);
  for (Iterator i = connections.iterator(); i.hasNext(); ) {
    Connection connection = (Connection)i.next();
    if (connection.getLineName().equalsIgnoreCase(lineName)) {
      if ((connection.getStation1().equals(station1)) &&
          (connection.getStation2().equals(station2))) {
        return true;
      }
    }
  }
  return false;
}
```

Subway
stations: Station [*] connections: Connection [*]
addStation(String) hasStation(String): boolean addConnection(String, String, String) hasConnection(String, String, String): boolean

```
class
Subway {
Sub-
way()
}
```
Subway.java

---

there are no Dumb Questions

Q: Wouldn't it be easier to write the hasConnection() method if we used a Line object, like we talked about a few pages ago?

A: It would. If we had a **Line** object, we could look up the line using the name passed into **hasConnection()**, and just iterate over the **Connection** objects for that line. So in most cases, **hasConnection()** would involve less iteration, and return a result faster, if we had a **Line** object.

We still decided not to use a **Line** object, though, because we've only added **hasConnection()** to help us test our classes. So adding a **Line** object just to make a test method return faster doesn't seem like a good idea. If we find that we need the **hasConnection()** method in other parts of our app, though, this might be something to come back and revisit later.

② Write a test class, called **LoadTester**, with a **main()** method that loads the Objectville Subway system from the text file we got from Objectville Travel, Inc.

③ Write code in **LoadTester** that checks a few of the stations and connections from the text file against the **Subway** object returned from **SubwayLoader**'s **loadFromFile()** method. You should check to make sure that at least three stations and three connections on three different lines were all entered correctly.

This code simply passes in the text file, and then tests a few stations and connections to see if they got loaded.

```java
public class LoadTester {
  public static void main(String[] args) {
    try {
      SubwayLoader loader = new SubwayLoader();
      Subway objectville =
        loader.loadFromFile(new File("ObjectvilleSubway.txt"));
      System.out.println("Testing stations...");
      if (objectville.hasStation("DRY Drive") &&
          objectville.hasStation("Weather-O-Rama, Inc.") &&
          objectville.hasStation("Boards 'R' Us")) {
        System.out.println("...station test passed successfully.");
      } else {
        System.out.println("...station test FAILED.");
        System.exit(-1);
      }

      System.out.println("\nTesting connections...");
      if (objectville.hasConnection("DRY Drive",
            "Head First Theater", "Meyer Line") &&
          objectville.hasConnection("Weather-O-Rama, Inc.",
              "XHTML Expressway", "Wirfs-Brock Line") &&
          objectville.hasConnection("Head First Theater",
                "Infinite Circle", "Rumbaugh Line")) {
        System.out.println("...connections test passed successfully.");
      } else {
        System.out.println("...connections test FAILED.");
        System.exit(-1);
      }
    } catch (Exception e) {
      e.printStackTrace(System.out);
    }
  }
}
```

You can use any stations and connections you like here.

class Load-
Tester {
main()

LoadTester.java

Test Puzzle Solution (cont.)

Your job was to test the **SubwayLoader** and our subway representation to make sure you can load a subway system from a text file.

4 Run your test program, and verify that we're really done with Iteration 1.

```
File Edit  Window Help  NotVeryExciting
%java LoadTester
Testing stations...
...station test passed successfully.

Testing connections...
...connections test passed successfully.
```

Tests are usually not really exciting to run... until you realize that they prove your software is <u>WORKING!</u>

BRAIN POWER

Try and write a test case that gets all the stations and connections in the Subway and prints them out, to verify your subway is loading the network correctly.

It's time to iterate again

We're done here.

Load network of subway lines

Our test proves that we really have finished up our first iteration. The "Load network of subway lines" use case is complete, and that means it's time to iterate again. Now, we can take on our next use case—"Get directions"—and return to the Requirements phase and work through this use case.

Get directions

Feature List	Use Case Diagrams	Break Up the Problem	Requirements	Domain Analysis	Preliminary Design	Implementation	Delivery

Once an iteration is complete, if there are more use cases or features to implement, you need to take your next feature or use case, and start again at the requirements phase.

But before we start Iteration 2...

Iteration 1

Iteration 2

It's been a <u>**LONG**</u> iteration, and you've done some great work. <u>**STOP**</u>, take a <u>**BREAK**</u>, and eat a bite or drink some water. Give your brain a chance to <u>**REST**</u>.

Then, once you've caught your breath, turn the page, and let's knock out that last use case. Are you ready? Then let's <u>iterate</u> <u>again</u>.

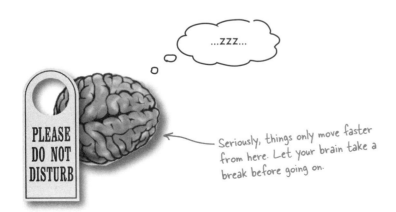

...zzz...

PLEASE DO NOT DISTURB

Seriously, things only move faster from here. Let your brain take a break before going on.

What's left to do?

We've made a lot of progress, on both our use cases, and
our feature list. Below is the feature list and use case
diagram we developed earlier in the chapter:

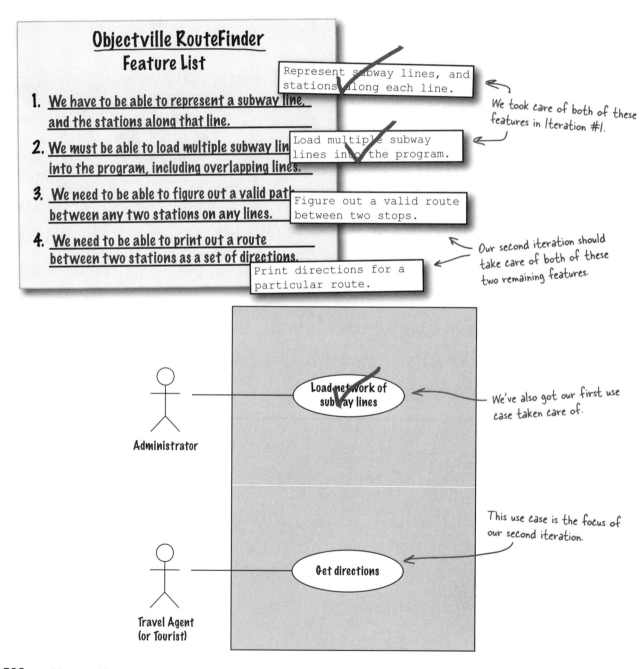

Back to the requirements phase...

Now that we're ready to take on the next use case, we have to go back to the requirements phase, and work through this use case the same way we did the first one. So we'll start by taking our use case title from our use case diagram, "Get directions," and developing that into a full-blown use case.

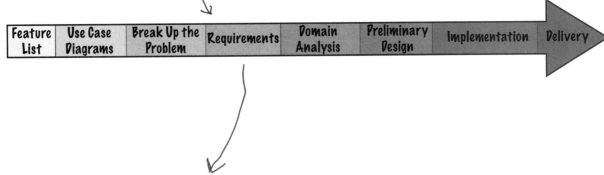

| Feature List | Use Case Diagrams | Break Up the Problem | Requirements | Domain Analysis | Preliminary Design | Implementation | Delivery |

Sharpen your pencil

Write the complete use case for "Get directions."

We're back to writing use cases again. This time, your job is to write a use case that allows a travel agent to get directions from one station to another on the Objectville Subway.

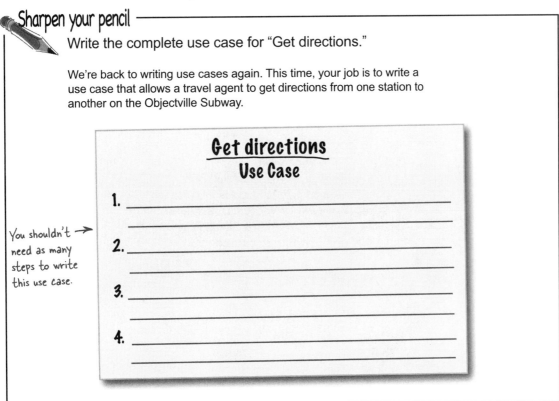

Get directions
Use Case

1. _____

2. _____

You shouldn't → need as many steps to write this use case.

3. _____

4. _____

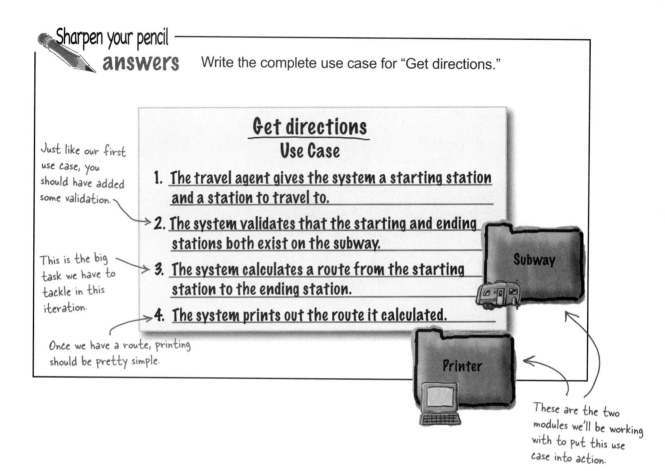

answers　Write the complete use case for "Get directions."

Get directions
Use Case

Just like our first use case, you should have added some validation.

1. **The travel agent gives the system a starting station and a station to travel to.**
2. **The system validates that the starting and ending stations both exist on the subway.**
3. **The system calculates a route from the starting station to the ending station.**
4. **The system prints out the route it calculated.**

This is the big task we have to tackle in this iteration.

Once we have a route, printing should be pretty simple.

Subway

Printer

These are the two modules we'll be working with to put this use case into action.

> I'm a little confused. We went to all that work to break our code up into modules, but our use cases involve code in **more** than one module. Why do we keep jumping back and forth between modules and use cases?

Focus on code, then focus on customers.
Then focus on code, then focus on customers...

When we started breaking our application up into different modules way back on page 502, we were really talking about the structure of our application, and how we are going to break up our application. We have a **Subway** and **Station** class in the Subway module, and a **SubwayLoader** class in the Loader module, and so on. In other words, we're focusing on our ***code***.

We've really been going back and forth between our code, and how our system is used, in both iterations.

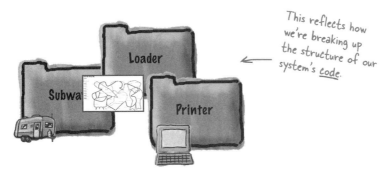

This reflects how we're breaking up the structure of our system's code.

But when we're working on use cases, we're focusing on how the customer <u>uses</u> the system—we looked at the format of an input file to load lines, and began to focus on the customer's interaction with your system. So we've really been going back and forth between our code (in the Break Up the Problem step) and our customer (in the Requirements step):

This step is about our code, and how we break up functionality.

This step is about how the customer uses our software.

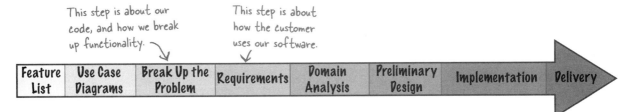

| Feature List | Use Case Diagrams | Break Up the Problem | Requirements | Domain Analysis | Preliminary Design | Implementation | Delivery |

When you're developing software, there's going to be a lot of this back-and-forth. You have to make sure your software does what it's supposed to, but it's your code that makes the software actually do something.

> ## It's your job to balance making sure the customer gets the functionality they want with making sure your code stays flexible and well-designed.

Analysis and Design Puzzle

It's time to take on more domain analysis and design for your system. Take the use case below, figure out the candidate classes and candidate operations, and then update the class diagram on the right with any changes you think you need to make.

Do some of these exercises look familiar? You use the same techniques in each iteration of your development cycle.

Get directions
Use Case

1. **The travel agent gives the system a starting station and a station to travel to.**

2. **The system validates that the starting and ending stations both exist on the subway.**

3. **The system calculates a route from the starting station to the ending station.**

4. **The system prints out the route it calculated.**

Nouns (candidate classes):

_____   _____   _____

_____   _____   _____

Verbs (candidate operations):

_____   _____   _____

_____   _____   _____

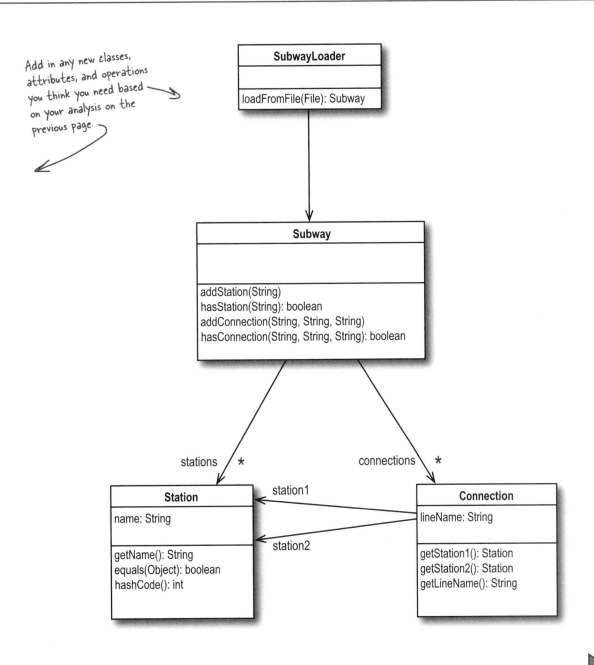

Add in any new classes, attributes, and operations you think you need based on your analysis on the previous page.

SubwayLoader

loadFromFile(File): Subway

Subway

addStation(String)
hasStation(String): boolean
addConnection(String, String, String)
hasConnection(String, String, String): boolean

stations *

connections *

Station

name: String

getName(): String
equals(Object): boolean
hashCode(): int

station1

station2

Connection

lineName: String

getStation1(): Station
getStation2(): Station
getLineName(): String

Iteration 1

Iteration 2

| Feature List | Use Case Diagrams | Break Up the Problem | Requirements | Domain Analysis | Preliminary Design | Implementation | Delivery |

We're taking these two phases on at the same time again.

Analysis and Design Puzzle Solutions

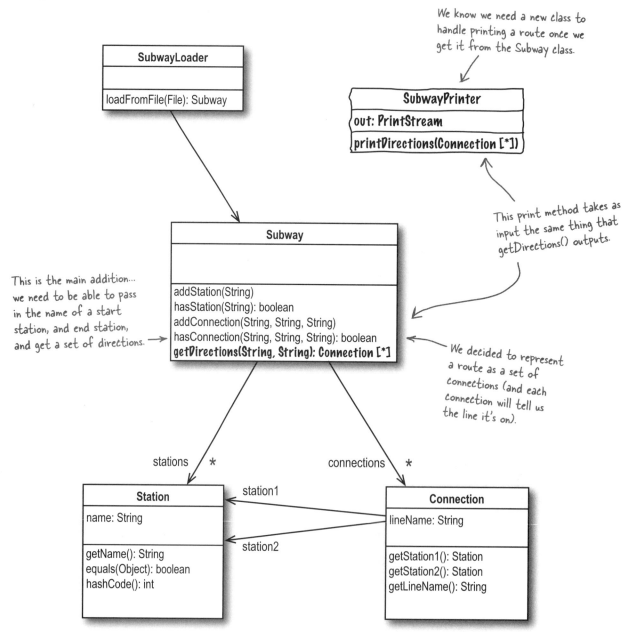

We know we need a new class to handle printing a route once we get it from the Subway class.

SubwayLoader

loadFromFile(File): Subway

SubwayPrinter

out: PrintStream

printDirections(Connection [*])

This print method takes as input the same thing that getDirections() outputs.

Subway

addStation(String)
hasStation(String): boolean
addConnection(String, String, String)
hasConnection(String, String, String): boolean
getDirections(String, String): Connection [*]

This is the main addition... we need to be able to pass in the name of a start station, and end station, and get a set of directions.

We decided to represent a route as a set of connections (and each connection will tell us the line it's on).

stations *

connections *

Station

name: String

getName(): String
equals(Object): boolean
hashCode(): int

station1

station2

Connection

lineName: String

getStation1(): Station
getStation2(): Station
getLineName(): String

* We didn't show the nouns and verbs... by now, you should be comfortable with that step, and be able to translate them into the class diagram shown here.

Iteration makes problems easier

The class diagram on the last page really isn't that much different from our class diagram from the first iteration (flip back to page 513 to take a look at that earlier version). That's because we did a lot of work that applies to **all** our iterations during our **first** iteration.

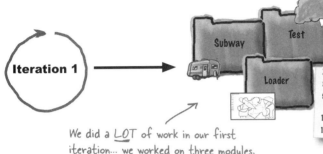

Load network of subway lines
Use Case

he administrator supplies a file of stations and lines.

he system reads in the name of a station.

he system validates that the station doesn't already exist.

he system adds the new station to the subway.

he system repeats steps 2-4 until all stations are added.

he system reads in the name of a line to add.

7. The system reads in two stations that are connected.

8. The system validates that the stations exist.

9. The system creates a new connection between the two stations, going in both directions, on the current line.

10. The system repeats steps 7-9 until the line is complete.

11. The system repeats steps 6-10 until all lines are entered.

We did a <u>LOT</u> of work in our first iteration... we worked on three modules, and completed an entire use case.

Once you've completed your first iteration, your successive iterations are often a lot easier, because so much of what you've already done makes those later iterations easier.

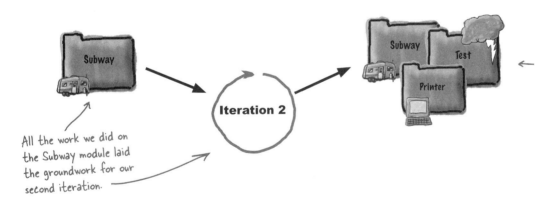

We still have plenty of work to do, but not nearly as much as we did in the first iteration. Most of the Subway module is done, and we've even got some tests in place.

All the work we did on the Subway module laid the groundwork for our second iteration.

We're ready to move to the implementation phase... but this iteration is moving a lot faster, and there's less to do, than the first iteration.

Feature List	Use Case Diagrams	Break Up the Problem	Requirements	Domain Analysis	Preliminary Design	Implementation	Delivery

Implementation: Subway.java

Figuring out a route between two stations turns out to be a particularly tricky problem, and gets into some of that graph stuff we talked about briefly back on page 515. To help you out, we've included some Ready-bake Code that you can use to get a route between two stations.

Ready-bake Code

Ready-bake code is code that we're already prepared for you. Just type it in as its shown here, or you can download a completed version of Subway.java from the Head First Labs web site.

```java
public class Subway {
  private List stations;
  private List connections;
  private Map network;

  public Subway() {
    this.stations = new LinkedList();
    this.connections = new LinkedList();
    this.network = new HashMap();
  }

  // addStation(), hasStation(), and hasConnection() stay the same

  public Connection addConnection(String station1Name, String station2Name,
                                  String lineName) {
    if ((this.hasStation(station1Name)) &&
        (this.hasStation(station2Name))) {
      Station station1 = new Station(station1Name);
      Station station2 = new Station(station2Name);
      Connection connection = new Connection(station1, station2, lineName);
      connections.add(connection);
      connections.add(new Connection(station2, station1,
                                     connection.getLineName()));
      addToNetwork(station1, station2);
      addToNetwork(station2, station1);
      return connection;
    } else {
      throw new RuntimeException("Invalid connection!");
    }
  }

  private void addToNetwork(Station station1, Station station2) {
    if (network.keySet().contains(station1)) {
      List connectingStations = (List)network.get(station1);
      if (!connectingStations.contains(station2)) {
        connectingStations.add(station2);
      }
    } else {
      List connectingStations = new LinkedList();
      connectingStations.add(station2);
```

We need a Map to store each station, and a list of all the stations that it connects to.

When we add connections, we need to update our Map of stations, and how they're connected in the subway's network.

Everything starting with this method down is new code.

Our Map has as its keys each station. The value for that station is a List containing all the stations that it connects to (regardless of which line connects the stations).

```
      network.put(station1, connectingStations);
   }
}

public List getDirections(String startStationName,
                          String endStationName) {
   if (!this.hasStation(startStationName) ||
       !this.hasStation(endStationName)) {
     throw new RuntimeException(
       "Stations entered do not exist on this subway.");
   }

   Station start = new Station(startStationName);
   Station end = new Station(endStationName);
   List route = new LinkedList();
   List reachableStations = new LinkedList();
   Map previousStations = new HashMap();

   List neighbors = (List)network.get(start);
   for (Iterator i = neighbors.iterator(); i.hasNext(); ) {
     Station station = (Station)i.next();
     if (station.equals(end)) {
       route.add(getConnection(start, end));
       return route;
     } else {
       reachableStations.add(station);
       previousStations.put(station, start);
     }
   }

   List nextStations = new LinkedList();
   nextStations.addAll(neighbors);
   Station currentStation = start;

searchLoop:
   for (int i=1; i<stations.size(); i++) {
     List tmpNextStations = new LinkedList();
     for (Iterator j = nextStations.iterator(); j.hasNext(); ) {
       Station station = (Station)j.next();
       reachableStations.add(station);
       currentStation = station;
       List currentNeighbors = (List)network.get(currentStation);
       for (Iterator k = currentNeighbors.iterator(); k.hasNext(); ) {
         Station neighbor = (Station)k.next();
         if (neighbor.equals(end)) {
           reachableStations.add(neighbor);
           previousStations.put(neighbor, currentStation);
           break searchLoop;
```

Here's the validation of the start and end stations that we referred to in our use case on page 534.

This method is based on a well-known bit of code called **Dijkstra's algorithm**, which figures out the shortest path between two nodes on a graph.

This first part of the code handles the case when the end station is just one connection away from the starting station.

These loops begin to iterate through each set of stations reachable by the starting station, and tries to find the least number of stations possible to connect the starting point and the destination.

```
            } else if (!reachableStations.contains(neighbor)) {
              reachableStations.add(neighbor);
              tmpNextStations.add(neighbor);
              previousStations.put(neighbor, currentStation);
            }
        }
      }
      nextStations = tmpNextStations;
    }

    // We've found the path by now
    boolean keepLooping = true;
    Station keyStation = end;
    Station station;

    while (keepLooping) {
      station = (Station)previousStations.get(keyStation);
      route.add(0, getConnection(station, keyStation));
      if (start.equals(station)) {
        keepLooping = false;
      }
      keyStation = station;
    }

    return route;
  }

  private Connection getConnection(Station station1, Station station2) {
    for (Iterator i = connections.iterator(); i.hasNext(); ) {
      Connection connection = (Connection)i.next();
      Station one = connection.getStation1();
      Station two = connection.getStation2();
      if ((station1.equals(one)) && (station2.equals(two))) {
        return connection;
      }
    }
    return null;
  }
}
```

Ready-bake Code

Once we've got a path, we just "unwind" the path, and create a List of connections to get from the starting station to the destination station.

This is a utility method that takes two stations, and looks for a connection between them (on any line).

> OK, this is just *ridiculous*. I spent 500 pages reading about how great OOA&D is so you can just give me the hardest code in the book? I thought I was supposed to be able write great software **on my own** by now.

Sometimes the best way to get the job done is find someone else who has already done the job for you.

It might seem weird that at this stage, we're giving you the code for getting a route between two stations. But that's part of what makes a good developer: a willingness to look around for existing solutions to hard problems.

In fact, we had some help from a college student on implementing a version of Dijkstra's algorithm that would work with the subway (seriously!). Sure, you probably can come up with your own totally original solution to every problem, but why would you want to if someone has already done the work for you?

Thanks, Felix Geller, your code really saved the day.

Sometimes the best code for a particular problem has __already__ been written. Don't get hung up on writing code yourself if someone **already has a working solution.**

You are HERE.

Feature List	Use Case Diagrams	Break Up the Problem	Requirements	Domain Analysis	Preliminary Design	Implementation	Delivery

What does a route look like?

The **getDirections()** method we just added to **Subway**
takes in two **String**s: the name of the starting station, and
the name of the station that a tourist is trying to get to:

XHTML Expressway

This is passed in as the starting station...

JSP Junction

...and this name is passed in as the destination station.

getDirections() then returns a **List**, which is filled
with **Connection** objects. Each **Connection** is one part
of the path between the two stations:

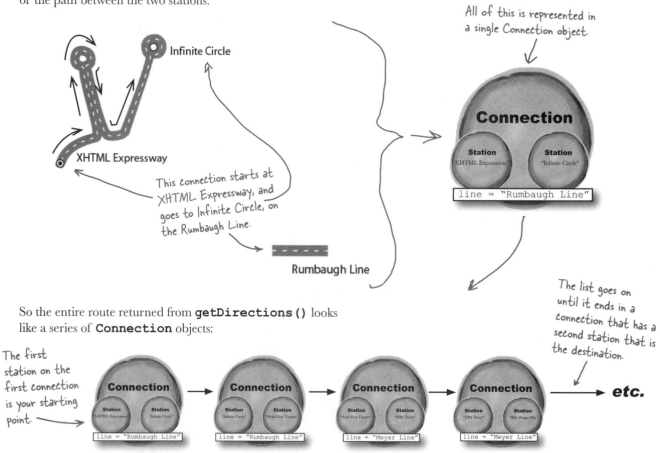

Infinite Circle

XHTML Expressway

This connection starts at XHTML Expressway, and goes to Infinite Circle, on the Rumbaugh Line.

Rumbaugh Line

All of this is represented in a single Connection object.

Connection

Station
"XHTML Expressway"

Station
"Infinite Circle"

line = "Rumbaugh Line"

So the entire route returned from **getDirections()** looks
like a series of **Connection** objects:

The list goes on until it ends in a connection that has a second station that is the destination.

etc.

The first station on the first connection is your starting point.

Connection

Station
"XHTML Expressway"

Station
"Infinite Circle"

line = "Rumbaugh Line"

Connection

Station
"Infinite Circle"

Station
"Head First Theater"

line = "Rumbaugh Line"

Connection

Station
"Head First Theater"

Station
"DRY Drive"

line = "Meyer Line"

Connection

Station
"DRY Drive"

Station
"Web Design Way"

line = "Meyer Line"

Printing Puzzle

You're almost done! With a working **getDirections()** method in **Subway**, the last feature to implement is printing those directions out. Your job is to write a class called **SubwayPrinter** that takes the data structure returned from **getDirections()**, which is a list of **Connection** objects, and prints out the directions. The directions should be printed to an **OutputStream**, supplied to the constructor of the **SubwayPrinter** class when an instance of the printer class is created.

Here's the class diagram for **SubwayPrinter** that you should follow:

SubwayPrinter
out:PrintStream
printDirections(Connection [*])

BONUS CREDIT: Go ahead and write SubwayTester, too, a class to test out loading the Objectville subway system, and then printing out directions.

Your output should look similar to this:

Begin by printing out the starting station.

You can get the line for this Connection using getConnection. Print the line and which station to head towards.

Print out each station on a line that is passed.

Anytime the line changes, print out the line and station to get off of...

...as well as the new line to get on.

```
File Edit Window Help ShowMeTheWay
%java SubwayTester "XHTML Expressway" "JSP Junction"
Start out at XHTML Expressway.
Get on the Rumbaugh Line heading towards Infinite Circle.
   Continue past Infinite Circle...
When you get to Head First Theater, get off the Rumbaugh Line.
Switch over to the Meyer Line, heading towards DRY Drive.
   Continue past DRY Drive...
When you get to Web Design Way, get off the Meyer Line.
Switch over to the Wirfs-Brock Line, heading towards Boards 'R' Us.
   Continue past Boards 'R' Us...
When you get to EJB Estates, get off the Wirfs-Brock Line.
Switch over to the Liskov Line, heading towards Design Patterns Plaza.
   Continue past Design Patterns Plaza...
Get off at JSP Junction and enjoy yourself!
```

The last thing you should have is a Connection with the destination station as the stopping point.

Printing Puzzle Solution

SubwayPrinter
out:PrintStream
printDirections(Connection [*])

Here's how we wrote the **SubwayPrinter** class. You might have come up with a slightly different approach to looping through the route **List**, but your output should match ours exactly for full credit.

```java
public class SubwayPrinter {
  private PrintStream out;

  public SubwayPrinter(OutputStream out) {
    this.out = new PrintStream(out);
  }

  public void printDirections(List route) {
    Connection connection = (Connection)route.get(0);
    String currentLine = connection.getLineName();
    String previousLine = currentLine;
    out.println("Start out at " +
      connection.getStation1().getName() + ".");
    out.println("Get on the " + currentLine + " heading towards " +
      connection.getStation2().getName() + ".");
    for (int i=1; i<route.size(); i++) {
      connection = (Connection)route.get(i);
      currentLine = connection.getLineName();
      if (currentLine.equals(previousLine)) {
        out.println("  Continue past " +
          connection.getStation1().getName() + "...");
      } else {
        out.println("When you get to " +
          connection.getStation1().getName() + ", get off the " +
          previousLine + ".");
        out.println("Switch over to the " + currentLine +
          ", heading towards " + connection.getStation2().getName() + ".");
        previousLine = currentLine;
      }
    }
    out.println("Get off at " + connection.getStation2().getName() +
      " and enjoy yourself!");
  }
}
```

Rather than printing directly to System.out, our class takes in an OutputStream at construction. That allows directions to be output to any output source, not just a console window on the user's screen.

We begin by printing the starting station...

...and the first line to get on, as well as the next station to travel towards.

This looks at the current connection, and figures out if a line change is required.

If it's the same line, just print the station name.

If the line changes, print out how to change lines.

Finally, we're through all the connections... get off the subway.

One last test class...

All that we need to do now is put everything together. Below is the **SubwayTester** class we wrote to load the Objectville Subway system, take in two stations from the command line, and print out directions between those two stations using our new **getDirections()** method and printer class.

We can't prove our software works without some test cases and test classes.

```java
public class SubwayTester {
  public static void main(String[] args) {
    if (args.length != 2) {
      System.err.println("Usage: SubwayTester [startStation] [endStation]");
      System.exit(-1);
    }
    try {
      SubwayLoader loader = new SubwayLoader();
      Subway objectville =
        loader.loadFromFile(new File("ObjectvilleSubway.txt"));

      if (!objectville.hasStation(args[0])) {
        System.err.println(args[0] + " is not a station in Objectville.");
        System.exit(-1);
      } else if (!objectville.hasStation(args[1])) {
        System.err.println(args[1] + " is not a station in Objectville.");
        System.exit(-1);
      }

      List route = objectville.getDirections(args[0], args[1]);
      SubwayPrinter printer = new SubwayPrinter(System.out);
      printer.printDirections(route);
    } catch (Exception e) {
      e.printStackTrace(System.out);
    }
  }
}
```

We want two stations passed in on the command line for this test.

We've tested this earlier, so we know that loading the subway works fine.

We also validate that the two stations supplied exist on the subway.

With two valid stations, we can get a route between them...

...and use our new SubwayPrinter class to print out the route.

Check out Objectville for yourself!

It's time to sit back and enjoy the fruits of your labor. Compile all
your classes for the Objectville Subway application, and try out
SubwayTester with a few different starting and stopping stations.
Here's one of our favorites:

```
File Edit  Window  Help  CandyIsKing
%java SubwayTester "Mighty Gumball, Inc." "Choc-O-Holic, Inc."
Start out at Mighty Gumball, Inc..
Get on the Jacobson Line heading towards Servlet Springs.
When you get to Servlet Springs, get off the Jacobson Line.
Switch over to the Wirfs-Brock Line, heading towards Objectville Diner.
  Continue past Objectville Diner...
When you get to Head First Lounge, get off the Wirfs-Brock Line.
Switch over to the Gamma Line, heading towards OOA&D Oval.
When you get to OOA&D Oval, get off the Gamma Line.
Switch over to the Meyer Line, heading towards CSS Center.
  Continue past CSS Center...
When you get to Head First Theater, get off the Meyer Line.
Switch over to the Rumbaugh Line, heading towards Choc-O-Holic, Inc..
Get off at Choc-O-Holic, Inc. and enjoy yourself!
```

Where do *YOU*
want to go in
Objectville today?

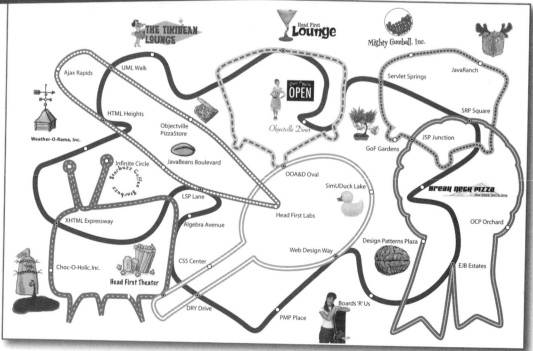

OOA&D Magnets

Way back on page 487, we asked you to think about where lots of different things you've been learning about fit on the OOA&D lifecycle below. Now that you've written another piece of great software, you're ready to take this exercise on, and see how we answered it, too. Go ahead and work this exercise again; did you change where you put any of the magnets after working through this chapter?

Oh, and don't forget, you can put more than one magnet on each phase, and there are some magnets you may want to use more than once.

Feature List	Use Case Diagrams	Break Up the Problem	Requirements	Domain Analysis	Preliminary Design	Implementation	Delivery

Scenario
Architecture
Test Driven Development
OO Principles
Encapsulation
Test Scenario
Analysis
Design Pattern
Requirements List
Textual Analysis
External Initiator
Commonality
Alternate Path
Alternate Path
Key Feature List
Class Diagram
Design Principles
Iteration
Architecture
Feature Driven Development
Cohesion
Variability
Delegation
Talk to the Customer

↖ Even though each magnet appears only once, you can use each one as many times as you like.

———→ This time, answers are on the next page!

OOA&D Magnet Solutions

Your job was to try and put the different magnets on the right phase of the OOA&D lifecycle, shown below. You could put more than one magnet on each phase; how do your answers compare with ours?

there are no Dumb Questions

Q: It seems like I could put almost every magnet on each phase... but that can't be right, can it?

A: That's exactly right. Although there are definitely some basic phases in a good development cycle, you can use most of the things you've learned about OOA&D, OO principles, design, analysis, requirements, and everything else at almost every stage of development.

The most effective and successful way to write great software is to have as many tools as you can, and to be able to choose any one (or more) to use at each stage of your development cycle. The more tools you have, the more ways you'll have to look at and work on a problem... and that means less time being stuck or not knowing what to do next.

> **OOA&D is about having lots of options. There is never one right way to solve a problem, so the more options you have, the better chance you'll find a good solution to every problem.**

Iteration #3, anyone?

No, we're not going to launch into any more design problems. But, you should realize that there is plenty more that you could do to improve the design of our RouteFinder application. We thought we'd give you just a few suggestions, in case you're dying to take another pass through the OOA&D lifecycle.

Make loading more extensible

Right now, we've just got a single class that handles loading, and it only accepts a Java **File** as input. See if you can come up with a solution that allows you to load a subway from several types of input sources (try starting with a **File** and **InputStream**). Also make it easy to add new input sources, like a database. Remember, you want to minimize changes to existing code when you're adding new functionality, so you may end up with an interface or abstract base class before you're through.

OOA&D and great software are ongoing projects... you can always add new functionality, or improve your design.

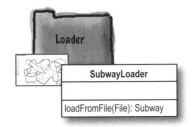

Allow different output sources (and formats!)

We can only print subway directions to a file, and the directions are formatted in a particular way. See if you can design a flexible Printing module that allows you to print a route to different output sources (like a **File**, **OutputStream**, and **Writer**), in different formats (perhaps a verbose form that matches what we've done already, a compact form that only indicates where to changes lines, and an XML form for other programs to use in web services).

Here's a hint: check out the Strategy pattern in Head First Design Patterns for ideas on how you might make this work.

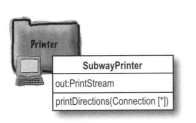

 # (the last) OOA&D Cross

Yes, it's a sad day: you're looking at the last crossword in the book. Take a deep breath, we've crammed this one full of terms to make it last a little longer. Enjoy!

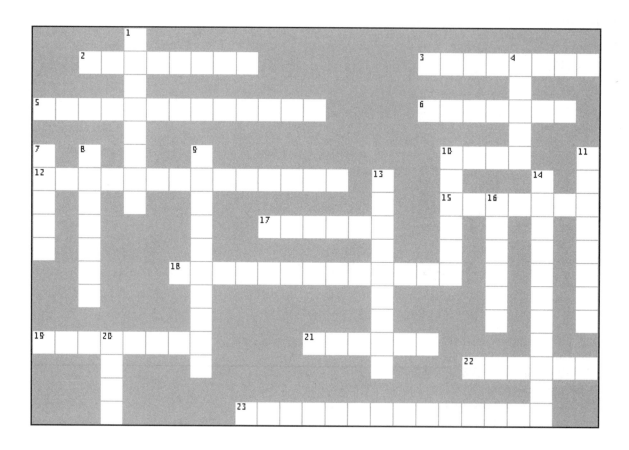

Across

2. All of your features should map to these, at least indirectly.

3. When you override equals() in Java, you should create a related implementation of this method.

5. Your features reflect this in your application.

6. You do this once you complete one feature or use case.

10. A feature list focuses on what your software _____.

12. When you complete this phase, you're either done or need to iterate again.

15. Break your application up into these, based on your app's functionality.

17. Understanding how a system is used should help you make better _____ decisions.

18. The approach to development we used in this chapter (3 words).

19. Never be afraid to use a _____ to a problem that someone else came up with.

21. Your design decisions are based on how this is used as well as good OO principles.

22. Iteration makes problems _____.

23. Each module in your application should have a single _____.

Down

1. Make a list of these to get your development started.

4. You usually create this type of diagram based on your domain analysis.

7. This iteration is usually the toughest.

8. OOA&D is about giving you lots of these.

9. You sometimes have to add a step to do this with your problem before writing use cases.

10. The kind of analysis that involves speaking to the customer in language that they understand.

11. This proves that your implementation is working.

13. The nouns in your use case are these types of classes.

14. You have to balance what the customer wants with your software's _____.

16. This is the stage where you apply good OO principles.

20. Use case diagrams focus on how your software will be _____.

Exercise
Solutions

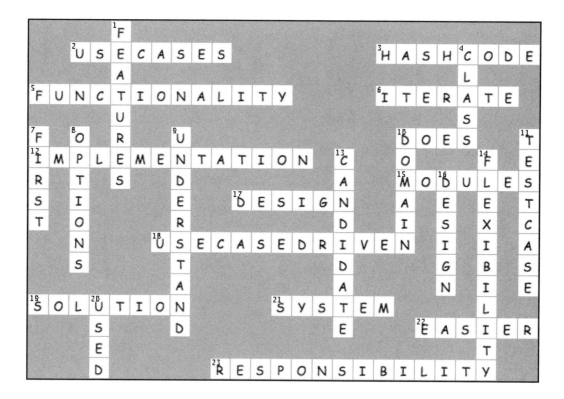

The journey's not over...

Now take OOA&D for a spin on your own projects!

We've loved having you here in Objectville, and we're sad to see you go. But there's nothing like taking what you've learned and putting it to use on your own development projects. So don't stop enjoying OOA&D just yet... you've still got a few more gems in the back of the book, an index to read through, and then it's time to take all these new ideas and put them into practice. We're dying to hear how things go, so drop us a line at the Head First Labs web site, http://www.headfirstlabs.com, and let us know how OOA&D is paying off for YOU.

appendix i: leftovers

The Top Ten Topics (we didn't cover)

Believe it or not, there's still more. Yes, with over 550 pages under your belt, there are still things we couldn't cram in. Even though these last ten topics don't deserve more than a mention, we didn't want to let you out of Objectville without a little more information on each one of them. But hey, now you've got just a little bit more to talk about during commercials of CATASTROPHE... and who doesn't love some stimulating OOA&D talk every now and then?

Besides, once you're done here, all that's left is another appendix... and the index... and maybe some ads... and then you're really done. We promise!

#1. IS-A and HAS-A

Lots of times in OO programming circles, you'll hear someone talk about the IS-A and HAS-A relationships.

IS-A refers to inheritance

Usually, IS-A relates to inheritance, for example: "A Sword IS-A Weapon, so Sword should extend Weapon."

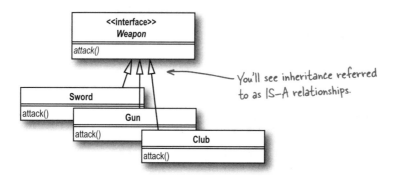

You'll see inheritance referred to as IS—A relationships.

HAS-A refers to composition or aggregation.

HAS-A refers to composition and aggregation, so you might hear, "A Unit HAS-A Weapon, so a Unit can be composed with a Weapon object."

This is sometimes referred to as a HAS—A relationship.

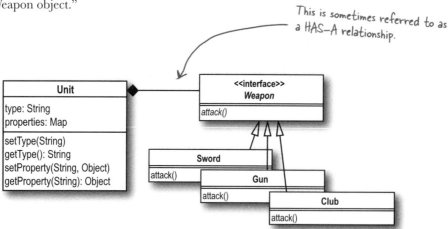

The problem with IS-A and HAS-A

The reason we haven't covered IS-A and HAS-A much is that they tend to break down in certain situations. For example, consider the situation where you're modeling shapes, like **Circle**, **Rectangle**, and **Diamond**.

If you think about a **Square** object, you can apply the IS-A relationship: **Square** IS-A **Rectangle**. So you should make **Square** extend **Rectangle**, right?

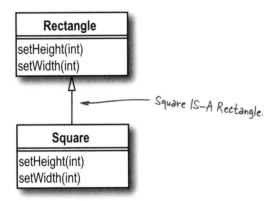

Square IS-A Rectangle.

But remember LSP, and that subtypes should be substitutable for their base types. So **Square** should be a direct substitute for **Rectangle**. But what happens with code like this:

```
Rectangle square = new Square();
square.setHeight(10);
square.setWidth(5);


System.out.println("Height is " + square.getHeight());
```

What does this method return? More importantly, what SHOULD it return?

The problem here is that when you set the width in **setWidth()** on **Square**, the square is going to have to set its height, too, since squares have equal width and height. So even though **Square** IS-A **Rectangle**, it doesn't *behave* like a rectangle. Calling **getHeight()** above will return 5, not 10, which means that squares behave differently than rectangles, and aren't substitutable for them—that's a violation of the LSP.

Use inheritance when one object <u>behaves</u> like another, rather than just when the IS-A relationship applies.

#2. Use case formats

Even though there's a pretty standard definition for *what* a use case is, there's *not* a standard way for writing use cases. Here are just a few of the different ways you can write up your use cases:

<u>Todd and Gina's Dog Door, version 2.0</u>
What the Door Does

1. Fido barks to be let out.
2. Todd or Gina hears Fido barking.
3. Todd or Gina presses the button on the remote control.
4. The dog door opens.
5. Fido goes outside.
6. Fido does his business.
   6.1 The door shuts automatically.
   6.2 Fido barks to be let back inside.
   6.3 Todd or Gina hears Fido barki[ng]
   6.4 Todd or Gina presses the butt[on on the] remote control.
   6.5 The dog door opens (again).
7. Fido goes back inside.
8. The door shuts automatically.

Here's the format we've been using so far. It's a simple, step-based format that works well for most situations.

This use case is in a casual style. The steps that the system follows are written out in paragraph form.

<u>Todd and Gina's Dog Door, version 2.0</u>
What the Door Does

Fido barks to be let outside. When Todd and Gina hear him barking, they press a button on their remote control. The button opens up the dog door, and Fido goes outside. Then Fido does his business, and returns inside. The dog door then shuts automatically.

If Fido stays outside too long, then the dog door will shut while he's still outside. Fido will bark to be let back inside, and Todd or Gina presses the button on the remote control again. This opens the dog door, and allows Fido to return back inside.

Any alternate paths are usually added to the end of the text in casual form, and presented in an "If–then" form.

Focusing on interaction

This format is a little more focused on separating out what is in a system, and how the actors outside of the system interact with your software.

This format focuses on what is external to the system (the actors), and what the system itself does.

Todd and Gina's Dog Door, version 2.0
What the Door Does

Remember, actors are external to the system. They act on, or use, the system.

Actor	System
Fido barks to be let out.	
Todd or Gina hears Fido barking.	
Todd or Gina presses the button on the remote control.	
	The dog door opens.
Fido goes outside.	
Fido does his business.	
Fido goes back inside.	
	The door shuts automatically.

In Todd and Gina's dog door, the system is pretty simple, and usually is just responding to the actions of Todd, Gina, and Fido.

Extensions

If Fido stays outside and the dog door shuts before he comes back in, he can bark to be let back in. Todd or Gina can press the button on the remote again, and he can return inside.

This format doesn't offer a very convenient way to handle alternate paths, so they're just added at the bottom of the use case.

A more formal use case

This is similar to the use case format we've been using, but adds some extra details.

Todd and Gina's Dog Door, version 2.0
What the Door Does

Primary Actor: Fido

Secondary Actors: Todd and Gina

Pre-condition: Fido is inside, and needs to use the restroom.

Goal: Fido has used the bathroom and is back inside the house, without Todd or Gina having to get up and open or close the dog door.

The actors are external forces that affect the system.

Pre-conditions detail any assumptions that the system makes before things get started.

Everything in the use case is geared towards accomplishing this goal.

Main Path

1. Fido barks to be let out.
2. Todd or Gina hears Fido barking.
3. Todd or Gina presses the button on the remote control.
4. The dog door opens.
5. Fido goes outside.
6. Fido does his business.
7. Fido goes back inside.
8. The door shuts automatically.

Extensions

6.1 The door shuts automatically.

6.2 Fido barks to be let back inside.

6.3 Todd or Gina hears Fido barking (again).

6.4 Todd or Gina presses the button on the remote control.

6.5 The dog door opens (again).

Alternate paths are also called extensions, and in this format, are listed below the main path steps.

These are the steps from the alternate path, but they're just listed separately.

All of these use cases say the <u>same thing</u>... it's up to you (and probably your boss) to decide which format works best for you.

#3. Anti patterns

We've talked a lot in this book about design patterns, and described them this way:

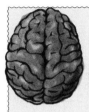

> **Design Patterns**
>
> *Design patterns are proven solutions to particular types of problems, and help us structure our own applications in ways that are easier to understand, more maintainable, and more flexible.*

But there's another type of pattern you should know about, called an anti-pattern:

> **Anti Patterns**
>
> *Anti-patterns are the reverse of design patterns: they are common BAD solutions to problems. These dangerous pitfalls should be recognized and avoided.*

Anti patterns turn up when you see the same problem get solved the same way, but the solution turns out to be a BAD one. For example, one common anti pattern is called "Gas Factory", and refers to designs that are overly complex, and therefore not very maintainable. So you want to work to avoid the Gas Factory in your own code.

We're actually not making this up! At your next serious development meeting, be sure to mention trying to avoid the Gas Factory.

Design patterns help you recognize and implement <u>GOOD</u> <u>solutions</u> to common problems.

Anti patterns are about recognizing and avoiding <u>BAD</u> <u>solutions</u> to common problems.

#4. CRC cards

CRC stands for Class, Responsibility, Collaborator. These cards are used to take a class and figure out what its responsibility should be, and what other classes it collaborates with.

CRC cards are typically just 3x5 index cards, with each individual card representing a class. The card has two columns: one for the responsibilities of the class, and another for other classes that are collaborators, and used to fulfill those responsibilities.

This class is the class you're determining responsibilities for.

Class: BarkRecognizer

Description: This class is the interface to the bark recognition hardware.

Responsibilities:

Name	Collaborator
Tell the door to open	DogDoor

List each job this class needs to do.

If there are other classes involved is this job, list them in this column.

Class: DogDoor

Description: Represents the physical dog door. This provides an interface to the hardware that actually controls the door.

Responsibilities:

Name	Collaborator
Open the door	
Close the door	

Be sure you write down things that this class does on its own, as well as things it collaborates with other classes on.

There's no collaborator class for these.

CRC cards help implement the SRP

You can use CRC cards to make sure your classes follow the Single
Responsibility Principle. These go hand in hand with your SRP
Analysis, as well:

SRP Analysis for _Automobile_

The	_Automobile_	_start[s]_	**itself.**
The	_Automobile_	_stop[s]_	**itself.**
The	_Automobile_	_changesTires_	**itself.**
The	_Automobile_	_drive[s]_	**itself.**
The	_Automobile_	_wash[es]_	**itself.**
The	_Automobile_	_check[s] oil_	**itself.**
The	_Automobile_	_get[s] oil_	**itself.**

If you've got a class that seems to violate the SRP, you can use a CRC card to sort out which classes should be doing what.

Class: Automobile

Description: This class represents a car and its related functionality

Responsibilities:

Name	Collaborator
Starts itself.	
Stops itself.	
Gets tires changed	Mechanic, Tire
Gets driven	Driver
Gets washed	CarWash, Attendant
Gets oil checked	Mechanic
Reports on oil levels	

Any time you see "Gets", it's probably not the responsibility of this class to do a certain task.

Technically, you don't need to list responsibilities that AREN'T this class's, but doing things this way can help you find tasks that really shouldn't be on this class.

#5. Metrics

Sometimes it's hard to tell how solid your design really is, because design is such a subjective thing. That's where metrics can help out: while they don't provide a complete picture of your system, they can be helpful in pointing out strengths, weaknesses, and potential problems. You usually use software tools to take as input your class's source code, and those tools then generate metrics based on your code and its design.

These metrics are more than just numbers, though. For example, just counting the number of lines of code in your application is almost a total waste of time. It's nothing but a number, and has no context (and also depends a lot on how you're writing your code, something else we'll talk about in this appendix). But if you count the number of defects per 1000 lines of code, then *that* becomes a useful metric.

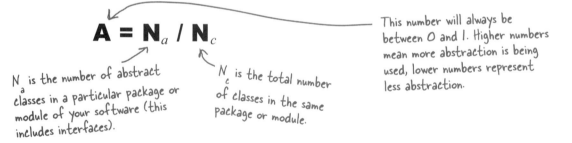

$$\text{defect density} = \frac{\text{errors found in code}}{\text{total lines of code} / 1000}$$

This number gives you some idea of how well you're writing your code. If it's high, look for design problems or inefficiencies.

You can also use metric to measure things like how well you're using abstraction in your code. Good design will use abstract classes and interfaces, so that other classes can program to those interfaces rather than specific implementation classes. So abstraction keeps one part of your code independent from changes to other parts of your code, at least to the degree that it's possible in your system. You can use something called the **abstractness metric** to measure this:

$$A = N_a / N_c$$

This number will always be between 0 and 1. Higher numbers mean more abstraction is being used, lower numbers represent less abstraction.

N_a is the number of abstract classes in a particular package or module of your software (this includes interfaces).

N_c is the total number of classes in the same package or module.

Packages that have lots of abstractions will have a higher value for A, and packages with less abstractions have a lower value for **A**. In general, you want to have each package in your software only depend on packages with a higher value for **A**. That means that your packages are always depending on packages that are more abstract; the result should be software that can easily respond to change.

Robert Martin's book called "Agile Software Development" has a lot more of these OO-related metrics.

#6. Sequence diagrams

When we were working on the dog door for Todd and Gina, we developed several alternate paths (and one alternate path actually had an alternate path itself). To really get a feel for how your system handles these different paths, it's helpful to use a UML **sequence diagram**. A sequence diagram is just what it sounds like: a visual way to show the things that happen in a particular interaction between an actor and your system.

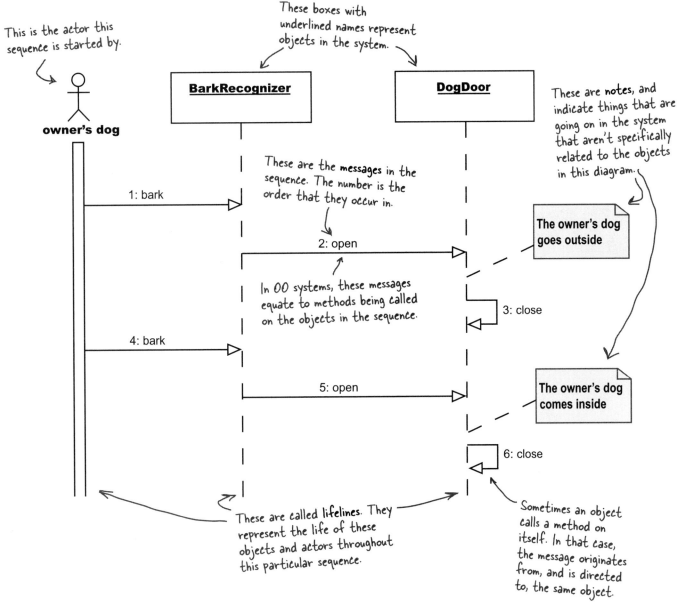

#7. State diagrams

You've already seen class diagrams and sequence diagrams. UML also contains a diagram called a **state machine diagram** or **statechart diagram**, which is usually just referred to as a **state diagram**. This diagram describes a part of your system by showing its various states, and the actions that cause that state to change. These diagrams are great for describing complex behaviors visually.

State diagrams really come into play when you have multiple actions and events that are all going on at the same time. On the right page, we've taken just such a situation, and drawn a state diagram for how a game designer might use Gary's Game System Framework. If game designers were going to use the framework, they might write a game that behaves a lot like this state diagram demonstrates.

Symbols commonly used in state diagrams

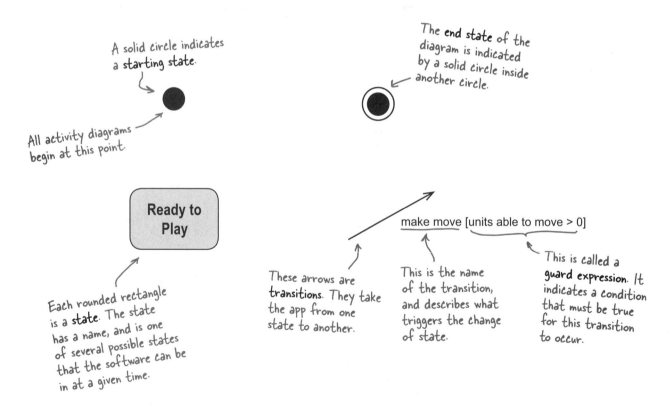

A solid circle indicates a starting state.

All activity diagrams begin at this point.

The **end state** of the diagram is indicated by a solid circle inside another circle.

Ready to Play

Each rounded rectangle is a state. The state has a name, and is one of several possible states that the software can be in at a given time.

These arrows are transitions. They take the app from one state to another.

make move [units able to move > 0]

This is the name of the transition, and describes what triggers the change of state.

This is called a guard expression. It indicates a condition that must be true for this transition to occur.

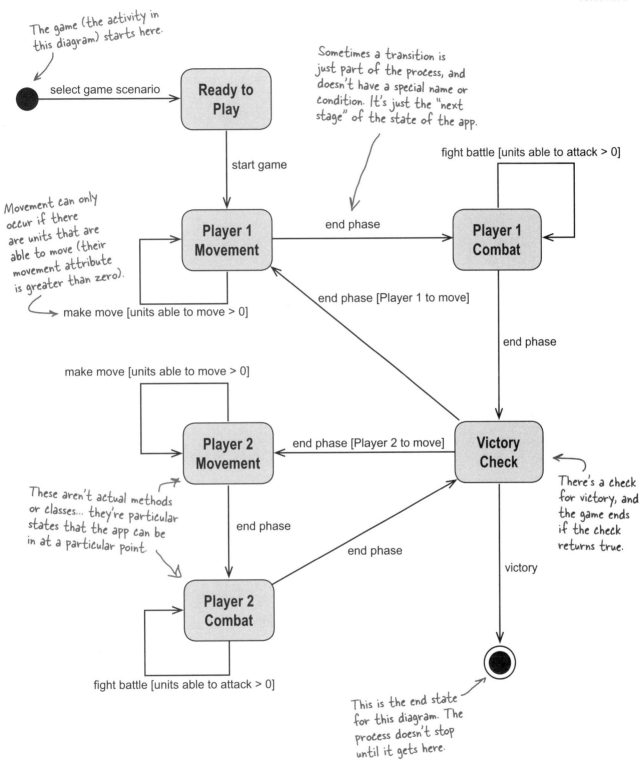

The game (the activity in this diagram) starts here.

select game scenario

Ready to Play

Sometimes a transition is just part of the process, and doesn't have a special name or condition. It's just the "next stage" of the state of the app.

fight battle [units able to attack > 0]

start game

Movement can only occur if there are units that are able to move (their movement attribute is greater than zero).

Player 1 Movement

end phase

Player 1 Combat

make move [units able to move > 0]

end phase [Player 1 to move]

end phase

make move [units able to move > 0]

Player 2 Movement

end phase [Player 2 to move]

Victory Check

These aren't actual methods or classes... they're particular states that the app can be in at a particular point.

There's a check for victory, and the game ends if the check returns true.

end phase

end phase

Player 2 Combat

victory

fight battle [units able to attack > 0]

This is the end state for this diagram. The process doesn't stop until it gets here.

#8. Unit testing

In each chapter that we're worked on an application, we've built "driver" programs to test the code, like **SubwayTester** and **DogDoorSimulator**. These are all a form of ***unit testing***. We test each class with a certain set of input data, or with a particular sequence of method calls.

While this is a great way to get a sense of how your application works when used by the customer, it does have some drawbacks:

1 You have to write a complete program for each usage of the software.

2 You need to produce some kind of output, either to the console or a file, to verify the software is working correctly.

3 You have to manually look over the output of the test, each time its run, to make sure things are working correctly.

4 Your tests will eventually test such large pieces of functionality that you're no longer testing all the smaller features of your app.

Fortunately, there are testing frameworks that will not only allow you to test very small pieces of functionality, but will also automate much of that testing for you. In Java, the most popular framework is called JUnit (http://www.junit.org), and integrates with lots of the popular Java development environments, like Eclipse.

---

there are no Dumb Questions

Q: **If the tests we wrote in the main part of the book made sure our software worked at a high level, why do we need more tests? Aren't those enough to be sure our software works?**

A: Most of the tests we wrote really tested a particular scenario, such as opening the door, letting a dog out, having another dog bark, and then letting the owner's dog back in. Unit tests, and particular the tests we're talking about here, are far more granular. They test each class's functionality, one piece at a time.

The reason that you need both types of tests is because you'll never be able to come up with scenarios that test every possible combination of features and functionality in your software. We're all human, and we all tend to forget just one or two strange situations now and then.

With tests that exercise each individual piece of functionality in your classes, you can be sure that things will work in any scenario, even if you don't specifically test that scenario. It's a way to make sure each small piece works, and one that lets you assume pretty safely that combining those small pieces will then work, as well.

What a test case looks like

A test case has a test method for each and every piece of functionality in the class that it's testing. So for a class like **DogDoor**, we'd test opening the door, and closing the door. JUnit would generate a test class that looked something like this:

```java
import junit.framework.TestCase;

/**
 * This test case tests the operation of the dog door by using the
 * remote button.
 */
public class RemoteTest extends TestCase
{
    public void testOpenDoor()
    {
        DogDoor door = new DogDoor();
        Remote remote = new Remote(door);
        remote.pressButton();
        assertTrue(door.isOpen());
    }

    public void testCloseDoor() {
        DogDoor door = new DogDoor();
        Remote remote = new Remote(door);
        remote.pressButton();
        try {
            Thread.currentThread().sleep(6000);
        } catch (InterruptedException e) {
            fail("interrupted thread");
        }
        assertFalse(door.isOpen());
    }
}
```

TestCase is JUnit's base class for testing software.

There's a method for each piece of functionality in DogDoor.

assertTrue() checks to see if the supplied method returns true, which it should in this case.

assertFalse() checks a method to ensure that it's NOT true.

This method tests for the door automatically closing, rather than just calling door.close(), which isn't how the door is usually used.

Test your code in context

Notice that instead of directly testing the **DogDoor**'s **open()** and **close()** methods, this test uses the **Remote** class, which is how the door would work in the real world. That ensures that the tests are simulating real usage, even though they are testing just a single piece of functionality at a time.

The same thing is done in **testCloseDoor()**. Instead of calling the **close()** method, the test opens the door with the remote, waits beyond the time it should take for the door to close automatically, and then tests to see if the door is closed. That's how the door will be used, so that's what should be tested.

#9. Coding standards and readable code

Reading source code should be a lot like reading a book. You should be able to tell what's going on, and even if you have a few questions, it shouldn't be too hard to figure out the answers to those questions if you just keep reading. Good developers and designers should be willing to spend a little extra time writing readable code, because it improves the ability to maintain and reuse that code.

Here's an example of a commented and readable version of the **DogDoor** class we wrote back in Chapters 2 and 3.

```java
/**
 * This class represents the interface to the real dog door.
 *
 * @author Gary Pollice
 * @version Aug 11, 2006
 */
public class DogDoor
{
    // the number of open commands in progress
    private int numberOfOpenCommands = 0;

    boolean doorIsOpen = false;
    /**
     * @return true if the door is open
     */
    public boolean isOpen()
    {
        return doorIsOpen;
    }

    /**
     * Open the door and then, five seconds later, close it.
     */
    public void open( )
    {
        // Code to tell the hardware to open the door goes here
        doorIsOpen = true;
        numberOfOpenCommands++;
        TimerTask task = new TimerTask() {
            public void run() {
                if (--numberOfOpenCommands == 0) {
                    // Code to tell the hardware to close the door goes here
                    doorIsOpen = false;
                }
            }
        };
        Timer timer = new Timer();
        timer.schedule(task, 5000);
    }
}
```

JavaDoc comments help people reading the code, and also can be used to generate documentation with Java's javadoc tool.

Method and variable names are descriptive, and easy to decipher.

This code is clear and spaced out.

Even variables used just within a single method are named for readability.

Any statements that aren't perfectly clear are commented to clarify.

Great software is more than just working code

Many developers will tell you that code standards and formatting are a big pain, but take a look at what happens when you don't spend any time making your code readable:

No comments at all here... it's up to the developer reading this code to figure everything out on their own.

No telling what these variables are for...

```
public class DogDoor
{
    private int noc = 0;
    boolean dio = false;

    public boolean returndio( ) { return dio; }

    public void do_my_job( )
    {
        dio = true;
        noc++;
        TimerTask tt = new TimerTask() {
        public void run() {
         if (--noc == 0) dio = false;
        }
        };
        Timer t = new Timer();
        t.schedule(tt, 5000);
    }
}
```

...or these methods. The names are not at all descriptive.

The lack of indentation and spacing makes things even harder to understand.

From a purely functional point of view, this version of **DogDoor** works just as well as the one on the last page. But by now you should know that great software is more than just working code—it's code that is maintainable, and can be reused. And most developers will not want to maintain or reuse this second version of **DogDoor**; it's a pain to figure out what it does, or where things might go wrong—now imagine if there were *10,000* lines of code like this, and not just 25 or so.

Writing readable code makes that code easier to maintain and reuse, for you and other developers.

#10. Refactoring

Refactoring is the process of modifying the structure of your code without modifying its behavior. Refactoring is done to increase the cleanness, flexibility, and extensibility of your code, and usually is related to a specific improvement in your design.

Most refactorings are fairly simple, and focus on one specific design aspect of your code. For example:

```
public double getDisabilityAmount() {
  // Check for eligibility
  if (seniority < 2)
    return 0;
  if (monthsDisabled > 12)
    return 0;
  if (isPartTime)
    return 0;
  // Calculate disability amount and return it
}
```

While there's nothing particularly wrong with this code, it's not as maintainable as it could be. The **getDisabilityAmount()** method is really doing two things: checking the eligibility for disability, and then calculating the amount.

By now, you should know that violates the Single Responsibility Principle. We really should separate the code that handles eligibility requirements from the code that does disability calculations. So we can *refactor* this code to look more like this:

```
public double getDisabilityAmount() {
  // Check for eligibility
  if (isEligibleForDisability()) {
    // Calculate disability amount and return it
  } else {
    return 0;
  }
}
```

We've taken two responsibilities, and placed them in two separate methods, adhering to the SRP.

Now, if the eligibility requirements for disability change, only the **isEligibleForDisability()** methods needs to change—and the method responsible for calculating the disability amount doesn't.

Think of refactoring as a checkup for your code. It should be an ongoing process, as code that is left alone tends to become harder and harder to reuse. Go back to old code, and refactor it to take advantage of new design techniques you've learned. The programmers who have to maintain and reuse your code will thank you for it.

> **Refactoring changes the internal structure of your code WITHOUT affecting your code's behavior.**

Speaking the Language of OO

It says here that you want to change my composition to aggregation, add some delegation, and that I'm not well-encapsulated. I'm totally lost, and I think I might even be insulted!

Get ready to take a trip to a foreign country. It's time to visit Objectville, a land where **objects do just what they're supposed to**, applications are all **well-encapsulated** (you'll find out exactly what that means shortly), and designs are easy to **reuse and extend**. But before we can get going, there are a couple of things you need to know first, and a few **language skills** you're going to have to learn. Don't worry, though, it won't take long, and before you know it, you'll be speaking the language of OO like you've been living in the well-designed areas of Objectville for years.

Welcome to Objectville

Whether this is your first trip to Objectville, or you've visited before, there's no place quite like it. But things are a little different here, so we're here to help you get your bearings before you dive into the main part of the book.

Welcome to Objectville! I picked up a few things I thought you might need to help make you comfortable right away. Enjoy!

We'll start with just a little bit of UML, so we can talk about classes easily throughout the book.

Then, we'll do a quick review of inheritance, just to make sure you're ready for the more advanced code examples in this book.

Once we've got inheritance covered, we'll take a quick look at polymorphism, too.

Finally, we'll talk just a bit about encapsulation, and make sure we're all on the same page about what that word means.

UML and class diagrams

We're going to talk about classes and objects a lot in this book, but it's pretty hard to look at 200 lines of code and focus on the big picture. So we'll be using UML, the **Unified Modeling Language**, which is a language used to communicate just the **details** about your **code** and **application's structure** that other developers and customers **need**, without getting details that *aren't* necessary.

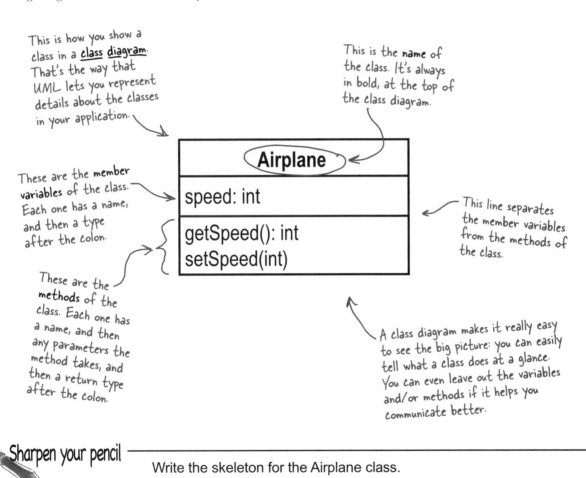

This is how you show a class in a <u>class diagram</u>. That's the way that UML lets you represent details about the classes in your application.

This is the **name** of the class. It's always in bold, at the top of the class diagram.

These are the member variables of the class. Each one has a name, and then a type after the colon.

Airplane

speed: int

getSpeed(): int
setSpeed(int)

This line separates the member variables from the methods of the class.

These are the methods of the class. Each one has a name, and then any parameters the method takes, and then a return type after the colon.

A class diagram makes it really easy to see the big picture: you can easily tell what a class does at a glance. You can even leave out the variables and/or methods if it helps you communicate better.

Sharpen your pencil

Write the skeleton for the Airplane class.

Using the class diagram above, see if you can write the basic skeleton for the Airplane class. Did you find anything that the class diagram leaves out? Write those things in the blanks below:

_____

_____

_____

Sharpen your pencil answers

Write the skeleton for the Airplane class.

Using the class diagram on page 577, you were supposed to write the basic skeleton for the Airplane class. Here's what we did:

```
public class Airplane {

    private int speed;

    public Airplane() {
    }

    public void setSpeed(int speed) {
        this.speed = speed;
    }

    public int getSpeed() {
        return speed;
    }
}
```

The class diagram didn't tell us if speed should be public, private, or protected.

Actually, class diagams *can* provide this information, but in most cases, it's not needed for clear communication.

There was nothing about a constructor in the class diagram. You could have written a constructor that took in an initial speed value, and that would be OK, too.

The class diagram didn't tell us what this method did... we made some assumptions, but we can't be sure if this code is really what was intended.

---

there are no Dumb Questions

Q: So the class diagram isn't a very complete representation of a class, is it?

A: No, but it's not meant to be. Class diagrams are just a way to communicate the basic details of a class's variables and methods. It also makes it easy to talk about code without forcing you to wade through hundreds of lines of Java, or C, or Perl.

Q: I've got my own way of drawing classes; what's wrong with that?

A: There's nothing wrong with your own notation, but it can make things harder for other people to understand. By using a standard like UML, we can all speak the same language and be sure we're talking about the same thing in our diagrams.

Q: So who came up with this UML deal, anyway?

A: The UML specification was developed by Rational Software, under the leadership of Grady Booch, Ivar Jacobson, and Jim Rumbaugh (three *really* smart guys). These days it's managed by the OMG, the Object Management Group.

Q: Sounds like a lot of fuss over that simple little class diagram thing.

A: UML is actually a lot more than that class diagram. UML has diagrams for the state of your objects, the sequence of events in your application, and it even has a way to represent customer requirements and interactions with your system. And there's a lot more to learn about class diagrams, too.

At this point, though, you just need the basics on page 577. We'll talk about other things you can show in a class diagram, and other types of diagrams, when we need them later in the book.

Next up: inheritance

One of the fundamental programming topics in Objectville is
inheritance. That's when one class *inherits* behavior from another
class, and can then change that behavior if needed. Let's look at how
inheritance works in Java; it's similar in other languages, too:

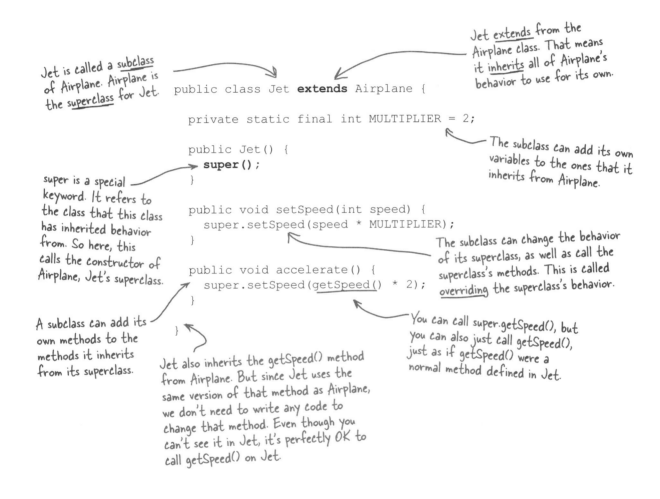

Jet is called a subclass
of Airplane. Airplane is
the superclass for Jet.

Jet extends from the
Airplane class. That means
it inherits all of Airplane's
behavior to use for its own.

```java
public class Jet extends Airplane {

    private static final int MULTIPLIER = 2;

    public Jet() {
        super();
    }

    public void setSpeed(int speed) {
        super.setSpeed(speed * MULTIPLIER);
    }

    public void accelerate() {
        super.setSpeed(getSpeed() * 2);
    }

}
```

The subclass can add its own
variables to the ones that it
inherits from Airplane.

super is a special
keyword. It refers to
the class that this class
has inherited behavior
from. So here, this
calls the constructor of
Airplane, Jet's superclass.

The subclass can change the behavior
of its superclass, as well as call the
superclass's methods. This is called
overriding the superclass's behavior.

A subclass can add its
own methods to the
methods it inherits
from its superclass.

Jet also inherits the getSpeed() method
from Airplane. But since Jet uses the
same version of that method as Airplane,
we don't need to write any code to
change that method. Even though you
can't see it in Jet, it's perfectly OK to
call getSpeed() on Jet.

You can call super.getSpeed(), but
you can also just call getSpeed(),
just as if getSpeed() were a
normal method defined in Jet.

> **Inheritance lets you build classes
> based on <u>other</u> classes, and <u>avoid</u>
> <u>duplicating</u> and <u>repeating</u> <u>code</u>.**

Pool Puzzle

Your *job* is to take code snippets from the pool below and place them into the blank lines in the code you see on the right. You **may** use the same snippet more than once, and you won't need to use all the snippets. Your *goal* is to create a class that will compile, run, and produce the output listed.

Output:

```
File Edit Window Help LeavingOnAJetplane
%java FlyTest
212
844
1688
6752
13504
27008
1696
```

```java
public class FlyTest {
  public static void main(String[] args) {
    Airplane biplane = new Airplane();
    biplane.setSpeed(_____);
    System.out.println(_____);
    Jet boeing = new Jet();
    boeing.setSpeed(_____);
    System.out.println(_____);
    _____;
    while (_____) {
      _____;
      System.out.println(_____);
      if (_____ > 5000) {
        _____(_____ * 2);
      } else {
        _____;
      }
      _____;
    }
    System.out.println(_____);
  }
}
```

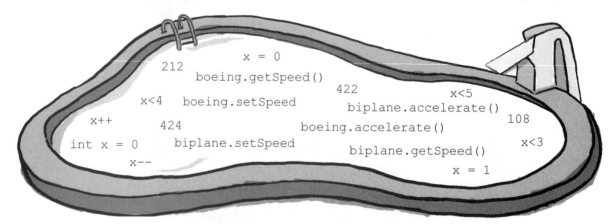

```
        x = 0
212
    boeing.getSpeed()
                        422              x<5
  x<4   boeing.setSpeed     biplane.accelerate()
 x++     424          boeing.accelerate()      108
int x = 0   biplane.setSpeed                    x<3
    x--                biplane.getSpeed()
                          x = 1
```

→ Solution on page 588

And polymorphism, too...

Polymorphism is closely related to inheritance. When one class inherits from another, then polymorphism allows a **subclass** to **stand in** for the **superclass**.

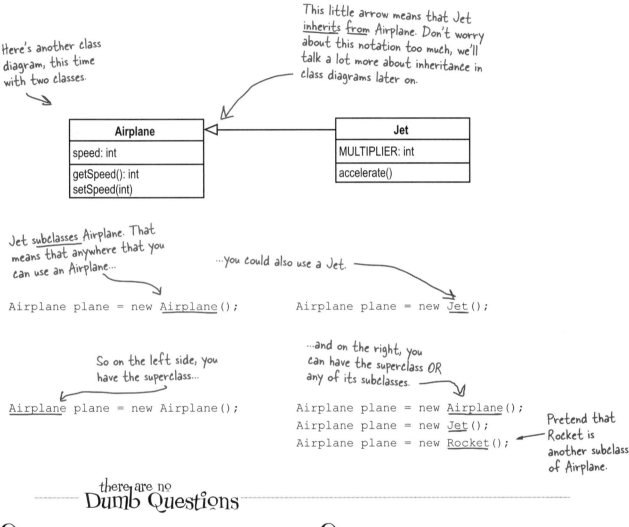

This little arrow means that Jet inherits from Airplane. Don't worry about this notation too much, we'll talk a lot more about inheritance in class diagrams later on.

Here's another class diagram, this time with two classes.

Airplane
speed: int
getSpeed(): int setSpeed(int)

Jet
MULTIPLIER: int
accelerate()

Jet subclasses Airplane. That means that anywhere that you can use an Airplane...

...you could also use a Jet.

```
Airplane plane = new Airplane();
```

```
Airplane plane = new Jet();
```

So on the left side, you have the superclass...

...and on the right, you can have the superclass OR any of its subclasses.

```
Airplane plane = new Airplane();
```

```
Airplane plane = new Airplane();
Airplane plane = new Jet();
Airplane plane = new Rocket();
```

Pretend that Rocket is another subclass of Airplane.

---

there are no Dumb Questions

Q: What's so useful about polymorphism?

A: You can write code that works on the superclass, like **Airplane**, but will work with any subclass type, like **Jet** or **Rocket**. So your code is more flexible.

Q: I still don't get how polymorphism makes my code flexible.

A: Well, if you need new functionality, you could write a new subclass of **Airplane**. But since your code uses the superclass, your new subclass will work without any changes to the rest of our code! That means your code is flexible and can change easily.

Last but not least: encapsulation

Encapsulation is when you **hide** the implementation of a class in such a way that it is easy to use and easy to change. It makes the class act as a black box that provides a service to its users, but does not open up the code so someone can change it or use it the wrong way. Encapsulation is a key technique in being able to follow the Open-Closed principle. Suppose we rewrote our **Airplane** class like this:

```java
public class Airplane {

    public int speed;

    public Airplane() {
    }

    public void setSpeed(int speed) {
        this.speed = speed;
    }

    public int getSpeed() {
        return speed;
    }
}
```

We made the
speed variable
public, instead
of private, and
now all parts
of your app
can access
speed directly.

Now anyone can set the speed directly

This change means that the rest of your app no longer has to call **setSpeed()** to set the speed of a plane; the **speed** variable can be set directly. So this code would compile just fine:

```java
public class FlyTest2 {
    public static void main(String[] args) {
        Airplane biplane = new Airplane();
        biplane.speed = 212;
        System.out.println(biplane.speed);
    }
}
```

We don't have to use
setSpeed() and getSpeed()
anymore... we can just
access speed directly.

Try this code out...
anything surprising in the
results you get?

Encapsulation
is when
you protect
information
in your
code from
being used
incorrectly.

So what's the big deal?

Doesn't seem like much of a problem, does it? But what happens if
you create a **Jet** and set its speed like this:

```
public class FlyTest3 {
    public static void main(String[] args) {
        Jet jet1 = new Jet();
        jet1.speed = 212;
        System.out.println(jet1.speed);

        Jet jet2 = new Jet();
        jet2.setSpeed(212);
        System.out.println(jet2.getSpeed());
    }
}
```

*Using Jet
without
encapsulation.*

*Using Jet with
encapsulation*

*Since Jet inherits from
Airplane, you can use the
speed variable from its
superclass just like it was
a part of Jet.*

*This is how we set and accessed the speed
variable when we hid speed from being
directly accessed.*

Sharpen your pencil

What's the value of encapsulating your data?

Type in, compile, and run the code for FlyTest3.java, shown above. What
did your output look like? Write the two lines of output in the blanks below:

Speed of jet1: _____

Speed of jet2: _____

What do you think happened here? Write down why you think you got the
speeds that you did for each instance of Jet:

_____
_____
_____

Finally, summarize what you think the value of encapsulation is:

_____
_____
_____

Sharpen your pencil answers

What's the value of encapsulating your data?

Type in, compile, and run the code for FlyTest3.java shown above. What did your output look like? Write the two lines of output in the blanks below:

Speed of jet1: _____**212**_____

Speed of jet2: _____**424**_____

What do you think happened here? Write down why you think you got the speeds that you did for each instance of Jet:

> **In the Jet class, setSpeed() takes the value supplied, and multiplies it by two before setting the speed of the jet. When we set the speed variable manually, it didn't get multiplied by two.**

You didn't have to write down exactly what we did, but you should have gotten something similar.

Finally, summarize what you think the value of encapsulation is:

> **Encapsulation protects data from being set in an improper way. With encapsulated data, any calculations or checks that the class does on the data are preserved, since the data can't be accessed directly.**

So encapsulation does more than just hide information; it makes sure the methods you write to work with your data are actually used!

Taking a college class in programming? Here's the official definition of encapsulation... if you're taking an exam, this is the definition to use.

the Scholar's Corner

encapsulation. The process of enclosing programming elements inside larger, more abstract entities. Also known as information hiding, or separation of concerns.

Q: So encapsulation is all about making all your variables private?

A: No, encapsulation is about separating information from other parts of your application that shouldn't mess with that information. With member variables, you don't want the rest of your app directly messing with your data, so you separate that data by making it private. If the data needs to be updated, you can provide methods that work with the data responsibly, like we did with the **Airplane** class, using **getSpeed()** and **setSpeed()**.

Q: So are there other ways to use encapsulation besides with variables?

A: Absolutely. In fact, in Chapter 1, we'll be looking at how you can encapsulate a *group* of properties away from an object, and make sure that the object doesn't use those properties incorrectly. Even though we'll deal with an entire set of properties, it's still just separating a set of information away from the rest of your application.

Q: So encapsulation is really about protecting your data, right?

A: Actually, it's even more than that! Encapsulation can also help you separate behavior from other parts of your application. So you might put lots of code in a method, and put that method in a class; you've separated that behavior from the rest of your application, and the app has to use your new class and method to access that behavior. It's the same principles as with data, though: you're separating out parts of your application to protect them from being used improperly.

Q: Wow, I'm not sure I'm following all of this. What do I need to do?

A: Just keep reading. Make sure you understand the exercise solutions on page 584, and you're ready for Chapter 1. We'll spend a lot more time on all of these OO principles and concepts, so don't feel like you need to get everything down perfectly at this point.

Encapsulation separates your data from your app's behavior.

Then you can control how each part is used by the rest of your application.

> Already gone through everything? Then you're definitely ready for the rest of this book. And welcome again to the **well-designed** part of Objectville... we love it here, I'm sure you will, too.

BULLET POINTS

- **UML** stands for the **Unified Modeling Language**.

- UML helps you communicate the structure of your application to other developers, customers, and managers.

- A **class diagram** gives you an overview of your class, including its methods and variables.

- **Inheritance** is when one class extends another class to reuse or build upon the inherited class's behavior.

- In inheritance, the class being inherited from is called the **superclass**; the class that is doing the inheritance is called the **subclass**.

- A subclass gets all the behavior of its superclass automatically.

- A subclass can **override** its superclass's behavior to change how a method works.

- **Polymorphism** is when a subclass "stands in" for its superclass.

- Polymorphism allows your applications to be more flexible, and less resistant to change.

- **Encapsulation** is when you separate or hide one part of your code from the rest of your code.

- The simplest form of encapsulation is when you make the variables of your classes private, and only expose that data through methods on the class.

- You can also encapsulate groups of data, or even behavior, to control how they are accessed.

OOA&D Cross

Take a moment to review the concepts in this appendix, and then you're ready to step firmly into the world of analysis, design, OO programming, and great software.

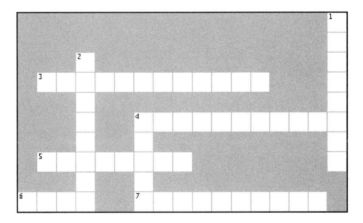

Across

3. This is when a subclass can substitute for its superclass.
4. Class diagrams don't show details about this part of our class.
5. A class that inherits from another class is this.
6. Encapsulation lets you do this to information.
7. A class that is inherited from is called this.

Down

1. Another term for encapsulation is separation of this.
2. Polymorphism helps make your code _____.
4. Use this kind of diagram to avoid wading through lots of code.

Pool Puzzle Solution

Your **job** was to take code snippets from the pool below, and place them into the blank lines in the code you see on the right. You **may** use the same snippet more than once, and you won't need to use all the snippets. Your **goal** was to create a class that will compile, run, and produce the output listed.

Output:

```
File Edit Window Help LeavingOnAJetplane
%java FlyTest
212
844
1688
6752
13504
27008
1696
```

```java
public class FlyTest {
  public static void main(String[] args) {
    Airplane biplane = new Airplane();
    biplane.setSpeed(212);
    System.out.println(biplane.getSpeed());
    Jet boeing = new Jet();
    boeing.setSpeed(422);
    System.out.println(boeing.getSpeed());
    int x = 0;
    while (x<4) {
      boeing.accelerate();
      System.out.println(boeing.getSpeed());
      if (boeing.getSpeed() > 5000) {
        biplane.setSpeed(biplane.getSpeed() * 2);
      } else {
        boeing.accelerate();
      }
      x++;
    }
    System.out.println(biplane.getSpeed());
  }
}
```

Here's our solution to the pool puzzle.

Exercise
Solution

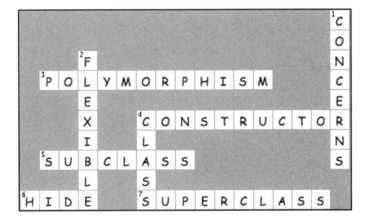

Index

Numbers

3DBoard, solving without inheritance 405

A

abstract base class 200–203, 212

abstracting behavior 205

abstraction 243

actors 294, 299, 300, 302

aggregation 208, 412–417, 414, 558
    versus composition 413

Airplane class 577

alternate paths 70, 85–87
    dog door 123
    dog door requirement changes 120
    questions and answers 125

analysis xiii–xxii, 145–196, 283
    identifying problems 148
    planning solutions 149
    textual 169
    use cases and 151

Analysis and Design Puzzle 510, 536–538

anonymous class 82

anti patterns 563

architecturally significant features 331

architecture
    defined 326–328
    purpose of 351
    three questions 332

Architecture Puzzle 340
    revisited 345
    solution 346–347

array of arrays 347

association 194

attributes 194

B

Bark object 158, 159
    multiple 165

BarkRecognizer.java 131, 132, 135
    Don't Repeat Yourself Principle 382

BarkRecognizer class 132, 135, 159
    delegation 161
    questions and answers 132
    recognize() method 160, 189

base classes, modifying 381

behavior
    of subclasses 241
    reusing from other classes 414

Be the Browser 333, 334, 365, 437, 438

big problems
    breaking into smaller pieces 281, 309, 310–314
    looking at 281
    versus little problems 280

Board class 346, 348, 349, 364

boolean property versus numStrings property 39

Bullet Points 106, 142, 191, 320, 372, 417, 475, 586

C

cancel() method (TimerTask anonymous class) 82

case diagrams, versus use cases 77

change 228
    constant in software development 115

changing requirements 115

checked exception 470

S

Better than e-books

Try it Free! Sign up today
and get your first 14 days free.
Go to *safari.oreilly.com*

Search
thousands of
top tech books

Download
whole chapters

Cut and Paste
code examples

Find
answers fast

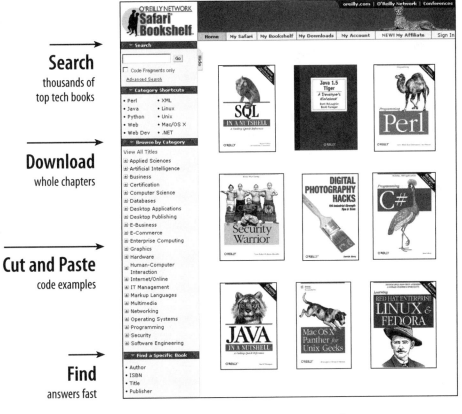

Search Safari! The premier electronic reference
library for programmers and IT professionals.

Related Titles from O'Reilly

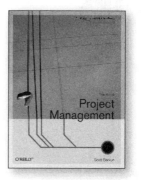

Software Development

Applied Software Project Management

Designing Interfaces

Essential Business Process Modeling

Enterprise Service Bus

Head First Design Patterns

Head First Design Patterns Poster

Head First Object-Oriented Analysis and Design

Learning UML 2.0

Practical Development Environments

Prefactoring

Process Improvement Essentials

The Art of Project Management

UML 2.0 in a Nutshell

UML 2.0 Pocket Reference

The O'Reilly Advantage

Stay Current and Save Money